The Vietnamese American 1.5 Generation

In the series

Asian American History and Culture,

edited by Sucheng Chan, David Palumbo-Liu, Michael Omi,
K. Scott Wong, and Linda Trinh Võ

A list of additional titles in this series
appears at the back of this book

The
Vietnamese American
1.5 Generation

STORIES OF WAR, REVOLUTION, FLIGHT,
AND NEW BEGINNINGS

Edited by Sucheng Chan

with contributions by students at the University of California

TEMPLE UNIVERSITY PRESS

Philadelphia

*To the memory of
the refuge-seekers from Vietnam
who lost their lives before finding safe haven*

Temple University Press
1601 North Broad Street
Philadelphia PA 19122
www.temple.edu/tempress

Copyright © 2006 by Temple University
All rights reserved
Published 2006
Printed in the United States of America

⊗ The paper used in this publication meets the requirements of the American National Standard for Information
Sciences—Permanence of Paper for Printed Library Materi-
als, ANSI Z39.48-1992

Library of Congress Cataloging-in-Publication Data

The Vietnamese American 1.5 Generation : stories of war,
    revolution, flight, and new beginnings / edited by
    Sucheng Chan.
        p.   cm. – (Asian American history and culture)
    Includes bibliographical references and index.
    ISBN 1-59213-500-5 (cloth : alk. paper)
    ISBN 1-59213-501-3 (pbk. : alk. paper)
    1. Vietnamese Americans—Biography.   2. Refugees—
United States—Biography.   3. Refugees—Vietnam—
Biography.   4. Vietnam—History—20th century.
[1. Vietnamese Conflict, 1961–1975—Personal narratives,
Vietnamese.   2. Vietnamese Conflict, 1961–1975—
Refugees.]   I. Chan, Sucheng.   II. Series.

E184.V53V55 2006
973'.04959200922—dc22
    [B]   2005055985

2 4 6 8 9 7 5 3 1

Contents

Part I: Historical Overview

Part II: Stories of War, Revolution, Flight, and New Beginnings

Preface

In early 1976, less than a year after the fall of Saigon, I gave a lecture in my introductory Asian American history class at the University of California (UC), Berkeley on why more than a hundred thousand Vietnamese had come to the United States. Having been an antiwar activist, what I said was rather critical of U.S. foreign policy, the American conduct of the war, and the behavior of the leaders who had governed the Republic of Vietnam (the official name of the country that Americans called "South Vietnam"), especially during the months before Saigon fell. At the end of that lecture, as well as after the lectures on the same topic that I gave in the following three years, the handful of Vietnamese students enrolled in each class rushed up to the stage to tell me that what I had said was "completely wrong." Some were so angry that their faces were flushed and tears welled up in their eyes. Others called me a Communist. A few even declared that someone with my perspective should not be allowed to teach at an American university.

I understood their rage. After all, some of the very politicians and military commanders I had called "corrupt" or "incompetent" were their fathers, uncles, or other relatives. Most of the Vietnamese students who took my courses in that early period of Vietnamese resettlement in the United States came from well-to-do families that had employed live-in servants, cooks, washerwomen, and chauffeurs in their homeland. Although some of their parents had managed to find jobs as bilingual teachers' aides or as interpreters in government offices and voluntary social service agencies that served refugees, a larger number, after their arrival, were forced to eke out a living in blue-collar or service occupations. Almost all blamed the United States for "abandoning" or "betraying" them. They rejected the idea that Vietnamese themselves, both those in the North and the ones in the South, *also* bore responsibility for the war's outcome.

The students' emotions were so intense and their objections so vocal that I quickly realized that if faculty members teaching Asian American Studies wished to draw Vietnamese students into our class-rooms, we had to find ways to come to terms with their vehemently anti-Communist political perspectives and their proclivity to adopt the most conservative currents in American political ideology. This fact created a dilemma for Asian American Studies faculty members, many of whom espoused antiestablishment and anticapitalist beliefs in those early years of the field's development. While I was among the faculty who held such views, I also believed strongly that Asian American Studies must be ecumenical both in terms of Asian paneth-nic inclusiveness and with regard to ideological openness. As a teacher who cared deeply about students, I tried my best to refrain from alien-ating any.

While I pondered how to deal with this clash of politics within our classrooms, Dr. Pham Cao Duong, a former professor of history at the National University in Saigon, submitted a proposal in 1978 to the Asian American Studies Program at UC Berkeley to establish what he called a "Vietnamese-in-America component" within Asian American Studies. He argued that such a curriculum "will be of great help not only to these new immigrants [who wish] to learn about and to re-search themselves, but also to those who have been working or plan to work with them."[1] Dr. Pham had apparently read the statement that seven Asian American Studies faculty had released a year earlier in the midst of a tumultuous internal struggle regarding the program's goals and future direction.[2] Echoing that statement, Dr. Pham stated that the major goals of the Vietnamese-in-America component he was proposing would be (1) educational work with students, (2) re-search on the Vietnamese community, and (3) fieldwork to enable students to participate in and to support the Vietnamese communities then sprouting up in America. However, because the Asian American Studies Program at UC Berkeley was still putting itself back on track after a year of turmoil, nothing came of Dr. Pham's proposal.

A few years later, however, the program did hire a Vietnamese faculty member, Chung Hoang Chuong, to teach a two-semester course on Southeast Asian refugees at UC Berkeley. He did so for about ten years. Professor Khatharya Um, a Cambodian American scholar, assumed responsibility for those courses in the early 1990s. San Francisco State University, UC Davis, UC Santa Barbara, UCLA, UC Irvine, and several other schools in California as well as in other states now offer courses on the refugees and immigrants from South-east Asia.

Before all this happened, back in the late 1970s I felt I had to do something to bring Vietnamese students into the Asian American Studies circle. Accordingly, I offered a course, Asian American Studies 171, "The Vietnamese Experience in America," in spring 1980. Undaunted by the paucity of published writings that could be assigned as readings, I told the students who enrolled in that class that I wanted to make a deal with them: in exchange for their efforts to teach me something about their families' experiences both before and after 1975, I would help them improve their writing and speaking abilities in English.

During the first six weeks, the students had to write an essay of five to seven pages each week. The assigned topics were their family histories before 1975, their memories of their childhoods, how the war had affected their daily lives, their departure from Saigon, the challenges they faced as they adapted to life in the United States, and their impressions and opinions of Americans. After completing the segments, using my comments as a guide, they revised and linked the six short pieces together into a single autobiography or family history. Three of the chapters in this book are from my collection of the papers that students in that class produced. Because the authors were in their teens when they left Vietnam, most of them could deftly analyze their own thoughts and feelings in addition to recounting events. Despite their relatively recent arrival, some students had a surprisingly good vocabulary because they used the dictionary often and learned many uncommon words that way.

In addition to writing their family histories, the students had to interview other Vietnamese in order to write reports comparing the interviewees' experiences and perspectives with their own. Then they gave oral presentations discussing the possible reasons for the similarities and differences between their views and those of others. With this exercise, I hoped to show them that the Vietnamese people are by no means homogeneous. For that reason, I pointed out, no individual can claim that his or her outlook represents *the* Vietnamese perspective on historical and contemporary events. What I was trying to do was to encourage them to be more tolerant of viewpoints other than their own.

To further emphasize the heterogeneity among Vietnamese, readings for the course included essays in which the authors expressed starkly divergent standpoints with regard to Vietnamese history and culture, as well as the thirty-year wars that engulfed Vietnam and its neighbors from 1945 to 1975. I no longer have a copy of the syllabus, but I remember that the class read an article on Vietnamese resistance to foreign intervention, "Vietnamese Nationalism: The Link with the Past," by Truong Buu Lam, a historian teaching at the University of Hawaii and one of the best known Vietnamese scholars in the United States at the time; an essay entitled "Confucianism and Marxism in Vietnam" by Nguyen Khac Vien, a medical doctor who eventually became a Marxist scholar and editor of *Etudes Vietnamiennes* and *Courrier du Vietnam*, both published in the Democratic Republic of Vietnam (Communist-ruled "North Vietnam"); and excerpts from *Reflections on the Vietnam War* by General Cao Van Vien and Lieutenant General Dong Van Khuyen, who had commanded units of the Army of the Republic of Vietnam (ARVN). The readings also included selections by French journalists and scholars such as Bernard Fall and Paul Mus, and short pieces by various American political leaders, soldiers who had fought in the war, antiwar activists, and journalists. Students had to turn in one-page comments on each of these readings. I was not asking for "book reports" that simply summarized the readings; rather, I wanted thoughtful critiques in which they evaluated each reading by "debating" each author whose work they read.

What I learned while teaching "The Vietnamese Experience in America" course at Berkeley was so heartwarming and eye-opening that I continued to assign autobiographies, family histories, and biographies as part of the course requirements in my introductory history courses in subsequent years. (Before I became convinced of the learning experience that writing such reflexive essays offered, I had been very wary of "touchy-feely" approaches to teaching.) Students of Asian ancestry wrote about themselves, while students of other ethnic origins interviewed Asian Americans and wrote their interviewees' biographies, analyzed the differences between their own experiences and those of their interviewees, and discussed what they had learned about Asian Americans in the process of writing their papers. Between 1980 and 1993, when I stopped assigning autobiographies because the enrollment in my introductory courses had become much too large for such an assignment to be feasible, I collected more than two thousand narratives written by Asian American students and by non-Asian students who interviewed them. Of these, approximately a hundred and fifty were autobiographies by Vietnamese and ethnic Chinese from Vietnam and some fifty were biographies written by their non-Vietnamese peers. Students who left Vietnam in 1975 wrote about a sixth of the Vietnamese autobiographies; individuals who fled from the late 1970s to the late 1980s as part of the "boat people" exodus penned the rest.

It may be asked why such "outdated" material should be published. The answer is simple: these life stories are valuable precisely because they are "old." They are eyewitness accounts of a war, a Communist revolution, and a refugee outflow seared into the memories of both Vietnamese and Americans. They document at an intimate personal level momentous events of great historical interest. While there are several anthologies of memoirs by refugees from Cambodia, Laos, and Vietnam in print,[3] I think the chapters in this book are more analytical than those already available because I encouraged my students to place their autobiographies within the context of the times in which they grew up and came of age. Several of the chapters in this book also reflect the fact that their authors had learned a number of sociological concepts—for example, social stratification, value system, age hierarchy, and role model—from my lectures and the required readings for the courses.

Choosing which papers to include in this volume has been very difficult because every paper contains interesting details and touching coming-of-age insights. My teaching assistants and I used to apologize to our students when we gave them a B, C, or D on their papers: we emphasized that the grades reflected how well written and organized their *papers* were, and not how valuable or significant we considered their *lives* to be. Still, I am certain that students who did not receive an A, A-minus, or B-plus must have felt hurt, depressed, or angry. Once again, I feel compelled to apologize to my former students—this time for not being able to include a larger number of accounts in this book because of space limitation.

Two criteria guided my selection process. First, I looked for papers that reveal the thoughts and feelings of the authors. I excluded accounts that read like "laundry lists" of what the authors had done or seen without any analysis of what those experiences meant. Second, I wanted as wide a range of experiences as possible to be represented. Each chapter contributes insight into events or places that are not discussed or are not told with as much detail in other chapters. In the headnotes, I identify what is most notable about each piece. I made sure there is material about the main refugee camps in as many of the countries of first asylum—Malaysia, Thailand, Indonesia, the Philippines, and Hong Kong—as possible. (Hong Kong was not a country but a British colony at the time, but it was usually counted as a "country" of first asylum.) As for variations over time, the authors of Chapters 11–16 left Vietnam in April 1975, while those who wrote Chapters 17–25 escaped as boat people between 1976 and 1986. In the early years of the boat people exodus, an estimated 70 percent of the refuge-seekers were ethnic Chinese living in Vietnam, but as time passed, more and more ethnic Vietnamese also sought refuge outside their country. This demographic change is reflected in the ethnicity of the contributors to this book. Another factor I kept in mind is gender balance: eight of the authors are women and seven are men.

The autobiographies are presented anonymously because even though many students gave me permission to publish their work when they submitted it I can no longer track them down to ask if they *still* wish to see their life stories in print. The writers attended four different campuses of the University of California where I taught— Berkeley, Santa Cruz, San Diego (as a visiting professor), and Santa Barbara. The chapters are arranged chronologically according to the authors' dates of departure from Vietnam. To further protect the authors' identities, I deleted place-names in Vietnam that the narrators had mentioned except for large geographic entities (North Vietnam and South Vietnam); the two capitals (Hanoi and Saigon); Dien Bien Phu because of its historical significance; and Vung Tau and Rach Gia, where many refuge-seekers went to make arrangements to escape by sea. However, I retained the titles that the authors had given their papers as the titles indicate what the authors themselves considered the most salient aspects of their lives.

Much as I admire my former students' indomitable spirit, there is a danger that these life stories may contribute to the misconception that *all* Asian Americans, including Vietnamese Americans, are a "successful model minority." Certainly, the authors fit that image but they are by no means a "representative sample" of the Vietnamese refugee and immigrant population as a whole. All the narrators were high achievers who, through fierce determination and perseverance, managed to master the English language well enough in a few short years to graduate from high school at or near the top of their classes, which qualified them for admission into a University of California campus. (The University of California considers for admission only the high school graduates in the top 12.5 percent of their graduating classes. The two University of California campuses in greatest demand—Berkeley and UCLA—turn down thousands of applicants with straight A grade point averages every year.) Benefiting from this education, all the authors were destined to become well-paid and respected professionals, thereby compensating for the downward mobility their families had suffered. Some families whose stories are told here experienced downward mobility not once, but twice, and in some cases, thrice—first, when they left North Vietnam in 1954, then after the Communists came to power in South Vietnam in 1975, and finally after they arrived in the United States.

Because I generally favor structural explanations over cultural ones, I am inclined to think that quite apart from the students' own determination and hard work, the pre-1975 socioeconomic status of their families very likely contributed significantly to their ability to overcome severe challenges in the United States. Their families possessed what sociologists call "class resources" and "human capital"—a conglomeration of higher education, pertinent work experience, an entrepreneurial drive, familiarity with Western ways of doing things, and experience with urban living.

The grandfathers of the authors of Chapters 13 and 15 were wealthy landowners in North Vietnam. One of the landlords was also a "mandarin." The prestige, power, and wealth of such landowning officials, who acquired their government positions by passing rigorous examinations on the Confucian classics, were similar to the elite social position that scholar-gentry in traditional Chinese society enjoyed. The grandfather of the author of Chapter 11 was a teacher in North Vietnam who became a government official after migrating south in 1954. The fathers in Chapters 14, 18, 21, and 23 were also government officials (two were employed by the South Vietnamese government and two by various agencies of the United States). The fathers in Chapters 13, 24, and 25 were South Vietnamese military officers. The mother in Chapter 15 likewise worked for the U.S. military as an office manager, while the mother in Chapter 11 worked for an American oil company. The fathers in Chapters 17, 19, 20, and 22 (three of whom were ethnic Chinese) were businessmen. The mother in Chapter 13 was also in business—she owned and ran a restaurant. Members of the extended family of mixed Chinese and Vietnamese ancestry whose story is told in Chapter 16 were health professionals even though the author's grandfather, who came from China, had begun life in Vietnam as a "coolie"—a common laborer. This is the only family whose members managed to retain, albeit with much effort, their occupational status in the United States. In short, a large majority of the authors' families were middle class. Aside from the grandfather in Chapter 16 who started life as a menial laborer, only three other families came from humble origins. The parents in Chapter 12 were both peasants (in the late 1960s the father became a security guard at an American consulate while the mother lived in a village with her children and continued to farm). The grandparents in Chapter 19 were fishermen, but the father was a traveling businessman. The father in Chapter 20 also grew up in poverty but had become a prosperous owner of an automobile dealership by the time the author was born.

The narrators are also distinguished by the fact that they belong to the "1.5 generation"—immigrants who come at a young age who retain their ability to speak, if not always to read and write, the ancestral language as well as Asian values and norms. Such individuals perform a unique bridging function, given their ability to understand both their elders and their American-born peers. They often act as cultural brokers, regardless of whether they wish to do so, between their grandparents, parents, aunts, and uncles, on the one hand, and the younger, usually American-born members of their families, on the other. As the narrators analyze their own experiences and ever-changing consciousness, they are quite conscious of the in-between spaces they occupy. They mediate not only between different generations in their families, but between American and Vietnamese ways of life and thought as well.

What is missing in this book are the experiences and voices of five other groups: elderly and adult refugees and immigrants who speak little or no English; former political prisoners released from re-education camps who paid the heaviest price of all in terms of suffering (the experience of one such prisoner is filtered through the eyes of his son in Chapter 18); members of the American-born second, or even third generation; *Viet Kieu* (overseas Vietnamese) whom some scholars characterize as transnational migrants who shuttle both physically and imaginatively between Vietnam and America; and youth who have not succeeded academically and socially as the narrators in this book have done. Among the last group, some became low-paid working people, while others dropped out of school, joined gangs, and hoped to become rich through criminal activities.

A subgroup within those who do not conform to the Asian American "model minority" stereotype are Amerasians, the mixed-blood children of American fathers and Vietnamese mothers. Even though in the late 1980s Congress passed an act to allow them to enter the United States with their mothers, stepfathers, and siblings, as a group Amerasians continue to encounter virtually insurmountable obstacles. People in Vietnam disdained and ostracized them; some of their mothers abandoned them; while most of the fathers long ago forgot about them. Most devastating of all, they had to fend for themselves from a very young age, living on the streets and receiving no education in post-1975 Vietnam. Thus, they entered the United States unprepared for either school or the world of work. (The bibliography contains titles of books that focus on those groups that are not included in this book.)

When I taught the "Vietnamese American Experience" course for the last time, at UC Santa Barbara in 2000, a year before I retired, I was shocked to discover that only one of the students in the moderately large class had been born in Vietnam and only one had been born in a refugee camp. All the others had been born in the United States. (The class also had two European American students whose fathers were Vietnam War veterans and who wanted to learn something about the tragic history of that long, long war.) How much has changed! When I first taught the course in 1980, all the students had been born in Vietnam and all of them had vivid recollections of the war and their escapes. In contrast, almost none of the Vietnamese students attending college in the twenty-first century have any personal memories of those years. That realization gave me the impetus finally to put together this collection of poignant life stories.

Editing this volume allowed me to retrace the steps in a journey toward understanding and tolerance that my Vietnamese students and I embarked on together a quarter century ago. Even though I still believe that American participation in the wars in Vietnam, Laos, and Cambodia was unjustified and the means the United States used to fight those wars were too brutal to be moral, my students have shown me how important it is never to forget the multifaceted human toll wreaked by war on both the victors and the vanquished. I shall always be grateful to them for sharing their life stories with me and reminding me that human connectedness is ultimately more important than ideology. One reviewer of the manuscript that became this book suggested that I be more "explicit and directive" in stating that my relationship to my students reflects "the expected pedagogical practice in Asian American Studies." However, I do not wish to make such a claim because teaching is an art more than a science. *How* we teach is intimately related to who we are. I do not have the right, therefore, to tell others to teach the way I did. Each teacher has to experiment and find approaches that seem most effective in terms of nurturing students and that feel most meaningful to herself or himself.

Two of my encounters with Vietnamese Americans in particular are etched in my memory. In 1988, when I was a visiting professor at UC San Diego, several students told me they felt frustrated and silenced because they were not allowed to express their true feelings about anything, especially with regard to their ancestral land. They said that their parents and other adults refused to tolerate any views other than the ones they themselves espoused. In contrast, having arrived in the United States when they were very young, the students' sense of who they were had been strongly influenced by American culture. They yearned for the freedom to express their thoughts and feelings. "Why don't you," I suggested, "write some short stories or plays in which the characters say what you yourself wish you can say? That way, if anyone criticizes you, you can respond it's just fiction." Such an outlet for expression had never occurred to them; they loved the idea and left my office elated.

A second interchange was more heartrending. After I had shown a film made by the first Western camera crew allowed into a reunified Vietnam, a freshman at UC Santa Barbara asked if he could borrow the videotape. He told me his father had just been released from a re-education camp in Vietnam and had been given an exit visa to join his family in America. He was extremely worried about how he would relate to his father, a complete stranger he had not seen since he was three years old. Because the film contained scenes of a re-education camp, he wanted to take a closer look. When he returned the videotape to me, he told me he had watched the four- or five-minute segment on the re-education camp almost twenty times with tears streaking down his cheeks. Three years later, just before he graduated from college, he dropped by to say goodbye to me and to thank me for helping him to get along with his father. "But I never did anything!" I protested. He explained that had he not seen the film, he, a young man who resented all authority figures, probably would have started fighting with his father right away. But after viewing the harsh physical settings in which his father, along with tens of thousands of former South Vietnamese government officials and military leaders, had been incarcerated—in his father's case, for more than a decade—he tried his best to be respectful as he and his father became reacquainted and told each other, bit by bit, about the lives they had each led during their long years of separation.

This book is primarily for Vietnamese American youths who would like to know a little something about their people's past. Written by students like themselves, the Vietnamese American voices in this book sing of anguish, bereavement, courage, and determination. Even more important, the authors chronicle how they became strong and eloquent young adults not in spite of, but rather, *because of* their tragedy-filled childhoods. Thus, their accounts should be inspiring, meaningful, and compelling to readers of other ethnic origins as well.

My contributions consist of correcting grammatical and spelling errors, rearranging sentences here and there to enable the narratives to flow more smoothly, deleting repetitious material, writing the ten chapters in Part I, and preparing the bibliography and videography. I anticipate that most readers will probably not be specialists in Vietnamese or Vietnamese American Studies; that is why I include a succinct presentation of the history of Vietnam and the successive stages of the refugee exodus so that readers can understand the larger historical, political, and social contexts within which the events described in the chapters in Part II occurred. The endnotes, many of which suggest additional readings, the bibliography, and videography are meant to facilitate the efforts of students, faculty, and other readers to explore in greater depth the specific topics that interest them.

Sucheng Chan
Goleta, California
July 2005

Acknowledgments

I express heartfelt thanks to my former Vietnamese American students who wrote the life stories in this book, as well as to many other students from Cambodia, Laos, and Vietnam who took my courses and taught me so much about the human costs of war and revolution.

I thank the two reviewers of the manuscript for their incisive and sensible suggestions that improved both the substance and organization of the book. I am especially grateful to Linda Trinh Võ who suggested I include a videography and sent me titles to augment the list I made.

I am beholden to Janet Francendese of Temple University Press, who has played a crucial role in disseminating scholarly knowledge about Asian Americans through her support of the Asian American History and Culture book series. I also appreciate the efforts of David Wilson, the production editor at Temple University Press; Joanne Bowser, the project manager at TechBooks, who guided the manuscript through the publication process; and Melissa Messina, who copyedited the book.

Vietnamese Names

In Vietnam, family names (what the British call "surnames" and Americans call "last names") precede given names (what Americans call "first names"). However, because of the relatively small number of family names in use, the Vietnamese people refer to each other by the last syllable in their given names. For example, Nguyen is the family name of President Nguyen Van Thieu, but he is known as "Thieu." The main exception is Ho Chi Minh (a pseudonym), who is always referred to as "Ho." Most Vietnamese living in the United States and other Western countries have adopted the Western naming sequence, with given names preceding family names. In this book, personal names are indexed according to family names. For example, President Ngo Dinh Diem is indexed under Ngo, even though he is always referred to as "Diem."

Well-known place-names in Vietnam, such as Hanoi, Saigon, Danang, and the name of the country itself, are written as polysyllabic words following Western conventional practice, but I transliterate each syllable in less well-known place-names (at least to American readers) like Ban Me Thuot and Rach Gia as a separate word.

"Ethnic Chinese in Vietnam," "Sino-Chinese," and "Chinese Vietnamese" are synonyms that refer to the ethnic origins, rather than the citizenship, of people of Chinese ancestry who live/d in Vietnam. Some of them are citizens of Vietnam (in its various historical, political, and geographic manifestations); others are citizens of China (either the People's Republic of China or the Republic of China on Taiwan); yet others reside in the United States and other nations, a portion of whom have become citizens of those countries.

"Montagnards" is the generic, collective name that the French gave several dozen ethnic groups who live in the mountains.

PART I

Historical Overview

Most of the English-language books and articles about Vietnam available to American readers deal with the U.S. involvement in the Vietnam War. However, that long, bitter, destructive, and very controversial war—a war that devastated the land in all parts of Vietnam and killed several million Vietnamese and some 58,000 Americans—is not the main focus of this study for three reasons. First, the existing literature on the war is voluminous and readers can easily find the pertinent studies. Second, it is impossible to synthesize a "balanced" and succinct account that reflects the perspectives of all the key players or of the authors who have written about them. Third, I believe we should view the history of Vietnam in its chronological totality to emphasize the fact that the Vietnamese have a long and complicated history—one that encompasses much more than the events that occurred in their country during the years when first the French and then the Americans fought wars on Vietnamese soil.

The chapters in Part I discuss several recurrent themes in Vietnamese history: foreign conquest and colonial rule, Vietnamese resistance to alien domination, and large population movements. Even though the wars against the French and the Americans stretched over thirty years, they were preceded historically by other deadly conflicts dating back more than a millennium. Similarly, though the refugee exodus from Vietnam that began in 1975 and ended only in 1997 was the largest outpouring of people Vietnam has ever witnessed, it was by no means the first or only large population movement in that country's history. Given these historical antecedents, a quick sketch of Vietnam's past will be instructive.

CHAPTER ONE

Vietnam before the Mid-nineteenth Century

Scholars generally agree that the ancestors of the Vietnamese orig-inated in the valleys of the Hong (Red) River and its tributaries in northern Vietnam—an alluvial plain that has sustained a significant portion of the country's population for several millennia. Archeol-ogists have discovered large ornamental bronze drums, as well as bronze arrowheads, javelin tips, cleavers, sickles, and fishhooks at Dong Son in Thanh Hoa province that provide evidence that the forebears of the Vietnamese people had entered the Bronze Age by the third millennium B.C.E. The Bronze Age in the Hong River valley and delta peaked in the seventh century B.C.E. The people there called themselves Lac, lived in small villages, grew rice in irrigated fields, hunted, and fished.[1] While Vietnamese claim the Lac as their ances-tors, some scholars have pointed out that the Lac were only one of many racial and ethnic groups, including Mongolian, Chinese, Thai, Austro-Asian, Melanesian, and Negrito, that amalgamated to form the Vietnamese people.[2] Among the ethnic groups that contributed to the evolution of Vietnam—the country as well as its people—the Chinese have exerted the greatest influence.

Chinese Colonial Rule and Vietnamese Resistance

The historical relationship between Vietnam and China has been a paradoxical one: after valiantly resisting Chinese domination for a thousand years, the Vietnamese dynasties established after the Chinese were driven out adopted many Chinese social, cultural, and political institutional forms mainly because the rulers recognized that the teachings of the Chinese philosopher, Confucius, were useful for exerting social and political control over their subjects. For that rea-son, Truong Buu Lam, a prominent Vietnamese historian teaching in the United States, thinks Vietnam should more properly be considered a part of East Asia rather than Southeast Asia because "from the Bronze Age down to the present, Vietnam has evolved within the Chinese world order, with Chinese cultural patterns and Chinese political institutions."[3] True enough, but an indigenous culture did exist centuries before Chinese imperial armies subjugated Vietnam and some of the Chinese ideas and practices the Vietnamese adopted were modified in the process of transplantation.

China began asserting its influence on the land that eventually became Vietnam in the third century B.C.E. when the founder of China's Qin dynasty, Qin Shi Huangdi, sent an army of half a million men to conquer and pacify the territory lying south of the Yangzi River and extending inland from the southeastern coast of China. People known by the generic name *Yueh* lived in that region. In 206 B.C.E., Chao To (Trieu Da in Vietnamese), the son of the Chinese governor of the Yueh region, founded a kingdom called Nan Yueh (which means southern Yueh and is pronounced Nam Viet in Vietnamese) that encompassed Guangdong and Guangxi provinces in southern China, the Hong River valley and delta, and the coastal strip stretching from the delta southward to what is now called central Vietnam.

In 111 B.C.E., China invaded Nam Viet and colonized it. During the next millennium, Chinese officials sent to govern the region divided it into provinces and districts, set up an administrative structure staffed mainly by Chinese appointees, sent tributes to the Chinese emperor, collected taxes from villagers, introduced the plow and the use of water buffalos as draft animals, opened schools to teach the Chinese language (which became the official language of Nam Viet) and the Chinese classics, erected buildings in the Chinese architectural style, and built roads, canals, and harbors with coerced Vietnamese labor.[4] An increasing number of Chinese settlers also came to farm and trade. The Chinese started calling the region An Nam (Pacified South)—a reflection of the Chinese perception that the region had become a subdued part of the Chinese empire. (In later years, the name Annam was used to refer only to the central part of Vietnam even though the French called all Vietnamese "Annamites.") As its rice acreage increased, Nam Viet became a prosperous region but the riches accrued to the Chinese empire and its colonial administrators and not to the Vietnamese people.

The Vietnamese chafed and seethed under the Chinese yoke. Revolts against Chinese rule punctuated the history of Nam Viet. The first uprising, in 39 C.E., was led by Trung Trac and Trung Nhi, two sisters whose husbands the Chinese had killed, according to conventional belief. Keith Taylor, however, observes that there is no documentary evidence that indicates their husbands had been killed, so he thinks the lore probably reflects the "patriarchal bias of later centuries, which could not countenance a woman leading a rebellion and being recognized as queen so long as her husband still lived."[5] The sisters and their army won their battles against the Chinese occupiers and established a kingdom in 40 C.E. with Trung Trac as queen. Even though a Chinese army led by General Ma Yuan with eight thousand regular troops and twelve thousand militiamen recaptured the territory two years later, the Trung sisters have come down in history as Vietnam's most cherished heroines.

Another uprising led by a woman, Trieu Au, took place in 248 C.E., but the Chinese crushed it also. The next notable revolt, led by Ly Bon, a descendant of Chinese settlers, occurred in 542 C.E. His armies fought to expel the Chinese from Nam Viet, his family's adopted land. His ethnic origins and his political allegiance reflect the complexities of the Vietnamese-Chinese connection: over the centuries, Chinese who lived in Vietnam became Vietnamized while Vietnamese became Sinicized.[6] Despite major uprisings in 590, 600, 722, and 791,[7] the Vietnamese failed to drive out their Chinese overlords until the tenth century, when Ngo Quyen successfully reestablished Nam Viet as an independent country in 939.

Vietnamese Dynasties

The dynasty that Ngo Quyen founded lasted barely thirty years. It was followed by the similarly short-lived Dinh (968–80) and Early Le (980–1009) dynasties. (The word *Early* is used to differentiate this first Le dynasty from another dynasty of the same name—the *Later* Le dynasty.) Emperor Tien Hoang of the Dinh dynasty incorporated Taoist and Buddhist priests into Nam Viet's administrative hierarchy, while an Early Le emperor helped proselytize Buddhism. The two faiths blended with indigenous animistic beliefs to form the Vietnamese variant of Buddhism, but scholars are not certain whether Buddhism initially came to Vietnam directly from India or via China.

The next dynasty, the Ly (1010–1225), renamed the country Dai Viet (Great Viet), established its capital, Thang Long (Rising Dragon), at the site now occupied by Hanoi, and in 1075 adopted the Chinese system of examinations that determined who would qualify for office at various levels of government. Henceforth, Vietnamese, rather than Chinese scholar-gentry, administered Vietnam. Since the main texts used in the examinations were the Confucian classics, Confucian values and norms spread among both the ruling class and those they ruled. Confucianism, which taught rulers and subjects, fathers and children, husbands and wives, elders and youth, and friends how to behave properly vis-à-vis one another in a hierarchical social system, became the foundation of Vietnamese culture, in which the extended family was, and still is, the fundamental social unit. Confucian doctrine favored the superordinate member in the first four dyads named above—that is, the rulers, fathers, husbands, and elders. Equality existed only among friends. Confucianists valued social harmony, which they believed would prevail only if people acted according to the norms appropriate to the statuses into which they had been born.[8] However, Buddhism, Taoism, and Confucianism did not completely erase preexisting Vietnamese practices. For example, women in Vietnam, like women in other parts of lowland Southeast Asia, enjoyed more rights than did women in China, Japan, and Korea, where patriarchal Confucian doctrine exerted a pervasive influence over the social structure. Vietnamese daughters could inherit property along with their brothers and could engage in business outside the home. Moreover, Vietnamese villages were not organized by clans or lineages as was the case in China.

The two dynasties that succeeded the Ly, the Tran (1225–1400) and the Later Le (1427–1788), continued to rely on Confucian tenets as part of their statecraft and adopted the court manners of China's Song dynasty.[9] After Emperor Le Thang Tong, who ruled from 1460 to 1497, promulgated the Le Code, Buddhism and Taoism lost their standing among the elite as Confucianism reigned supreme.[10] Commoners, however, continued to adhere to the syncretized form of those religions. More important, despite the formal adoption of Chinese orthodoxy, the Vietnamese made sure that future generations would never forget the humiliation of a thousand years of Chinese rule. In 1407, during China's Ming dynasty, the Chinese reconquered Vietnam and held it once again in its grip. A landowner and official named Le Loi and a military commander named Nguyen Trai teamed up to lead a guerrilla war against the Chinese and drove them out of the country in 1427.[11] Since then, the Chinese have never succeeded in reimposing their domination over Vietnam.

The Vietnamese Colonization of Champa and the Mekong Delta

Soon after the Vietnamese regained their independence, they themselves embarked on a centuries-long campaign to expand their territory and colonize other lands. They began a slow but steady southward march to conquer Champa, a kingdom occupying the southern half of what eventually became Vietnam. Dai Viet and Champa engaged in a seesaw series of battles over the course of several centuries: sometimes the Vietnamese held the upper hand, at other times the Cham did. Both the Vietnamese and the Khmer (Cambodians) were interested in annexing Champa, a wealthy realm. Its strategic location along one of the major trade routes in the South China Sea enabled international trade to flourish there. The Vietnamese finally captured the capital of Champa in 1471, but it took them two more centuries to vanquish the remaining pockets of the Cham kingdom at the end of the seventeenth century.[12]

The Vietnamese also started moving into the marshy lands of the Mekong Delta that belonged to the Angkor kingdom in Cambodia. During the reign of Emperor Le Thang Tong, Vietnamese officials started sending soldiers to the delta to open up sparsely populated land for rice cultivation. The state gave these soldier-peasants tools to clear and cultivate the land, buffalos to pull their plows, seed grain for planting, and enough food to sustain them until the first harvest. The colonists were organized into groups called *don dien* and were exempted from paying taxes during the first seven years.[13] Army deserters and bandits also found their way to the delta in search of, if not quick fortunes, then at least a livelihood. The Cambodians who remained in the delta after the Vietnamese captured it bit by bit call themselves Khmer Krom and still refer to the region as Kampuchea Krom (Lower Cambodia).[14] The Mekong Delta, after the swamps were drained—first on a small scale by the Vietnamese settlers and later on a large scale by the French—became and remains the most fertile and productive arable region in the country. The southward march to conquer, colonize, and settle lands belonging to other kingdoms was the first large and prolonged population movement in Vietnam's history.

While they were expanding their territory, the Vietnamese had to fend off two major invasions. After Kublai Khan conquered China and established the Yuan dynasty in 1279, the Mongols tried to invade Dai Viet, Champa, and Cambodia. Approaching the three countries by land and by sea, a Mongol army numbering half a million men sacked the Dai Viet capital but a smaller Vietnamese army of about two hundred thousand troops led by Tran Hung Dao managed to repel the invaders in 1284. The Mongols tried again to take Dai Viet three years later, this time with three hundred thousand warriors. Again they failed despite occupying Thang Long (Hanoi) briefly three separate times during these two campaigns.[15]

Upon the Chinese departure in 1427, Le Loi established a new dynasty known as the Later Le dynasty, which lasted for three and a half centuries. However, by the latter part of the sixteenth century that dynasty began to decline. Two powerful families, the Trinh *chua* (lords) in the north and the Nguyen *chua* in the south, came to dominate the country even though Le emperors remained nominally on the throne. Feuds, intrigues, and assassinations kept both sections of the country in turmoil, while a series of civil wars between the Trinh and the Nguyen wracked the countryside and reduced the common people's lives to abject misery. Vietnam was split in two when the Nguyen built two rows of walls stretching from the sea to the mountains in a location where the country was less than fifty miles wide, thereby preventing the Trinh armies from breaching that line of defense. That historical precedent of dividing Vietnam into two halves would be repeated centuries later in 1954.

A revolt led by three brothers from the village of Tay Son in Binh Dinh province that began in 1771 brought down the house of Nguyen in 1777, the house of Trinh in 1786, and the Later Le dynasty in 1787. The Tay Son soldiers took the land of the gentry and distributed it to peasants. They burned tax registers to give commoners reprieve from the heavy levies that had burdened them. One of the Tay Son brothers proclaimed himself emperor in 1788. The Tay Son forces defeated a Chinese army that marched into Vietnam in response to the Le emperor's call for help,[16] but the Tay Son kingdom lasted only until 1802. In that year Nguyen Phuc Anh (commonly called Nguyen Anh by Western scholars), who had managed to escape in 1777 as the Tay Son army killed the members of his extended family, the Nguyen chua, founded the Nguyen dynasty.[17] During his reign and those of his successors, Europeans became the greatest threat to Dai Viet's independence.

Enter the Europeans

The Portuguese were the first Europeans to reach Southeast Asia. They built a seaborne empire consisting of a string of coastal trading stations stretching from the Iberian Peninsula to Africa, the Arabian Peninsula, India, across the Indian Ocean, through the Straits of Malacca, on to the spice islands of Southeast Asia, and northwards across the South China Sea to China and Japan. Goa, in India, served as the headquarters of that empire. In Dai Viet, the Portuguese set up their first trading station, which also functioned as a Catholic mission, at Faifo (now called Hoi An) located a few miles south of present-day

Danang, in 1535. They established another one in Thang Long a decade later. In the seventeenth century, however, the Dutch captured many of Portugal's trading posts and gained control over the sea-lanes as they vied with the English for supremacy in Southeast Asia.

Though the Portuguese carried out their colonizing activities for the glory of God, it was the French who became the main propagators of Catholicism in Vietnam. French Jesuits established a mission at Faifo in 1614 and one at Thang Long in 1626 despite Portuguese objections. A missionary, Alexandre de Rhodes, was stationed at Faifo from 1627 to 1630, during which he converted several thousand Vietnamese to Catholicism and wrote a catechism in the Vietnamese language. He learned Vietnamese so well that he could preach in it. He also created a Romanized script for the Vietnamese language, using diacritical marks to indicate the tones of Vietnamese words. Known as *quoc ngu* (national language), this script is still in use today. In 1630, the Vietnamese authorities forced Rhodes to leave but he managed to reenter Dai Viet in the mid-1640s and proselytized there for several more years before returning to Europe in 1649, where he published a Latin-Vietnamese dictionary, a history of Tonkin (the northern part of Vietnam), and a map of Dai Viet. In 1658, he secured the Pope's blessing for a plan to train Asian priests to serve their compatriots. French priests slated to undertake this task were educated in a seminary established in 1663 in Paris, which became an integral part of the Société des Missions Etrangères (Foreign Missions Society).[18]

The first French Jesuit missionaries sent out by the Société des Missions Etrangères reached Dai Viet in 1669. Missionary work was full of dangers: Vietnamese authorities sometimes imprisoned the proselytizers, while some common people killed local Christian converts and burned church buildings from time to time.[19] The French central government did not offer the missionaries any protection. Instead, the French Navy, which had imperialistic ambitions, became their champion. The missionaries, naval officers, and merchants affiliated with the French East India Company actively lobbied for the reestablishment of a French colonial and commercial presence in Asia after the British drove the French out of India.[20]

The Nguyen Dynasty

The French became entangled in Vietnam's political affairs when the French apostolic vicar at Ha Tien (located near the Vietnamese-Cambodian border), Pierre J. G. Pigneau (commonly known as Pigneau de Behaine in honor of Behaine, his birthplace), befriended

Nguyen Anh, who was only fifteen years old when he escaped the Tay Son massacre of his extended family. When the Tay Son armies marched north to attack the territory controlled by the Trinh chua, Nguyen Anh slipped back into Cochinchina (the name the Portuguese gave the southern part of the country—a name that the French later adopted) and rallied enough supporters to capture Gia Dinh (Saigon and its vicinity). He proclaimed himself king of Cochinchina and ruled for four years before the Tay Son ousted him in 1782. He found sanctuary in Siam (today's Thailand), where he met up again with Pigneau, who offered to seek help from the French government on his behalf. However, Pigneau failed in this mission. By the time he returned to Saigon in 1789, Nguyen Anh had already been back there for a year. It took the young warrior another thirteen years to complete the military campaigns that brought the entire country under his control in 1802. He renamed the country Vietnam, ascended the throne as the Gia Long emperor, and chose Hue as his capital, ruling a unified Vietnam that for the first time covered the entire eastern section of the large peninsula known as mainland Southeast Asia.[21]

Gia Long ruled as a Confucian monarch. He revised the Le Code and brought it into conformity with the Qing Code in China. He founded a National Academy in Hue to train the sons of officials and other ambitious young men in the Chinese classics. Though he was friendly to and rewarded a small number of Frenchmen who had supported him during his military campaigns, he did not grant any Western powers the commercial privileges they sought. He allowed Western merchants to trade only at selected ports under a state-controlled Merchant Superintendency, but he did instruct his officials to aid foreign vessels shipwrecked along Vietnam's coastline, which is more than a thousand miles long. He also allowed Catholic missionaries to travel around the country to preach even though he had issued an edict in 1804 that branded Catholicism a dangerous foreign doctrine.[22]

Gia Long died in 1820. His successor, Minh Mang (also transliterated as Ming Menh), was also a staunch Confucianist but, unlike his father, he felt no debt of gratitude to the French. He persecuted both foreign and local Catholics, executing half a dozen of the former and punishing the latter when they refused to renounce Christianity. He broke diplomatic relations with France in 1826. However, after the First Opium War between China and Britain erupted in 1839, Minh Mang, fearful that Vietnam might suffer a similar fate as China's, tried to make peace with the French. Before anything came of his overtures, he died in 1841. His successor, Thieu Tri, who ruled from

1841 to 1847, continued the efforts to rid the country of Christians by expelling (but not executing) missionaries. In response, French naval vessels bombarded Danang (which the French called Tourane) to spring French missionaries out of jail.[23] Catholics in France demanded that their government retaliate against Vietnam's actions.[24] Thieu Tri's successor, Tu Duc, who ruled from 1848 to 1883, likewise opposed the presence of Christians, but he stopped harassing them after 1862 when Vietnam and France signed the Treaty of Saigon.

Scholars have interpreted Vietnam's reaction to Christianity in opposite ways. An older generation of scholars, relying mainly on French sources, tend to depict the Vietnamese rulers' anti-Christian actions as "Oriental" xenophobia. In contrast, Mark McLeod, who reads Vietnamese and has plumbed the archives of the Nguyen dynasty, offers a more nuanced interpretation. He argues that the Vietnamese rulers had good reason to see Christians in a negative light. A Christian convert, Le Van Khoi, led an insurrection that broke out in the southern part of the country in 1833 and lasted several years. French missionaries, Vietnamese Catholic converts, and King Rama III of Siam, who sent his armies to attack Vietnam, all supported this rebellion. Some two thousand Vietnamese Catholics led by a Vietnamese priest aided the Siamese invaders. This was by no means the only antidynastic effort in which Christians participated. Thus, in McLeod's (and my) view, the Nguyen rulers had reason to be wary of a foreign religion whose adherents attempted to overthrow the dynasty.[25] The missionaries' presence encouraged other Frenchmen, who desired not only converts but also an empire, to go to Vietnam to see what riches might be found there.

CHAPTER TWO

French Colonial Rule and Vietnamese Resistance

By the middle of the nineteenth century, the French were no longer concerned just with protecting their missionaries but also with acquiring an empire in Southeast Asia in the name of *mission civilisatrice* (civilizing mission), the underlying assumption of which was that Europeans, who thought they possessed moral superiority, should "uplift" and "civilize" nonwhite and non-Christian peoples by colonizing them. A more basic concern was that in the age of imperialism, each of the major European countries desired an empire of its own in order to enhance its national stature. Dissatisfied with the concessions they had gained at the end of the First Opium War (1839–42), which China lost, the British again went to war with China in 1856. France joined Great Britain in the Second Opium War (1856–60), which China also lost. The two victorious nations extracted additional concessions from a prostrate China.[1]

The Creation of French Indochina

Simply acquiring concessions—small enclaves controlled by the Western powers in China—did not satisfy the French desire for glory. So, they set about colonizing Vietnam. They sent an expedition to Danang in August 1858 with fourteen ships and two thousand and five hundred men.[2] They also persuaded the Spanish, the colonial masters of the Philippines, to join the expedition against the Vietnamese by sending four hundred and fifty Catholic Filipinos. The combined forces attacked Danang but when they went ashore they could not proceed into the hinterland because the Vietnamese, led by General Nguyen Tri Phuong, had built trenches and walls to impede the enemy's advance.[3] The invaders then sailed to Saigon, which they took in February 1859. Thus began the French conquest and colonization of Vietnam, Cambodia, and Laos, which they eventually amalgamated into an entity called *Indochine Française* (French Indochina).

Before the French forces could make their way into the countryside beyond Saigon, they were summoned back to China to participate in the Second Opium War. They left a small contingent in Saigon, but those troops failed to make additional advances until January 1861 when the French returned with seventy ships and three thousand and five hundred men who had just completed the campaign in China. Not only did they take Saigon, but they also captured three provinces lying between Saigon and the Vietnamese-Cambodian border. In light of the European superiority in firepower and, more important, because a rebellion led by a Catholic convert, Pierre Le Duy Phung, aimed at toppling the Nguyen dynasty had erupted in northern Vietnam, Emperor Tu Duc felt compelled to sign the Treaty of Saigon forced upon him by the French in June 1862, ceding the three provinces, as well as Poulo Condore island, to France. He hoped that Vietnam would regain the provinces later through diplomatic negotiations. The treaty forced Vietnam to open three ports to European ships and merchants, allow missionaries to spread Christianity, permit French ships to sail up the Mekong River, give up the right to cede any territory to other countries without French permission, and pay the French an indemnity of four million Mexican silver dollars—the international currency of choice at the time.[4]

However, the Vietnamese people, some groups led by scholars, others by commoners, resisted the imposition of French rule. Fearing further incursions by the French, the Hue court suppressed these uprisings.[5] In the words of David G. Marr, "the Nguyen dynasty was strong enough to contain domestic dissent and retain power for itself, but worried enough about its underpinnings—its sources of support—to be unwilling to take really appropriate defensive measures." The French, for their part, "forced concessions from the court, tied them down solemnly in treaties, and then proceeded if necessary to 'safeguard' the Nguyen from popular wrath."[6] The emperor and his officials ordered Truong Dinh, leader of a local resistance group in Cochinchina, to stop fighting by enticing him with an official position. Truong Dinh declined the appointment, but he died in 1864 when one of his former associates betrayed him to the French.[7] It took the French four years to pacify the three provinces they had acquired.[8] To consolidate their hold over the delta, the French wrested another three provinces from Vietnam in 1867. They named the six delta provinces Cochinchina and ruled the region as a direct colony. Given the leading role that the French Navy had played, the governors of Cochinchina from 1862 to 1879 were all admirals.[9]

In 1863, the French coerced King Norodom of Cambodia to allow them to turn his country into a French protectorate.[10] Next, France imposed protectorates over Tonkin and Annam in 1883. Because Tu Duc died without a natural male heir (he had three adopted sons) that same year, struggles to determine who would be his successor preoccupied the Hue court as the French grabbed northern and central Vietnam. Once again, it was the common people, often led by officials, who resisted the French advances. On July 5, 1885, the regent, Ton That Thuyet, whisked Ham Nghi, the thirteen-year-old emperor, out of Hue and took him into the mountains of central Vietnam. From his hideout, Ham Nghi issued an edict called *Can Vuong* (Loyalty or Aid to the King) in which he granted royal "permission" for local uprisings to take place. Couriers distributed copies of the edict to all the provinces. The subsequent acts of resistance, known as the Can Vuong Movement, lasted until the 1890s even though the French captured Ham Nghi in 1888 and sent him into exile in Algeria, another French colonial possession.[11]

The second-highest ranking court official to participate in the Can Vuong Movement was Phan Dinh Phung. He and Cao Thang, a former bandit, built a network of bases in the mountains of central Vietnam, gathered and hid food supplies, acquired weapons and ammunition, and trained peasants to spy on the French. Cao Thang died in battle in 1893. The French tried to threaten Phan Dinh Phung by holding his brother hostage, but he declared: "If I saved my brother, who would save all the other brothers of our country?" As Hue-Tam Ho Tai puts it, "Phan was rare, if not unique, among his contemporaries in speaking of his compatriots as his brothers, and in suggesting that love of country . . . was the wellspring of his struggle."[12] Refusing to leave his mountain base, he died of hunger and dysentery in 1896.

Colonial Exploitation

By the time that Tonkin and Annam came under French control, French private citizens had entrenched themselves in Cochinchina. They became very rich, owning thousands and thousands of acres of rice land cultivated by Vietnamese tenants and landless laborers. Soon, Cochinchina became the world's third largest exporter of rice (after Thailand and Burma). However, French colonial authorities forbade the rice growers in Cochinchina to export rice to Annam and Tonkin, thereby making life in those two regions of Vietnam extremely difficult.[13] Moreover, the French owners of the de facto fiefdoms in Cochinchina had no desire to contribute to the common budget of a proposed Indochina Union, so they resisted efforts to create a central administrative structure for the three regions. Even though a single governor-general was appointed to administer Cochinchina, Annam, Tonkin, Cambodia, and after 1893, Laos,[14] in fact he never gained much control over Cochinchina. Meanwhile, the authority of the Vietnamese emperors, who were allowed to remain on the throne, extended over only the court in Hue. Not surprisingly, the French, who now controlled royal succession, placed only pliable candidates on the throne.[15]

Unable to raise much revenue from Cochinchina, the French colonial administrators resorted to levying heavy taxes, especially on the sale of salt, alcohol, and opium, which they made into state monopolies. To maximize the income from these three monopolies, they imposed quotas to force each Vietnamese community, both rural and urban, to consume annually specified amounts of alcohol and opium, an addictive drug.[16] Every Vietnamese also had to pay a head tax. In addition to using Vietnamese corvée labor (unpaid coerced labor) to grow rice in Cochinchina, the French employed Vietnamese to mine for coal, zinc, tin, and tungsten in Tonkin. In the early twentieth century, after the automobile was invented and rubber became a crucial commodity for making tires, the French established rubber plantations in northern Cochinchina, southern Annam, and eastern Cambodia.[17] Working conditions in the mines and plantations were so odious that they can best be described as living hells.[18] The French also developed tea and coffee plantations to increase the profits made by exporting such cash crops and set up small factories to manufacture textiles, paper, sugar, matches, bicycles, and other light items for the local market.

As landownership became more and more concentrated in the hands of French *colons* (colonists) and a small number of Vietnamese landlords, the number of tenants and landless laborers increased. They had barely enough grain left to keep themselves alive after turning over as much as 70 percent of their harvests to landlords and moneylenders.[19] A new class also emerged during those years—educated Vietnamese who found jobs as lower-echelon civil servants, clerks, translators, schoolteachers, and employees in French-owned enterprises. Having a higher opinion of the Vietnamese than of the Cambodians and Laotians, the French staffed their colonial administration in Cambodia and Laos with Vietnamese civil servants. As their livelihood depended on the continued existence of a colonial regime, many of these people became collaborators of the French.

Intellectual and Cultural Ferment

By the end of the nineteenth century, the French had put down all armed uprisings. Vietnamese resistance did not end, however. Instead, it took new forms. A small number of intellectuals began looking for ideas from other countries—particularly China, Japan, and France— to help them make sense of their country's plight. The intelligentsia read the works of Kang Youwei and Liang Qichao, the two leaders of the Reform Movement in China, sought help from the Japanese, and read the writings of French thinkers such as Montesquieu and Rousseau. David Marr proposes that the despair felt by this new generation can be summed up in the concept *mat-nuoc* (losing one's country), which refers not only to the loss of Vietnam's sovereignty but also of its "soul" or sense of Vietnamese peoplehood.[20] The loss was symbolized by the fact that the French had even erased the country's very name, Vietnam, from the face of the earth.

The two most notable Vietnamese scholar-patriots in the first twenty-five years of the twentieth century were Phan Boi Chau (1867–1940) and Phan Chu Trinh (1872–1926), who fought with pens rather than swords or guns. They and their like-minded colleagues, also born in the 1860s and 1870s, received their early education in the Chinese classics and did not discover other sources of knowledge until they were adults. But because they were well versed in Chinese, they could quickly absorb the "new learning," including selected Japanese and European writings, through Chinese translations of them. After Japan defeated Russia in the Russo-Japanese War (1904–05), Vietnamese patriots looked increasingly to Japan as a model of how an Asian country could retain its sovereignty while selectively using Western knowledge, especially science and technology, to strengthen itself.

Phan Boi Chau founded the Duy Tan Hoi (Reformation Society) in 1903, persuaded Prince Cuong De, a direct descendant of Emperor Gia Long, to serve as a symbol around whom partisans might rally, wrote many books and pamphlets, and urged an increasing number of Vietnamese students to study abroad in order to learn modern ideas and methods. Small donations from a handful of Japanese and Chinese political leaders and rich Vietnamese in Cochinchina, who remained patriots even as they accommodated themselves to life under the French, financed the activities of the Dong Du Movement (Eastern Study or Travel Movement—"Eastern" referred to Japan). Phan Boi Chau also gained some adherents among Buddhist and Taoist priests who, unlike other Vietnamese, could travel relatively freely around the country to help spread the message. A Japanese politician persuaded Phan Boi Chau to bring Prince Cuong De to Japan as a student. Liang Qichao, who was residing in Japan at the time, published some of Phan Boi Chau's early writings, including *Viet Nam Vong Quoc Su* (History of the Loss of Vietnam) and a pamphlet that encouraged Vietnamese students to study abroad and well-heeled Vietnamese to support them financially. These publications had to be smuggled into Vietnam but they apparently reached audiences in all parts of the country. Some sympathizers opened hotels and other businesses in order to make money to support the students. These enterprises also served as drop-off and dissemination points for Phan Boi Chau's publications.[21]

Unfortunately for the Dong Du Movement, Japan and France signed a treaty in 1907 to support each other's "territorial rights." Under French pressure, the Japanese government expelled Cuong De, Phan Boi Chau, and other Vietnamese students. Phan Boi Chau continued to write and publish as he lived in exile in Siam and various places in China. After China's 1911 Republican Revolution ended the Qing dynasty, he became an advocate of a republican form of government and formed the Viet Nam Quang Phuc Hoi (League for the Restoration of Vietnam), in which many Vietnamese living in exile in southern China became members. At the request of the French governor-general of Indochina, the Chinese authorities arrested him in 1914. He spent three years in a Chinese jail in Guangdong province, during which he wrote prolifically. In 1925 the French caught up with him again and took him back to Vietnam to be tried. He was sentenced to life imprisonment at hard labor, but the new French governor-general, a socialist, commuted his sentence to house arrest for life.[22]

Phan Chu Trinh, an equally influential intellectual, was against using violent means to oust the French. He placed less emphasis on action, as Phan Boi Chau did, and more on transforming and revitalizing Vietnamese culture and psychology. In addition to French colonialism, he blamed Vietnam's imperial system for the country's ills. He argued that the Confucian examination system should be abolished and called for the establishment of modern schools and businesses, as well as the adoption of Western dress and appearance (by appearance, he meant that Vietnamese men should cut their long

hair and long fingernails). He called those Vietnamese who collabo-
rated with the French "parasites" and castigated the colonial regime
for exploiting Vietnamese workers and treating them as though they
were not human beings. However, he opposed seeking support from
Japan and China and believed that violent attempts to overthrow the
French colonial regime would fail.

Enamored of French Enlightenment thinking, Phan Chu Trinh believed that the French could guide the Vietnamese along the road to
progress until they were ready for self-rule. Despite his obvious belief
in the mission civilisatrice, the French colonial authorities arrested
him in 1908, along with many other scholar-gentry resistance leaders, in the aftermath of demonstrations and protests that erupted in
various parts of Vietnam, and sent them to the penal colony on Poulo
Condore island. After he was released in 1911, Phan Chu Trinh spent
the next fourteen years in exile in France. While there, he and others
formed an organization, Dong Bao Than Ai (Fraternity), composed of
individuals from French colonies in Asia and Africa who were studying or working in France. After World War I broke out, the French
security organization, the Sûreté, in a sweep to lock up members of
subversive groups, arrested him and kept him in jail until 1915. Upon
his release, he eked out a living and continued to write. Returning to
Vietnam in 1925, he died of tuberculosis the following year. Tens of
thousands of people used his funeral as an occasion to demonstrate
very publicly their growing hostility to French rule.[23]

Phan Boi Chau and Phan Chu Trinh were but the two best-known
individuals who searched for ways to regain Vietnam's independence.
For all his efforts to promote direct action, Phan Boi Chau's mindset
was still embedded in traditional Confucian ideals. As for Phan Chu
Trinh, despite his wide readings and prolific writings, he was wedded
to a cultural idealism that failed to analyze how concrete social, economic, political, and institutional changes might be achieved. In this
protean period, thousands of other Vietnamese, including women,
likewise searched for ways to save and regenerate their country. They
examined and evaluated not only all facets of Vietnamese society but
also how various philosophical and political currents emanating from
Asia and Europe might be applicable to their own country. Given the
fact that only an estimated 10 percent of the school-age population
in the 1920s and 1930s received an education,[24] the thousands of
young people who debated and participated in anti-French activities
is truly astonishing—a fact that gives them an historical importance
far out of proportion to their small numbers. They included conservative cultural restorationists, advocates of a constitutional monarchy,

supporters of a republican form of government, proponents of direct action, reformers who believed in gradual change, anarchists for whom freedom was paramount, socialists who emphasized the well-being of collectivities rather than individuals, and Communists concerned about class oppression. As Hue-Tam Ho Tai argues, it is in "the interplay between cultural discourse and political action" that the origins of the Vietnamese anticolonial revolution can best be understood.[25]

As traditional patriotism evolved into modern nationalism, a wide array of political parties came into being. The Dang Lap Hien (Constitutionalist Party) demanded more educational opportunities for Vietnamese; greater participation in administrating the country; higher pay for workers; freedom to assemble, publish, and travel; and assimilation into French society rather than Vietnamese independence. The Viet Nam Quoc Dan Dong (Vietnamese Nationalist Party—usually referred to by its initials, VNQDD) advocated the use of militant methods to achieve national liberation from colonial rule. The Tan Viet Cach Menh Dang (Revolutionary Party of the New Vietnam—usually abbreviated as Tan Viet) was anti-French, had Marxist leanings, and later renamed itself the Dong Duong Cong San Lien Doan (League of Indochinese Communists). Members of the Thanh Nien Cao Vong Dang (High Aspirations Youth Party), often called the Nguyen An Ninh Secret Society after its founder, believed that national awakening would have to come from within. Nguyen An Ninh was the only intellectual who sought support from peasants as well as educated youth.[26]

Of the panoply of cultural, intellectual, and political options available, it was Marxism-Leninism—both as an ideology and as an organizational blueprint for carrying out revolutions—that guided those who eventually succeeded in forcing the French to give up their colonies in Indochina. Because of its central importance in the history of twentieth-century Vietnam and the hostility of diasporic Vietnamese ethnic communities toward the current Communist regime in their homeland, it is necessary to discuss in some detail how Communism was introduced into Vietnam and its complex relationship with modern Vietnamese nationalism.

CHAPTER THREE

Communism and Nationalism

During the twentieth century, many educated people in colonized countries found Marxism-Leninism (Communism) attractive because it purported to offer a "scientific" analysis of history and, in its Leninist form, suggested methods that could be used to guide their nationalist—that is, anticolonial—struggles even though the original formulation addressed the problem of overthrowing capitalism, rather than colonialism. Karl Marx explicated "laws" of historical development and prophesied that the proletariat (workers) would eventually prevail over capitalists who oppressed them. Vladimir Lenin's exegesis of Marxist theory gave hope to aspiring nationalist revolutionaries in countries where the working class was either nonexistent or very, very small by arguing that a vanguard political party—the Communist Party—could nevertheless lead a revolution in the name of workers. The successful 1917 Russian Revolution seemed to confirm the correctness of Lenin's analysis. Then, China's revolutionary leader, Mao Zedong, made Marxism-Leninism applicable to agrarian societies by emphasizing that peasants could play a significant role alongside workers and radical intellectuals to defeat Western colonialism and to transform Asian societies dominated by landlords, moneylenders, and bureaucrats.

Ho Chi Minh's Role in the Vietnamese Revolution

Among Vietnamese, Ho Chi Minh (a pseudonym)[1] played the paramount role in spreading Communist ideology and organizational methods to Vietnam even though he lived abroad for some three decades. Similar to what Mao Zedong was doing in China, Ho applied Marxism-Leninism "creatively" to the specific conditions in Vietnam. Born around 1890 into a patriotic, impoverished but

respected scholar-gentry family in central Vietnam, he met Phan Boi
Chau when the latter visited his father. He recalled later that the patriotism of his father and Phan Boi Chau inspired him. He attended
the Imperial Academy in Hue and taught school briefly before finding a job as a cook's assistant on a French ship in 1911. He spent
two years at sea, visited many ports in Africa and Europe, worked in
London during World War I, and in 1917 moved to Paris, where he
participated in the political activities of Vietnamese and people from
other French colonies then living in France. He made friends with
French trade unionists and pacifists and was the first Vietnamese to
join the *Jeunèsses Socialistes* (Young Socialists) in France.

Ho first emerged as a public figure in 1919 when he sent a petition
to the victorious Allies of World War I meeting in Versailles to hammer out the political settlements of the war. Buoyed by U.S. President
Woodrow Wilson's declaration of the "Fourteen Points" that promised
self-determination or even complete emancipation for the former
colonies of the Austro-Hungarian and Ottoman empires, Ho and his
copetitioners, including Phan Chu Trinh, who was then in exile in
France, asked that the colonies in French Indochina be allowed to
send representatives to the French parliament; that the colonized
people be granted the freedom to speak, assemble, and publish;
amnesty for and the release of political prisoners; and equality
with Frenchmen.[2] The Allies ignored the petitions submitted by the
Vietnamese and by people from other countries colonized by the
European powers.

Undaunted, in the following years Ho wrote many articles, pamphlets, and even plays; helped form the Intercolonial Union to gather
together patriots from other colonized countries; and founded and
edited *Le Paria* (The Pariah), the organ of the Intercolonial Union. He
joined the French Socialist Party because some of its members showed
sympathy for anticolonial struggles. He became a founding member of
the French Communist Party established in December 1920. Reading
Lenin's "Theses on the National and Colonial Questions," in particular, enhanced his conceptual clarity. As Jean Lacouture phrased it,
Lenin's writings enabled Ho to see how "national emancipation via
international revolution" might be achieved.[3]

Some time in late 1923 or early 1924, Ho went to Moscow, where
he received political training at the University for Toilers of the East
run by the Comintern (Third Communist International), after which
he became a Comintern agent. He was assigned as Mikhail Borodin's
secretary-interpreter when the Comintern sent Borodin to Canton to
guide the revolutions in China and elsewhere in East and Southeast

Asia.[4] Southern China had long been a sanctuary for Vietnamese would-be revolutionaries as they evaded the dragnet of the French Sûreté. The well-traveled and multilingual Ho, who by this time could speak, read, and write Vietnamese, Chinese, English, French, and Russian, found a group of eager activists, many of them followers of Phan Boi Chau, in cosmopolitan Canton upon his arrival.

The Introduction of Communism

In spring 1925, Ho Chi Minh established the Viet Nam Thanh Nien Cach Menh Dong Chi Hoi (Vietnamese Revolutionary Youth Association—Thanh Nien for short), the first explicitly Marxist-Leninist organization among Vietnamese. He recruited members and instructed them in revolutionary theory and strategy. He enrolled many of them in the Whampoa Military Academy in Canton and sent a few to study at the Soviet Military Academy and the University for Toilers of the East in Moscow. Even though Marxist theoreticians in Moscow denigrated the revolutionary potential of peasants, Ho understood the agrarian nature of Vietnamese society well enough to know that peasants absolutely could not be left out of the anticipated revolution. What was needed in Vietnam, he said, was a two-stage revolution. First, there must be a "national bourgeois revolution" led by a patriotic (that is, anticolonial), urban middle class to change a "feudal" society (an agrarian society controlled by landlords) into a capitalist one, in which private property and the profit motive reigned supreme. Only after such a bourgeois revolution succeeded could a socialist revolution to collectivize agriculture and industry occur, in order to transform a capitalist economy and society into a Communist one.[5] This analysis differed from the Comintern's policy during certain periods.

In 1927, China's Guomindang (Chinese Nationalist Party) leaders turned against their erstwhile ally, the Chinese Communist Party, arresting and killing many of the latter's members. That event had a profound effect on Thanh Nien, whose members could no longer function safely in Canton. Ho fled to Moscow while other Thanh Nien members dispersed elsewhere. The Guomindang arrested and imprisoned the Thanh Nien members who remained in Canton. The crisis in China, as well as the Dutch colonial government's repression of Communists in Indonesia, led to a change in the Comintern's "line." (In Marxist jargon, "line" refers to the analysis of a situation and the proposed policy to deal with it.) The Comintern abandoned its strategy of building "united fronts" (within which Communist and non-Communist parties worked together) and instructed Communist and socialist parties around the world to purge their "petty bourgeois elements" (merchants, teachers, students, journalists, clerks, and civil servants) and to "proletarianize" their organizations so that workers could occupy leadership positions. Soviet leader Joseph Stalin claimed that a "revolutionary tide" was rising in "the East" and instructed Communist cadres in that part of the world to organize workers and lead strikes and mass demonstrations.

In Vietnam, the Thanh Nien members who were still at large tried to find work in factories so that they could form unions and Communist cells.[6] In Hong Kong in May 1929, at the first (and only) congress of Thanh Nien, those members who wanted to follow Ho Chi Minh's strategy of first-nationalism-then-socialism and others who stressed the primacy of the socialist revolution clashed openly. As a result of the ideological schism, the Vietnamese leftists splintered and formed three different Communist parties. Greatly disturbed by the factionalism, the Comintern sent Ho Chi Minh to Hong Kong to convene a "unification" meeting in February 1930. Ho's diplomatic skills, authority, and patience brought results: the three parties agreed to merge into a single organization, the Dang Cong San Viet Nam (Vietnamese Communist Party). The Comintern, however, was displeased with the nationalism implied by the word *Vietnamese* and ordered the party to rename itself the Dang Cong San Dong Duong (Indochinese Communist Party—ICP for short).[7]

In deference to the Comintern's new line, ICP leaders argued that instead of a *sequential* two-stage revolution, the two stages would now take place simultaneously as *parallel* revolutions. To carry out a worker-led-and-controlled socialist revolution, the ICP would rely on "mass organizations" to be organized among identifiable groups in society, such as workers, peasants, soldiers, intellectuals, women, ethnic minorities, and youth.[8] The new Comintern line eclipsed Ho Chi Minh's analysis and strategy; he became virtually invisible during most of the 1930s.

Political Repression during the 1930s

The 1930s was a time of social and political turmoil in Vietnam and of ideological vicissitude among Vietnamese anti-French groups. In February 1930, the VNQDD led a mutiny of soldiers stationed at Yen Bay and other military posts in the Hong River valley. The French easily suppressed the uprising overnight. This abortive act almost destroyed the VNQDD as the French arrested, imprisoned, and killed a large number of its members. The party never completely recovered but those members who managed to escape to China kept it alive. Meanwhile, the Great Depression, which had worldwide repercussions, made the lot of Vietnam's urban and rural poor even more destitute than it already was. In March 1930, more than a thousand workers at a rubber plantation in southern Vietnam rioted. Their example was followed by workers at a cotton factory and a match factory in central Vietnam who went on strike. Angry peasants pillaged government offices, rich people's houses, marketplaces, and even Buddhist temples. Those in Nghe An and Ha Tinh provinces (often called the Nghe Tinh region—a combination of the two provincial names) formed village organizations that Communist historians have called "soviets." They seized communal land that used to be available for the common use of villagers but had been taken over by landlords under French aegis. The organizers of these soviets burned tax rolls, distributed rice from government granaries, and reduced the rents of tenant farmers. The French suppressed the uprisings with brutality.[9]

During the unrest, the French colonial government arrested an estimated fifty thousand activists and kept a fifth of them in jail until the mid-1930s. The repression decimated the ICP. Those who were not killed were jailed at Poulo Condore and other prisons from six to fifteen years and many of them died during their incarceration. However, there was an unanticipated and unintended consequence to imprisoning so many anticolonial activists together: under the leadership of jailed ICP members, the prisoners studied Marxism systematically and assiduously, analyzed and evaluated the reasons for their successes and failures, and in the process developed an ironclad discipline and cohesion that would serve them well in the years to come.

Meanwhile, the British, fearing the influence of the peripatetic Ho Chi Minh on their own colonies in Southeast Asia, tracked down, arrested, and imprisoned him in Hong Kong. However, a left-wing British lawyer, Frank Loseby, and the International Red Aid, a Communist legal defense organization, successfully pressured the British government to release him in December 1932.[10] British colonial authorities arrested Ho a second time while he was passing through Singapore but again released him. Ho eventually made his way to Moscow in 1933 via Shanghai and Vladivostok. In 1938, when the Russians permitted him to return to Asia, he traveled a circuitous route, several hundred miles of the journey on foot, until he reached Yunnan province in southwestern China.[11]

While Ho was leading a relatively quiet existence in Moscow in the 1930s, momentous events were taking place in Europe and Asia that affected Vietnam. As Adolf Hitler began his conquest of Europe, the Comintern once again changed its line. Now it encouraged Communist parties around the world to lure "progressive" members of the middle class into their ranks. Stalin promulgated a new policy in 1935, instructing Communist parties everywhere to form "anti-fascist popular fronts" to fight Nazism and protect the Soviet Union. In France, a Popular Front government led by a socialist came to power in 1936. Its policies toward France's colonies were more benign than those of its predecessors: it ordered thousands of political prisoners, including leaders of the ICP in Vietnam, to be released from jail. However, when Nazi Germany and the Soviet Union signed a mutual defense pact in August 1939 and Hitler's army invaded Poland the following month, the French government, worried about a potential combined German-Soviet invasion, dissolved the French Communist Party, confiscated its property, and arrested its leaders, so that the latter could not act as a "fifth column" (saboteurs within a country at war working to support its enemies) should an invasion indeed occur.

In light of what was happening in France, the governor-general of Indochina cracked down on the ICP, suppressed a revolt in northern Vietnam, and put down an uprising of peasants and soldiers who attacked French military posts in the Meking Delta. In December 1940 and January 1941, the colonial authorities arrested almost six thousand people, including over two thousand ICP members, and threw them in prison. Of those, more than a hundred, among them key ICP leaders, were executed and all left-wing publications were henceforth banned.[12] To cope with the new situation, the ICP decided to establish a new organization, the Anti-Imperialist National United Front, to rally and unite people from all social classes to fight for Vietnam's national liberation from French colonial rule.[13]

World War II and the Japanese Occupation

Developments in Asia had an equally profound impact on Indochina. During the 1930s, Japan began to expand its empire beyond Korea, which it had annexed in 1910, by encroaching on and occupying larger and larger areas of China. Failing to halt the Japanese advance, the Chinese central government moved its capital westward to Chongqing, Sichuan province, in southwestern China. Because supplies, including war materiel, were being transported to south-western China via the railroad that linked the port of Haiphong in northern Vietnam and the city of Kunming in Yunnan province, China, Japan demanded that the French colonial government shut the railroad down. The French responded by restricting the shipment of all arms but continued to use the railroad to send textiles, trucks, and gasoline to China. As soon as the Japanese southward sweep across China brought them to the Vietnamese-Chinese border, they bombed the railroad to cripple its operation.

When Hitler invaded and occupied France in June 1940, those French leaders who decided to collaborate with the Nazis set up a government in the health-resort town of Vichy. The Vichy government and Japan signed a protocol, which allowed the Japanese to station up to twenty-five thousand troops in French Indochina and to use its airports and naval bases in exchange for Japan's recognition of France's right to retain Cochinchina, Tonkin, Annam, Cambodia, and Laos as colonies. For that reason, Indochina was not a theater of war during the Second World War. However, the Japanese milked the French colonies by requisitioning a very large quantity of rice (between six hundred thousand and a million tons per year) to feed their troops, by imposing a Japanese monopoly on Indochina's export of corn, coal, rubber, and minerals, and by demanding monetary re-muneration for the costs of "common defense" in Indochina.[14] The Japanese allowed French officials and their Vietnamese civil servants to retain control of the day-to-day operation of the colonial govern-ment so long as they did not contravene Japan's interests.

It was in the midst of such rapid changes in the international balance of power that Ho Chi Minh reappeared in southwestern China. There, he linked up with, among others, Vo Nguyen Giap and Pham Van Dong, two of the most important Communist leaders in the years to come. In an effort to win allies, Ho tried to gain the cooperation and support of local Chinese military commanders and political leaders, as well as Vietnamese nationalists who kept filtering across the border into southwestern China, many of whom came to rejoin or join for the first time the VNQDD. Despite enormous privation, the thousand or so ICP members who were still alive and not in jail managed to augment their ranks with several thousand people.[15]

The ICP formed a broad-based organization, the Viet Nam Doc Lap Dong Minh (Vietnamese Independence League—Viet Minh for short) in May 1941. To camouflage its own leading role within the front, the ICP encouraged non-Communists to run for office and sev-eral were elected to leadership positions. The Viet Minh's stated goal was to unite "all social classes, revolutionary parties, patriotic groups of the people, in order to expel the Japanese and French, render Vietnam completely independent, and create a Democratic Republic of Vietnam."[16] It formed mass organizations called "national salvation associations" that would include even "patriotic landlords" and "progressive Frenchmen" and strengthened its efforts to win over and organize ethnic minorities living in the mountainous areas in northern Vietnam, some of whom had joined the ICP during the earliest years of its existence.

Unimpeded by the Japanese presence, the French continued to hunt down Communists and demolished one of the two Viet Minh rural bases along the Vietnamese-Chinese border, as well as ICP cells among workers in the factories of Hanoi, Haiphong, and Saigon, the rubber plantations of southern Vietnam, and the mines of northern Vietnam.[17] At the same time, however, in a symbolic effort to mollify conservative Vietnamese nationalists and keep them pro-French, the governor-general allowed the flag of the Nguyen dynasty to fly alongside the French one. The Japanese, on their part, also tried actively to win over certain groups, particularly the Cao Dai and the Hoa Hao, two religious sects that the French had tried to suppress, as well as anti-French but non-Communist political parties.[18]

To counteract French and Japanese efforts to gain adherents, Chinese regional leaders convened a meeting in Liuzhou, Guangxi province, China, in October 1942 to which all Vietnamese organizations then operating in China were invited. The participants established an umbrella organization, the Viet Nam Cach Menh Dong Minh Hoi (Vietnamese Revolutionary League—Dong Minh Hoi for short), to which the Chinese gave a monthly stipend. In exchange, the Dong Minh Hoi's member organizations were expected to gather intelligence on Japanese troop movements and other information that might prove useful to China's war against Japan. However, when the component groups, which often squabbled with one another, failed to produce the results the Chinese desired, the local Chinese military commander, who had arrested and imprisoned Ho Chi Minh shortly after the Viet Minh was formed, released him from captivity in 1943 and, in a startling turn of fortune for Ho, made him head of the Dong Minh Hoi when he agreed to ask his followers to gather the kind of information the Chinese wanted.[19]

CHAPTER FOUR

The 1945 August Revolution

By mid-1943, when World War II appeared to be turning against the Germans in Europe and the Japanese in the Pacific, the Viet Minh decided the time had come to prepare for a nationwide insurrection. Although the ICP leaders who controlled the Viet Minh still stressed the paramount importance of political work—that is, propaganda and organizing people—they paid increasing attention to building a military force to be formed, initially, of small, mobile guerrilla units. Since 1940, Chu Van Tan, a member of the Nung ethnic group who had joined the ICP during the early days of its existence, had been building up a small "national salvation" guerrilla force composed almost entirely of ethnic minorities. By 1944, it had about three hundred men. The Viet Minh authorized Vo Nguyen Giap, a former history teacher who would soon become the most important Vietnamese Communist military leader, to organize Vietnam Liberation Army Armed Propaganda Units to do both political and military work.[1] The two groups combined in early 1945 to form the kernel of the Vietnamese People's Liberation Army that helped bring the Communists to power.

On the Road to a "General Insurrection"

As the end of World War II seemed imminent, the Japanese in Indochina carried out a coup d'état on March 9, 1945: they arrested and imprisoned all French colonial officials and military commanders and disarmed all troops under French command. The Allied landing in Normandy, France on June 6, 1944, soon brought an end to the Vichy government. The Free French, under General Charles de Gaulle, reestablished the French Republic and announced that France intended to reclaim its colonies in Indochina and Africa. Even though the Japanese knew they might lose the war, still, they did not wish to see the French recolonize Indochina (or the British recolonize Burma, Malaya, and Singapore; the Dutch Indonesia; and the Americans the Philippines). So, they urged Southeast Asian leaders to declare independence. In response, Emperor Bao Dai abrogated the treaties that the French had used to turn Cochinchina into a direct colony and Annam and Tonkin into protectorates and proclaimed that Vietnam was once again a unified and independent country. Bao Dai asked Tran Trong Kim, a historian and conservative nationalist, whom the Japanese had kept in protective custody during the war, to form a government. However, the Japanese never formally recognized that government.[2]

The ICP moved with alacrity to take advantage of this unexpected development. One thing that played into their hands was a famine that had begun in 1943 in northern and central Vietnam for several reasons. First, the Japanese were hoarding the bulk of the rice harvest for their own use. In preceding years they had also forced farmers in northern and central Vietnam to use rice land to grow peanuts, oil seeds, cotton, and jute for military use, thereby decreasing the acreage of rice planted in those two regions. Second, the French had forbidden rice to be shipped from the Mekong Delta—that usually produced a rice surplus relative to its population—to central and northern Vietnam. Third, American bombs and torpedoes had severely disrupted the shipment of all goods by land and by sea. Fourth, the weather wreaked havoc: heavy floods were followed by a severe drought. By early 1945, an estimated two million people had starved to death. Neither the French nor the Japanese did anything to help the people, who in desperation ate whatever was available—tree bark, insects, and even old leather shoes. To deal with the situation, Viet Minh propaganda teams led attacks on government granaries and distributed rice to the people. The ICP instructed its cadres that antifamine relief work and efforts to increase agricultural production of such supplementary staples as yams and corn would be their most important tasks under the current circumstances.[3] As David Marr observes, "[o]utraged at the wielders of power who had permitted such horrors to occur, the survivors were open to Viet Minh explanations and exhortations." Huynh Kim Khanh is even more emphatic: "It is not an exaggeration to say that the campaign against the famine was largely responsible for the Viet Minh rise to power in Bac Ky [northern Vietnam] and northern Trung Ky [central Vietnam]."[4]

While the cadres were busy ameliorating the travails caused by the famine, ICP leaders pondered how they might take power when five thousand of their members were still in jail and their combined military force numbered only several hundred men armed with only a handful of old weapons. Party leaders, under the cloak of the Viet Minh front, decided to adopt a combined military and political strategy. The two existing military forces were unified under the command of Vo Nguyen Giap, who by then had successfully recruited three thousand Vietnamese troops who had served in the French Indochina Army before the Japanese coup of March 1945. To enlarge their weapons cache, Viet Minh forces seized weapons and ammunition from the armories of the incarcerated French colonial administration. The first Viet Minh "liberated zone," made up of six northern provinces, came into being in June 1945. Viet Minh adherents systematically moved first into villages, then small towns, and finally large cities. They encountered virtually no resistance as they took over the administration in each locality, raised the Viet Minh flag over government buildings, and formed mass organizations.[5]

In light of the Viet Minh's rapid advance, Tran Trong Kim and his cabinet resigned at the beginning of August 1945. After the United States dropped atomic bombs on Hiroshima and Nagasaki, Japan surrendered unconditionally on August 15. In anticipation of the Japanese surrender, ICP leaders, meeting in a hut at Tan Trao from August 13 to 15, issued a call for a "general insurrection for wresting power from the hands of the Japanese fascists and their puppets before the arrival of Allied troops."[6]

The 1945 August Revolution

Vo Nguyen Giap's armed units moved rapidly toward Hanoi and took that city on August 19 as crowds chanted slogans and sang songs that the Viet Minh had taught them. The Vietnamese People's Liberation Army met no resistance because the French were locked up, the Japanese had surrendered, and the nationalist parties either were in disarray or had joined the Viet Minh. Moving southward, Viet Minh forces seized Hue and Danang in central Vietnam on August 23 and Saigon in southern Vietnam on August 26. The situation in southern Vietnam posed a great challenge to the Viet Minh because there, the Cao Dai and Hoa Hao religious sects, the Binh Xuyen (a mafia-like group), the Trotskyites, and various pro-French organizations hung on to whatever power they wielded. In villages and small towns, people took matters into their own hands, forming "liberation committees," deposing local officials, seizing weapons, and punishing their former oppressors. As they swept over the country, Viet Minh cadres rounded up several thousand pro-French and pro-Japanese "traitors," "reactionaries," and members of various minor political parties and executed these "enemies of the people," while detaining persons of lesser importance.[7]

Emperor Bao Dai abdicated on August 30, turning over the twin symbols of the Nguyen dynasty—a golden sword and the imperial seal—to a Viet Minh delegation, marking an end to the Nguyen dynasty that Nguyen Anh, the Gia Long emperor, had founded in 1802. On September 2, with Viet Minh flags and banners in several languages waving all over Ba Dinh Square in Hanoi, half a million people gathered to hear Ho Chi Minh proclaim Vietnam's independence and the establishment of the Democratic Republic of Vietnam (DRV). Ironically, in view of later developments, Ho began his speech with sentences borrowed from the American Declaration of Independence. Several Americans (agents of the Office of Strategic Services, the forerunner of the U.S. Central Intelligence Agency) with whom Ho had become acquainted attended the ceremony.[8]

The Viet Minh formed a provisional people's government on August 24 that included several non-Communists in leadership positions in order to underscore its united-front, populist character.[9] Ho Chi Minh asked Bao Dai, who became "Citizen Vinh Thuy" upon his abdication, to serve as a "supreme political advisor" to the provisional government. The ex-emperor agreed to do so. The provisional government asked all civil servants of Vietnamese origin to remain at their posts and technicians and workers to continue running plantations, mines, factories, and business enterprises. They ordered all armed groups to disband and to enroll in the Vietnamese People's Liberation Army. To win popular support, as one of its first acts the government abolished the most onerous taxes and lifted restrictions on the transportation of rice. Meanwhile, the Japanese handed over public buildings and communication facilities to the provisional government.[10]

The French Recolonization of Vietnam

The Viet Minh did not have long to savor their victory. At the Potsdam Conference in July 1945, the Allies had decided that British forces should accept the Japanese surrender in Vietnam south of the sixteenth parallel, while Nationalist Chinese troops should accept the Japanese surrender north of the sixteenth parallel. However, the Allies did not inform the French government in liberated Paris of these arrangements until mid-August. The first contingent of a thousand troops from India (at the time a British colony) under British command came by air and landed at Tan Son Nhut Airport in Saigon on September 12, 1945.

The following day, British General Douglas Gracey, commander of the Allied forces responsible for occupying southern Vietnam, arrived with orders to "secure the Saigon area" by disarming Japanese troops, evacuating Allied prisoners of war, catching and arresting criminals, and protecting facilities of military or civil importance. Gracey not only disarmed the Japanese but the Viet Minh as well. More important, he rearmed the main unit of the French Indochina Army, thereby initiating the process that enabled the French to return to power even though that was not a task Gracey was authorized to carry out. He imposed martial law and a curfew, banned public meetings, forbade the Vietnamese to publish newspapers, and announced that anyone caught looting or engaging in any kind of sabotage would be summarily shot.[11]

Even though a number of Free French agents had parachuted into southwestern China and Indochina before World War II ended, France was short of manpower and had neither the weapons to arm its troops nor ships to transport them to faraway Indochina. Therefore, without Gracey's assistance at this critical juncture, it would have taken France a lot longer and far more effort to recolonize Indochina. The first contingent of French troops, accompanied by a British naval convoy, finally arrived in Saigon in early October. Their commander, Philippe Leclerc, immediately set out to reconquer Cochinchina. The Viet Minh and their sympathizers scattered to the countryside, while the Cao Dai surrendered to the returning French. Meanwhile, Admiral Georges d'Argenlieu, the new high commissioner for Indochina, removed from service those colonial administrators he suspected of having been Vichy sympathizers and lost no time in forming close bonds with French rubber plantation owners and businessmen. Great Britain and France signed an agreement on October 9 declaring that the French colonial administration had the sole right to govern Vietnam south of the sixteen parallel. British troops remained until January 1946, after which the French were on their own.[12]

The Chinese troops assigned to accept the Japanese surrender in Vietnam north of the sixteen parallel began arriving in late August. They were from Yunnan and were commanded by General Lu Han. Viet Minh leaders were apprehensive about what these soldiers might do because their lack of discipline—indeed, rapacity—was well known before they even crossed the Chinese-Vietnamese border. However, the Chinese had an attitude opposite to that of the British: they did not wish to see the French recolonize Indochina. Therefore, they allowed the Viet Minh forces to keep their weapons but confiscated the arms of resident Frenchmen. They remained in northern

Vietnam until June 1946, pulling out only after France agreed to return the territories and cancel the trade concessions it had imposed
on China after the Second Opium War and to exempt goods being
shipped to China on the Haiphong-Kunming Railroad from customs
and transit duties.[13]

Along with the Chinese troops came leaders of the VNQDD, the
Dong Minh Hoi, and smaller political parties that had spent the
war years in China. These anti-Communist nationalists charged that
Viet Minh members were not "real nationalists" and began to install
themselves in power at the village, county, and provincial levels even
though Viet Minh cadres were already serving in those capacities.
To deal with the situation, the ICP made a momentous decision: it
formally dissolved itself on November 11, 1945. By camouflaging the
Viet Minh's true nature, its leaders hoped to draw in a broader range
of groups committed to regaining Vietnam's independence. However,
ICP members remained organized in Marxist study groups. Cognizant
of the threat posed by both the French and the Chinese, Ho Chi
Minh struck a deal with the VNQDD and the Dong Minh Hoi: he offered to set aside fifty seats for the former and twenty for the latter in
the national assembly to be formed after the elections the Viet Minh
had scheduled for January 1946. The elections took place peacefully.
Half of the individuals elected to the national assembly did not even
belong to any political party. Intellectuals, peasants, workers, former
officials of the Nguyen dynasty, conservative nationalists, and Communists all had representatives. Ho became president, the head of the
Dong Minh Hoi became vice president, and a high-ranking member
of the VNQDD became the foreign minister.[14]

Roadblocks to Independence

The immediate postwar period posed an enormous dilemma for Ho
Chi Minh. He knew that Viet Minh forces were not strong enough to
prevent the French recolonization efforts when the economy was in
dire straits and Leclerc's army was making its way northward, yet he
wanted to preserve the Viet Minh's political gains. He decided, therefore, that his government had no choice except to negotiate with
France. However, he also knew that his own lieutenants, as well as
the anti-French non-Communist nationalists, would strongly oppose
such negotiations. When the end of World War II seemed imminent,
France had offered to make Cambodia, Laos, Tonkin, Annam, and
Cochinchina into "free states" within a French Union (an association

of France and its colonies) as well as an Indochinese Federation (a confederation of the five territorial entities that made up French Indochina). But what did "free state" really mean? According to the French, each "free state" would have its own government, including a parliament and an army, and control its own economy. However, the French would retain control of foreign affairs and the right to station troops there. The Vietnamese, in contrast, wanted *full* sovereignty, as well as the reunification of Cochinchina, Annam, and Tonkin into a *single* country called Vietnam. Despite these differences, Ho Chi Minh and Jean Sainteny, the representative of the French government who had been talking to Ho since October, signed an agreement on March 6, 1946, indicating that implementation details would be left to further negotiations scheduled to take place at Fontainebleau, France, in the near future. Ho, as well as the Chinese occupation forces, also agreed to let the French bring their troops to the north, where they would be allowed to disembark in Haiphong harbor. Many Vietnamese were stunned by the concessions Ho made. In response, he swore to his people that he had not betrayed them, that the arrangements would be only temporary, that they were necessary for the survival of the DRV, and that some time soon Vietnam would indeed achieve full independence.[15]

In May 1946, Pham Van Dong led a delegation to France to hammer out the details of the March 6 agreement. Ho Chi Minh also traveled to France but not in an official capacity. While the negotiations were going on at Fontainebleau, d'Argenlieu took decisive action to separate Cochinchina from whatever arrangements might result from the negotiations. On May 30, he announced that the southern part of Vietnam would now be known as the Autonomous Republic of Cochinchina. This announcement threw a monkey wrench into the process of drafting a treaty to be signed by France and the DRV. Then, at the beginning of August, d'Argenlieu convened a conference to which he invited representatives not only from Cochinchina but also from Cambodia, Laos, and "southern Annam," in the process revealing that his territorial ambition encompassed more than just Cochinchina. Furious at d'Argenlieu's unilateral moves, Pham Van Dong rejected the draft treaty on September 10 and returned to Vietnam. Four days later, hoping to salvage something from the months of effort, Ho, who had remained in France, and Marius Moutet, the French minister in charge of "overseas France," signed a modus vivendi, in which they agreed to cease all acts of hostility and to resume negotiations in January 1947.[16] But the promised negotiations never resumed because a small incident that occurred two months later escalated into all-out war.

CHAPTER FIVE

The First Indochina War

When a French patrol boat captured a Chinese junk carrying petroleum into Haiphong harbor, which the French were blockading, in mid-November 1945, Viet Minh shore batteries fired shots at the French boat. Angered by this action, on November 23 the commander of French forces in Haiphong gave the Vietnamese two hours to leave the French quarter, the Chinese quarter, and the docks. When the two hours expired, French troops bombarded the Vietnamese quarter, killing some six thousand people. At the beginning of December, the French demanded that the Vietnamese withdraw all their military forces from Haiphong and announced that henceforth all roads into Haiphong would be controlled by the French. Hoping to avert a war, Ho Chi Minh sent an appeal to the French government in Paris, but to no avail. The conflict quickly spread to Hanoi. When the French parachuted troops into the capital, the Vietnamese lobbed grenades at them. Meanwhile, the DRV government prepared to evacuate both cities. When the French tried to disarm the Vietnamese militia in Hanoi on December 19, in retaliation the Vietnamese cut off electricity and the water supply. Four days later, the French imposed martial law on all of northern Vietnam and a part of central Vietnam. Ho Chi Minh, for his part, declared a state of emergency in the DRV (whose geographic boundaries had never been specified). Marius Moutet, who had signed the modus vivendi with Ho in March, arrived on December 25 to investigate the situation on the ground. Two days later, he announced that it would be impossible to negotiate with the DRV because "before any negotiations . . . it is necessary to have a military decision." Radiating out from Hanoi, the fighting spread to the countryside. The First Indochina War had begun.[1]

Negotiating and Fighting

The war lasted eight years during which the French held the cities while the Viet Minh dominated the countryside. Negotiations and fighting proceeded simultaneously. In search of an alternative to the DRV, the French tried to persuade Bao Dai to return to head a new government, but Bao Dai told them that he would expect even more concessions than Ho Chi Minh had asked for. As news of what the French were trying to do spread, many groups, including the VNQDD, the Dong Minh Hoi, the Cao Dai, the Hoa Hao, Catholics, and former court officials, proclaimed their undying loyalty to Bao Dai. These groups, which had never got along with one another, nonetheless formed a National Union Front in February 1947 and pledged allegiance to the former emperor. Even Ho Chi Minh contacted Bao Dai to indicate the DRV's interest in taking "joint action" with the man who had once been designated as its "supreme political advisor." Bao Dai coyly announced that he would go home if his people really wanted him to do so. The government in Paris also signed on to the "Bao Dai solution." Still, Bao Dai equivocated.[2]

Finally, in May 1948, Bao Dai expressed his support for a provisional government to be formed by General Nguyen Van Xuan, one of the few Vietnamese to have acquired French citizenship. Perhaps because the general had served as vice president and the minister of national defense of the French-installed Autonomous Republic of Cochinchina, he enjoyed no respect. One after another, individuals he invited to serve in his cabinet declined to do so; those who eventually agreed to serve had little or no political experience. The provisional government accomplished very little with one significant exception: it persuaded the French to renounce the separate status of Cochinchina and to recognize that Tonkin, Annam, and Cochinchina composed a single "associated state" within the French Union. In July 1948, Bao Dai, General Nguyen Van Xuan, and a small entourage met with the French high commissioner for Indochina on a boat anchored in Ha Long Bay. They signed an agreement to formalize France's acceptance of Vietnam's territorial integrity as a single country. Thus, from 1948 on, though Vietnam was now one country, there existed two governments within its territory—the DRV and the government headed by Bao Dai. The latter, however, controlled no territory and its titular head continued to live in Hong Kong.[3]

The DRV continued to grow in strength even though it received no international diplomatic recognition. Its troops fought with weapons smuggled in from China, Thailand, and the Philippines. Holed up in the mountains and the marshlands, the DRV nevertheless managed to develop a self-sufficient though primitive economy. Technicians dismantled and moved to the countryside or built from scratch small factories to manufacture needed goods. Communist cadres exhorted peasants to increase agricultural production and to plant supplementary staples. By looking after the daily needs of ordinary Vietnamese, the DRV gained popular support. At the same time, it eliminated its opponents without any qualms. By the time the Ha Long Bay Agreement was signed, the DRV controlled a large part of northern Vietnam, most of the narrow strip of land along the central coast, and the rural areas, marshlands, and jungles of southern Vietnam. The French controlled only the large cities.

The French hoped to turn the tide, politically if not militarily, by pressuring Bao Dai to return to Vietnam, but he responded that he would not do so without a clear agreement on how Vietnam's independence would be "perfected." Finally, the French relented and signed an agreement with Bao Dai at the Elysée Palace in Paris on March 8, 1949. The Elysée Accords stipulated that the French National Assembly would pass a law to change the legal status of Cochinchina so that it could become a part of the new country, the name of which would be the State of Vietnam. France promised to support its application to become a member of the United Nations. The State of Vietnam could send diplomats to a handful of countries approved by France, send representatives to the French Union, of which it was now a constituent state, and raise an army and police force to maintain law and order and uphold its *internal* sovereignty. France, however, would continue to control Vietnam's foreign policy and its military interactions with other nations. French property in Vietnam would be protected, while French technicians were given priority for jobs in Vietnam's enterprises. French nationals who committed crimes would not be subject to Vietnamese law but could be tried only under French law. The State of Vietnam also signed a military convention with France in December 1950 to place its newly created national army under French command.[4]

The People's Republic of China Enters the Picture

The international balance of power changed in favor of the DRV in October 1949 when the Chinese Communist Party came to power.

Suddenly the DRV had an ally, the People's Republic of China (PRC), north of the border. The PRC granted diplomatic recognition to the DRV—the first country to do so—in January 1950. The Soviet Union followed suit two weeks later. In July of the same year, the PRC sent a Chinese Military Advisory Group to the DRV consisting of seventy-nine battle-hardened officers of the Chinese People's Liberation Army. (The United States sent its first Military Assistance Advisory Group to the State of Vietnam two months after the Chinese group arrived in the DRV.) From then on, the Chinese not only supplied the Vietnamese Communists with weapons but also trained their military officers in three-month-long courses.[5]

Up to that point, General Vo Nguyen Giap's regular army and guerrilla units had only a small number of weapons captured from the French and the Japanese, a few pieces left by a handful of American troops who had parachuted into Vietnam in the last phase of World War II, and whatever could be smuggled into the country. He had a few trucks but no mechanics to maintain them. Even though the DRV's factories hidden in the jungles could produce grenades, mines, and cartridges for rifles, they could not manufacture heavy military equipment. Chinese aid now solved the problems inherent in the DRV's lack of heavy armaments as its fighters battled troops under French command. Most of the latter were not Frenchmen; they were Vietnamese and soldiers imported from French colonies in Africa.[6]

At the beginning of 1950, Vo Nguyen Giap decided to launch his first major offensive to push French forces completely out of northern Vietnam. His troops captured all the remaining provinces in that part of the country that were not yet in DRV hands. Phillip Davidson, a retired lieutenant general of the U.S. Army and a military historian, points out that the localities that Giap targeted for attack were well chosen. The border forts the French had erected in Vietnam's northern frontier were set so far apart that the soldiers manning each post could not expect speedy reinforcements from the other posts should it come under attack. This allowed Giap to lay waste to each one in any sequence he pleased. Attacking these isolated fortifications also offered a psychological advantage: the certainty of victory boosted the morale of Giap's troops. By late October, only one border fort remained in French hands. In the course of eight months, the French had lost six thousand men out of the ten thousand guarding these border posts.[7]

The following year, however, when Vo Nguyen Giap tried to evict the French from the northern section of the Hong River delta, French General Jean de Lattre de Tassigny, who had built a string of twelve hundred fortified structures in the area, not only repelled the DRV

forces but also dealt them a decisive defeat. Giap had hoped to conquer the delta, a productive rice-growing area, because he had problems securing enough rice to feed his troops. The DRV leaders were
also aware of and concerned about the increasing amount of economic and military aid the United States was giving the French and
they wanted to strike before U.S. equipment enabled French military commanders and their Vietnamese and African troops to build
up their capabilities. Unfortunately for the DRV's troops, they had no
place to hide in the rice paddies as French airplanes pounded them
from the air. They lost an estimated twenty thousand men in these
engagements in open fields.[8]

Now that the DRV's back was covered by the PRC, its leaders decided
to allow a Communist party to resurface in February 1951 under
the name Viet Nam Lao Dong Dang (Vietnam Workers' Party—Lao
Dong for short). The party platform was quite moderate, calling only
for rent reduction rather than land confiscation and redistribution.
However, as Vo Nguyen Giap's troops suffered heavy casualties, the
need to replenish the DRV's armed units became urgent, which meant
the leaders had to find ways to motivate an increasingly large number
of peasants to join the fight or at least to serve as porters. Thus, in
early 1953, the Lao Dong decided to step up the "anti-feudal" part
of its revolution. The party divided peasants into four categories:
proletarian peasants (landless farm laborers), poor peasants, middle
peasants, and rich peasants, depending on the amount of land they
cultivated. The first three groups would receive allotments of the land
confiscated from landlords, "reactionaries," and religious institutions
that owned more land than they could use. The families of soldiers
killed in action would also be eligible for redistributed land.[9]

As the war dragged on, the French public became weary of its toll
and an increasingly vocal opposition to it soon emerged.[10] More and
more politicians called for a negotiated settlement of what appeared
to be an unwinnable war. Proposals to grant full independence to
Indochina were no longer denounced as unpatriotic. Keenly aware of
the shifting attitudes in France, various political groups in Vietnam
began debating their country's future. In September 1953, the leader
of the Cao Dai sect decided to organize a national conference to work
out what the State of Vietnam should bargain for during projected
talks with the French government. The conference participants who
met in October tried to define a new relationship between Vietnam
and France. Then Bao Dai headed a delegation to Paris to tell the
French government that if it wished the war to end, it must grant full
independence to Vietnam.[11] (Bao Dai ignored the fact that it was DRV

troops that were doing the actual fighting.) In response, the French government announced that the war in Indochina would be placed on the agenda of a conference to be held in Geneva, Switzerland, beginning in April 1954. France, Great Britain, the United States, the USSR, and the PRC would attend to discuss the future of partitioned Berlin, the political settlement of the Korean War (1950–53), and the situation in Vietnam.[12]

Dien Bien Phu

In response to the announcement that Vietnam's fate would be discussed at the Geneva Conference, Vo Nguyen Giap decided to launch immediately an all-out offensive in northwestern Vietnam close to the Laotian border. A year earlier, to prevent the Vietnamese People's Liberation Army from making further advances, the new French commander-in-chief, General Henri Navarre, had laid out a three-pronged plan. First, the French would secure the Hong River delta by driving out Giap's forces in those areas the latter controlled; second, they would attack areas held by the DRV in the central coastal area of Vietnam; and third, they would try to wipe out the DRV's main forces in northern Vietnam.[13] However, Giap refused to allow Navarre to determine the order of battle. He decided not to commit his main forces to fight the French in the delta, having learned a bitter lesson about the disadvantages of fighting in open plains. Instead, he wanted to confront the French in the mountainous areas of northwestern Vietnam and northeastern Laos. He knew that Navarre had begun to send troops to that remote corner of Vietnam to prevent Giap's men from capturing Luang Prabang, the royal capital of Laos. (Laos also had an administrative capital at Vientiane.) Navarre had no choice except to defend Luang Prabang because the Laotian king refused to be evacuated from his capital.

The spot where Navarre chose to make his stand was Dien Bien Phu, a fairly broad valley situated along one of the main routes between Vietnam and Laos. It had an airfield, which meant that supplies could be brought in by air instead of over mountain paths. The crest of the mountains surrounding the valley was six to seven miles from the airfield, so Navarre thought that it would be impossible for enemy mortars to reach his troops unless the attackers descended the slopes that faced the valley, in which case the French could fire at them. On November 20, 1953, the first French paratroopers moved into Dien Bien Phu. Around the same time, Giap coordinated a massive effort to dismantle and haul heavy artillery, piece by piece, up the mountains surrounding Dien Bien Phu where they were reassembled and placed into positions pointing at the valley below. Trucks transported the heaviest pieces of military hardware (supplied by both China and the Soviet Union); even more important, some one hundred thousand fleet-footed porters recruited from ethnic minority groups living in the area whom the Vietnamese Communists had won to their side, supplemented by peasants brought in from elsewhere in Vietnam, carried the lighter pieces on their backs for some two hundred miles from the Chinese-Vietnamese border over rugged, treacherous terrain. The porters also hauled enough food to feed more than one hundred thousand soldiers and themselves for several months.[14]

By the beginning of March 1954, Giap had fifty thousand combatants and fifty-five thousand support personnel assembled. In contrast, Navarre had sixteen thousand men in place. The Communists dug several hundred miles of trenches so that they could advance toward the outer perimeters of the French garrison without being shot at or blown up. They also dug long tunnels inside the mountains through which heavy artillery could be moved from one position to another as the battle progressed. By the end of March, Giap's men had destroyed the airfield by heavy shelling. The French garrison was now trapped and food and munitions had to be parachuted to them. On May 7, the Vietnamese forces charged at the French troops from all directions. The eleven thousand French troops still alive and uninjured surrendered. Casualties were high on both sides: at least fifteen hundred troops under French command died and four thousand were wounded; eight thousand to ten thousand Vietnamese Communist soldiers met their end, and twenty-five thousand were wounded.[15]

The 1954 Geneva Conference

The news of the French debacle stunned the world. By coincidence, the political leaders attending the Geneva Conference had scheduled discussions about Indochina to begin on May 8; the news of France's defeat at Dien Bien Phu thus dominated the agenda. The DRV delegation, led by Pham Van Dong, pressed hard for full independence and a French promise to withdraw all troops under French command. The delegations from the DRV and the State of Vietnam both insisted strenuously that Vietnam must not be partitioned. The DRV representatives, in particular, felt that their victory at Dien Bien Phu gave them the right to claim all of Vietnam. However, the Chinese and Soviet foreign ministers, Chou Enlai and Vyacheslav Molotov, respectively, exerted enormous pressure on the DRV delegates to accept a compromise: Vietnam would be temporarily partitioned at the seventeenth parallel and the future of the country would be determined by a general election to be held in July 1956.[16] In later years, when relations between the Vietnamese Communists and the Chinese Communists became bellicose, the Vietnamese would recall with bitterness how China and the Soviet Union had betrayed them at Geneva. After the Geneva Accords, signed in July 1954, the DRV became known in common parlance as "North Vietnam." In 1955, the State of Vietnam changed its name to the Republic of Vietnam and was commonly called "South Vietnam."

Two population movements occurred during the First Indochina War. Between 1946 and 1948, an estimated fifty-five thousand Vietnamese sought refuge in Thailand. These refuge-seekers did not come directly from Vietnam; rather, they were ethnic Vietnamese residing in Laos and Cambodia who fled from those two countries to escape the fierce fighting between French and Vietnamese Communist forces. Approximately forty-five thousand came from Laos and the rest from Cambodia. However, their ancestral homes were in northern Vietnam and their political sympathies were with the Viet Minh. Even though the Thai government allowed them to remain in northeastern Thailand, it was wary of their presence. In 1959, the governments of Thailand and the DRV held talks on neutral territory in Yangon (formerly called Rangoon), the capital of Myanmar (formerly named Burma), and signed an agreement to repatriate the refugees, whose numbers had increased to more than seventy thousand by then because of their high birthrate and the additional Vietnamese who had slipped into Thailand since the late 1940s. By 1964, about half had been repatriated to North Vietnam; the Hanoi government unilaterally ended the repatriation when the United States became more deeply involved in the Vietnam War.[17]

A second outflow involving more than a million people occurred in 1954–55. For both Korea and Vietnam, the Geneva Accords stipulated that people who wished to move from the northern half of the country (governed by Communists) to the southern half (ruled by pro-Western leaders) and vice versa could do so within a three-hundred-day period. More than nine hundred thousand people from North Vietnam, a majority of whom were Catholics and well-to-do people who did not wish to live under a Communist government, moved to the Republic of Vietnam. French airplanes and American, French, and British ships transported about eight-ninths of them, while the rest used their own means to reach their destinations. At the same time, somewhere between one hundred and thirty thousand and one hundred and forty thousand Communist cadres, military personnel, and their dependents moved north in Soviet and Polish ships.[18] However, somewhere between ten thousand and fifteen thousand Communist cadres remained in South Vietnam where they would play a significant role in the next war.

CHAPTER SIX

The American Involvement in Vietnam

The Second Indochina War (which Americans call the Vietnam War) involved American combat troops on the ground from 1965 to 1973, so most Americans assume that the United States got entangled in Vietnam only in the 1960s. In reality, American participation in the affairs of Vietnam had begun two decades earlier.[1] Not only were there Americans on the ground, but as the First Indochina War progressed, the United States funded a larger and larger portion of France's military expenditures. By 1954, the United States was paying 78 percent of the French war cost.[2] American policy-makers felt compelled to shore up the French military efforts during the First Indochina War, not because they supported French colonialism per se, but because they themselves were fighting an anti-Communist Cold War. The United States needed France to act as a strong bulwark against Soviet expansionism in Europe; helping the French hold on to their colonies in Indochina was part of the bargain.

The Ngo Dinh Diem Government

Though Bao Dai remained the titular head of South Vietnam, the man who really ruled the country after the Geneva Convention was Ngo Dinh Diem, whose ancestors had converted to Catholicism in the seventeenth century. Born in 1901 in central Vietnam and educated in the Chinese Confucian classics as well as in a French school in Hue, Ngo Dinh Diem graduated at the top of his class in the School of Law and Administration in Hanoi and became a provincial governor when he was only in his twenties. The French colonial administration persuaded Bao Dai to appoint him as the minister of the interior in 1933, but he resigned after only three months in office when he realized that French rule circumvented any meaningful action that Vietnamese officials might take. Declaring that he could not act against the interests of Vietnam, he became known as an ardent nationalist.[3]

The French Sûreté kept Diem under surveillance as he lived quietly in Hue in the years following his resignation. In 1950 he left Vietnam. During his travels, he met Wesley Fishel, a political science professor from Michigan State University, who invited him to the United States. A devout Catholic, Diem spent a year each in two Maryknoll seminaries as the guest of New York's Cardinal Francis Spellman. Though he lived in cloistered settings, he made regular trips to New York City and Washington, D.C., where some prominent Americans, including U.S. Supreme Court Justice William O. Douglas and Senators Mike Mansfield, John F. Kennedy, and Hubert H. Humphrey, befriended him. (In later years, Mansfield was known as "Diem's godfather.") These men became the core members of the American Friends of Vietnam, a pro-Diem support group. In meetings with U.S. officials, Diem emphasized his Catholic faith, which led one official to declare, "Catholic leadership in government [in Vietnam] is the only way to assure a national government free of communist influence."[4] Diem's visibility increased as journalists published laudatory articles about him. In June 1954, Bao Dai, who was then living in France, summoned Diem to see him. Bao Dai actually disliked Diem, but seeing growing American support for him, the former emperor, without consulting anyone, asked Diem to return to Vietnam as prime minister and to form a government. Aware that Diem had no popular following, Bao Dai wrote a check for a million piasters to pay people to go to the airport to welcome Diem home, but only five hundred Catholics showed up to greet him.[5]

Neither the State of Vietnam nor the United States had signed the Geneva Accords. Instead, in September 1954, the United States created the Southeast Asia Treaty Organization (SEATO)—a misnomer, as only one Southeast Asian country, Thailand, was a member. The other members in the pact were the United States, Great Britain, France, Australia, New Zealand, and Pakistan. In addition, even though Cambodia, Laos, and Vietnam were not members, SEATO pledged itself to defend them should their national security be threatened. President Dwight Eisenhower promised to help Diem build a non-Communist society in South Vietnam and authorized the Joint Chiefs of Staff to send advisors to train the South Vietnamese army.[6]

Now that Communists ruled China and both the Korean War and the First Indochina War had ended in military and political stalemates, American foreign policy-makers became extremely paranoid about

Communist expansion in Asia. Thinking in geopolitical terms, they envisioned countries as dominos; if one domino fell, it would set in motion the collapse of the ones lined up next to it. They supported the staunchly anti-Communist and devoutly Catholic Diem because they thought he could be a counterweight to Ho Chi Minh. The U.S. Central Intelligence Agency sent Edward Lansdale, an expert in psychological warfare, on loan from the U.S. Air Force to the CIA, who had played a key role in exterminating Communists in the Philippines, to Vietnam to undertake covert counterinsurgency measures against the DRV and the Communist cadres who had stayed behind in South Vietnam when their comrades moved north following the signing of the Geneva Accords.[7]

To consolidate his power, Diem brutally suppressed the two powerful religious sects, the Cao Dai and the Hoa Hao, as well as the Binh Xuyen underworld.[8] He then engineered a referendum, held in the fall of 1955, in which South Vietnamese voters were asked to choose between himself and Bao Dai as the head of state. Diem received a majority of the votes and became both head of state and prime minister. The Geneva Agreements had stipulated that North Vietnam and South Vietnam should hold consultations in 1955 to prepare for the elections slated for 1956. But Diem declared, with U.S. support, that since his government had not signed the agreements, he was not bound by their terms. Instead of preparing for elections, he accelerated efforts to hunt down Communists, whom he dubbed "Viet Cong," as well as other dissidents. Ironically, the jail on the penal island, Poulo Condor, that the French had used to incarcerate anti-French activists, once again filled to the brim, this time with anti-Diem opponents. Wesley Fishel of Michigan State University arranged to send faculty from that campus' School of Police Administration to train Diem's police on contract with the CIA. Diem's brother, Ngo Dinh Nhu, kept watch over the police, army officers, and civil servants to ensure their loyalty while Madame Nhu served as official hostess for the bachelor Diem.[9]

To cope with Diem's campaign to annihilate Communists, in 1957 the Lao Dong party authorized its southern colleagues to take armed measures to defend themselves. Some four thousand "regroupees" (cadres and soldiers who had gone north in 1954 and 1955) started moving back to South Vietnam. North Vietnam formed Group 559 in May 1959 to infiltrate cadres and weapons into South Vietnam and to set up a base camp in the Central Highlands, a mountainous region. Men and women walked hundreds of miles along a network of footpaths in the jungles dubbed the Ho Chi Minh Trail that ran along the Laotian-Vietnamese and Cambodian-Vietnamese borders. They transported munitions on bicycles each carrying a load of several hundred pounds. A second group, Group 759, organized in July of the same year, sent supplies southward by sea. In December 1960, the National Front for the Liberation of South Vietnam (NLF) came into being.[10]

To control the rural population, the Diem government instituted a Strategic Hamlet Program in 1962 to pacify the countryside. The government rounded up villagers and forcibly moved them into compounds surrounded by barbed wire and stockades, often located a long distance from their fields. The blueprint for this program of coerced relocation came from Sir Robert Thompson, the secretary of defense in British Malaya, where a Communist insurgency raged in the 1950s. The aim of the program was to offer an attractive alternative to the Communists: protecting the rural population by training and arming village militia, uniting the people, and promoting social and economic development in the countryside.[11] In fact, strategic hamlets became yet another instrument used to hunt down and kill Communists. The government even bombed rural areas to drive peasants into the strategic hamlets.

Given these repressive measures, opposition to the Diem government grew apace. The dissidents who caught international attention were South Vietnam's Buddhists. Diem had forbidden all flags except the flag of South Vietnam to be flown in public. In defiance of this ban, thousands of Buddhist demonstrators gathered and waved hundreds of banners to celebrate Buddha's birthday in May 1963. The police fired into the crowd, killing one woman and eight children. A stampede broke out and many people were injured. Diem claimed the Buddhist monks were Communists. Even larger demonstrations followed the first. Then, on June 11, a Buddhist monk poured gasoline on himself and lit a match to burn himself to death. His self-immolation was perceived as the ultimate act of protest; that fiery image was broadcast on television screens around the world. The U.S. ambassador to South Vietnam urged Diem to be more conciliatory; instead, in August Ngo Dinh Nhu ordered his forces to attack Buddhist pagodas and to arrest the monks inside. Even Diem's most ardent American supporters, both in and out of the U.S. government, began to question whether it was wise to continue supporting his regime. When several South Vietnamese generals indicated that they were planning a coup to topple the government, the United States gave them its covert approval. The bodyguard of one of the coup plotters murdered Diem and Nhu on November 1, 1963. By then, the number of American military advisors in the country had increased from several hundred to fifteen thousand.[12]

Political Instability and the Beginning of the American Quagmire

The deaths of Ngo Dinh Diem and Ngo Dinh Nhu did not bring peace or reform to South Vietnam. One short-lived government followed another. The twelve-man Military Revolutionary Council headed by General Tran Van Don and General Duong Van Minh that carried out the coup was itself in power for only two months. On January 30, 1964, General Nguyen Kanh ousted the council. However, Nguyen Kanh's regime lasted only a year. In February 1965, Phan Huy Quat, a civilian, took over the reins of government and remained in power until June when a group of young generals chose Air Force Marshal Nguyen Cao Ky as prime minister and Army General Nguyen Van Thieu as head of state. Elections held in September 1967 legitimized Ky and Thieu; the two would remain the dominant political leaders in Saigon until 1975. Thieu and Ky had opposite personalities: the former was cautious and secretive, while the latter was flamboyant, outspoken, and always eager for action. Though they served together as president and vice president, in time they became bitter rivals. In 1971, Thieu pushed aside Ky, as well as other high-ranking military and political leaders, and instituted one-man rule.[13]

Three weeks after the death of the Ngo brothers, President John F. Kennedy himself was assassinated. During his administration, Kennedy had been reluctant to send combat troops to Vietnam and preferred, instead, to use military advisors and U.S. Army Special Forces (the "Green Berets") to support the Army of the Republic of Vietnam (ARVN) and to train South Vietnam's own Special Forces. American advisors accompanied ARVN troops on their combat missions, while American helicopters provided air cover. The Green Berets went to the Central Highlands of South Vietnam to recruit ethnic minorities to whom the French had given the generic name *Montagnards*, placed them into Civilian Irregular Defense Groups, and trained them to attack Communists hiding in the jungles. Soon after Kennedy's death, beginning in January 1964, the United States also carried out a series of covert military operations in North Vietnam, "inserting" South Vietnamese agents trained by the United States into territory north of the seventeenth parallel. The pilot who flew some of the first missions (at a dangerously low altitude to evade North Vietnamese radar) was none other than Nguyen Cao Ky.[14]

In light of the political instability in South Vietnam, Kennedy's successor, Lyndon B. Johnson, listened more and more to those military commanders and civilian advisors who argued that the United States should take drastic action by attacking North Vietnam directly. Johnson was not yet convinced that bombing raids over North Vietnam should be launched, but he authorized increased air and naval surveillance as well as commando raids to destroy North Vietnam's transportation and communication infrastructure. In addition, American planes started flying sorties over the eastern border of Laos to drop bombs on the Ho Chi Minh Trail with the hope of disrupting the North Vietnamese supply line to the South. Johnson increased the number of American advisors in South Vietnam to twenty-three thousand, appointed General William Westmoreland to head the Military Assistance Command—Vietnam (an enlarged version of the original Military Assistance and Advisory Group), and augmented economic aid to South Vietnam.[15]

The Second Indochina War

As part of the increased surveillance efforts, a U.S. destroyer, the *Maddox*, which had been ordered to sail from its home base in Japan to the Gulf of Tonkin in July 1964, was patrolling off the coast of North Vietnam to collect electronic surveillance data on August 2. It encountered three North Vietnamese boats that charged at it in a V-formation and fired some torpedoes that missed their target before quickly veering off. The *Maddox* returned fire and, aided by planes from the aircraft carrier the USS *Ticonderoga*, chased the torpedo boats away. Then, on August 4, the *Maddox*, now joined by the *Turner Joy*, reported that their radars and sonars had picked up signals that seemed to indicate the two destroyers were under attack. It was a stormy night and there was no actual sighting of the torpedo boats. Nevertheless, the American ships fired their guns into the darkness for several hours. On August 5, President Johnson ordered retaliatory attacks against North Vietnam. Planes from the *Ticonderoga* and the *Constellation*, another aircraft carrier, destroyed four North Vietnamese bases, two dozen patrol boats, and oil storage depots. To this day, there is still no agreement over whether there was an actual attack against the American ships that night. But Johnson did not hesitate to ask Congress to pass a resolution to give him broad powers to take "all necessary measures to repel any armed attacks against the forces of the United States and to prevent further aggression."[16] This Tonkin Gulf Resolution, passed by the Senate 88 to 2 and by the House of Representatives 466 to 0, enabled the United States to fight an undeclared war in the years to come.[17]

Not yet willing to commit American ground troops, Johnson authorized an air war that began in late 1964 to destroy North Vietnam's capacity to arm and support the insurgency in South Vietnam. In Operation Barrel Roll that began on December 14, American planes flew eight sorties a week to bomb the Ho Chi Minh Trail. (The bombing of the Ho Chi Minh Trail would intensify exponentially in subsequent years.) Bombing raids over North Vietnam began with Operation Flaming Dart in retaliation for a Communist attack against U.S. billets in Pleiku. On March 2, 1965, Operation Rolling Thunder was launched, during which U.S. planes bombed North Vietnam almost daily, initially at targets below the eighteenth parallel and eventually striking farther north to areas south of the nineteenth parallel. By May, U.S. planes were bombing roads, bridges, power plants, moving vehicles (especially trucks), and military installations as far north as the twentieth parallel. The following month, they bombed airfields, supply depots, and military bases up to the twenty-first parallel. Soon, dams and waterways in the upper Hong River delta and around Hanoi and Haiphong, as well as factories and missile sites, also became targets. In 1966, an average of three hundred bombers a day destroyed more roads, railroads, bridges, and petroleum storage depots. The following year, North Vietnam's major steel manufacturing plant, its only cement factory, and its most important thermal power plant and electric transformer, as well as a host of smaller industrial plants, rail yards, and army barracks, were all hit repeatedly.[18]

The total number of sorties flown was twenty-five thousand in 1965, seventy-nine thousand in 1966, and one hundred and eight thousand in 1967. Johnson ordered a partial halt to the bombing campaign on October 30, 1968, but regular bombing runs resumed in 1972 during the Nixon administration as part of a carrot-and-stick strategy to pressure North Vietnam to relent during secret talks in Paris in which the two sides searched for a negotiated political settlement to the war. By then, the bombing raids had destroyed or severely damaged virtually all of North Vietnam's industrial and transportation infrastructure. During the entire course of the war, more than a million tons of bombs were dropped on North Vietnam, 4 million tons on South Vietnam, 1.5 million tons on Laos, and 500,000 tons on Cambodia. These amounts greatly exceeded the total tonnage dropped on Nazi Germany and the countries it occupied during World War II.[19] Four times as many bombs were dropped on South Vietnam as on North Vietnam because the fundamental concern of the United States was to preserve South Vietnam as a non-Communist, pro-American country.[20] For that reason, it was more important to obliterate the "Viet Cong" in the South than to vanquish North Vietnam per se. However, since it was North Vietnam that sustained the insurgents in the south, it, too, had to be reduced to rubble.

Bombs were not the only things dropped on the enemy. U.S. planes also dropped napalm, a gel that sticks to human bodies as it burns; white phosphorus incendiary bombs; chemical defoliants and herbicides that strip leaves from trees in order to destroy the canopy provided by the dense tropical jungle so that pilots could see more clearly what or who was moving on the ground below; and poisonous antipersonnel gases.[21] But the air war and the use of chemical and biological agents had an unanticipated effect: the high-technology brutality fueled a nationwide antiwar movement in the United States that became an impediment to continuing a controversial war with no end in sight. Students, professionals, working people, religious leaders, draftees who refused to go to Vietnam, members of Congress, and, in time, veterans who had fought in the war all raised their voices to demand that the United States get out of the war.[22]

North Vietnam coped with the unprecedented destructiveness of American firepower by evacuating major population centers; dispersing industrial production, a great deal of which was hidden in caves and manmade tunnels; decentralizing decision making; mobilizing more than half a million people to repair roads, rails, bridges, and the most vital installations; assigning responsibilities to all able-bodied men, women, and children; and exhorting the entire nation to participate in a "people's war of national resistance" against a mighty enemy.[23]

Despite all the damage caused by the air war and the infusion of more and more American advisors, the battles on the ground in South Vietnam were not going well. As ARVN soldiers became demoralized, the desertion rate rose as the war progressed. In 1964, seventy-three thousand men deserted from ARVN; the following year, the number was one hundred and thirteen thousand. Lyndon B. Johnson finally gave in to the demands of the hawks in his administration and sent the first American combat troops to South Vietnam—two marine battalions that landed at Danang on March 8, 1965. By the end of that year, U.S. troop strength in South Vietnam stood at two hundred thousand. There were four hundred thousand American troops in the country by the end of 1966, five hundred thousand by the end of 1967, and five hundred and forty thousand by the end of 1968. Despite the massive American presence and assistance to shore up ARVN, the number of deserters from ARVN exceeded one hundred thousand every year except 1967 until the war ended. Two years after the United States withdrew its troops, the number of deserters from ARVN peaked at two hundred thousand in 1975.[24]

The Tet Offensive

In January 1968, during the lunar New Year that Vietnamese call Tet, North Vietnamese troops and the "Viet Cong" launched major attacks against dozens of cities and towns in South Vietnam. The central committee of the Lao Dong party had been preparing for such an offensive for some time. In the weeks before the planned offensive, sappers (specially trained commando units) began infiltrating into the urban areas with their weapons hidden in carts and trucks filled with agricultural products. The Communists committed eighty-four thousand men (sixty-seven thousand in main units and seventeen thousand guerrillas) to this campaign. In the middle of the night on January 30, Communist forces attacked and took six cities and towns in central Vietnam but those attacks were premature. General Vo Nguyen Giap had initially planned the attack for the night of January 29–30 but later changed the date to January 30–31. However, because of poor communication, not everyone was aware of the change. This snafu in timing resulted in many deaths because the premature attacks alerted U.S. and ARVN forces to what the Communists intended to do. General Westmoreland went to see President Thieu and asked him to order all Vietnamese military personnel, who had gone home to celebrate Tet—a celebration that lasts for days—back to their posts, but many did not return. The Communists attacked thirty-six out of forty-four provincial capitals, sixty-six county seats, and many military bases. The heaviest fighting—hand-to-hand combat in the streets—took place in Saigon and Hue. It lasted for two weeks in the former and almost four weeks in the latter before the Communists were beaten back. The number of Communist casualties was extraordinarily high: forty-five thousand combatants, including thirty-two thousand deaths, out of eighty-four thousand. Not only did military personnel perish, so did important political cadres. South Vietnam lost two thousand soldiers and the United States one thousand.[25]

While on the face of it the Tet Offensive was a stunning defeat for the North Vietnamese and the "Viet Cong" (the armed units of the latter were virtually decimated), paradoxically it became an immense psychological defeat for the United States. That the Communists could launch such a massive offensive when U.S. military and political leaders had been trying to convince the American public that the war was going well multiplied the doubts that many individuals already harbored about the wisdom of continuing the war. The death toll of American troops was rising; the United States was spending two billion dollars per month on the war; and even Westmoreland sounded sober about future prospects. In a report submitted to the Joint Chiefs of Staff on February 27, 1968, Westmoreland pointed out that the Military Assistance Command—Vietnam faced three problems. First, logistical support north of Danang was difficult because of foggy weather along the central coast and the need to concentrate U.S. forces in the demilitarized zone around the seventeenth parallel and in Hue. Second, ARVN units were pinned down in stationary positions defending large population centers and military bases—a situation that gave the mobile Communist forces a strategic advantage. Third, half of all U.S. forces were deployed in the region immediately south of the demilitarized zone (the so-called I Corps zone), leaving the rest of South Vietnam vulnerable to future attacks. Based on this pessimistic assessment, Westmoreland requested additional troops.[26] Burdened by the inability of the United States to win the war despite the massive input of men and military materiel, President Johnson announced that he would not run for a second term. He also ended all bombing raids over North Vietnam. Richard M. Nixon won the presidency in 1968 with a promise to find a way to exit from Vietnam "with honor."

The Nixon Strategy: Vietnamization and Secret Negotiations

The strategy Nixon adopted, called Vietnamization or the Nixon Doctrine, was to turn the fighting over to South Vietnamese troops. The United States would continue to provide advisors and hardware. After meeting with President Thieu on Midway Island in the middle of the Pacific Ocean in June 1969, Nixon announced that a first batch of twenty-five thousand American troops would be withdrawn immediately. By the end of December, sixty thousand American soldiers had left Vietnam. Though the war would not end for another four years, the drawdown continued apace. By the end of 1970, there were only two hundred and eighty thousand American troops left in South Vietnam. A year later, there were only one hundred and forty thousand. The last American troops left on March 29, 1973.[27]

To protect South Vietnam's flank as American troops departed, Nixon authorized a bombing campaign over eastern Cambodia that began on March 18, 1969. The objective was to destroy not only that segment of the Ho Chi Minh Trail (which by this time was no longer a trail but a network of paved highways) that ran along the Vietnamese-Cambodian border, but also the sanctuaries in Cambodian territory to which Communist troops retreated whenever U.S. and ARVN forces chased them in hot pursuit. Nixon kept the bombing raids over Cambodia a secret. In the next fourteen months, B-52s flew 3,630 sorties in an attempt to destroy what Americans called COSVN (Central Office for South Vietnam)—the headquarters of the "Viet Cong." There was indeed such a base but Americans were mistaken when they assumed it remained in one location. In fact, the Communists moved COSVN from place to place depending on circumstances. Then, on April 29, 1970, thirty-two thousand U.S. troops and forty thousand ARVN troops invaded Cambodia. When Nixon announced the invasion on national television, antiwar activists erupted in furor. Nixon, however, kept his promise to limit the duration of the invasion. U.S. forces withdrew from Cambodia by the end of June, but ARVN troops remained.[28] To cut the Ho Chi Minh Trail into unconnected segments, U.S. and ARVN troops also invaded southern Laos in early 1971, but that did not achieve the desired goal, either.[29]

What forced the war to continue for four more years after the promulgation of the Nixon Doctrine was the slow pace of negotiations. Henry Kissinger, Nixon's national security advisor and later secretary of state, met secretly in Paris with Xuan Thuy, the North Vietnamese representative, in August 1969 to explore how negotiations might proceed. More formal talks, still secret, began on February 20, 1970, with Le Duc Tho. Among many sticking points, the most recalcitrant one involved the status of South Vietnam. The United States wanted it to remain an independent, non-Communist country, while the North Vietnamese pointed out that the 1954 Geneva Accords had affirmed that Vietnam was a single nation. North Vietnam indicated it would negotiate in earnest only after all American troops left South Vietnam, while the United States insisted that no progress could be expected until all North Vietnamese troops left South Vietnam. So it went, back and forth, for three long years.

In January 1972, Nixon made public, for the first time, that secret talks had been taking place since 1969. When Kissinger and Le

Duc Tho reached preliminary agreement, South Vietnamese President Thieu was furious and insisted on revising the draft agreement extensively. In November of that year, talks resumed during which Kissinger presented the dozens of amendments that Thieu demanded, but North Vietnam refused to consider them. So, the talks broke down again but they resumed in December when the United States bombed Hanoi and Haiphong, including heavily populated areas, without mercy. Kissinger and Le Duc Tho reopened talks. This time, the two sides each made important concessions and came up with an agreement that was mutually acceptable. But that agreement was not acceptable to Thieu. The major concession the United States made was to accept a cease-fire-in-place, which meant that North Vietnam would not have to move its troops out of South Vietnam.

The cease-fire-in-place gave North Vietnam a great advantage because a year earlier it had launched an Easter Offensive against South Vietnam and captured extensive territory. Hanoi's objective was to demonstrate by such an offensive that ARVN could not fight well on its own. The combined Communist forces (that is, regular troops and guerrillas from both North and South Vietnam) participating in the Easter Offensive numbered two hundred thousand. During the first phase of the campaign, North Vietnamese troops struck the provinces south of the demilitarized zone. It took them only two days to capture all twelve military bases that the United States had turned over to ARVN. During the second phase, the Communist forces attacked the Central Highlands and the central coast. In the third phase, the campaign targeted the provinces north of Saigon and those in the Mekong Delta.[30] In retaliation for this major military incursion and to exert utmost pressure on North Vietnam at the negotiating table, Nixon authorized the mining of Haiphong harbor in May 1972 and resumed heavy bombing of North Vietnam.

Even though Nixon offered South Vietnam two billion dollars' worth of military equipment and assured Thieu that the United States would take "swift and retaliatory action" should North Vietnam violate the 1973 Paris Peace Agreement, Thieu refused to accept the terms. Despite Thieu's vociferous objections, the cease-fire went into effect on January 27, 1973—the day the agreement was signed in Paris. In the next two months, the United States speedily dismantled its bases, exchanged prisoners with the Communists, and left South Vietnam to its own fate. Without a pause, the war, now a civil war, resumed.

During the Second Indochina War, the ground fighting and the massive tonnage of bombs, napalm, and defoliants displaced some twelve million people in South Vietnam—about half the total population of the country at the time—from their homes. There are no statistics on how many people were forced to leave their homes in North Vietnam, but it safe to say that the percentage of people displaced there must have been much, much higher, as retreating to the countryside was a key strategy that North Vietnam's leaders used to survive. Because these millions of displaced people had not crossed international boundaries, they did not come under the mandate of the United Nations High Commissioner for Refugees (UNHCR), which, strictly speaking, is supposed to protect only refugees. (In international law, refugees are defined as persons *outside* of their own countries who are unable or unwilling to return home because of a well-founded fear of persecution by their own governments.) A number of international relief organizations, most notably Catholic Relief Services, the International Rescue Committee, the International Committee of the Red Cross (ICRC), and an evangelical Christian organization called World Vision, tried to assist as many of the displaced persons as their resources allowed.[31] No one foresaw that some of these same organizations, along with other voluntary agencies, would soon play a major role in resettling the refuge-seekers who fled from Vietnam, Laos, and Cambodia in 1975 and in subsequent years.

CHAPTER SEVEN

The Fall of Saigon and Its Aftermath

As North Vietnamese troops routed ARVN forces in the Central Highlands, President Nguyen Van Thieu ordered his army commanders on
March 15, 1975, to abandon the area and to retreat southward to establish a more defensible front line. The highest-ranking general in the
region vehemently protested Thieu's order, saying it was immoral to
retreat before the battle was even joined. But Thieu stood firm—
the fall of Ban Me Thuot, which sits astride the intersection of two
main highways (one running north-south and the other west-east),
on March 12 had apparently shaken him to the core. Tens of thousands of civilians, many of them family members of the ARVN troops,
joined the soldiers as they all rushed southward. By April 22, a quarter
million people had fled from Hue and were converging on Danang
whose residents also started to flee. Masses of panicky people clogged
the roads; civilians and military personnel filled every available boat,
some of which they had commandeered, to take them to ports farther
south. Danang fell on March 29.

On March 31, North Vietnam's military and political leaders formally launched the "Ho Chi Minh Campaign," the goal of which was
to capture Saigon, they hoped, by 1976. But ARVN disintegrated and
the South Vietnamese government collapsed a whole year earlier than
anyone expected. Following ARVN's pell-mell retreat, one hundred and
fifty thousand to two hundred thousand Communist troops speedily
followed them. Sensing imminent victory, North Vietnam announced
on April 15 that it would guarantee the safe evacuation of Americans.
By April 21, one hundred and fifty thousand to two hundred thousand
Communist troops had amassed on the outskirts of Saigon.[1] Saigon
"fell" on April 30.

Americans, North Vietnamese, and South Vietnamese have all discussed reasons for why events turned out the way they did. An examination of how Americans have sought to understand their "defeat" is

beyond the scope of this chapter, while the accounts by North Vietnamese leaders are laced with Communist jargon that makes them less than useful. The retrospective analyses of several South Vietnamese military and political leaders, however, are illuminating.

The "Final Collapse"

In contrast to the triumphalist accounts published by North Vietnamese generals,[2] those written by South Vietnamese generals and diplomats are more measured and surprisingly free of rancor. Instead of simply blaming the United States for abandoning South Vietnam, they cast the military defeat within the larger context of South Vietnamese politics—particularly the weaknesses of the Thieu regime.

Bui Diem, former secretary of state and South Vietnam's ambassador to the United States (1967–72), discloses how he had tried repeatedly to persuade Thieu "to broaden the government and remove the incompetence and corruption that stigmatized it in American eyes." He recalls telling Thieu that "we also needed these things for our own health. Corruption and nepotism debilitated the armed forces and government equally." But Thieu preferred to surround "himself with weak and incompetent people who were corrupt and incapable of challenging him." Above all else, "Thieu sought loyalty above ability." The United States was partly to blame for this state of affairs because "South Vietnamese corruption and political reforms were simply not high on the American list of priorities." Instead, what preoccupied American policy-makers was South Vietnam's ability to fend off Communist assaults. Bui Diem notes that Americans were arrogant and made no efforts to understand the Vietnamese. However, even as he declares that "the manner in which the United States took its leave was . . . an act unworthy of a great power," he realizes that "[t]he South Vietnamese people, and especially the South Vietnamese leaders, myself among them, bear the ultimate responsibility for the fate of their nation."[3]

Nguyen Cao Ky, former Vietnamese Air Force marshal, prime minister, and vice president, also discusses the political conditions that led to the Thieu regime's demise. (Between the 1971 presidential election and the fall of Saigon, Ky was not in power. Rather, he was enjoying civilian life while developing a large farm using modern agronomy. Therefore, he could criticize Thieu without implicating himself.) In two books, Ky pinpoints corruption as one of South Vietnam's major problems. He devotes an entire chapter in each book to recounting his own unsuccessful efforts to wipe out corruption while he was prime minister. Fond of dramatic gestures, Ky had a corrupt ethnic Chinese businessman publicly executed in Saigon's central market as he began his anticorruption campaign. Ky says that about ten merchants controlled the entire country's price of rice, the basic staple, by hoarding or flooding the market as they saw fit, caring only about their profits rather than the well-being of the populace. Businessmen similarly manipulated the gold market. Furthermore, during the years of American involvement, a black market in American PX (military post exchange) goods flourished. As salaries were low, many South Vietnamese, in connivance with U.S. troops, bought or stole PX merchandise and resold them on the black market. Some became "PX millionaires." Even more detrimental, a drug market thrived because heroin processed from opium poppies grown in the highlands of mainland Southeast Asia is of excellent quality and at that time was very cheap. According to Ky, even though some officials were not corrupt themselves, many of their wives took advantage of their husbands' high positions to accept bribes. One lucrative source came from parents who wanted their sons to dodge conscription: they offered large bribes to officials to remove their progeny's names from the list of potential draftees.[4]

The currency market was likewise a source of corruption: Ky claims that in the early 1970s an annual average of half a billion dollars in U.S. aid was lost through "illegal currency rackets." However, when Ky told President Richard Nixon that "ninety percent of the money [U.S. aid] disappears into the pockets of corrupt American and Vietnamese officials," Nixon's response was, "Um, that's a very serious matter. . . . We need to know more about this. Send me a memo about it."[5] This anecdote makes the same point as Bui Diem does—American leaders were not really concerned about the decay of South Vietnamese society; all they cared about was winning the war militarily.

Another weakness, in Ky's eyes, was that "we never achieved the standing or appearance of an independent, self-governing country. . . . We never produced a leader to unite the country. . . . The North had one in Ho Chi Minh; . . . Neither Diem, nor Thieu . . . won the hearts of even the South Vietnamese. The Americans controlled the fighting of the war. American aid financed the country; without it we could not survive."[6] Thus, after the United States withdrew its troops in 1973 and the amount of U.S. aid dwindled, the South Vietnamese armed forces, which had been groomed to fight a high-technology war, could no longer carry on. Consequently, morale sagged.

Tran Van Don, a leader of the coup that removed Ngo Dinh Diem and Ngo Dinh Nhu, confirms that Ky indeed did try to stamp corruption by preventing the illicit trade in rice, gold, currency, U.S.-supplied fertilizers, and PX goods, but notes that Ky failed because "he was lazy" and did not put enough effort into the crusade. In 1974 and 1975, as the American "money base dried up," observes Don, "the government had to print more and more piasters to finance budgetary deficits and the rate of inflation really accelerated."[7] Like Ky, Don also believes that South Vietnam suffered as a client regime: Thieu "survived in power for about ten years by pleasing the Americans."[8]

Then, speaking as a general, Don claims that "we did not adopt the correct military strategy to deal with the inexorable Communist steamroller. We spread our forces too thin, trying to maintain a presence in and defend each province town, an ambition clearly beyond our capability. Although by this time we had an armed force of over one million men . . . [w]e had also become used to American military methods which are fine when you have all the supplies and equipment needed to fight an American-style war. On this, too, we failed to reckon with the facts of life in 1974."[9] Don exonerates the behavior of ARVN troops who shed their uniforms and weapons as they retreated. He points out that the soldiers' wives, children, and other family members lived "in and around the tactical positions. . . . Our troops were naturally motivated to protect their families and individual possessions" in the face of North Vietnam's unstoppable onslaught.[10]

As for the United States, Don thinks its most reprehensible act was to hold secret negotiations with North Vietnam: "The United States came into South Vietnam to help us defend our freedom. As a foreign government, the United States was not entitled to substitute for us in negotiations with the enemy, especially on questions of an essentially political nature."[11]

The author who goes into the greatest detail about the military reasons for South Vietnam's "final collapse" is General Cao Van Vien, the last chairman of South Vietnam's Joint General Staff. Like Don, Vien argues that the troops themselves should not be blamed for the disintegration of ARVN: "The separation of families seriously affected the morale of our troops who, out of impatience and anxiety, deserted their units to look for parents, wives, and children. . . . The troops withdrawing to Danang were more concerned with their dependents than with their units and the enemy. Given this chaotic situation, it was a matter of each individual trying to solve his own personal problems and those of his family."[12]

Vien concludes by crisply listing a dozen reasons for the collapse: (1) The United States forced South Vietnam to accept the Paris Agreement, which was "much too disadvantageous to its survival"; (2) the pledge of continued support that Nixon gave Thieu could not be honored because of the Watergate scandal and Nixon's impeachment and resignation; (3) the cutoff of U.S. military aid "seriously affected the combat capability and morale of our troops and population"; (4) Thieu made a crucial strategic error when he ordered troops to withdraw southward; (5) South Vietnam's leaders failed to perceive that the United States had changed its strategy in Asia from confronting Communism to accommodating it; (6) there was no national unity in South Vietnam—a nation "riddled by corruption and sometimes ineptitude and dereliction"; (7) having been taught to fight a "rich man's war, . . . when military aid was reduced, our forces plummeted from a state of material abundance to one of privation" and did not know how to fight a "poor man's war"; (8) South Vietnam's "mobilization policy succeeded only in meeting about half of all manpower requirements . . . [and] achieved [only] modest results in our effort to reduce the desertion rate"; (9) "both the civilian government and the armed forces made regrettable errors" when they assigned and promoted officers "based on family or clan connections and more on personal trust than ability, achievements, or integrity"; (10) in terms of cooperating with the U.S. armed forces, "we never achieved unity of command and thus violated one of the basic principles of war"; (11) "[t]he war pursued by the Communists . . . was not purely military; it was a total war fought on other fronts as well: political, economic, diplomatic, etc."; and (12) "[o]ur enemy was determined, persistent, and experienced. . . . During his long years of struggle, a single, continuous, and unchanging politico-military strategy dictated his conduct of the war." Vien ends his recitation by observing that "[t]he advantages and disadvantages, strengths and weaknesses of both sides added up to the final collapse of South Vietnam."[13]

These are sober and evenhanded evaluations. By offering them, the authors show that they have looked hard at the reasons for their country's defeat. By publicly owning up to their own responsibilities, they are helping salve the pain and transcend the tragedy in which all South Vietnamese have been engulfed.

The April 1975 Evacuation

As the South Vietnamese government seemed about to fall, the United States hastily prepared to evacuate not only Americans and their dependents but at-risk Vietnamese as well. The U.S. government moved quickly to deal with the whirlwind developments in Southeast

Asia. On April 8, the State Department began to consult with committees in the House of Representatives and the Senate about using the attorney general's parole authority to admit refugees.[14] On April 14, the attorney general agreed to admit the Vietnamese and Cambodian dependents of U.S. citizens under parole. The government also asked UNHCR and the Intergovernmental Committee for European Migration (ICEM), originally established to aid displaced Europeans after World War II, to help find countries that might be willing to accept Indochinese refugees. Four days later, President Gerald Ford created an Interagency Task Force, composed of officials from a dozen federal agencies, and asked it to plan for the reception of Indochinese refugees. A week after that, the attorney general extended parole to high-risk Vietnamese and to Cambodians who were abroad at the time.

On April 21, South Vietnamese President Thieu resigned and delivered a televised farewell speech, in which he praised himself and expressed enormous resentment toward the United States. An American aircraft flew him to exile in Taiwan on April 26. His successor, Tran Van Huong, served for only a few days. He was, in turn, succeeded by Duong Van Minh on April 28, to whom fell the task of negotiating a cease-fire and a political settlement with the victorious Communists.

Until the last minute no one knew exactly how many people would be evacuated from South Vietnam. State Department officials, when asked by the International Relations Committee of the U.S. House of Representatives and by the Committee on the Judiciary of the U.S. Senate in mid-April, could not give a precise figure.[15] As the collapse of the Saigon government appeared imminent, an arbitrary figure of one hundred and thirty thousand evacuees was chosen, with one hundred and twenty-five thousand slots for Vietnamese and five thousand for Cambodians. Part of the uncertainty came from the fact that Graham Martin, the U.S. ambassador to South Vietnam, refused to make evacuation plans public because he did not wish to provoke widespread panic that might hasten the fall of the Thieu government.[16]

Evacuation by fixed-wing aircraft began on April 1 but it went slowly because many "non-essential" Americans who were told to leave refused to do so until their Vietnamese dependents received authorization to accompany them. Such authorization took time to obtain because the South Vietnamese government required people to apply for exit permits and passports before letting them leave and American officials said they must wait for visas if they wished to be admitted into the United States. However, once it was known that North Vietnamese troops had reached the edge of the capital, evacuation moved into high gear on April 22. Sympathetic American officials based at Saigon's Tan Son Nhut Airport cut as much red tape as they could. In the following eight days, U.S. aircraft lifted out about seventy-five hundred people a day. That operation ended a week later. On April 28, North Vietnamese pilots, whom a South Vietnamese defector had trained, flew four airplanes to Saigon—planes that had been left behind by the retreating South Vietnamese army—and dropped bombs on Tan Son Nhut Airport. Though interrupted, the evacuation nevertheless continued. The following day, Communist rockets and artillery shelled the airport with great accuracy, blowing up buildings and parked airplanes. But it was fleeing pilots of the South Vietnamese Air Force who finally destroyed the runways when, right after takeoff, they dropped the ordnance their planes were carrying in order to reduce the load on board because their planes were jammed with passengers—families and friends—whom they flew to U.S. airbases in Thailand.[17] Once the runways were disabled, fixed-wing aircraft could no longer take off or land, so giant helicopters had to be used to haul people out on April 29 and 30. The helicopters managed to lift out 7,014 people before Saigon fell on the morning of April 30.

These last-ditch evacuation efforts were chaotic. So many South Vietnamese planes and helicopters tried to land on the flight decks of the U.S. aircraft carriers anchored in the South China Sea that they had to be pushed into the ocean to make room for others to land.[18] Tens of thousands of Vietnamese who were definitely at risk failed to be evacuated[19] while some who were not at risk bribed their way out. More than one hundred and thirty thousand Vietnamese managed to escape before North Vietnamese troops entered Saigon. Over seventy-three thousand of them did so by sea. Men in the Vietnamese Navy spirited their families and friends to safety in their ships. Twenty-six South Vietnamese naval vessels showed up with some thirty thousand passengers at the U.S. naval base at Subic Bay in the Philippines the first week of May. Other Vietnamese commandeered whatever boats they could and made their way to the waiting ships in the South China Sea or to the nearest ports in Vietnam's neighboring countries.[20]

When the governor of Guam heard that Philippine President Ferdinand Marcos refused to let the United States house the refugees in the latter's country, he offered his island's hospitality. Overnight, Navy Seabees, aided by a wide variety of civilians, including tourists vacationing in Guam, erected a tent city capable of housing fifty thousand people at a time. The first planeload of refugees touched down on the tarmac only two hours after construction began. Over the next six months, officials of the U.S. Immigration and Naturalization Service (INS—now renamed as the Bureau of Immigration and Customs Enforcement within the U.S. Department of Homeland Security) and the Public Health Service examined and interviewed the refugees on Guam, as well as smaller numbers brought to the American military bases at Subic Bay and Wake Island, before they were allowed to leave for four reception centers on the U.S. mainland. Camp Pendleton in California opened as the first reception center on April 29, Fort Chaffee in Arkansas on May 2, and Eglin Air Base in Florida on May 4. A fourth military base, Fort Indiantown Gap in Pennsylvania, was hastily added on May 28 to relieve the overcrowding at the other three centers.

Resettling the Evacuees

Over the next seven and a half months, U.S. officials and staff from a dozen voluntary agencies worked to find sponsors for the refugees. That task was completed by the end of 1975. The Interagency Task Force set October 31 as the deadline for moving Vietnamese and Cambodians who were still stranded around the world into the refugee system. The Subic Bay processing center closed on July 6, the one on Wake Island on August 1, Eglin Air Force Base on September 15, the Guam processing center and Camp Pendleton on October 31, Fort Indiantown Gap on December 15, and Fort Chaffee on December 20. The Interagency Task Force disbanded itself on December 31.[21] The work of resettling the first wave had been completed.

During the resettlement process, about nineteen hundred Vietnamese and over four hundred Cambodian evacuees decided they wanted to return to their homelands. UNHCR provided the Vietnamese would-be repatriates in Guam with a refurbished cargo ship, the *Thuong Tin I*, that took 1,546 people to Cam Ranh Bay in late October even though Vietnamese authorities had not agreed to accept them.[22] The Provisional Revolutionary Government (PRG), formed in 1969 to administer areas in South Vietnam already under Communist control, governed the former Republic of Vietnam pending the reunification of the two halves of the country. PRG officials accused the repatriates of being CIA agents and placed them in "re-education" camps upon their arrival. (The nature of these camps will be discussed below.) The U.S. government and UNHCR did not grant the wishes of several hundred Vietnamese who had already been flown to the U.S. mainland who also desired to be repatriated. Despite U.S. attempts to "internationalize" the resettlement, other countries agreed to take in only about fifteen thousand people—a tenth of the total number. The largest number went to France and Canada. Few countries came forward to help because everyone viewed the exodus as an American problem. Even the UNHCR played only a relatively peripheral role.

The Quiet Beginning of the "Boat People" Exodus

Refuge-seekers continued to leave Cambodia, Laos, and Vietnam after the American evacuation and resettlement efforts ended. The first of the "boat people" escaped from Vietnam and found their way mainly to Malaysia. Smaller numbers also landed in Thailand, Indonesia, Singapore, and the Philippines. Until October 1975—the U.S. deadline for placing refugees into American processing centers—the United States admitted all the refuge-seekers from Vietnam who fled by sea. That is why there were virtually no "residue" refuge-seekers left in Southeast Asia by late 1975.

The American public did not hear much news about the first batches of people who escaped in boats in 1976 and the early months of 1977 because journalists paid little attention to them. Their number was very small compared with the number of "land people" from Laos who were entering Thailand during this period. Also, officials in the countries of first asylum where they landed preferred to keep their arrival as quiet as possible because they feared a far larger exodus might ensue if people in Vietnam found out that their compatriots had managed to reach safe haven with ease.

Relatively few people escaped from Vietnam in the two years after the Communist victory because within a few days of capturing Saigon, the new authorities announced on the radio that certain groups of people—elected officials from the national assembly down to the village level, civil servants, members of non-Communist political parties, military officers, policemen, employees of various counterinsurgency programs, religious leaders, professors, teachers, writers, and artists—should gather at specified locations to attend "re-education" sessions. Local Communist cadres told people that they had to attend courses that would last anywhere from three to thirty days. Even those whose ranks required them to attend for more than a few days were told to bring along only a week's rations. This misled people into thinking that the sessions would not last long. Since the individuals singled out for re-education thought it best to cooperate, most of them reported to the stations as told. To their surprise, soldiers packed them into covered vehicles, from which they could not see where they were going, and transported them to re-education camps, where they were subjected to hard labor, a near-starvation diet, and political indoctrination. While some low-ranking civil servants and noncommissioned officers indeed were kept for only three days of "thought reform classes," a majority of the political prisoners remained incarcerated for years. However, when inmates became so ill that it looked as though they might soon die, the camp wardens released them to avoid a high death toll.

Most of the re-education camps were in the southern part of Vietnam, but the PRG sent high-ranking officials and military officers of the fallen regime—those deemed to have "committed serious crimes against the people"—to camps in northern Vietnam, where both the environment and the treatment the prisoners received were harsher. Thus, in one fell swoop, virtually all the potential opponents of the new government were removed from society. There is no consensus about how many people were "re-educated." The government claimed that they numbered only forty thousand to fifty thousand, but a former ARVN officer who made a systematic study of the camps estimated there were somewhere between three hundred and forty thousand and four hundred thousand.[23] Since the incarcerated people were the very ones who might have tried to leave the country once they realized that resistance would not be feasible, their confinement reduced the number of potential escapees.

A second reason for the relatively small boat people outflow from late 1975 to early 1978 is that initially life for many residents in the former South Vietnam did not change drastically. Communist leaders did not try to reunify the two halves of the country immediately because their first priority was to increase agricultural and industrial production. They knew that the million or so ethnic Chinese living in the southern half of the country had, for centuries, dominated rice milling and wholesale and retail trade. Even though they stood in the way of the country's intended socialist transformation, to remove them abruptly would severely disrupt the distribution system and cause economic chaos. Although the government issued new currency in 1975, it set no ceiling on how much of the old currency people could exchange for the new, so those with money, gold, and other valuables could still hoard them. The black market in Western-manufactured goods continued to flourish in Ho Chi Minh City (formerly Saigon).

After the country was reunified on July 1, 1976, and adopted a new name—the Socialist Republic of Vietnam—the pace of change quickened. Le Duan, the First Secretary of the Lao Dong party, announced that Vietnam could wait no longer to embark on its march toward socialism. For socialist reconstruction to proceed, he said, the "comprador bourgeoisie" and the "remnants of the feudal landlord class" must be eliminated, economic enterprises must be nationalized, and large land holdings confiscated. The overall goal was to merge the economies of the two halves of the country into "a single system of large-scale socialist production."[24] Thus, owners of large and medium-sized businesses that the government confiscated became "nonproductive" persons overnight. To enable them to be "productive" again, Le Duan explained, they would be sent to "New Economic Zones" (NEZs) to till the soil. NEZs were set up on uncultivated land in remote regions and life there was extremely harsh. Those who dared to escape from an NEZ and returned to the cities without authorization would be committing a crime. Such people would be deprived of food rations and other necessities of life.

In light of these punitive measures, middle-class people—both ethnic Chinese and Vietnamese—who feared they might be penalized because of their class backgrounds began to escape by sea. One or two dozen people paid boat owners to take them away in small boats measuring perhaps no more than twenty feet in length. They sneaked out to sea under cover of darkness. The shore patrol imprisoned those they caught, but as soon as people were released, many tried to escape again. Journalists first took note of the small number of refuge-seekers from Vietnam who sailed to Thailand's east coast in mid-1976. While Thailand allowed them ashore, the island nation of Singapore prevented such boats from docking.[25]

As the number of boats increased, in late 1977 Thailand and Malaysia started pushing boats back to sea after giving food, water, and fuel to the passengers on board. Thai and Malaysian officials feared that domestic unrest might result should even larger numbers arrive. As one official put it, "People in camps get good food and medical treatment while sitting around with nothing to do all day. Prices in the local market go up, and the farmer ploughing the field over the fence is likely to ask himself what the Government has done for him recently."[26] Malaysia, which received many more boat people than Thailand did, pointed out that its capacity to care for refuge-seekers had been pushed to the limit as the country had already resettled fifteen hundred Cham from Cambodia (fellow Muslims whom Malaysian Muslims welcomed) and was providing

asylum to ninety thousand Muslim Filipinos displaced by the fighting between separatist Muslim groups and the Philippine central
government.[27] (In time, Malaysia would take in almost ten thousand
Cham refuge-seekers from Cambodia, accepting even those who had
originally shown up in other countries of first asylum.) Indonesia, the
Philippines, and Hong Kong, where the number of boat arrivals was
smaller, continued to provide temporary asylum, but Singapore and
Japan resolutely turned all away.

U.S. Executive and Legislative Responses

As the outflow grew in size—it reached an average of fifteen hundred
people a month by the spring of 1978[28]—the United States adopted
ad hoc measures to deal with both the land and boat people. With
the approval of Congress, in the spring of 1976 the attorney general
paroled eleven thousand people into the United States under an
"Expanded Parole Program." On August 11, 1977, he authorized another fifteen thousand parolees to enter under the "Indochinese Parole
Program." Of the fifteen thousand, eight thousand spaces were allocated to land people housed in Thai camps and seven thousand to boat
people scattered in various countries around Southeast Asia. Then,
on January 25, 1978, the attorney general extended parole to an additional seven thousand boat people. But the number of new arrivals
kept outpacing the additional resettlement slots offered by the United
States and other countries. In an attempt to solve the problem once
and for all, the United States announced a "Long Range Parole Program" on June 14, 1978, to admit twenty-five thousand people, half
from inland camps in Thailand, and the other half from boat people
camps. Barely six months later, the total had to be increased to 46,875
because of an unanticipated large outflow. Of the additional 21,875
slots, 17,500 were reserved for Vietnamese boat people and 4,375 for
Cambodians. Congress took further action by enacting Public Law
95-412, which allowed approximately five thousand unused spaces
under the 1965 Immigration Act's seventh preference (for refugees)
to be used for boat people who had reached Thailand.[29]

Given that the number of Indochinese refuge-seekers in Southeast Asian camps greatly exceeded the number of resettlement slots
available, the U.S. State Department delineated four categories to
prioritize whom to admit. Priority I was for people with close relatives in the United States. Priority II was for former employees of

U.S. government agencies in Vietnam, Laos, and Cambodia. Priority III was for people who had been "closely associated with U.S. policies or programs." This category included people who had held positions before 1975 in the governments or armed forces of South Vietnam, Laos, and Cambodia; or worked for American firms or organizations; or received training in or by the United States. Priority IV was a catchall category that included anyone who had not yet been accepted by another country for resettlement or who did not qualify for admission under Priorities I, II, and III, and who, "for compelling reasons, should be granted parole on humanitarian grounds." (In later years, the number of priorities would be expanded to six.) To give an indication of what kinds of people were being admitted, of the fifteen thousand slots authorized in August 1977, 7 percent went to Priority I, 5 percent to Priority II, 85 percent to Priority III, and 3 percent to Priority IV.[30]

As it became apparent that there would be no possibility in the near future for the Indochinese refugees admitted into the United States to return to their homelands, Congress enacted Public Law 95-145 to allow them to change their status from "parolee" to "permanent resident." President Jimmy Carter signed the act in October 1977. Applicants had to be natives or citizens of Vietnam, Laos, or Cambodia, although their spouses or children could be of other nationalities. They must have been paroled into the United States as refugees before January 1, 1979, or been admitted in various visa categories before March 31, 1975. They must also provide evidence that they had been physically present in the United States for two years. Furthermore, the applicants had to be "otherwise admissible" under INS regulations. However, INS could waive certain requirements with regard to literacy, communicable diseases, and the applicants' likelihood of becoming "public charges." Lawmakers included this provision because they knew that some refugees were illiterate, suffered from tuberculosis and other diseases, and very likely would need public assistance or "welfare" to survive. INS, with the help of hundreds of voluntary agency staff members, processed the applications.[31]

When Thailand and Malaysia started pushing boats back to sea, thousands of boat people simply anchored offshore and continued living on their boats under extremely overcrowded conditions. Their plight, especially the fate of those who drowned, began to attract mass media attention. Because greater international attention was focused on them, the U.S. State Department and INS, aided by the staff of voluntary agencies, processed boat people much more quickly than land people even though all the parole programs were supposed to be implemented in an evenhanded manner. During this period, boat people usually waited in first-asylum camps for only a few months before they were flown to resettlement countries, whereas tens of thousands of land people who had been living for years in camps in Thailand had to keep on waiting.[32] This is a prime example of how the mass media can shape perceptions of which groups of sufferers most deserve the world's sympathy and charity.

CHAPTER EIGHT

The Plight of the Ethnic Chinese in Vietnam

Between 1978 and 1989, several developments affected the outflow of refuge-seekers from Vietnam: that country's persecution of its ethnic Chinese residents, the Vietnamese invasion and occupation of Cambodia that led to China's retaliatory invasion of Vietnam, the reactions of Vietnam's neighbors that became countries of first asylum against their will, and the responses of countries of second asylum (which are also called resettlement countries or "third countries"). The United States was the country of second asylum that took in the largest number of refugees. It had historically dealt with refugee flows in an ad hoc manner, but the "boat people" exodus forced Congress to debate and pass the 1980 Refugee Act—the first act ever passed to deal specifically with refugees. UNHCR, for its part, tried to maintain its neutral stance, but it, too, had to modify its approach in the face of the almost insoluble problems created by the massive and widely publicized outflow of desperate people.

Punitive Measures against the Ethnic Chinese

The lives of ethnic Chinese living in both the southern and northern parts of Vietnam changed for the worse in 1978. On March 24, the Hanoi government announced that henceforth all "bourgeois trade" in the south would be abolished. Up to this point, only large and medium-sized enterprises had been nationalized; the new policy applied to small traders and even itinerant peddlers who had not been affected by the earlier reforms. On the evening of March 23, cadres summoned hundreds of youth to emergency ward committee meetings and taught them how to take an inventory of the goods in the shops and homes of businesspeople they were assigned to visit the following morning. Armed soldiers accompanied the young people as they went about their task in Cholon—the Chinese enclave in Ho Chi Minh City—and elsewhere. The speed with which the raid was carried out prevented the shopkeepers from dispersing their goods, currency, and gold bars among relatives and friends as they had done during a previous inspection. Communist leaders launched this campaign because they believed it would be impossible to control the price of rice and other goods without breaking the economic hold of the ethnic Chinese merchants. Some thirty thousand small businesses closed as a result of the raid. Officials told the merchants that they and their families should prepare to move to NEZs.[1] Then, in May, the government carried out a second currency exchange but this time it placed a ceiling on the amount that could be exchanged. Thus, in one fell swoop, whatever hoarded riches that remained were wiped out.[2]

Even before launching the reforms in the south, the Hanoi government had already begun to impose greater economic and political restrictions on the hundred thousand or so ethnic Chinese in northern Vietnam. First, it cracked down on the cross-border smuggling that had been going on ever since the DRV was established in 1954. Ethnic Chinese were at the center of an illicit trade between the DRV and the PRC. Even though both countries had Communist governments and socialist economies, China was not at war as Vietnam was, which meant that such consumer goods as cigarettes, liquor, and herbal medicines were more readily available north of the border. The ethnic Chinese could be smugglers because, as foreigners, they had greater freedom of movement than the citizens of North Vietnam did. To evade detection, smugglers brought goods acquired in China back to Vietnam along rough mountain paths that linked the two countries instead of taking the train. By selling them for a small profit, smugglers were able to achieve a higher standard of living than peasants and workers earning low government salaries could ever hope to enjoy. When caught, the smugglers simply bribed the cadres, who were not immune to corruption given their own meager wages and Spartan living conditions. Other Vietnamese also profited when they helped distribute the goods. When the supplementary income that smuggling provided dried up as a result of the crackdown, people began to leave the country, especially after the government announced that possessions that could not have been acquired on the basis of one's salary were henceforth subject to confiscation.[3]

Next, the government changed its policy on the citizenship status of the ethnic Chinese. Unlike the situation in the former South Vietnam, where the government had, in 1956, forced most of the Chinese living there to opt for South Vietnamese citizenship by barring noncitizens from certain occupations, the Communist parties in China and in North Vietnam had agreed in 1955 that the ethnic Chinese in the latter country could retain their Chinese citizenship.[4] Since the Hanoi government did not put any pressure on its ethnic Chinese residents to give up their Chinese citizenship, most of them did not try to acquire Vietnamese citizenship because they wanted to avoid the draft. (During Vietnam's thirty-year war for independence, citizens of North Vietnam did not enjoy the privilege, as the ethnic Chinese did, of being exempted from conscription.) However, as tensions mounted between China and Vietnam, cadres began to tell the ethnic Chinese that aliens, especially those living near the Vietnamese-Chinese border, would have to move inland. This meant that unless the Chinese became citizens of the Socialist Republic of Vietnam, thereby subjecting them to the draft, not only would they have to leave their homes but they might also end up in the jungle. Instead of being forced into the wilderness, many of the affected people demanded that they be repatriated to the People's Republic of China.[5]

China's Response

In response to these developments in Vietnam, China initially simply expressed concern over what was happening. However, the verbal jostling between the two countries quickly turned nasty. In contrast, as journalist Nayan Chanda pointed out, China's officials had said almost nothing when ethnic Chinese merchants in Laos lost their means of livelihood in 1976 as a result of the Laotian government's nationalization of economic enterprises. Nor did China protest when the Khmer Rouge persecuted and killed large numbers of ethnic Chinese in Cambodia. This discrepant behavior seemed to indicate that China criticized Vietnam because of the growing antagonism between China and the former Soviet Union, now Vietnam's major supporter, rather than any concern for the well-being of the ethnic Chinese in Vietnam.[6]

Even though both the Soviet Union and China had given extensive support to North Vietnam during the Second Indochina War, once the war was over Vietnam developed a warmer relationship with the Soviet Union but became increasingly hostile to China. The Soviet Union and Vietnam signed a twenty-five-year friendship treaty in November 1978. Because China strongly supported the radical Khmer Rouge (Communist) regime in Cambodia, which ruled that country from April 1975 to January 1979, Vietnamese leaders mistrusted China's intentions in Southeast Asia: was China trying to establish a sphere of influence in mainland Southeast Asia or perhaps even to colonize the countries there? In December 1978, Vietnam invaded Cambodia and ousted the Khmer Rouge regime on the pretext of stopping the Khmer Rouge regime's massive killings of its own people. China retaliated by invading Vietnam in February 1979. With this brief "punitive" war, China was apparently warning the Soviet Union that it should not assume it could expand its influence in Southeast Asia without contestation.[7]

The first groups of ethnic Chinese to cross the border into China were from northern Vietnam but soon more and more people from southern Vietnam also made the overland trek. Many ethnic Chinese who had been sent to the NEZs escaped and joined the northward movement.[8] By early August 1978, one hundred and sixty thousand ethnic Chinese from all over Vietnam had entered China's southern provinces. Overwhelmed by this influx, China announced that henceforth it would admit only those who had obtained certificates issued by the Chinese embassy in Hanoi. Then China abruptly closed the crossings along the Chinese-Vietnamese border, stranding thousands of people who had not yet crossed.[9] Officials of the two countries sat down to negotiate in an attempt to resolve the conflict, but after the double invasions,[10] the outflow resumed apace. Before the exodus ended, more than a quarter million ethnic Chinese residents of Vietnam, plus a smaller number of Vietnamese, many of whom were trying to dodge the draft, had gone to China, which became the second Communist country to seek financial help from UNHCR to support the refugee population. (The first Communist country to ask for help from UNHCR was Vietnam when tens of thousands of refuge-seekers from Cambodia fled the murderous Khmer Rouge regime and entered Vietnam in search of sanctuary.)

The Reactions of the Southeast Asian Countries of First Asylum

An increasing number of refuge-seekers from Vietnam also fled by boat to neighboring countries in Southeast Asia. Whereas only about twenty thousand boat people had found their way there in the two and a half years between mid-1975 and the beginning of 1978, that same number arrived during the first few months of 1978.[11] Between January and September, total arrivals in the region numbered forty thousand. Henceforth, the heaviest burden of sheltering the refuge-seekers shifted from Thailand to Malaysia as the northeast coast of the Malay Peninsula is only a short distance from the coast of southern Vietnam.

At a meeting on June 20, 1978, the foreign ministers of the countries that composed the Association of Southeast Asian Nations (ASEAN)—at the time Thailand, Malaysia, Singapore, Indonesia, and the Philippines—discussed the importance of taking a united stand on a number of issues, one of which was what policy to follow in dealing with the outflow of refuge-seekers from Indochina. Because of their geographic location, these Southeast Asian countries became countries of first asylum regardless of whether they were willing to shoulder the burden of coping with the exodus. The ASEAN countries were concerned because the number of boat people kept rising, especially in Malaysia. In August, 8,000 boat people landed in Malaysia; in November, 20,000 did; by December, the country was hosting 48,000. The number kept spiraling despite the fact that 20,000 boat people had been resettled in the three and a half years from mid-1975 to the end of 1978—15,000 of them in 1978—and seventy-two boats carrying an estimated 7,200 people had been towed back to sea. By June 1979, there were 76,500 boat people in the refugee camps in Malaysia even though in the first six months of that year more than 22,000 had been resettled in countries of second asylum and two hundred and seventy-five boats carrying almost 49,000 people had been towed back to sea.[12]

The Malaysian government wanted as little contact as possible between the boat people and the local population in order to prevent the inmates from bribing their way out of the camps and disappearing among the villagers and fishermen in the vicinity of the camps. Accordingly, they housed half of the refuge-seekers under severely crowded and miserable conditions on Pulau Bidong, a rocky island located twenty-three miles off the northeastern coast of peninsular Malaysia, and the rest on two other islands. There was no commercial ferry service between the peninsula and the islands; so, the government itself had to ship all supplies, including drinking water, to the islands. During the monsoon season, high seas made the transportation of needed supplies a dangerous task but it was worth the trouble for there was no chance that any of the refuge-seekers confined on the islands could escape. Those en route to resettlement countries stayed in a transit camp near Kuala Lumpur, Malaysia's capital.[13]

The growing numbers reached Malaysia at a time when the country was dealing with severe flooding from heavy rains during the northeast monsoon and the outbreak of foot-and-mouth disease among cattle and swine fever among pigs. Northeastern Malaysia, where the bulk of the boat people landed, was the poorest region in the country. The local people became angry when they saw huge quantities of food being shipped to the refugee camps and threw rocks at the arriving boats. As a foreign ministry official complained, "The U.S. attitude is full of sympathy for the refugees—but we are the ones stuck with the massive social and security problems the refugees bring."[14]

The "social and security problems" referred to the delicate ethnic balance in Malaysia. During the almost two centuries that Malaysia (at that time known as Malaya) was under British colonial rule, large numbers of Chinese immigrants settled there to work in the tin mines, rubber plantations, and in retail trade. In time, ethnic Chinese merchants and professionals dominated Malaysia's national life even though Chinese Malaysians composed only 35 percent of the total population. To reduce the Chinese dominance, the postindependence government set aside quotas for the largely rural Malays (who represented 45 percent of the population) in government employment and in higher education to facilitate their social and economic advancement. In the late 1960s, "race riots" broke out between the ethnic Chinese and the indigenous Malays. To avoid future eruptions, the government did not want anything to upset the numerical balance among the Chinese, the Malays, and the Indians (who composed 10 percent of the population). Since approximately two-thirds of the boat people who arrived in 1978 and the first half of 1979 were ethnic Chinese, the country's leaders understandably worried about the demographic and social impact of the influx.

Malaysia's opposition political parties criticized the central government and asked how the country could expect to handle an armed invasion or even its Communist insurgents (most of whom were ethnic Chinese who had been fighting against the government since the 1940s) if it could not even keep unarmed refuge-seekers away. In response, Prime Minister Hussein Ong announced in January 1979 that Malaysia would not accept any more would-be refugees. He was worried, he said, about Communist infiltration—that is, the possibility that the Vietnamese government might be "sending out Communist agents" disguised as refugees to destabilize his country.[15] Home Minister Ghazali Shafie proclaimed that Malaysia's first priority should be "the survival of our country and our people." He suspected that the exodus was not a simple flight: "To move from one area to another in Vietnam you need documents. Why is it so simple for the boat people?" Foreign Minister S. Rajaratnam of Singapore voiced his suspicion another way: he observed that the Vietnamese government must be deliberately forcing people out because few Vietnamese had fled "even at the height of the [Vietnam] war."[16]

Whereas a vast majority of the boat people who landed in Malaysia was from southern Vietnam, many of those who escaped from northern Vietnam found a shorter route to Hong Kong, which eventually housed the second-largest number of boat people. Hong Kong first encountered Vietnamese boat people in May 1975, when a Danish ship that had picked up four thousand people in the South China Sea brought them there. It took three years to get this first batch of refuge-seekers resettled. Only 191 refuge-seekers reached Hong Kong in 1976 and 1,007 in 1977, but almost nine thousand arrived in small boats in 1978.[17] Some were ethnic Chinese merchants in Vietnam who, through their coethnic contacts in Hong Kong, had put money into Hong Kong bank accounts to pay for their journey.[18] By spring 1979, densely populated Hong Kong was housing seventeen thousand boat people. The local people resented them tremendously because the Hong Kong government was very tough in the way it handled would-be refuge-seekers from the People's Republic of China: Hong Kong's border guards caught and deported them to the Chinese mainland without mercy. By allowing the Vietnamese boat people to stay, its critics said, the Hong Kong government was following a double standard, showing far greater leniency to the refuge-seekers from Vietnam than those from China. Members of Hong Kong's Legislative Council were also angry: they felt that Great Britain was doing nothing to relieve Hong Kong, its crown colony, of its burden yet gave the colony no authority to deal with the situation on its own.[19] Despite these complaints, no one foresaw that the worst was yet to come.

CHAPTER NINE

An International Refugee Crisis

In the fall of 1978 and the early months of 1979, the simmering resent-ment felt by the people and their leaders in the countries of first asylum boiled over into fury when refuge-seekers showed up in large ships, each carrying several thousand passengers, in Malaysia, Indonesia, the Philippines, and Hong Kong. Their appearance marked a turning point not only in terms of what was happening in Vietnam but also in how the outflow would be perceived and handled by the countries of first asylum. The first large ship to show up was the *Southern Cross*, an 850-ton freighter with a Honduran registration, which took 1,250 "boat people" from southern Vietnam to Malaysia in September 1978. Malaysian officials refused to let it dock and a navy patrol boat es-corted it out beyond the country's territorial waters. Singapore also denied the ship permission to dock, so it sailed to Indonesia and delib-erately ran aground on the beach of an uninhabited island, where the passengers scrambled ashore. The ship's officers radioed Indonesian authorities and claimed that the ship was beyond repair. UNHCR per-suaded Indonesia to grant temporary asylum to the passengers, who were placed into a UNHCR holding camp and eventually resettled.[1] Thus began a new phase of the refugee exodus.

Allegations of "Refugee Racketeering"

Given the success of the *Southern Cross*, the same overseas Chinese syndicate that had arranged the first load tried next to carry 2,504 passengers from Vietnam to Hong Kong on the *Hai Hong*, which weighed 1,586 tons and flew a Panamanian flag. However, when a typhoon started blowing over the South China Sea, the ship changed course. Instead of heading north to Hong Kong, it went south toward Indonesia. As it approached its destination, the captain radioed the

UNHCR regional office in Kuala Lumpur and claimed that he had picked up more than 2,000 refuge-seekers from small boats in the open sea. The story roused the suspicion of Indonesian officials who ordered the ship to leave. It showed up next on November 9 at Klang, a port on the west coast of the Malay Peninsula, but marine police prevented it from docking. After supplying the ship with provisions and tending to the sick people on board, Malaysian officials, like their Indonesian peers, told the captain the ship had to leave. The UNHCR's regional representative in Kuala Lumpur asked that the passengers be treated as refugees, but the Malaysian government refused to abide by UNHCR's request. The ship lay at anchor while negotiations were carried out. The UNHCR office sent food to feed them while they waited for decisions. Malaysian officials finally allowed immigration officials from the United States, France, and Canada to board the ship so that they could process the passengers. As soon as resettlement places had been lined up for everyone on board, the passengers were allowed to disembark to await flights overseas.[2] Indonesia and Malaysia resented the intervention of UNHCR and the Western countries. In the coming years, tensions marred the working relationship among all the parties involved as they dealt with the dilemma created by the massive outflow of refuge-seekers from Vietnam, Laos, and Cambodia.

More large ships carrying refuge-seekers from Vietnam continued to show up in the countries of first asylum. The 4,200-ton *Huey Hong* carried 3,318 people from Vietnam to Hong Kong in December 1978. The 1,235-ton *Tung An* brought 2,300 to the Philippines in January 1979 and remained anchored in Manila Bay for seven months pending an agreement on what to do with the passengers. As fewer than 7,500 boat people had landed in the Philippines in the three and a half preceding years, the sudden appearance of 2,300 was a shock. Philippine legislators hastily pushed through new shipping and immigration regulations to deter "refugee racketeers." The 3,506-ton *Skyluck* sailed into Hong Kong in February 1979 with 2,651 passengers after it had already disembarked 600 in Palawan, an island belonging to the Philippines. Hong Kong authorities arrested the captain, the officers, and the crew and put them on trial as the ship sat at anchor for five months. Like their peers in the Philippines, authorities in Hong Kong also stiffened the penalty against refugee racketeers.[3] During this period, surveillance planes flying over Vietnam reported that other large ships were lined up along the Vietnamese coast, apparently waiting to take additional shiploads of refuge-seekers out. Exasperated leaders in the countries of first asylum asked why the Communist Vietnamese army that had beaten the Americans and held back the Chinese

People's Liberation Army during the border war could not stop a "mere fleet of refugee boats."[4] The answer soon became clear.

Investigators working in several countries, with a newly created Refugee Ship Unit in Hong Kong taking the lead, discovered that trafficking in refugees had become a lucrative business in Vietnam. It was being carried out with the active participation of officials, who even built transit camps along the coast to house the refuge-seekers as they waited to board ship. However, people had to get to these camps on their own. Though permits were required to travel from one locality to another, some corrupt cadres, for a large fee, were willing to issue travel documents to indicate that the individuals carrying them were headed for the NEZs. The Public Security Bureau even administered the outflow at the embarkation points. Ethnic Chinese in Singapore, Hong Kong, Taiwan, and Vietnam made the actual arrangements for the journey. They employed captains and crew of several nationalities. Depending on what locality would-be refuge-seekers departed from, each adult ethnic Chinese passenger had to pay two taels of gold as an "application fee," five to eight taels as an "exit fee," and two taels for the actual passage. (One tael equals 37.79 grams of gold, the value of which fluctuated in the world market.) Children older than five paid half price; those under five traveled free of charge. Departing people also had to "donate" their houses and land to the government. Vietnamese had to pay a surcharge (usually 50 percent above the amount charged the ethnic Chinese). So, some Vietnamese bought fake documents to indicate they were Chinese. Prisoners in re-education camps who wished to get on a departing boat could also buy their release from camp for anywhere between five and twenty-five taels of gold.[5]

When all this information became public, the countries of first asylum were appalled. One question that everyone asked was, should people who could afford such expensive passage and who left in such an organized manner under the aegis of the Vietnamese government be considered refugees? To almost everyone, the answer was no. Even Indonesia, which had not turned away small boats up to this point, declared it would take in no more. The issue then became what to do with the ones who had already arrived. The United States—which saw itself as a strong advocate for the human rights of people seeking refuge from Communism—Great Britain acting on behalf of Hong Kong, other Western resettlement countries, the ASEAN countries, and UNHCR all agreed that something had to be done if the principle of first asylum was to be preserved. The solution was a conference convened by UN Secretary General Kurt Waldheim in Geneva on July 17–19, 1979.

The 1979 Geneva Conference

Waldheim invited seventy-one nations to attend; sixty-five accepted the invitation. The participants agreed on a three-pronged solution. First, Vietnam would place a temporary moratorium on "illegal" departures and would facilitate legal departures through the Orderly Departure Program (ODP) that had been set up two months earlier under a Memorandum of Understanding between the Socialist Republic of Vietnam and UNHCR, in which several dozen nations eventually participated. The United States announced that three categories of people could enter the United States via ODP: close family members of Vietnamese and ethnic Chinese from Vietnam already in the United States, former employees of U.S. government agencies, and other individuals "closely identified" with the U.S. presence in Vietnam before 1975.[6] Second, the countries of first asylum would stop turning people away and continue to give them temporary asylum. Third, the countries of second asylum would increase their intake. Dozens of countries, including those that agreed to take just a few dozen or a few hundred, pledged a total of more than 260,000 resettlement spaces. (At that time, there were 372,000 refuge-seekers in first asylum camps, of whom 202,000 were boat people.) Densely populated Japan, which was extremely reluctant to take in any refuge-seekers at all, pledged to pay for half of UNHCR's expenses in this endeavor. Indonesia and Malaysia each donated land, on Galang Island and the Bataan Peninsula, respectively, to build regional refugee processing centers to relieve the demographic pressure on Thailand, Malaysia, and Hong Kong.[7] A third regional processing center was set up in Phanat Nikhom, Thailand, adjacent to an existing UNHCR holding center. Those who qualified as refugees and thus were approved for resettlement would be given English lessons and "cultural orientation" in the processing centers before departing for their new homes.

The Geneva Conference brought immediate results. On August 9, Hanoi announced that its officials had already arrested four thousand people involved in organizing the departure of refuge-seekers and that some of them might be executed. Moreover, the Vietnamese government would provide UNHCR and resettlement countries "all necessary facilities" to process ODP applicants.[8] In the three months following the conference, not only did the total number of boat arrivals decline, but the boats did not contain any ethnic Chinese at all— ample proof that the Vietnamese government did indeed have control over the ethnic Chinese outflow.[9] However, critics claimed that what the conference participants did was to enter into "an unwitting collaboration to repress and contain rather than rescue the victims of tyranny."[10] They pointed out that ironically, by asking Vietnam to stop the outflow, the conference participants, including UNHCR itself, were violating the 1948 Universal Declaration of Human Rights that guarantees freedom of movement to individuals, including the right to leave the countries in which they live.

Not everyone was happy with what the conference accomplished. The countries of first asylum continued to resent the fact that the United States and UNHCR put so much pressure on them to offer asylum to *everyone* who showed up while immigration officials from the United States and the other Western resettlement countries reserved the right to *select* whom they would admit. The fear was that it would be the "dregs"—the criminals, drug addicts, physically handicapped, and people without any transferable skills—who would be left behind in Southeast Asia as a "residue." As one Thai official declared, "There is no need to preach to us about humanity any longer because we have been choked with humanity." The Hong Kong government was even more bitter: even though Hong Kong was sheltering 35 percent of the boat people, it was allocated only 13 percent of the resettlement slots pledged at the 1979 Geneva Conference. Declared one official, "One cannot blame people in Hong Kong for drawing the conclusion that help would be greater if policies were harsher. We should not be penalised [sic] by receiving a lower rate of resettlement than countries which have taken a less humanitarian line."[11]

As time passed, it became apparent the countries of first asylum had a right to worry. Even though the boat people outflow was diminishing, it did not cease entirely. In May 1980, more than ten thousand five hundred landed in the countries of first asylum. While that figure was only a fifth of the number who had arrived in May 1979, it was still large. Despite the stepped-up pace of resettlement, the refugee camps continued to house almost ninety seven thousand boat people a year after the conference.[12] Officials in the countries of first asylum feared that the attention given to ODP, which enabled people to leave directly from Vietnam, might reduce the number of boat people slated for resettlement.[13]

Changes in U.S. Refugee Policy

The crisis also led to significant changes in U.S. refugee policy. In the months preceding the Geneva meeting, President Jimmy Carter had busily shored up the leadership role of the United States in the international effort to solve the refugee problem. In February 1979, he created a position for a U.S. Coordinator for Refugee Affairs to enhance cooperation among those departments in the federal government that were dealing with the refugee influx. He sent a bill to Congress in March asking legislators to consider passing a refugee act. In April, he further increased the annual parolee quota, which had already risen from fifty three thousand to eighty four thousand. Two months later, in an attempt to exert moral pressure on other potential resettlement countries, he announced that the United States would increase its intake to one hundred sixty-eight thousand a year or fourteen thousand per month.[14]

Congress debated various versions of a proposed refugee act for a year before passing the 1980 Refugee Act on March 17, 1980. The act (P.L. 96-212) was the first piece of U.S. legislation to address refugees explicitly apart from regular immigration policies. It began by declaring that "it is the historical policy of the United States to respond to the urgent needs of persons subject to persecution in their homelands" and that "the objectives of this Act are to provide a permanent and systematic procedure for the admission to this country of refugees of special humanitarian concern to the United States, and to provide comprehensive and uniform provisions for the effective resettlement and absorption of those refugees who are admitted." It then laid out the administrative structure to implement these objectives.[15]

The act brought the U.S. definition of "refugee" in line with that adopted by the United Nations in 1951, thereby removing the ideological and geographic biases that had been an integral part of how the United States had treated refugees in the past. Before 1980, American policy-makers considered only those people who had escaped from Communist countries and certain regions of the Middle East as refugees. People who fled repressive right-wing governments did not qualify as refugees. The 1980 Refugee Act also spelled out, for the first time, procedures for dealing with asylum-seekers who had already set foot on American soil. It removed the president's authority to use parole to admit large groups of people. To determine how many refugees would be admitted each year and from which regions of the world, the executive branch and Congress must consult one another annually to reach a mutually acceptable ceiling.[16] However, since the U.S. State Department continued to play a leading role in deciding how many to take in and from where, foreign policy considerations continued to dominate the U.S. refugee admission process. The State Department's priority system continued to be used, which meant that refuge-seekers were first reviewed to see if they would fit one of the priorities before interviewers tried to determine if they qualified as refugees based on the new definition.[17] In other words, political persecution was not always the key criterion even after the United States adopted the United Nations definition of refugee.

For that reason, the United States and UNHCR did not always see eye to eye with regard to how refuge-seekers from Vietnam, Laos, and Cambodia should be treated. As Charles Keely has pointed out, not one, but two separate "refugee regimes" existed during the Cold War and even after it ended. One regime centers on UNHCR as the lead agency. Those who work within the UNHCR system accept the 1951 United Nations Convention on the Status of Refugees and the 1967 United Nations Protocol on the Status of Refugees as the basic international laws pertaining to refugees. UNHCR relies on the governments of the affected nation-states and on voluntary agencies to serve as its "operational arms." It attempts to treat refugees from various parts of the world in a politically neutral way and recognizes three durable solutions: repatriation, local integration, and resettlement. Its preferred option is to repatriate refugees to their countries of origin once it is safe for them to return.[18] The second refugee regime centers on the United States, with only a minor role for UNHCR. During the Cold War, U.S. refugee policy was a component of the anti-Communist strategy of containment. Instead of promoting repatriation, the United States favored resettlement in Western, democratic countries to underscore the oppressiveness of Communist rule.[19] American officials strongly objected to proposals to repatriate the Vietnamese boat people.

The Still-Unsolved Boat People Crisis

According to UNHCR statistics, by November 1980 forty nations had resettled three hundred thousand out of the three hundred seventy thousand boat people in Southeast Asian and Hong Kong camps. However, in 1987 and 1988 the number of boat people crept up again, partly because the Thai government, with U.S. assistance, had managed to reduce the number and brutality of pirate attacks[20] against the boat people in the Gulf of Thailand during the preceding years, and partly because processing under ODP had stalled. As a large backlog of ODP applications built up, the Vietnamese government unilaterally suspended all processing in January 1986 and did not restart it until September 1987. At that time, the U.S. embassy in Bangkok had six hundred seventy thousand ODP applications on file awaiting adjudication.[21] Only people whose names appeared on both the list of a resettlement country and the list prepared by the Vietnamese government could leave. The problem was that Vietnam saw the ODP as yet another channel through which it could get rid of ethnic Chinese and other groups it did not want, while the United States, where about three-quarters of ODP applicants wished to go, wanted to facilitate the emigration of individuals who either had family members already resettled in the United States or who had been persecuted because of their former relationship to the United States.[22]

As a new boat people crisis loomed on the horizon, Thailand announced in January 1988 that it would no longer offer first asylum to any future arrivals and started pushing boats back to sea. Its coast guards pushed off an estimated three thousand two hundred boat people in 1988. What disturbed Thai officials above all was that the boat people had found a new route to the east coast of Thailand: they traveled overland across Cambodia and then boarded boats at the Cambodian port of Sihanoukville, whence they sailed a short distance to Thailand.[23] Malaysia, which had suspended first asylum since 1979, announced in April 1988 that it would close the camp at Pulau Bidong and that henceforth, all boat people would be considered "illegal immigrants" subject to deportation. As more and more began to arrive in Malaysia (two thousand eight hundred in March and three thousand four hundred in April, compared with only one thousand five hundred per month in 1985 in all the countries of first asylum combined), Malaysian naval officers pushed several thousand back to sea. Some of these people had found their way to Malaysia after being pushed away from Thailand.[24] But the largest number of boat people was now going to Hong Kong,[25] which became the locale for the most intractable problems from 1989 onward.

CHAPTER TEN

Ending the Indochinese Refugee Exodus

A second Geneva Conference held on June 13–14, 1989, and attended by over seventy countries came up with a Comprehensive Plan of Action (CPA) to deal with the continuing outflow of refuge-seekers. At that point, despite the huge numbers resettled since 1979, the number of "boat people" in the countries of first asylum had risen again to more than one hundred thousand.[1] There were also still more than seventy thousand refuge-seekers from Laos and seventeen thousand from Cambodia living in UNHCR holding centers in Thailand. In addition, about three hundred thousand Cambodians being cared for by the United Nations Border Relief Organization remained in so-called border camps at the Thai-Cambodian border. That is, the fate of approximately half a million refuge-seekers from Vietnam, Laos, and Cambodia still hung in the balance.

The Comprehensive Plan of Action

The CPA stipulated a cutoff date after which all arrivals would be subjected to "refugee status determination" or screening. June 16, 1988, was the cutoff date for Hong Kong; March 14, 1989, for Thailand and Malaysia; March 17, 1989, for Indonesia; and March 21 for the Philippines. After these dates, boat people from Vietnam, all of whom had been accorded presumptive refugee status up to this point, lost that privilege. Unlike the past, when they were accepted as refugees (according to the UN definition of that word) simply by virtue of having shown up on the shores of the countries of first asylum, they now had to undergo a regionwide screening process aimed to separate "political refugees" from "economic migrants." Refuge-seekers whom screeners determined had bona fide reasons to fear persecution should they return to their homelands would be classified as refugees and resettled abroad, while the rest would be considered economic migrants and would be repatriated to the countries whence they came. The latter received financial assistance to enable them to reintegrate into the societies they had fled. Officials in each of the countries of first asylum and in Hong Kong would carry out the screening, while UNHCR representatives played an advisory role by training screeners and monitoring interviews. UNHCR could also review "screened out" cases and arrange to resettle those persons if UNHCR thought they qualified for refugee status even though screeners in the countries of first asylum had turned their petitions down. What made repatriation under CPA possible was that in December 1988, Vietnam, which had up to that point refused to take back anybody who had escaped, signed an agreement with UNHCR, promising not to prosecute boat people who returned. UNHCR representatives could visit the returnees to ensure that they suffered no reprisals. Under the CPA, Vietnam also agreed to facilitate the legal departure of aspiring emigrants via ODP.[2] Unlike the agreements made at the 1979 conference, which only dealt with the Vietnamese boat people, the 1989 CPA applied to all Laotian "land people" as well. However, Cambodians in Thailand were left out of consideration.

The next seven years witnessed the movement of several groups of refuge-seekers. First, more than one hundred thousand boat people were either resettled abroad or repatriated to Vietnam, at first voluntarily and later involuntarily. Second, more than two hundred fifty thousand Amerasians and former "re-education" prisoners and their families emigrated directly and legally from Vietnam to resettlement countries via the ODP. Third, about ten thousand lowland Lao and sixty thousand Hmong who were still in Thailand, many of whom refused to move anywhere, were resettled, repatriated, or left in a limbo state as illegal immigrants on Thai soil. Fourth, the United Nations repatriated more than three hundred sixty thousand "border Cambodians" to their homeland. The United States terminated its refugee admission program for Cambodians in 1994 and the Laotian and Vietnamese refugee admission programs in October 1997.[3] People from Vietnam, Laos, and Cambodia who have come to the United States since then have entered as immigrants or as humanitarian parolees, and not as refugees.

These efforts to deal with the seemingly never-ending outflow of refuge-seekers occurred within a changing political context that included several significant developments, all of them related to Vietnam. The country had suffered a series of poor harvests in the mid-1980s and its economy was in dire straits. In December 1986, more moderate leaders came to power and set about reforming the economy under a comprehensive program called *doi moi* (renovation) in order to make the country more prosperous even as it remained socialist. They reintroduced private enterprise and decentralized management but retained one-party rule.[4] Vietnam's new desire to improve relations with the West, particularly with the United States, was manifested in its increasing willingness to release the remaining re-education prisoners for resettlement and to cooperate with the United States to search for American prisoners of war and military personnel still missing in action. The thaw between Vietnam and the United States culminated in the 1994 lifting of the U.S. trade embargo against Vietnam and the reestablishment of diplomatic relations between the two countries in 1995.

During the same period, the United States also changed its attitude with regard to an important issue—repatriation as a durable solution for refuge-seekers from Communist countries. Up to this point, the U.S. government had strenuously resisted proposals and efforts to repatriate the Indochinese refuge-seekers but it finally acquiesced to the necessity of repatriating those who did not qualify for refugee status. By 1989, every country, including the United States, and every relief organization that had helped deal with the Indochinese exodus was suffering from extreme "compassion fatigue." Everyone wanted the flow to stop and the people still in the refugee camps to be removed. Once aspiring Vietnamese refuge-seekers realized that the CPA meant business, the outflow of boat people ceased. Compared with the seventy thousand who arrived in Southeast Asia and Hong Kong in 1989 before the CPA went into effect, only 41 persons showed up in 1992.[5] Henceforth, Vietnamese who wanted to leave had to apply through the ODP.

The resettlement and repatriation of refuge-seekers in first-asylum camps and the emigration of Vietnamese via the ODP were two sides of the same coin. In fact, the countries of first asylum feared that the large number of people being channeled through the ODP would cut into the number who would be resettled out of the first-asylum camps. Despite such worries, the number in the countries of first asylum did gradually decrease. About 80,000 Vietnamese and 44,000 Laotians (lowland Lao, Hmong, and other hill-dwelling people combined) were resettled in the years following the 1989 Geneva Conference. Of this total, 51,670 were people who had arrived before the cutoff dates, all of whom were given presumptive refugee status; the rest were people who arrived after the cutoff dates but who were "screened in."[6] The United States took in 40 percent of the former and 50 percent of the latter.[7]

Hong Kong's Dilemma

Hong Kong encountered the most intractable problems under the CPA for several reasons. First, the boat people influx into Hong Kong continued unabated even after the CPA was implemented. So, unlike the Southeast Asian countries of first asylum, the number of refuge-seekers from Vietnam who reached Hong Kong continued to increase rather than decrease. Second, many of the boat people who landed in Hong Kong came from northern Vietnam and few of them had prior relationships with any of the Western resettlement countries and thus did not qualify for resettlement under the priorities used by the receiving nations to select refugees. Third, Hong Kong officials worked under a severe time constraint because China insisted that all the refuge-seekers from Vietnam, regardless of their ethnic origins, must be removed from Hong Kong before the colony was due to be handed back to China on July 1, 1997. Fourth, those who refused to be repatriated held demonstrations and engaged in hunger strikes and other forms of protest that garnered a great deal of mass media attention. Human rights groups from around the world took up their cause and issued scathing reports on the situation in Hong Kong. The glare of publicity tied the hands of Hong Kong's officials and made it even more difficult for them to deal with the tense and potentially explosive situation.[8]

That the most intractable problems should occur in Hong Kong is ironic. In the early years, Hong Kong was considered a model first-asylum location because it did not push back any boats. Moreover, it housed the refuge-seekers in "open camps." Though the quarters in such camps were extremely crowded, their inhabitants could move about freely during the daytime, look for paid employment outside, and enroll their children in school in the community at large. However, after large ships each carrying several thousand people began to show up, Hong Kong changed its policy and introduced "closed camps" in July 1982. Hong Kong's Correctional Services Department, which ran its prisons, administered the closed camps. The residents in closed camps were not allowed to seek employment and their children could not attend schools outside the camps. Because of the extremely high population density in Hong Kong and the scarcity of land, several of the camps were situated in the middle of the city. The worst conditions existed in those camps that were housed in old factories. They had inadequate cooking, washing, toilet, sewage, and exercise facilities. Within these warehouse-like buildings, each family was allocated a wire cage in which they slept, ate meals, and kept their meager belongings. The cages were not high enough for adults to stand up in because three tiers of such cages were piled one on top of another on each floor. While residents in the open camps found some relief during their excursions outside the camps, those detained in closed camps lived under truly appalling conditions. As a result of international criticism, Hong Kong eventually "opened" the closed camps one by one in 1989 and 1990.[9]

Still, Hong Kong was the destination of choice for a majority of Vietnamese boat people in the late 1980s. Whereas only 3,395 appeared in 1987, the number rose to 18,449 in 1988 and 34,507 in 1989.[10] A full year before the CPA went into effect, Hong Kong had instituted its own screening process on June 15, 1988. Screened in people lived in closed camps as they awaited resettlement while those screened out were incarcerated in detention centers, where life was even harsher than in the closed camps. At the beginning of August 1988, a Hong Kong delegation went to Vietnam to negotiate the possible return of the screened out people. News of this initiative led to the first of what turned out to be a series of hunger strikes by the incarcerated people who declared they would rather die than return to Vietnam. Time and time again, both the boat people and their wardens resorted to violence in their confrontations with one another. It did not help that some of the facilities were controlled by gangs that formed in the camps. That the camps housed people from both northern and southern Vietnam, many of whom viewed one another with suspicion, also exacerbated tensions.[11]

Hong Kong's officials were caught in a bind. As a British colony, Hong Kong could not take action on its own behalf; yet, its "mother country," Great Britain, refused to admit more than a token number of boat people. The rate of resettlement out of Hong Kong's camps was lower than that of any other country of first asylum because so many of the boat people in Hong Kong simply did not qualify for refugee status. Furthermore, whenever the Hong Kong government tried to do something to ameliorate the plight of the boat people, it faced protests from local residents, who resented the double standard the government accorded refuge-seekers from China (who were routinely arrested and deported) versus those from Vietnam (who were allowed to stay). For example, on August 6, 1988, the government announced it planned to build a new detention center in the New Territories (the part of Hong Kong situated on the Chinese mainland). The very next day, angry villagers demonstrated against the plan. Later that month, another group of Hong Kong residents protested the policy of allowing the children of boat people to enroll in local schools and criticized the government for "wasting" millions of dollars of taxpayers' money caring for the escapees from Vietnam. In September, yet another group protested the government's decision to open some of the closed camps.[12]

The greatest controversy involved the Hong Kong government's attempt to repatriate those refuge-seekers who failed to qualify for refugee status but who refused to return to Vietnam voluntarily. When more than a hundred policemen forcibly placed fifty-one boat people on an airplane in the wee hours of December 12, 1989, under a program of "mandatory repatriation," an international outcry arose. Consequently, Hong Kong had to refrain from forcing people to return to Vietnam while continuing to negotiate with the Vietnamese government. In September 1990, the latter agreed to accept "those, while not volunteering to return, are nevertheless not opposed to going back."[13] Even the United States did not object to such a plan. As might be expected, the detained people became more belligerent in their refusal to leave.

To make matters worse, new boatloads continued to arrive. Investigators soon discovered that the monetary assistance given to repatriates (U.S. $360 per person) had itself become an incentive. People who took the money, returned to Vietnam, and then escaped to Hong Kong a second time in order to collect more money became known as "double backers." To reduce the financial magnet, the sum was reduced to $50 per person and only "the most deserving persons" would get it. To deal with the unending dilemma, Hong Kong's officials asked voluntary social service agencies to leave, stopped offering classes for children, eliminated income-generating activities, and limited the amount of remittances that people could receive from their families and friends abroad.[14]

Track II

As Hong Kong and the Southeast Asian countries of first asylum worked with great determination to end the boat people outflow and to ensure that no "residual" Indochinese population would remain as the CPA's screening efforts drew to a close, the U.S. Congress threw a monkey wrench into the process. The House of Representatives considered a bill to prohibit U.S. funds from being used to repatriate Vietnamese or Laotians. Congressman Christopher Smith, chair of the Subcommittee on International Operations and Human Rights of the Committee on International Relations of the House of Representatives, held hearings because he was "by no means confident that wrongly screened out refugees will be safe upon their return to Vietnam or Laos." He declared emphatically, "There is one fundamental principle on which we cannot compromise: the number of genuine political and religious refugees who are forcibly repatriated because of a defective screening process must be zero."[15] Even though the House bill never became law, news of this development nevertheless quickly reached people in the refugee camps and raised the hopes of those who refused to be repatriated.

After much negotiation, in January 1997 Vietnam and the United States agreed on a procedure called the Resettlement Opportunities for Returned Vietnamese (RORV), or Track II for short. Under it, any repatriated Vietnamese who had been in a refugee camp before October 1, 1995, or who had registered for voluntary repatriation before June 30, 1996, would be given a chance to be interviewed by American INS officials *in Vietnam* to determine whether they would qualify as people "of special interest" to the United States.[16] Those who refused to return to Vietnam would not have this opportunity. The program began in April 1997 and continued until the end of 2001. American officials interviewed more than twenty thousand applicants during this period and almost all of them were eventually admitted into the United States.[17]

By the end of 1996, all the camps except those in Hong Kong had closed. Even though almost 15,000 people left Hong Kong for Vietnam in 1996 (more than 8,000 of them voluntarily and the rest involuntarily through the Orderly Return Program), 7,640 remained, of whom 1,345 had been granted refugee status. In 1997, despite China's insistence that all refuge-seekers from Vietnam must be removed by June 30, 1,800 were still in Hong Kong at year's end. Unable to get rid of them, the Chinese government, which now governed Hong Kong, announced in February 2000 that the last of the boat people would be allowed to apply for permanent residency status.[18] The only other country in which nonrefugee boat people have gained permanent residency is the Philippines. In 2005, the U.S. government allowed some of the boat people still in the Philippines to immigrate to the United States—a final gesture to bring closure to the Indochinese exodus.

Groups of "Special Humanitarian Concern"

While the CPA was resettling or repatriating the boat people in Hong Kong, Thailand, Malaysia, Indonesia, and the Philippines, which had large populations of these people, as well as those in Japan, Korea, Macao, and Singapore, which had small numbers, an even larger movement was occurring via the ODP. The ODP allowed three groups of people to emigrate directly from Vietnam: those who wanted to rejoin family members who had been resettled abroad, Amerasians, and former re-education prisoners. Even though the ODP applicants had also experienced enormous trauma after 1975, at least they did not spend many bleak years in refugee camps outside of Vietnam.

Amerasians—the mixed-race children of American military personnel and Vietnamese women—were first allowed to immigrate to the United States in 1982 under the Amerasian Immigration Act, which applied to children not only in Vietnam but also in Korea, Thailand, the Philippines, and elsewhere. Under that act, Amerasian children could enter the United States but they could not bring their family members with them. For that reason, only about 4,500 left Vietnam via the ODP between 1982 and 1987, despite their oppressed existence there. Called *bui doi* (the dust of life) or *con lai* (half-breeds), almost everyone in Vietnam discriminated against them. Not only did their American fathers abandon them, so did some of their Vietnamese mothers. In addition to being mixed-race, they were also "children of the enemy." Other children teased them mercilessly while adults avoided contact with them lest they themselves become tainted.[19]

The Amerasian Homecoming Act that Congress passed in December 1987 removed the hurdle embedded in the 1982 act. The new legislation allowed Amerasians born between January 1, 1962, and January 1, 1976, as well as their mothers, stepfathers, and siblings or half-siblings to enter the United States as immigrants, while entitling them to the same benefits as refugees.[20] As a separate bilateral program, the number of Amerasians to be admitted each year would not be counted against the annual ceilings for the regular refugee admission program.[21]

Amerasians accepted for resettlement spent six to nine months at the Philippine Refugee Processing Center, where they enrolled in English-language classes and cultural orientation and vocational training programs, before being flown to the United States. The United States paid for the construction of an Amerasian Transit Center in Ho Chi Minh City, where Amerasians who applied to the Amerasian

Resettlement Program could stay while waiting to hear if they would be admitted. Initially, the acceptance rate was almost 90 percent. However, as evidence of fraud surfaced, the rate plummeted to only 5 to 10 percent of those who applied. The fraud involved Vietnamese who either did not qualify as family reunification cases or who did not wish to wait to emigrate via the ODP. These people "bought" Amerasians who became their "golden passports" for entry into the United States. Some Amerasians allowed themselves to be bought because they were so poverty-stricken that they could not afford the cost of transportation to Ho Chi Minh City, where the interviews were conducted, or to pay local government officials to place their names on interview lists and later, after they had been accepted for resettlement, the required exit fees. Some "fake families" who got to the United States this way abandoned the Amerasian youths once they landed in America.

Because of the existence of such fraud, interviewers increasingly insisted on seeing documentation that proved the applicants indeed had American fathers. However, when the Communists came to power, fearful mothers with mixed-race children often destroyed whatever photographs of, or letters from, their American husbands or lovers that they still possessed. Because of the fraud and the lack of documentation, an unknown number of genuine Amerasians failed to gain admission into the United States.[22] Still, almost ninety thousand Amerasians and their family members came between 1982 and 1999.[23]

As for the re-education prisoners, after years of negotiations the U.S. and Vietnamese governments finally agreed in July 1989 on the conditions under which released detainees could be resettled in the United States under the Released Re-education Detainees Program (also known as Humanitarian Operation). The negotiations dragged on for a long time because initially Vietnam insisted that the United States take everyone who had been reeducated, while American officials, fearful that the cohort might number several million if family members were also included, refused to accept this condition. The agreement that was finally reached included only those individuals who had spent three or more years in re-education camps.[24]

The first large batch of "re-eds," as staff members in voluntary agencies called them, and their family members—a total of some 7,000 persons—arrived in the United States in 1990. The acceptance rate for re-eds was high: 82 percent. More than 166,000 re-eds and their family members entered the United States in the 1990s.[25] Their lives, however, have not been easy. In many families, where the wives and children who had arrived earlier had become quite independent, husbands and fathers found it difficult to adjust to their loss of social status and power not only within their own families, but also in society at large.[26]

With Amerasians and former re-education detainees joining the legal emigrant stream, the number of people leaving Vietnam via the ODP for resettlement in dozens of countries around the world in the years immediately following the 1989 Geneva Conference was substantial: a total of 39,000 left legally in 1988, 43,200 did so in 1989, 70,400 in 1990, 70,000 in 1991, and 80,600 in 1992.[27] The number of ODP emigrants who came to the United States varied from 70 to 80 percent of the worldwide total. The percentage taken in by the United States was so much higher for those who departed via ODP than for people resettled out of first asylum camps because the Amerasian and re-ed subprograms within the ODP were solely an American undertaking and American officials did not attempt to pressure other nations to take them in.

The influx from the Amerasian and re-ed subprograms within the ODP was largest in the early 1990s. In fiscal year 1991, of the 42,800 ODP spaces available, 15,000 went to Amerasians and 19,000 to re-eds. In the following fiscal year, American officials reserved 18,500 slots for Amerasians and 20,000 for re-eds out of a total of 40,100 slots. In FY 1993, the 40,000 ODP allocations included 16,000 Amerasians and 22,000 re-eds. In FY 1994, even though the total number of ODP slots slated for the United States declined to 36,000, fully 30,500 went to re-eds and only 3,500 to Amerasians, with the remaining 2,000 for all other applicants. In FY 1995, the 32,000 ODP spaces went entirely to Amerasians (1,000) and re-eds (31,000). Not even one space was allocated to other categories of aspiring Vietnamese emigrants. The large-scale processing of Amerasians ended in 1993 but it took some years for all those approved for resettlement to be flown to the United States. Processing for the final group of re-eds took place in 2000. As these two subprograms terminated, the overall ODP number declined year by year. Moreover, with the resumption of diplomatic relations between the United States and Vietnam, an admission program separate from the general procedures that all aspiring immigrants have to follow could no longer be justified. The ODP program ended on September 30, 1999, after having resettled half a million people from Vietnam (including about 15,000 Cambodians who had sought refuge in Vietnam) in the United States and another 150,000 in other countries during the two decades of its existence. Remaining ODP cases destined for the United States were turned over to the Refugee Re-settlement Section in the U.S. consulate established in Ho Chi Minh City in 1999.[28]

The U.S. Congress in late 2001 made one last attempt to broaden the categories of Vietnamese who could be admitted into the United States as persons of "special humanitarian concern." The lawmakers granted eligibility for "in-country processing" to the adult, unmarried sons and daughters of former re-education detainees who had been incarcerated for three or more years or of the latter's widows who were already in the United States or who were "awaiting departure formalities" from the Vietnamese government. This law modified the refugee act and the provisions used to admit former re-eds in two ways. First, under normal circumstances, to qualify as refugees individuals must have left their countries of origin. Second, up to this point, re-eds could bring only their spouses and unmarried children under the age of twenty-one with them. The adult children, like their minor siblings, are called "derivative refugees." Congress gave them a two-year period in which to apply for admission into the United States as "immediate relative immigrants."[29]

Thus ends the story of why and how so many refuge-seekers from Vietnam have come to the United States. How they have adapted to life in America since their arrival is another story—one that I will tell in my next book. Meanwhile, the autobiographies in Part II offer glimpses of how young, college-educated Vietnamese Americans confronted and overcame adversity with courage and fortitude as they forged new beginnings for themselves and their families.

PART II

Stories of War, Revolution, Flight, and New Beginnings

"I was born in Vietnam into a world at war. Our life was war. We lived and breathed war. We waited for peace, longing night after night, longing and longing in the darkness only to see flares burst into bombs and hear the weeping of people who had lost their relatives.... Women had to be brave as they said goodbye to their men one by one as they left to fight. There remained only the fields, the bare houses, the responsibility of supporting what was left of their families. They did the work of men. And always, there was the unbearable waiting—waiting for their men, knowing some may never come back....

"For more than twenty years, my mother never had a quiet night; she knew nothing but the sound of artillery shells as lullabies to put her babies to sleep. Children grew up learning to hate, to fight, to kill. There was nothing but war. Every time the word 'peace' was mentioned, there would suddenly be an emptiness, a loss of purpose and direction ... [even though] we were sick and tired of a war that was thirty years long, a war that took away our loved ones, our hearts, our feelings, and destroyed everything we had ever lived or worked for....

"Memories of the past still bring pain. Sometimes I wish the past would leave me alone but deep down I know that no matter what, I will never forget it or get it out of my mind. . . . I want my younger brothers to be happy like normal kids; I want them to enjoy life, to grow up in peace and with love . . . I don't want them to go through what I have been through, to see what I have seen, to hear what I have heard. I dream of going home to a land of peace. I want to be a teacher so that I can teach little children how to laugh, to love, to live life to the fullest. I want to teach them to fly kites over green ricefields on a clear day under a blue, blue sky. I don't want them to play with guns and bombs. I want to travel from the south of Vietnam to the north, singing to everyone that peace is here once again . . . with each other's help we will rebuild everything . . . I want to be so strong that nothing else can hurt me, not ever again."

[This lyrical lament was written in 1980 by a student at the University of California, Berkeley, whose family had escaped from Vietnam in a small boat in 1976 as one of the first batches of "boat people."]

CHAPTER ELEVEN

A Tragedy: From Vietnam to America

The author, a thoughtful and observant young man, and his family left Saigon on April 25, 1975, on a U.S. military transport plane when he was seventeen years old. He wrote this account in 1980 based on the notes he took during his journey. Like the narrator's family, many of the people who fled just before Saigon fell had originally come from North Vietnam. Almost a million people, a large percentage of whom were Catholics or landowners, had left the North for the South in 1954–55 as permitted by the 1954 Geneva Agreements. These second-time refuge-seekers had a deeply ingrained fear of and hatred for Communism based on their earlier experiences. The author reveals how American and South Vietnamese officials at Saigon's Tan Son Nhut Airport took matters into their own hands to enable a significant number of people to be evacuated in the week before Saigon fell despite the red tape and indecision of the American and South Vietnamese governments. The narrator's mother, the breadwinner in the family, managed to get the requisite papers because she had worked for an American oil company. This account also provides a close look at life in the reception centers at Wake Island and Camp Pendleton.

In 1938, my grandfather graduated from junior high school and received a diploma that was at that time, so far as I know, the highest degree that a Vietnamese could obtain under the strict French colonial educational policy. The French considered "less educated Vietnamese" to be more amenable to their control. After his graduation, my grandfather taught in the superior primary school in Hanoi. He was well respected by other people. He married my grandmother who became a housewife. Shortly afterwards, my mother was born. My grandfather could not accept the fact that the French had colonized his country in the nineteenth century, so he left his teaching position to join the guerrilla forces, the Viet Minh, who were resisting the French colonial administration in Vietnam. After a number of years, however, he became disillusioned as he observed the bloody confrontations between those Vietnamese who had become Communists and those who thought of themselves as nationalists. So, he left the Viet Minh and returned to teaching. In terms of socioeconomic standing, my family's status was average.

After the Viet Minh defeated the French at Dien Bien Phu in 1954, the Geneva Agreements divided Vietnam into two parts—North and South. In the North, the Communists began a campaign to execute individuals who were accused of having committed social crimes (for example, for being "rich"). My grandmother was forced to watch many so-called people's trials that were conducted without giving the accused any defense counsel and to attend Communist demonstrations. Also, religious people were prevented from attending church. Since the 1954 Geneva Agreements allowed people from both regions to migrate at will during a three-hundred-day transitional period, my family left for the South along with about a million other people. As refugees, they had no property and little money. After reaching South Vietnam, my grandmother sold miscellaneous groceries and my grandfather became a government official. My mother and uncle attended high school while holding concurrent part-time jobs to cope with the difficult living conditions.

Shortly after, my mother met my father, whom she knew through his famous poetry published in Saigon. They married when my mother was in senior high school. My brother was born a year later. The family moved to another town in 1958, where I was born. A few years after that, we returned to Saigon. Due in large part to the volatile and unstable social climate, my father fell into a pattern of gambling and drinking while continuing to write poetry. His excesses eventually resulted in a heartbreaking divorce, a rare phenomenon regarded as undesirable in Vietnamese society where everyone was supposed to observe strict moral and cultural traditions. My mother then moved to another city where she worked as a clerk in an American oil company. I continued to live with my grandmother in Saigon in order to attend a good school there. As a result, I got to know my grandmother extremely well.

I was born into a family whose status rose from middle class in 1954 to a much higher position in subsequent years despite my parents' divorce. Fortunately, I was still too young to be affected by the divorce psychologically, especially since my father came to visit my brother and me once in a while. I was ignorant of what "divorce" meant in terms of my family's public image. My grandparents' love gave me a feeling of normalcy. After my mother moved to her new job, my life entered another period of change.

In 1966, when I was eight years old, I was sent to an elementary school in the town where I was born. My brother went with me. Living in a dormitory enabled me to understand the importance of community activities and responsibilities. There, I was strictly disciplined and lived according to a fixed schedule. My classmates and I were allowed to see a movie every Thursday night and to go shopping downtown every weekend. The group leaders taught us lessons in courage and premanhood responsibilities. They held weekend programs such as games between school teams during which we threw pinecones at each other. We also went on adventures in the jungles and mountains, all of which toughened me and gave me valuable training. I developed the courage to conquer all obstacles as I attempted to achieve my life goals.

It was here, in the school dormitory, where I first heard Communist rockets flying overhead in the night sky. But I was not scared at all. I remained at that school until the beginning of 1968, and then returned to a province on the northern edge of Saigon, where I once again lived with my grandmother. No sooner had I rejoined my grandmother than the Viet Cong launched the Tet Offensive with an endless series of explosions. Even though I stayed inside the house, I saw many intensely blazing flames in all directions. I was enormously shocked as these eruptions added more casualties to the war's death toll. Although my life was in danger, I tried to control myself and to remember all the lessons in courage and strength I had learned in school. I recall running to my friend's home as bullets whizzed over my head. Only after the battle was over could I return to my grandmother's house.

That I remained with my grandmother rather than return to the school I used to attend to complete my elementary education gave me a childhood moral education that was uniquely determined by my grandmother. In terms of politics, I was brought up by a woman whose direct experience with Communism had been unpleasant. My parents, in contrast, had only limited experience with the Communists. Had they raised me, my political views might have been different. During my childhood, the horrible stories my grandmother told me about the Communists were reinforced by the news and commentaries broadcast on television that showed images of people being buried alive and villages and cities being shelled. These scenes terrified and astonished me. My grandmother and the mass media, therefore, shaped my perspective on the Vietnam War.

My childhood was full of mental strain. It was not like the childhoods of people who lived in other places during other times. I was emotionally stressed by the war at a very young age. Sometimes I acted my age—lively and loving life—but at other times I felt as though I were dead whenever I thought about the tremendous destruction of my country as people on both sides of the conflict pursued the goal of exterminating each other. I hated the Communists, but at the same time I realized I could not join the Army of the Republic of Vietnam and kill fellow Vietnamese. I saw the war as irrational, absurd, and beyond understanding.

I began to search for a philosophy of life when I turned sixteen. I was readily fascinated by any person who could discuss politics, especially about North Vietnam and its ideology. As I searched for a light to guide my life, my high school teachers and some of my friends helped me attain a higher level of analysis and judgment. I still remember two stories that my teachers told my classmates and me. I was deeply impressed by their profound philosophy that eventually became a part of the foundation of my own thinking. One was narrated by my history teacher when I was in the ninth grade. He told us about his miserable life as a young and enthusiastic soldier during World War II, trying to fight for what he sincerely believed in—freedom for his people living under French colonialism. The battles left him wounded but he said, "I am proud of those wounds." Then he asked us to ponder a question: "Why do *we*, Vietnamese, have to fight against one another as enemies when *we*, in the past, had always fought together to drive out hostile foreign invaders?" This question all of a sudden left me with a broken heart. For the first time, I felt emotionally disturbed by the simple question, "Why are we fighting?" As I questioned the wisdom of both the North and South Vietnamese leaders, I wanted to become a politician. I could no longer believe in the reasons for war so long as it involved "we killing ourselves." I came to believe that the leaders of both sides put their political ambitions above their duty to serve their people. I felt that the Vietnamese people would not want, in their deepest feelings, to kill each other regardless of how different their ideologies were. This is an idea I have held until now.

Another story that impressed me came from a teacher who had a PhD in sociology. I heard this story while I was in the eleventh grade. Just like the question that my other teacher had asked, what this sociologist said became a second building block in my philosophy of life. He told our class about the "dirty bribery" that some South Vietnamese officials were willing to accept while hiding their own corruption. He concluded, "I know what I am saying today may lead to my arrest. But I accept it! Because once I dare to say what I think, I have no more fear. If they don't arrest me today, they will have reason to fear that I'll arrest them someday."

When I heard such defiance, I really worried about his safety. At the same time, however, his stand became a principle in my own life. Most of my close friends' parents were from the North, but not all of them shared my ideals. I tended to associate more with friends who were concerned about politics than those who just wanted to enjoy life. I formed better relationships with friends who were poorer than me as their lower living standard gave them broader experiences in society, endowing them with honesty and self-respect. I don't know whether my observations were always correct, but it appeared to me that many people born with inherited wealth almost always denied the war's existence and continued to enjoy themselves.

Growing up in a somewhat unusual family in which many abrupt and unhappy changes occurred during my childhood gave me an increased level of understanding about life and the Vietnam War. I was strongly affected by my grandmother's moral teachings, as well as by the perspectives of my teachers and friends as we discussed social and political issues. My family helped polish my moral values and deepened my religious beliefs; my friends provided more analytical insights into the practical issues of how to build a better society. My family's influence emerged as a result of my natural trust in them, while my friends' influence came from our shared concepts and efforts to evaluate intellectually existing social problems. Despite these influences, I retained a lot of independence—I assessed what I saw and relied on my own ability to pass judgments.

On the evening of April 21, 1975, Nguyen Van Thieu suddenly went on Channel 9, the Saigon television station, to announce his resignation as president of the Republic of Vietnam. His televised speech lasted hours and was a shocking yet exciting moment for me. It took a while after his sudden resignation before I actually realized how significant this event would be for the people of South Vietnam. Until that announcement, Thieu had been very stubborn about remaining in office. His stepping down had many potential implications. As soon as he resigned, as I learned later, there began a steady flow of Vietnamese citizens out of the country as political refugees. During the next few days, anxiety gripped my immediate family members and other relatives. However, the face of Saigon did not seem to have been altered in any way. Traffic continued to jam the streets and businesses remained open. But rumors of many Vietnamese fleeing via the so-called bridge of evacuation flights were confirmed as I noticed that some people in my neighborhood were no longer there. Apparently they had left secretly. The front doors of their homes were shut and there was no sign of life within.

In my family, my older brother tried to flee Vietnam by going to the port of Vung Tau, nearly fifty miles southeast of Saigon. He risked riding past a portion of the highway between Vung Tao and Saigon that was increasingly disrupted by Viet Cong guerrillas. The normalcy of life in Saigon was only a disguised image, reflecting the worries that people with anti-Communist sentiments tried to hide. I knew for sure that I could not stand living under a Communist regime that had been responsible for shooting tens of thousands of refugees fleeing on Highway 1 in 1972 and for numerous acts of terrorism that I had either heard about or seen on television. I had also personally seen the physical damage and human casualties resulting from the Viet Cong's tactics.

On April 25, after failing twice to get a visa from the American embassy in Saigon, my mother finally obtained an exit permit for our family and visas directly from the South Vietnamese and American authorities, respectively, in Saigon's Tan Son Nhut Airport (TSN) where evacuation flights were departing. Obviously, only those Vietnamese like my mother who had prior contacts with Americans were given permits. Why did my family decide to leave Vietnam? First, my family had come from the North during the 1954 exodus. At that time, local Communist cadres threatened (when there were no international observers around) to punish anyone who dared to leave the North. In other words, the Communists were ready to wreak their vengeance on those who dared to "vote with their feet." My grandparents were among the people who were being watched by the Communists. So, the members of my family had to sneak their way to the American naval ships waiting in Haiphong harbor that took people who wished to move to the South. As my grandparents' experiences with Communism had been so negative and intense, my entire family was certain that we could not live under Communism. Moreover, having been refugees once, my family was less hesitant to become refugees again.

Second, news broadcast on television kept reminding us that the Viet Cong had committed an endless series of brutalities against South Vietnam's soldiers and civilians. Equally important, we knew that the Communists denied religious freedom to people under their rule. As for me, I disapproved of a political system with no opposing parties, as was the case not only in North Vietnam but in South Vietnam as well. The latter government was rife with corruption because its officials knew the public would not dare to criticize them. They initiated all kinds of programs without any input from opposing parties.

Third, we knew that a Communist government would restrict literary and artistic expression, so that all literature, art, and music would reflect only the "wisdom of the party" and "our great Uncle Ho." For example, if someone wrote a romantic poem, he or she would be punished for being "weak" and for failing to follow the Communist Party's guidelines. In contrast, I believe that human beings possess emotions that need to be expressed, and it is this trait that makes man superior to other living things on earth.

At that time, I was very much concerned about the reunification of Vietnam and the reconstruction of the country. At the same time, I realized that military rule under Communism would not allow people to act with any more freedom than under the corrupt regime of Nguyen Van Thieu. Uncertain about the future, I thought I had better choose to live in a political system that does not have those repugnant characteristics. My family's decision to leave was unanimous but we could carry out that decision only because of my mother's efforts at the last minute.

I shall now talk about what life was like en route and what my feelings were during that period. I shall excerpt passages from a story I wrote five years ago. This story, written immediately after the long flight to America, accurately reflects my emotions during that short but intense period.

April 25, 1975

Around 1:00 P.M., my mother came home and announced that our family would be leaving for TSN Airport in two hours. She had just received approval from South Vietnamese and U.S. officials at TSN for our evacuation. I should have been happy because my life would be safer when we left the chaos of war behind. But I asked myself, what about my people? Should I leave behind my people with whom I had been living for seventeen years? Should I leave behind those with whom I had shared moments of joy as well as distress? Would my memories of them fade in time? No! I would rather die with them! But "die with them" was only in my mind, not in my actions. I knew too much about Communism to remain in Vietnam; I had no grounds to dismiss the Communists' past cruelty. Oh, shame! God, forgive me! I am lying to myself, my people, and my country. I am betraying my majestic nation. How can my sin ever be forgiven? How can it be forgotten? How?

But there was no time for me to spin my thoughts further. Everybody in the house urged me to hurry up and put the things we wished to take with us in bags. We could take only a small fraction of our household property. We thought someday we would return to Vietnam. I hid a small statue of Holy Mary in my bag. I prayed, "Holy Mary, be with me and save my people." Then, we left. I did not even have a minute to tell my friends that I was going. But honestly, my mind had already begun to think of our trip to a new land. I wondered whether the United States would be willing to receive us. What would the "free world" be like? Thousands of questions accumulated in my mind.

By 4:00 P.M., we had finished packing and were ready to move. When we stepped outside the house, all our neighbors stared at us strangely, but in an instant some of them understood what we were doing. They asked "Where are you going?" even though I suspect some of them already knew the answer. I kept silent. I could not hurt them by saying we were leaving the country and they would be the ones who would be subjected to every risk. One of our relatives wept upon seeing us depart. Before our car started moving, I called back, though not very loudly, "I'll pray for you. We won't leave you forever. We will come back someday." As our car moved slowly into the street, I felt my heart breaking and bleeding.

At the airport, I saw thousands of Vietnamese crowded together. I tried looking for my friends among these people. But I saw no one I could recognize. As we waited for our departure, my family looked for a place to rest as my grandmother and mother were both exhausted. After finding them a shaded area, I wandered around. I tried to perceive every aspect of every object in sight. I knew it might be the last time I would see these objects. Or, even if I could see them again, who knew if it would be next week, next month, or next year? Were we bidding a last farewell that day? To suppress my emotions, I took deep breaths.

After many hours of hanging around, I was truly tired. I went back to where my family was and lay down on the ground. But I could not fall asleep. As group after group of people walked toward the waiting airplanes, I knew I would soon be out of my homeland. It wasn't an illusion. How sad it was to think of such a departure without the certainty of return. Our flight number finally appeared on a square piece of cardboard. We stood up, still very tired. We had to avoid stepping on people lying in our path as we walked to the steel door. Passing that door, after presenting our legal papers, we walked through a small, dark lane to a place where a bus was waiting. It was 4:15 A.M. now—twelve hours since we had left our house. We and all the other people had to be rechecked before we were allowed to board the bus. As the bus drove toward the runway, the scenery was barely visible—seen for the last time, engulfed by darkness.

April 26, 1975

Far, far away, great black "ghosts" lay dormant in the night. One of those "ghosts" suddenly woke up and began to rattle. It turned out to be a giant military transport plane waiting to evacuate us. Just then, another plane landed, its wheels touching the runway with a menacing shriek. I did not know which airplane would take us. I guessed it was the one that had just started its engines running a few minutes before. Our bus slowly came to a stop where that plane was. I forced my eyes to open more widely to look at my illuminated watch. It was 5:00 A.M. precisely. The sound of the plane's engines conveyed strength. As it growled louder and louder, our eardrums felt as though they were being punched through.

An order was given. We rushed into the airplane as quickly as we could because the very hot exhaust produced by the jet engines blasted forcefully in our faces. I first stepped on the floor of this transport plane at exactly 5:06 A.M. Soon, "boom! click!" and the door was closed and locked. Our uncertain destiny began to unfold. The plane took off at 5:25 A.M.—the moment we no longer belonged to the land of Vietnam but only to its airspace. I looked down through the glass window. Behind me, I heard an American voice telling me to sit down, but I pretended not to hear and remained standing. I felt so much pain as my eyes stayed glued to the shrinking blue lights on the runway. Below, Saigon, the capital of South Vietnam, emerged as flickering fireflies— so magnificent and lovely. The glow came from streetlights and the light coming out of tall buildings. Everything looked as peaceful as the green river in a poem I once read. I felt hot on my cheeks as I could hold back my tears no longer. Adieu forever! Around me, everybody's eyes were closed. Were they sleeping or were they weeping for their fate?

Although very tired, I tried to stay awake. In my mind a new world, the so-called free world, appeared. I visualized it as splendid, beautiful, and fairy-tale-like. I had thought that even a war-torn country like mine was attractive; a world free of war and devastation must surely be even more magnificent. While thinking thus, I finally fell asleep.

When we landed at Clark Air Base in the Philippines my watch pointed to 9:23 A.M. We had arrived at the base that the United States maintained there. Everything on that base belonged to Americans. All of us, some fifty to sixty refugees, were led to a waiting room. I took a careful look at the huge building and the polite flight attendants in it. Everything was quiet. Suddenly, I missed my country so much. As we waited hour after hour, somebody gave us some cookies and light beverages. I felt very tired and in need of sleep. It wasn't until the evening that we were taken to another big building filled with cots lined up in rows. It looked like a hospital but without the medical equipment. Half an hour later, an American soldier called us to dinner. Two buses picked us up and took us to the dining room. It was a wonderful meal—we were *so* hungry.

After eating, we were taken back to our new "house." There, we lay down in repose. Five Red Cross volunteers appeared and gave each of us several envelopes and sheets of paper. I let my words flow out as much as time allowed. I wrote down everything I could remember of the trip, as well as my thoughts about it. I hoped my words would calm the turbulence in my mind as I thought about my country's political and military problems.

By 7:35 P.M., the sky had already turned dark. We left the Philippines that night for Wake Island. Our original destination was supposed to be Guam, but since Guam was already full of refugees, we changed our destination to Wake Island. We enjoyed the flight on a Boeing 747, which was so different from the cargo plane we had been on. During the flight, I sat next to a window so my soul could float back to Vietnam. Memories of my homeland surged as sweet and romantic music played in my mind. I felt so sad.

April 27–30, 1975

After five and a half hours, we arrived on Wake Island. The local time was 5:06 A.M. My watch told me it was 1:06 A.M. in Saigon. We lived on this beautiful island for four days. It was so peaceful there that we almost forgot about our difficult lives. We slept in simple wooden buildings surrounded by trees. We lived with nature, which alleviated some of our wounded feelings. The free dining room stayed open twenty-four hours a day and was always full of people. I remember one early morning I went miles away to help make beds and prepare additional housing for new waves of refugees. Only one American and several Vietnamese young men did the work. We worked continuously from morning until 3:00 or 4:00 P.M. without any food or water. We were exhausted but also happy that we could do something for our people. One night, I walked across an empty field in the dark to see a free movie. I got lost on the way back. I also remember hot afternoons and cool evenings on a bridge where I watched some

American soldiers catch inedible fish just for sport. On another night, alone on this wild island, I walked and walked. I was very sad as I thought of my country and my friends. No place can make me feel as wonderful as my country can. It may be poor in material wealth but it is richer than anywhere else in the world in terms of human love. Our idyllic stay on Wake Island ended on Wednesday afternoon. We boarded a C-141 military transport plane that flew us to Honolulu. We arrived there four and a half hours later. The local time was 11:21 P.M.

April 29, 1975

Having crossed the international dateline, it was still April 29, not 30, in Honolulu when we arrived sleepy and exhausted. In the waiting room, I glanced over someone's shoulder at the newspaper he was reading. The headline said, "Saigon Surrenders, Communist Tanks Enter the City." [It was already April 30 in Saigon.] I felt myself falling apart. I wanted to cry but did not. I told myself that I had to be strong and to remain calm. Looking at me, no one would guess that my heart had shattered to pieces. I lost not only my country but also everything I had loved. We have paid too high a price for thirty years of struggle. Thirty years of bones and blood. And what did we end up with? A shameful defeat. April 30, 1975, made all our people's past sacrifices meaningless. The shame of April 30, 1975, will never fade until our people regain full human rights. For my God, my valiant people, and a million dead soldiers, I would never stop struggling for the freedom of our people. I had a lot of dreams; now I lost them all. But I knew that to master destiny meant I had to overcome its consequences, not in the form of appeasement or compliance, but in avoiding a complete psychological breakdown.

I was suddenly very, very tired. Fatigue, coupled with hunger, made me sleepy. Fortunately, fifteen minutes later, someone delivered packages of food and drinks to all the people who had been on the plane with me. But I could not eat all the food even though I was very hungry. Most of the refugees paced around the waiting room and did not try to sleep. I guessed they were in the same condition as I was: we were all in shock over the loss of South Vietnam and realized there was no hope of ever seeing our relatives again. I talked to a Red Cross volunteer; he was pleasant and kind. I thought talking to him would help calm my soul. He gave me his address for future contact. I kept hoping that all my people would make it through the dark days ahead.

April 30, 1975

We continued our journey on the C-141 around 2:45 A.M., but some technical problems developed and our plane had to return to the runway for repairs. An hour later, it took off again but was forced to land a second time for the same reason. The passengers were led back to the waiting room. Our faces showed few signs of blame or grievance because we knew we were the recipients of our hosts' generosity. As we waited, we tried to create more affinity among ourselves.

At 9:30 A.M., we were given the signal to board a new C-141. Half an hour later, the plane took off. I was so fatigued that I slept during the entire flight. After five and a half hours, we arrived on the mainland of the United States. Our plane touched down in the state of California, well known for its beautiful climate and economic prosperity. As dusk approached, we boarded a military bus for Camp Pendleton, a marine base. We arrived there at midnight. It was extremely cold. The big and tall people took us small and short people into the housing they had prepared for us in structures called "hemispheric cylinders." Immediately, I climbed up a bunk bed and fell asleep. For many years, my sleep had been punctuated by explosions and gunfire. So, when I woke up and heard explosions nearby, I felt confused. "Am I still in Vietnam?" I asked myself. It turned out that the noise came from the American marines' target practice. The other refugees and I were still obsessed with the long, dreaded nightmare that was the Vietnam War. Hearing the shots made me miss my country to an unbearable degree—a country where cannon shells could be heard whizzing through the wind every night.

May 1, 1975

The noise outside woke me up but I was so exhausted that I went back to sleep, pulling the thick blanket over my head to muffle the sounds. Just as I was about to fall asleep again, my destiny as a refugee again pierced my consciousness. I opened my eyes. The alien surroundings of Camp Pendleton heightened my anxieties. I quickly jumped out of bed and went outside. The fog was thick and damp. I washed my face and brushed my teeth quickly before joining the stream of Vietnamese making their way to a big dining room that could accommodate four hundred people at a sitting. I had not eaten anything for almost a day. When we got to the dining room, I saw that most of the seats were taken but I eventually found an empty seat. After breakfast, I went back to bed because I felt so chilled in the fog. A few moments later, my brother also came back from the dining room and told me he had seen a friend of mine in another "hemispheric cylinder." He and I immediately found our way there. How happy I was to see my friend! But because we had no addresses to exchange, I lost touch with him after we both left the camp.

Early that evening, my family and many others were taken to another location by a military bus. After driving about fifteen minutes, the bus stopped in front of some buildings. It was here that my family would have to take care of some paperwork if we wished to leave the camp. I felt sad because I could foresee the day when I would be separated from my people here in Camp Pendleton. I knew I would be extremely lonely once I left the camp because all of America would be new to me.

May 2, 1975

The paperwork took my mother hours to complete. I had nothing to do except watch our bags. I ate a sandwich outside in the thick fog. I thought of my country. The chilly air froze my body but it could not freeze my burning love for my people still living in Vietnam. What penalties were the Communists inflicting on them? Or were they enjoying the happiness the Communists had promised? I simply could not believe that they would be happy. Our tragic departure from Vietnam underlined our objection to Communism. If the Communists had been kind, we would not be here now. We did not leave our country in search of economic gains; we left because we wanted basic human rights. We wanted to live in freedom. Even though we shall be living in a foreign country, our hearts will always be pointed toward the compatriots we left behind. We shall pray for our people, even those victorious Communists, for we know in our hearts that those Vietnamese who fought for the Communist cause are still our brothers and sisters—sons and daughters of our common motherland. We are *all* victims of war. The noise around me brought me back to reality. Quickly I ran back into the building to make sure our bags were still there. Our entire family had seven bags—two large and five small.

At two o'clock in the morning, we took a bus to another area of Camp Pendleton, where hundreds of tents had been set up close together. Here resided new waves of refugees. I guessed they must have come via Guam because I had not seen any of them while I was on Wake Island. I wanted to express my sympathy to my fellow refugees but did not make any sound to disrupt their rest. In fact, most of them were not sleeping. They looked cold and miserable. Whoever said we came to the United States for economic reasons? Maybe some rich Vietnamese did, but the rest of us, we came buried in sadness and homesickness. We came to avoid Communist "re-education camps."

An American soldier invited all those who were hungry to follow him to a dining room about two thousand feet away. We walked in a daze along a dark path. There were hundreds of Vietnamese refugees about my age in the dining room. After eating, I returned to where my mother was.

"Go to the back of the bus! Go to the back." These words were uttered by the bus driver repeatedly as refugees boarded the bus. The bus left at 4:15 A.M. according to my watch. It rolled along the highway in complete darkness. The quiet was eerie. There was total silence on the bus. What was there to say? In a new world, our fate was perhaps already predetermined. I missed Vietnam. We were sad simply because today was no longer yesterday. We felt isolated. Occasionally, the buzz of insects broke the silence momentarily. Ahead of the fast-moving bus, we saw pieces of what seemed like shining phosphorus. I had never seen such a sight before but I did not ask what they were.

The bus slowed down as we approached Los Angeles. Groups of refugees got off the bus at one stop after another. Then, it was our turn to get off. The bus driver, seeing my "funeral" face, smiled. I said, "Thank you," and stepped down. It was not as cold here as in Camp Pendleton. We walked to the American Airlines terminal where some people were waiting for their flights. I looked into the street and saw only a few passersby. Los Angeles must be a dead city, I thought. We had been told we were going to Detroit. Many questions popped up in my mind. What is Detroit like? Is it cold? Will it be a sad place for us to live in? Will Americans welcome us or hate us for being refugees? Do they think we are parasites in their country? These thoughts made me desperate.

The main reason I felt sad was that I did not want to be separated from the other Vietnamese refugees. I wanted to live near them. Among them, my native sentiments could be preserved. I had just lost my country; must I also lose contact with my fellow refugees? If I had to live apart from my people, I was certain I would feel lost among the vast number of Americans. I knew that eventually I would become Americanized. But no! Vietnamese can never become Americans. Vietnamese must remain Vietnamese. Our culture has to survive in order to help us retain our distinctiveness as a people. As long as Vietnam exists, we shall continue to live and die for it.

"We will be taking off for Detroit in three minutes. Please fasten your seat belts," said the sweet voice of the American Airlines flight attendant. The sun was shining brightly. I could see clearly the shadow of the plane's wing on the ground below.

Living among Strangers

By 1966, the increasing number of foreigners, especially military and civilian Americans, in South Vietnam had brought Western technology and investment to many cities and towns. My first impression of Americans, when I was seven, was very favorable. I was very curious about these "strangers." I perceived American men and women as elegant and friendly people. From inside my home, I watched through the window as children joyfully gathered around Americans who were "talking with smiles." At that time, I was not yet old enough to see any cultural differences between Americans and Vietnamese. All I noticed was a language barrier and the obvious physical discrepancy between the tall Americans and the short Vietnamese. I also noticed that all Americans, including low-ranking soldiers, seemed to enjoy a luxurious lifestyle.

As I grew older, I chose English as my foreign language option in high school as I dreamed of going abroad for higher education someday. I also took English classes at a school established by the Vietnamese-American Association. Learning English was very popular among a lot of Vietnamese students in those days. After several years of study, I began to understand, though barely, slowly spoken conversations in English. It was at this stage in my life that I developed a serious interest in how and why Americans were involved in the Vietnam War. As I followed the war's development and the American impacts on it, I became disillusioned. On the one hand, they talked of freedom; on the other, they bombed "the hell" out of many villages as they attempted to destroy their enemy. They often did not respond to calls from South Vietnamese soldiers for air support, which resulted in the loss of many lives among those they called "allies." That hypocrisy reflected the American disrespect for Vietnamese lives. The American presence led to other developments that changed South Vietnamese society. The most tragic example was the transformation of thousands and thousands of young women into prostitutes. As old traditions and moral values were pushed aside, the Vietnamese social structure entered a period of crisis.

However, my attitude toward Americans in Vietnam was not hostile. I still thought of them as crucial allies who sometimes made mistakes as they helped South Vietnam resist the invasion from the North. I saw Americans and their country through the eyes of the generous, polite, and well-disciplined officers and civilians whom I met and through the images projected in American and European films and television shows. Before I left Vietnam, I thought of America as a rich country where people lived easy, romantic lives.

Immediately after arriving in the United States, my impression of America did not change at all. On the contrary, I developed an even more favorable view of the country as I saw and appreciated its natural wonders. However, it took no more than a month for me to realize that Americans are isolated people because individualism reigns supreme in their society. This realization was what led me to a state of near psychological breakdown and endless homesickness—feelings that persisted for more than a year before they subsided. As time passed, I slowly transformed my homesickness into unconditional sympathy for every compatriot I met. I read a large number of newspapers and magazines, particularly articles that analyzed what was going on in Vietnam and other world events. I even read Communist theories and tried to understand their practices.

Slowly, I became more and more critical of Americans as I began to see how the dollar divides different groups of Americans. I became aware of the persistence of racial discrimination and the oftentimes crookedness of the judicial system. In my eyes, Americans are no longer as omnipotent as I had once thought. As I increased my knowledge of the world, I broadened my outlook and began to wish that a person, regardless of his or her race, national origin, or sex, could possess equal dignity as any other human being. I gained greater insight into what the French philosopher Jean Paul Sartre once said: "A man is himself meaningless. It is his devotion to certain ideals that makes him different from animals."

As far as Vietnamese moral and cultural values are concerned, I have been trying to maintain myself as a Vietnamese, speaking Vietnamese at home and in school, deliberately avoiding mixing up Vietnamese and English words as some of my peers do. I borrow Vietnamese books that discuss Vietnamese customs, art, music, and poetry. I also read about the ancient and modern history of Vietnam, of which I am proud, to maintain my sense of nationalism. I continue to polish my Vietnamese by writing letters to my friends who are still in Vietnam, in an effort to express myself as best as possible.

Sometimes, I write essays purely for myself, analyzing various topics so that I can sharpen my mind. I attend meetings to exchange ideas about our country. Finally, I participate in cultural events to help Americans understand that we are a distinct people with a profound culture. Though I have lost my country, everything about Vietnam will remain in my heart and continue to shape my life.

CHAPTER TWELVE

A Journey Called Freedom

The author left Saigon with her family on April 28, 1975, in a U.S. cargo plane when she was seven years old. Unlike many of the urbanites evacuated as Saigon was about to fall, the narrator and her family came from rural origins. Her parents were farmers and the family was Catholic. However, after Americans became involved in the war in Vietnam, her father found a job as a security guard at the American consulate in a city in the northern part of South Vietnam. While he worked in the city, the author, her mother, and siblings moved to a village situated in a forest when the South Vietnamese government allocated small plots of land to those willing to till the soil there. South Vietnam's leaders believed that placing a significant number of inhabitants in the area would make it more difficult for Communist troops to capture it. As an employee of the U.S. government, the author's father and his family qualified for evacuation. They left because they believed that a Communist government would persecute Catholics. This account paints a memorable picture of village life. Also notable is how religion and the small size of the Oregon town in which the author's family resettled helped ease their adjustment after they arrived in the United States. This essay was written in 1988.

Why? Why Vietnam? I asked the world as I recalled the history of Vietnam and the sadness that spread over the land with the fall of Saigon. Vietnam has a history of being oppressed by a succession of conquerors. Living in a country that rarely had its own rulers, Vietnamese watched the fall of Saigon with the same emotions as their ancestors had felt when the country was passed from one foreign ruler to the next. Is the Communist victory going to be any different from Chinese imperial rule, French colonialism, or Japanese occupation?

Growing up in Vietnam, my birthplace and homeland, the fall of Saigon affected me very deeply just as it affected the rest of the people in South Vietnam. Despite the fact that I left Vietnam when I was only seven and have lived in the United States for almost thirteen years, I still consider Vietnam as my home. Memories of my country still have an effect on my life, as shown in the way I speak, act, and feel. It has been very hard to adjust to life in America because I came from a small village in Vietnam. As I sit on my couch staring at the inside of an average American house, I remember a time when television was a treat and carpeted floors did not exist. Even though my memories of Vietnam grow fainter with each passing day, I can still remember its beauty and pain.

Before the fall of Saigon, life in the rural area where I lived was peaceful and untouched by modern technology. Although I was born in a city, my most memorable days were spent in the countryside where I lived during the latter half of my childhood. My earliest memory goes back to the place where I was born, a city located in the northern part of South Vietnam. My father was a security guard at the American consulate there. Sometimes he took me along when he went to work, gave me a shower, and put me to sleep while he worked. When I was three years old, I encountered an American for the first time. I remember my father taking his bicycle, which was parked outside our house, as he got ready to go to work. He allowed me to ride on the back. Holding tightly on to the seat, I looked up and saw the afternoon sun shining brightly through the trees lining both sides of the street, which was paved with tar—an indication we were in a city. Coming to the downtown area, the hustle and bustle of cars, motorcycles, bicycles, and pedestrians surrounded my father and me. There were shops everywhere, selling clothing, shoes, jewelry, household utensils, meat, and vegetables. I saw many merchants with their wares, mothers bargaining for the lowest prices, and children running between everybody's legs. It was a normal, noisy city except for the bombings that could be heard once in a while. Yet, that too was common and everyone learned to ignore the fact that the bombs may soon come closer.

The American consulate was located in the middle of downtown. As we got to the entrance, a Vietnamese security guard checked my father and me before he admitted us through the iron gates. Holding on firmly to my father's hand, I followed him into a lounge that had beds and showers. There, we took a shower, my father and I together, and then my father changed into his uniform while I settled down on a nice comfortable bed with a mattress. The simple house we lived in did not have the luxury of showers and beds with mattresses. This was true of most other Vietnamese houses as well. My father went outside to start work as I lay down to take a nap.

I was jolted from my restful nap by a strange noise. As I opened my eyes slowly, I heard the deep rumbling of a man's voice, so unlike the soft pitch of a Vietnamese's voice. My eyes wandered toward the doorway and took in the massive frame and flaming red hair of a strange man. I did not know who he was and assumed he was a monster. His strange foreign voice and huge body reminded me of stories about monsters that ate little girls. Fear gripped my body. In a flash, I was under the bed as I hid from this monster. I stayed beneath the bed and watched his huge feet coming closer and closer toward me. My heart pounded faster and faster. But the feet turned and walked out of the room. A little smile tugged at the corner of my mouth as I thought I had outsmarted the ugly monster. Still afraid, I stayed under the bed until my father came for me. So ended my first contact with an American.

A few years after this incident, my family moved to a village south of the city where we had lived. Since the city had little land, all the houses there were squeezed together, so the thought of moving to another place where land, especially farmland, was abundant, was tempting to country folk like my parents, who had both been born on farms and had been farmers before they moved to the city two years before I was born. The South Vietnamese government had announced a plan: families who were willing to move to the village would be given a few acres of farmland and a house. The government wanted people to inhabit unoccupied areas in South Vietnam in order to make it more difficult for the Communists to infiltrate or even invade our country. The village we moved to was directly north of Saigon, so it was an ideal place where the Communists could station their troops if they wished to attack Saigon. Moreover, there was a forest in the area in which Communist troops could hide.

The decision to move came abruptly. Since we are Catholics, my parents decided to join other Catholics who wished to settle in that particular village. However, my father could not come with us because he had to keep his security guard job with its modest pay and benefits. Mother would have to take care of us six children on her own—a tough job but not too hard for a strong-willed woman to manage.

Village life was peaceful and simple. The houses were made for practical use rather than for outside appearance. Made of clay, wood, and hay, they were affordable. The wealthy people's houses had red tile roofs. The roofs of poorer people's houses were made of woven banana or coconut leaves. Our first house on the outskirts of the village was built of wood and it had a tin roof. It was a typical Vietnamese house with lots of plants and trees around it. We had our own well.

Like many houses in Vietnam, ours had a big yard full of fruit trees that produced mangos, bananas, papayas, and sugarcane.

We lived in our first house for only a couple of months. When the Communists shot bullets through our house, we were forced to move farther into the village. Our second house was much smaller than the first. The walls were made of woven banana leaves and the floor was dirt. We considered it only a temporary dwelling until we could build a bigger house. Our temporary house had two rooms—a bedroom and a living-dining room. The bedroom had two beds. It was customary in Vietnam for young children to sleep with their parents and for the older children to share beds. My younger sister and I shared my mother's bed until my youngest brother was born. Then I had to move to the older children's bed. Five of us shared a big bed made of wood and covered with a reed mat. Kitchens in Vietnamese rural houses are never inside the main house but are separate from the living quarters so that smoke will not fill up the house. Since we did not have modern electric appliances, such as a stove, we cooked over a wood-burning fire.

Life in the rural area was slow. We took one day at a time. Spiritual values overshadowed materialistic ones. The country folk usually wore black or brown shirts and pants—ideal colors for working in the fields. People always left their houses open; there were no locks on the doors and guests were always welcome. However, the custom of welcoming guests was not restricted to the rural areas alone.

Schools in Vietnam were very strict. Elementary schools ran from eight in the morning until four in the afternoon with a lunch break from noon to two in the afternoon. The long lunch break gave us time for a siesta, another custom that many Vietnamese share. In elementary school, severe punishment, such as spanking, was inflicted if students did not learn their lessons. Since my elementary school was too poor to purchase books, we copied down each lesson in a notebook. We had to memorize whatever we had copied down each day and recite it the next day. At the end of the school year, those students who failed their tests would not be promoted to the next grade—a great shame to the students and their families. High schools in the rural areas were in session from eight in the morning to one in the afternoon six days a week so that the students could help their parents with farmwork in the afternoon.

On our plot of land my mother grew rice, sweet potatoes, and corn. We children helped in the fields after school. At harvest time, the whole village gathered to help each family for a day. They did this in return for labor on their own farms. Since my father was not there to help us, my mother had to hire laborers to harvest the crops. Farmworkers worked from dawn to dusk. They only had Sundays off.

Festivals were always lots of fun as the whole village took part, bringing food and laughter to share with everyone. During the lunar New Year, Tet, and the summer festival, my father came home to visit. Tet was the most popular holiday in Vietnam. Celebrations lasted from a week to a month. There were fireworks, dragon dances, and lots of food. Happiness filled the air. Children received little red envelopes with money inside. These were symbols of good luck for both the children and the adults who gave them the gifts.

The simple life in our village differed from the fast-paced life in cities, especially a big city like Saigon. My brothers, sisters, and I played outside, roaming the countryside as we grew up without the strict discipline of a father. But we were good children. We tried not to be too troublesome because our mother had lots of work to do in the fields. I used to daydream a lot, especially about the big orange ball in the sky. My mother told me stories about the sun's home, which she said was located in the middle of the forest behind our village. I dreamed of going on a search to find the home of the sun. However, my mother told me another story about the forest. She said that men with green faces lived there. (These men, green monsters, were actually the Viet Cong hiding in the forest.) So, she did not allow me to go search for the sun's home.

My sheltered life in the village left me unprepared for the evacuation in April 1975. Unaware of the war around me, I was caught off guard when my family left our cozy home and hurried to Saigon. I remember my sister came to pick me up from my second-grade class. Oblivious of the situation at hand, I was happy to leave school early. However, all the classes were dismissed because of an emergency: news had spread that the cities north of us had been captured and we were next in line as the Viet Cong and North Vietnamese troops marched south toward Saigon. Our village would soon become the site of an upcoming battle. We felt hopeless when we heard that the South Vietnamese army could not hold the Communists back. In a state of panic, we villagers quickly evacuated our homes and tried to find a sanctuary as we moved toward Saigon. However, Communist troops were already blocking the main road to the capital, so the only hope for us was to go by sea.

What fun, I thought, we are going on a vacation. Riding the village's overcrowded truck toward the ocean, I did not notice how glum the other passengers' faces were. I noticed neither the scared faces of my older sisters nor the worried one of my mother. Even the babies did not cry. We hoped to meet Father at a harbor along the coast. From there, we planned to rent a boat and sail to another coastal town and then travel by land to Saigon. We assumed that from Saigon we could board a U.S. airplane and fly to the United States because my father was working for the Americans. Two days after we left our village, we heard about the bloody battles being fought. Many wild stories about the torture used by the Viet Cong reached our ears. One especially popular story said that the Viet Cong chopped off the arms and legs of everyone they captured and ate them. My oldest brother, who was about twenty, had stayed behind in the village to help the South Vietnamese army. Later, we found out that he died of bullet wounds four days after we evacuated that village. The news of his death took us by surprise. Mother was torn apart when she heard that her oldest son had died. We tried to comfort her but she was inconsolable.

Finally, Father arrived. However, we could not leave right away because the weather was terrible. The waves were too strong. The disaster that befell each boat that tried to leave the shore made it very clear that the ocean was dangerous. Many people perished as their boats were tossed by waves and flipped over. After a few days, the storm subsided. We were ready to go. Father rented a boat that my family and several other families shared. We sailed down the coast on this overcrowded boat. Standing on the boat's deck, we saw many dead bodies floating on the water. Through my seven-year-old eyes, I could not understand why there were so many bodies of adults as well as children. I thought those people must be swimming and I secretly envied them; I wanted to go swimming, too.

Upon arriving at our destination, we saw huge crowds of people. Everyone wanted to go to Saigon to find shelter. Desperate to leave, Father looked for a taxi but found none. So we joined thousands of other pedestrians who were walking to Saigon. It took us an entire week to get from our village to Saigon—a normal drive of two hours by bus. We lost most of our luggage on the way—some fell off the boat and others were stolen. By the time we got to Saigon, I was very fearful. My parents told us we were going to visit my aunt but I never understood why we had to go by boat and to walk instead of taking a bus.

As soon as we reached Saigon, we rushed to the airport. Father knew his family would have no chance to live a peaceful life in Vietnam once the Communists captured Saigon, as he, along with the rest of South Vietnam, thought they surely would. Many military men and politicians were trying to flee. The rich and the educated were likewise trying to escape. They all knew that they would have no future once the Communists took over the country. They would be jailed and even executed. My father was neither rich nor a politician, but he knew that if we stayed in Vietnam, we would have to abandon our religion. Many Catholics feared they would be persecuted or even put to death. Also, my father worried that he might be separated from his family as he had worked for a U.S. consulate. He felt, therefore, it was crucial that we leave the country.

Fortunately, we were able to board a U.S. military cargo plane, despite all the families who were shuffling and pushing to get on that plane. On April 28, 1975, two days before the fall of Saigon, our plane took off. In it, many Vietnamese families were tightly packed together on the floor. My family joined the crowd on the floor. Some people who were not used to flying got sick and threw up. It was awful. After a few hours, the plane landed on an American military base in the Philippines. I was so relieved when we landed. While in the Philippines, we heard the news that the Communists had captured Saigon. In the following days, thousands of South Vietnamese who knew how oppressive the Communists would be also tried to escape. Since the United States no longer sent planes or helicopters to evacuate them, they left by whatever boats they could find.

We stayed in the Philippines for only a few days before we were flown to Guam. The Philippine government refused to take in any refugees permanently. Before we flew to Guam, we got immunization shots and had to fill out some forms. We did not stay in Guam long; our next destination was Camp Pendleton. My family was among the first batch of Vietnamese to arrive there. At Camp Pendleton, I saw how different everything looked compared to Vietnam. All we saw were hills and a brown desert landscape—so different from the green scenery in my village. I and my younger brother and sister adjusted to life in Camp Pendleton much more easily than did my parents and older sisters simply because we were younger. My busy days in that camp helped me overcome my fear. Since I enrolled in an English as a Second Language (ESL) class, I could play with other children my age.

My family was not completely alone. My aunt's family had traveled with us. There were thousands of families in Camp Pendleton. Each family slept in a tent with cots. We ate in a large tent that was known as the mess hall. I found it difficult to adjust to American food. We even tried to cook our own food but we almost burned our tent down with the fire we started. The marines in the camp taught us to speak English. They played with us children and gave us toys and candy. Never had I eaten so many sweets or sipped so many soda pops, both of which were consumed only on festive occasions in Vietnam. I remember how happy I used to be whenever Father came to visit us in the village and brought candy for the children. How good the candy tasted then. What tasted even better were the apples, pears, and peaches—fruits that do not grow in Vietnam—that we ate in Camp Pendleton. But the adults were sad because our simple life in Vietnam had vanished. It was replaced by fear and confusion.

We stayed in the camp for a month before we found a sponsor. My aunt's family found a sponsor first. A Catholic parish in Oceanside, a city near Camp Pendleton, sponsored them. A few days later, a Catholic parish in Oregon agreed to sponsor us. An older couple would take us in. My father jumped for joy when he heard that we would have Catholic sponsors. We had no idea that the climate in northern Oregon was very cold. It was cold on the bus that took us to Oregon. After a long trip, we stopped at a place called Mt. Angel. People fed us and gave us clothes. Our sponsors had found us a beautiful big house in Woodburn, Oregon. We were the only Vietnamese family there. How lonely we felt at first! None of us spoke English except my father and my older sister who knew a few words. We could not eat the American food that our sponsors gave us. We did not know where to buy rice or fish sauce. There were no Vietnamese around to show us where to buy such things. Everything was so strange to us. We did not know how to use the stove or the bathroom. All these things took time to get used to, especially if one came from an area with no electricity and where wells were the only source of water. My father knew about electricity but he was not comfortable using it. For months, we felt lonely living in a totally alien environment.

After several months, we finally felt we could cope with our environment despite the difficulties. Life no longer seemed so bad because we had "real" beds to sleep on. We were amazed that each member of our family had his or her own bed. However, the two youngest children, my two-year-old sister and eight-month-old brother, continued to sleep with my mother while my father had his own bed.

At first, my family was in the news practically every day. Journalists described us as one of the first Vietnamese families in the United States, let alone Oregon. At Christmas, we had a live Christmas tree and made traditional Vietnamese lanterns using sticks and transparent paper of different colors. Inside each lantern was a candle. When we lit the candles in all the lanterns, they glowed in bright beautiful colors. The people in Woodburn were fascinated and many came to our house to see the lanterns. My father also made a big nativity scene, just as every Catholic family in Vietnam used to do.

We lived in Woodburn for a year. All the school-age children in my family went to a Catholic school. My father found work as a gardener while my mother stayed home to take care of us children. The government and social service agencies gave us money and helped us adjust. In time, our lives were peaceful again. I made many friends in school. Because we did not know English, my sisters and I were placed at grade levels below what our age would have determined. I was eight years old but I entered the first grade. However, I was the smallest person in the class. My classmates were fascinated with the little Vietnamese girl who had just arrived from another country and who couldn't speak a word of English. In this little town, most of the residents were Euro-Americans, with a sprinkling of Asians, Mexicans, and Blacks. All my classmates tried to teach me English but for some reason I refused to speak it. All I would say was "thank you" and "I'm fine." However, because I was surrounded by Euro-Americans, my initial fear of strangers eventually subsided even though I continued to be very shy.

Although I did not know English, first grade was easy for me. The school allowed me to skip the second grade and go directly into the third grade the following year. My English had become more proficient by then and much of my shyness had vanished. By then, I was slightly more willing to speak English because when my communication skill was nil, life was very boring. I did not attend third grade in Woodburn, however, because we moved to Mt. Angel, where a few Vietnamese families had settled. Mt. Angel had a population of a thousand people at the time, while Woodburn had only six hundred. Mt. Angel has a name to fit the place: 80 percent of the people were Catholics. There was a convent on the outskirts of town and a monastery located on a hill. In the center of the town stood a big Catholic church. Even though the other parishioners were not familiar to us, the religion was. The fact that most of the Euro-Americans we came in contact with were Catholics helped my family feel more at ease.

At school, I felt very different from everyone else. Although all my classmates were very nice to me, I felt their niceness was not due to friendship. They did not know how to treat me. I was not like them. There were two other Vietnamese students in my elementary school but I did not know them, either. I kept to myself and only spoke when other students asked me questions. It was not until my third year in the United States that I started coming out of my shell. I began making friends and was even invited to a birthday party. That all the other girls in my class had also been invited did not dampen my excitement. Birthdays are not celebrated in Vietnam, so this was a new experience for me.

Actually, life in Mt. Angel was not too dramatic a change from Vietnam. Although we had indoor plumbing and electricity, we never locked our doors because everybody in the town was friendly. We lived in a two-story house and had two acres of land around us full of fruit trees—apples, plums, cherries, and pears, rather than the banana, mango, and papaya trees we had in Vietnam. We felt very lucky to have this roomy house and lots to eat. Our situation differed from those of many other Vietnamese who had come to the United States who were crammed into small apartments or houses. Besides, my father found a job as a gardener instantly, our sponsors fully supported us, and the Catholic community in Mt. Angel helped us as much as possible. They donated clothes, food, and money. The Vietnamese community in that town grew quickly; most of the newcomers were also Catholics. The convent had sponsored all of them. We even had a Vietnamese priest who came to say mass in Vietnamese every Sunday. Unlike California, where there were thousands of Vietnamese families, Mt. Angel's Vietnamese community grew from one family to about twenty to thirty families. Our small number kept us close and we supported each other.

The worst aspect of Oregon was the terrible weather. It was so cold and windy. It even snowed in winter. We got sick constantly from the cold, damp weather. Whenever one of us got sick, germs spread to everyone else in the family. Unused to this climate, our bodies became skinny and our skin turned pale. We looked almost like walking skeletons. Although our diet improved once my father planted traditional Vietnamese vegetables and herbs with seeds he had brought from the home country, our health did not improve.

In September 1978, we moved to Oceanside where my aunt lived. We were attracted by California's warm climate and the large Vietnamese communities there. Although the fast-paced life in California is very different from that in Mt. Angel, and many Californians are Black, Mexican, and Asian, we found it much easier to adjust to life in California because by then we had already been in the United States for more than three years. However, the students in California were a lot more rowdy, but that made life more interesting. Schoolwork was easy for me. Unlike in Vietnam, nobody spanked me when I had not learned my lessons. By the time I entered junior high school, I tried as hard as I could to be the top student in my class. I graduated from high school as one of the top ten students in a very competitive school.

Our family has changed a great deal since we first entered the United States. Family is still an important part of our lives, despite the fact that most of the children are now grown up, some are married, and some have moved to other cities to work. Ironically, one of the reasons we left Vietnam was to keep our family intact. Father constantly stresses Vietnamese culture—he expects us to speak Vietnamese, eat Vietnamese food, and celebrate Tet. As a result, I grew up in two environments: a Vietnamese one within my home and an American one outside the home. Even though I have been in the United States for thirteen years, I still keep my Vietnamese heritage inside me. I know I always will. No matter what hardships I encounter, I shall always remember the saying, "A journey of a thousand miles begins with a single step." This is the story of my journey, a journey that made me into the person I am today: a Vietnamese American.

CHAPTER THIRTEEN

My Autobiography

The author left Saigon with her family on a U.S. naval vessel on April 29, 1975, when she was thirteen years old. Amid the chaos, her father was left behind. In despair, the narrator's mother almost returned to Vietnam when the United Nations High Commissioner for Refugees provided a ship to those who had arrived in Guam but wanted to return to their homeland. At the last minute, however, the mother removed her name from the repatriation list when she realized how her children might be adversely affected. Sponsored by a Guamanian family, the author's family lived on Guam for three years, unlike most refugees who spent only days or weeks or at most months on that island while they were "processed." Like many people who fled as Communist troops amassed around Saigon, the author's family originated in North Vietnam where her grandfather was a wealthy landowner who took two-thirds of the crops that his tenants grew. Still, the author claimed he was a kind landlord. Her grandmother, who decided to leave the North in 1954 even though her husband chose to remain, and her mother, who worked in a restaurant in San Francisco to support her family after their arrival, both illustrate the strength and independence of Vietnamese women. This account was written in 1980.

My maternal grandfather was born in North Vietnam. He was the richest landlord in the city where he lived and was considered a member of the elite. Every harvest season, he collected the rent and debts that his tenant farmers owed him. Even though he had power and authority, he never mistreated his tenants. Usually, he took two-thirds of the crops they had harvested, but if they did not have enough left to feed their families, he put off collecting whatever they owed him until a future harvest. Therefore, on special occasions like Tet, the Vietnamese New Year, my grandfather's house was full of gifts that the tenant farmers brought him.

My grandfather had two wives; my grandmother was his second. At that time, in the 1920s, the second wife was called a concubine.

Whether a man had one or more concubines depended on his economic status. My grandmother got along with the first wife and her children. She never had to cook or clean house. She was never mistreated and her children were treated equally and had the same rights as the children of the first wife. When my grandfather died, his property would be equally divided among all the children of both wives.

In 1954, Communist revolutionaries defeated the French. The Geneva Agreements divided Vietnam into two regions, North and South. The North became a Communist society under Ho Chi Minh and the South was ruled by Emperor Bao Dai. People in North Vietnam could choose to live in either North or South Vietnam. My grandfather knew about the Communist policies of land reform, collectivization of agriculture, and industrialization. He knew that his land and houses would be redistributed as part of the reconstruction of the country. Still, he decided to stay because he wanted to die in the land where he was born. He was about sixty-five years old at the time.

However, my grandmother decided to go to South Vietnam. She felt insecure about whether there would be freedom under a Communist government. So, she took all her children—my mother, aunts, and uncles—to the South. She brought along a small sum of money and she and her children traveled to South Vietnam on an American ship. During the evacuation, the ship's crew gave the passengers enough food to eat.

My mother dropped out of school after finishing the eleventh grade and went to work in a restaurant in order to help support the family. After working hard and saving her earnings, my mother bought a restaurant of her own. A few years later, she bought a hotel. She was very successful in her business career. Most of the employees in her restaurant and hotel were my aunts and uncles from both my maternal and, after she married my father, paternal sides of the family. She seemed to trust family members more than outsiders. All of them worked as members of one big family and got along very well together.

My paternal grandparents are South Vietnamese. They owned an automobile repair shop in Saigon. They had twelve children; my father is the oldest son. Even though my father has a college degree, he did not have a large income. He was in the army and worked with Americans. My mother helped him a lot with our family finances. Deeply concerned about the education of his children, my father tutored my brothers and me every night from the first grade through high school. Whenever I had questions, he would be the one I would ask.

My three younger brothers and I were sent to the best schools in Saigon. My parents wanted all of us to achieve a high educational level. My father did not allow us to go out or to watch television frequently, while my mother, who had suffered the disadvantages of a low socioeconomic status after she, her siblings, and her mother moved to Saigon, kept reminding us of her own experiences. My parents were very strict. Whenever I wanted to go out—to a movie, for instance—I had to ask permission from one of them ahead of time. Whenever I did something wrong, I knew I would be punished. As my mother was in charge of the family budget, whenever I needed spending money, I went to her. I had to explain why I needed money; my mother did not want to give me money for "bad" movies or nonsensical books.

My family was very close to my maternal aunt's family because my aunt worked for my mother and they spent all their weekends together. We went swimming, had picnics, or went to movies. My cousins and I got along pretty well. We went to the same school and spent time together after school.

My maternal grandmother was respected by everybody in the family. She was a loving and caring woman and taught me to obey my parents. She also took care of me when I was young. Often she took me to school and sometimes watched television with me in the evenings. I had a very close relationship with her and loved her as much as I loved my parents. When I grew older, she moved to my uncle's house to help take care of her other grandchildren there.

I did not get to know my paternal grandparents as well as my maternal grandmother, but we visited both sides of the family on national holidays. During Tet, family members from both my father's and mother's sides got together for a special dinner and worshipped our ancestors. The dinner often fed more than a hundred people.

I went to a Catholic school—one of the best girls' schools in South Vietnam. I studied very hard and served as a class officer from the fifth through the eighth grades. My classmates and I all studied hard and competed with each other but we were not jealous of or hostile to any classmate who did better than the rest of us. I felt that school was my second home where I had fun with my classmates. In class, we respected our teachers and we listened to them as we did our parents. I was always one of the top five students. My parents were very proud of me, an honor student. They rewarded me by giving me books, clothes, or some money. They wanted me to become a doctor or a pharmacist. They expected me to support them when they grew old. In Vietnam, the family is the main structure in society. Old parents live with the

family of one of their sons or daughters. Family relations are considered more important than anything else. Even though we are now in
the United States, I intend to support my parents in their old age.

Growing up in a war-torn country, I understood that Vietnam was
a poor country that had suffered a great deal during thirty years of
war. The government paid attention only to the war and the power of
its army. So much money was spent on the war that we did not have
many public schools and public hospitals, or much public housing.
Even a private school like mine had few laboratories or facilities for
physical education. For girls, it was all right if they failed their high
school examinations, but for boys, those who failed would be drafted
into the army. Vietnamese young men were under severe pressure,
because those who joined the army might be killed or, even if they
survived, become handicapped.

Before the war, most families depended on agriculture for survival.
I think about 90 percent of the population were farmers. But during
the war, many rice fields and coconut and rubber plantations were
bombed. Farmers had to leave the countryside and move to urban
areas. Even though I lived in the capital city, Saigon, which was not
bombed until the last stage of the war, I still had some idea of what the
war was like by reading newspapers and listening to the radio. I also
saw many tragic situations around me: people suffered from hunger,
unemployment, and lack of shelter. I considered myself lucky because
I could go to school while some other children could not afford to
do so. That fact further motivated me to study hard so that I could
attain a high social status in the future.

Every member of my maternal grandmother's family knew about the
Communists—their ideology and the social structure they imposed
on North Vietnam. We had all heard many stories told by northerners
who had escaped. Citizens in the North had no right to speak out
against the government. The government nationalized everything, so
there was no free enterprise. The land redistribution policy worked
only in theory; in reality, the government took charge of and controlled all the land. One of my uncles, who did not leave the North
in 1954, was imprisoned because of his political opposition to the
Communist government, but he managed to escape. After he came
south, he joined the Army of the Republic of Vietnam. He told us
about the cruelty of the Viet Cong.

In early 1975, the North Vietnamese soldiers captured many cities
in South Vietnam. The South Vietnamese army fought back and
tried to keep the most important regions of the South even though
they had few guns. However, when the army failed to win battles,

President Nguyen Van Thieu commanded the generals and captains to send their soldiers back to Saigon. No one could understand why the president made that decision. Disobeying his command, some generals stayed behind with their soldiers to fight to the last. Other soldiers hurriedly took off their guns and uniforms, put on civilian clothes, and joined the stream of people moving southward toward Saigon. Many people walked for miles and miles. Others went in private ships by paying a large amount of money or gold. Thousands of people died along the way from hunger and thirst. The Communists managed to take over many parts of South Vietnam without fighting with the Army of the Republic of Vietnam, whose troops had retreated. With hundreds of thousands of people all converging on Saigon, the city was in serious trouble. Schools and churches became temporary shelters for the people flooding into the city.

Before Saigon fell, many generals, admirals, soldiers, and sailors left Vietnam on their military airplanes or ships. The army no longer protected Saigon. On April 26, 1975, the Communists bombed Saigon's airport, which destroyed the runways so that no planes could take off. The Viet Cong also set some houses in the central part of the city on fire.

My family was desperate because we had no way to leave Saigon. Finally, my mother found a way. We left on an American ship in the late evening of April 29, 1975. We had only two or three hours to pack our valuables. After we got on the ship, all our clothes and valuables were stolen. Everyone in my family was left with only the clothes he or she was wearing. My father was left behind because he had gone to look for other possible ways to escape and we could not find him anywhere before we boarded the ship. My mother hoped that he would escape later but my father is still in Vietnam.

There were about five thousand people jammed into the ship when it was designed to hold only about a thousand. We had hardly any space to sleep. The members of my family took turns lying down. We received only one meal a day because there was not enough food for five thousand people. After sailing for five days, we arrived at Subic Bay in the Philippines. The next day we flew to Guam on an American airplane. We stayed in a tent city at Orote Point that had been built to house Vietnamese refugees temporarily. It was so hot during the day and so cold at night in Guam. We were fed three meals a day but we had to stand in line for long hours to get the food. We were provided with toothpaste, soap, baby food, and much more. Each tent housed about fifteen persons. There were only a small number of toilets and not enough water for bathing.

My mother was very sad and worried because my father was still in Vietnam and we had lost all our clothing and money. She did not know how we would survive in a new environment in the United States. Feeling depressed and discouraged, she signed up to return to Vietnam when she found out that a ship was being repaired and loaded with provisions to take those who wished to go back to Vietnam. But after a few days, my mother thought about her children's future. She knew that she was now the head of the family and if she returned to Vietnam by herself, our family would fall apart. So, she restrained herself and tried to accept the tragic situation and removed her name from the list of people who wished to go back to Vietnam.

When my mother and my aunt found jobs as interpreters in the camp, our two families were moved to another "camp" in the Tokyo Hotel, where the families of interpreters were housed. My mother and aunt worked as interpreters for six months, moving from one campsite to another. We children stayed in the Tokyo Hotel where the living conditions were very comfortable. We had three meals a day and the food was better than the food in the other camps. We did not have to stand in line waiting for food and we could watch a movie almost every night. Every once in a while, we were allowed to have a party. Sometimes, we could go shopping if we went in a group. That made us very happy.

I enjoyed living in the hotel and I made many friends there. We went to English class together and played badminton and volleyball. I tried to get to know my friends as well as possible because I thought it might be the last time we would live in a community of Vietnamese. I knew that after we got to America, we would be scattered all over the United States. Furthermore, we would be busy working to earn a living in the new society. All of us thought of the United States as a land of milk and honey with lots of jobs and opportunities for everyone.

After living in the Tokyo Hotel for six months, a Guamanian family offered to sponsor us. So, we decided to remain in Guam. My family and my aunt's family moved into the same house provided by our sponsor. My mother and aunt found jobs in the same restaurant. After a few months, we had saved up enough money to move out of the house our sponsor had put us in. We found two houses that were near each other for our two families. The government provided us with food stamps and welfare.

We lived in Guam for almost three years. We were comfortable there, but my mother and aunt eventually decided to move to California because it has a better climate and the largest Vietnamese population outside of Vietnam. My mother had some close friends in San Francisco, so that was where we went. My family is still living in San Francisco. My aunt's family is in a house close by. My mother works in a restaurant. All of us like California a lot because its weather is really nice, there is a large Asian population, and Asian food is readily available. Being among Chinese, Japanese, Koreans, and especially Vietnamese, we feel that it would be harder for white Anglo-Saxons to discriminate against us.

When we were still in Vietnam, my mother's restaurant served many American soldiers. It was in this restaurant where I first had some contact with Americans. Through the eyes of a young girl, Americans seemed to be the richest people in the world. They ate the best food and drank a lot, spending an enormous amount of money and leaving large tips. In fact, because the U.S. dollar was worth a lot more than Vietnamese money, the large sums they spent were not an extravagance. With the salary that U.S. soldiers earned at that time, they could live in Vietnam like rich men. They bought a lot of canned food, candy, clothes, and soap that Vietnamese sold on the black market. The way they spent money confirmed the image that I had got from movies and television of America's wealth and power. I also appreciated the fact that Americans had come to help my country in the war against Communism.

However, I began to develop a negative impression of Americans when many Vietnamese became corrupted by the U.S. dollar. For example, many bars and nightclubs opened to cater to American soldiers. Young girls worked in the bars because there they could earn higher salaries than could university professors. The number of prostitutes multiplied. The number of drug users also increased tremendously.

Having lived in Guam and the United States for almost five years now, I am getting to know what American society is really like. I am impressed by the materialistic world of the American people. They can buy all kinds of cars, houses, clothes, and cosmetics. They are always trying to satisfy their materialistic needs, which they regard as absolutely necessary constituents of their lives. I have also learned that the United States is a nation consisting of all the different races in the world. In theory, America is a country that is open to everybody, but in reality, it is a country dominated by the Anglo-Saxon race. Blacks and Asians are regarded as minority groups and they have a hard time fighting for equal rights in America. They suffer from discrimination and racism because the Anglo-Saxons do not regard these minority groups as "real" Americans. If individuals from these minority groups want to be recognized as Americans, they have to work very hard to raise their racial status and to fight against cultural and racial barriers. I think minority groups such as Vietnamese, Chinese, and Koreans should unite and work together for our rights in order to have a voice in American society.

More than one hundred and fifty thousand Vietnamese are living in the United States today. We seem to have grouped together in the states with warm weather and easy living, such as California, Texas, and Florida. When I am asked what my Vietnamese identity means to me, I find it hard to answer that question. I left Vietnam when I was thirteen years old, but I do know some basic facts about Vietnam's four-thousand-year history. The Vietnamese mind has been deeply influenced by Taoist, Confucian, and Buddhist concepts. All three are important. The main Taoist idea is harmony. Confucianism is concerned about social structure. Buddhists believe in reincarnation. These principles form the foundation of Vietnamese traditions, customs, and manners. Even though Vietnam was dominated by the Chinese for a thousand years and by the French for a hundred years, the Vietnamese people still kept their own social system and cultural values. They enriched their culture with new ideas without sacrificing their own traditions. For example, the Vietnamese people had designed a distinctive system of writing, but after coming into contact with Western civilization in the nineteenth century, they adopted a new writing system based on the Roman alphabet. But the grammar and vocabulary of the language remain the same.

Living in America, however, has changed some Vietnamese points of view because we are a highly adaptable people. We are adopting both the good and bad sides of American culture. On the one hand, we are adopting a new, liberal way of living. For example, women are supposed to have rights equal to those of men in America; there is supposed to be no sexual or age hierarchy among Americans. Members of a family are more open in their relationships with one another. Individuals are independent and make friends with all kinds of people, regardless of their social status. On the other hand, we have also adopted some of the materialism of America. We go to discotheques, smoke cigarettes, and watch harmful movies. In some families, husbands and wives no longer respect each other.

As for me, I think I still have a strong sense of being Vietnamese. I try to cultivate Vietnamese culture by reading and writing Vietnamese. When I have a family, I will teach my children whatever Vietnamese philosophy and way of life that I know. I will teach them to speak, maybe even to write, the Vietnamese language so that they will understand Vietnamese traditions. I hope all the Vietnamese in the United States and elsewhere in the world will do the same thing to maintain our language and culture.

Right now, like many other young Vietnamese, I am trying my best to do well in school. I feel lucky to have an opportunity to pursue higher education, so I am taking advantage of that. I shall never forget that millions of people are being victimized by the Communists in Vietnam. I want to be a voice for those whose basic human rights are not respected by the Communist regime. I shall inform the world that many people are suffering in so-called re-education camps, which are in fact concentration camps. When Vietnam is no longer ruled by Communists, I shall return to my country and use my knowledge and skills to help reconstruct it.

CHAPTER FOURTEEN

How It Feels to Be an Asian American

The author left Saigon with her family on April 29, 1975, on a U.S. helicopter that flew them to a dock where they boarded an American ship when she was four years old. Her family belongs to the Chru ethnic group—one of several dozen mountain-dwelling ethnic groups that the French colonial government called collectively "Montagnards." The U.S. Army's Special Forces, formed in 1952 and commonly known as the "Green Berets," recruited many Montagnards into Civilian Irregular Defense Groups to fight against North Vietnamese and Viet Cong forces. The author does not indicate in what capacity her father worked for the U.S. government. However, the fact that she was born in Saigon would seem to indicate that the United States also employed some Montagnards in the cities. The narrator keeps her Chru heritage alive by trying to live as close to nature as possible even in America. Despite the family's rushed departure, her father remembered to take along the seeds of various plants that grow in Vietnam and he planted these fruits and vegetables in his backyard after the family arrived in the United States. The family also raised all kinds of animals. The author, who obviously has learned to identify with other Asian Americans, as well as other peoples of color, wrote this piece in 1989.

What is it like to be an Asian American? How do Asian Americans feel and live? These questions are often asked of me. I tell people that an Asian American is an Asian immigrant or an American-born person of Asian ancestry who is accustomed to America's lifestyle yet proudly preserves his or her ethnic culture. Like all other ethnic groups, Asian Americans have advantages and disadvantages. Some advantages are our beautiful customs and traditions, our pride in our uniqueness, broader views about society, and a sense of belonging to two cultures. Disadvantages include discrimination, confusion over our identity, and the hardships involved in making transitions and adaptations to life in America. As an Asian American, I understand both the advantages and disadvantages.

When I look back at my early childhood, I recall some events in my homeland. I was born in Saigon in 1971. My family later moved to a city in the northern part of South Vietnam. I remember the mountains and dirt roads as we traveled there from Saigon. I also remember the beautiful Chru tribe my father belonged to. My father, his parents, and his brothers and sisters were raised in the mountains of central Vietnam. Since the Chru still live and strive in that environment, they are very close to nature. They live simple, nonmaterialistic lives. Even though I was only four years old when we left Saigon, I can still remember the jungles and mountains where my father grew up. I sat by anthills and played with the ants all day. I also loved catching snakes, birds, and fish. Because of my love for the jungle, my father called me "Shabo," jungle boy, even though I was a girl. One of my father's friends told me I was a true daughter of the mountains. To this day, I love animals and nature passionately.

On April 29, 1975, a date that forever changed my family's history, Saigon was on the verge of collapsing as Communist troops assaulted the city. That morning, when we heard the news, my family quickly packed our passports, family papers, photographs, and a few sentimental family souvenirs. My maternal grandmother, grandaunt, granduncle, and his children, however, refused to leave. They wanted to stay behind to take care of our home and my great grandmother, who was too fragile to travel. As we left our house and loved ones, we all cried for fear of not seeing each other again. We had barely two hundred dollars to take with us. My parents, sister, brother, paternal grandmother, uncle, aunt, twenty cousins, and I rushed to the airport on foot. I can still recall my little two-month-old sister clinging to my mother's blouse as we ran toward the airport. Hundreds of other people were also making their way there; we all worried about being shot or killed. I still remember the tears in people's eyes. There were many scenes of blood and chaos along the way. This is all I can remember about the evacuation. The other details that follow are based on stories that my parents told me.

When we arrived at the airport, we lined up to get on an American helicopter. Since my father had worked for the American government, the names of his blood relatives were all on the passengers' lists. However, some of my cousins' names were not on the list. The soldiers told my father that we had to leave them behind because they were not my father's blood relatives. Even though my father begged and begged the soldiers, they would not relent. As the helicopters were about to leave, one of my older cousins told us to go ahead without them. He said not to worry because we would all see each other again in America. As we boarded the helicopter, we felt guilty and sorrowful, but we had no choice. We all knew we had told ourselves a lie in order to cover up our fears, sorrow, and pain. My father was certain that this would be the last time we would see our relatives and that we would never see the mountains, jungles, animals, and birds of my homeland again.

As the helicopter we were on took off, we saw hundreds of people shoving to get on the other helicopters. Some helicopters that had too many people collapsed. Our helicopter flew to a dock. We got out and climbed up a ship by a rope ladder that swayed. My mother told me that I almost fell off but luckily an American soldier grabbed me. My father was worried that my grandmother would also fall because she was eighty years old and very frail, but she managed to make it. On the ship, some people tried to steal other people's possessions. Everyone was scared of our uncertain future. My mother had only a few bottles of milk to feed my baby sister, so she had to ration the milk. Fortunately, a kind American soldier found more milk for my sister. Had we not reached Guam after sailing for a little more than a week, my sister would have died. We stayed in a camp in Guam for a week, where we had medical check-ups and immunization shots. The surroundings of the camp were filthy. The outdoor toilets smelled terrible as they filled up with urine. I was shocked when my mother told me years later about the unsanitary conditions there.

When my family arrived in the United States, we felt joyful to be alive and safe, because some people who had come with us on the journey died en route. We settled in Santa Barbara, California, where my parents applied for and received social security cards that would allow them to work. Some of my relatives decided to go their separate ways so that we could find jobs more easily. Only my parents, brother, sister, grandmother, and two of my cousins and I remained in Santa Barbara, where the Catholic Church had found a cheap house for us. The first week was really difficult. We did not know where any place was and we could not speak English. Fortunately, only a week after we arrived in Santa Barbara the government offered my father a job, which he accepted immediately. However, because that job did not give us enough money to buy food and pay for other expenses, my father found a second job at a pizza parlor. Every night, he cleaned the whole facility. This was a job that made my father feel ashamed and dishonored. I still remember my father coming home late at night wearing his uniform and bringing leftover pizza for our dinner. We survived on the leftover pizza because we did not have enough money to buy all the food we needed. My mother, too, worked very hard to earn money as a cook and seamstress. My parents each worked two shifts, one in the daytime and one at night, in order to provide their children with a decent life in America.

During this transitional period, I had a lot of emotional problems. I went to a school that had very few Asians. I was the only Asian girl in the first grade and felt very alienated and different from everyone else because of my looks, language, and lack of familiarity with everything. I did not know English, so some of the children teased me. They ridiculed me not only because of my accent but because of my culture as well. They made fun of how my family lived, ate, and socialized. In third grade, one of the boys told everybody that I ate dog meat. When I heard this, I cried all day. Some of the teachers were not sympathetic toward me, either. One thought I was deaf or mute because I could not understand what she said in English. I thought the teachers must be right, so I considered myself inferior to my classmates. I became quiet and reserved. I found it difficult to talk and open up to people, even to my parents. I constantly feared that if I talked, people were going to mock me. So I remained silent, shy, and embarrassed. Every day I asked God why he had not made me White. As I grew up, I realized it was terrible to think of myself that way, but children are very self-conscious about what others think of and say about them.

During my elementary school years, I developed a deep hatred toward society. Why must people be so prejudiced and cruel? I longed to go back to my homeland. Even though I remembered it only vaguely, I still had a deep desire to go back there to live close to nature. My father was correct in naming me Shabo. I belong in the mountains, not in a modern society. My father and I raised animals and cultivated plants in our backyard to enable us to feel more at home. We raised chickens, ducks, pheasants, quails, cockatiels, parakeets, and pigeons. We also had a pond for fish. We planted orange, lime, plum, and pear trees, as well as many vegetables. My father and I dreamed of owning a farm someday.

Another problem I encountered was the difference between the Vietnamese and American lifestyles. Being raised in a strict Asian family, I found it hard to fit into America's liberal society. My parents were shocked at the way American parents raise their children, giving them far more freedom and rights than parents in Asia do. My parents never let me have a say in any family discussions. If I talked back to them, I was punished. I felt it was unfair that my American classmates could get away with behavior for which I would be punished. I envied their independence. My parents never allowed me to spend a night at a friend's house or to associate with children of the opposite sex. Not only were my parents overly protective of me, they also always expected me to be the best student in my class all the way through high school. These strict rules were barriers that made it difficult for me to make friends with Americans whose customs were so different. Therefore, the few friends I had were Asians.

I often felt confused and bewildered. As I grew older, I had to fight hard against becoming too Americanized because I did not want to become materialistic and modern. Despite my efforts, I began losing my Vietnamese and Chru cultures. The worst thing was that I did not see this transformation in myself until I reached junior high school when I realized I could neither read nor write a correct sentence in Vietnamese. Also, I was so busy with schoolwork and a part-time job that I did not realize I was becoming less spiritual. All I cared about was getting good grades and bringing money home to help my parents.

My parents also had difficulty adapting to American society because the language, customs, and way of thinking in the United States are so different. It was especially hard for my mother, who had to learn English while taking care of the children when my father was at work. Even though her English was poor, she still had to take us to doctors' appointments and go grocery shopping. Both my parents' ability to survive amazed me.

It was not until eleventh grade that a series of events enabled me to see how I was losing my identity and becoming too materialistic. First, as I spent less time with my birds and plants, some of them became very sick. Because of my irresponsibility, Polly, one of my birds, died. I suddenly realized that if I did not take care of my own soul, I, too, might die. After Polly's death, I tried harder to live closer to nature and to preserve my culture by asking my parents questions.

A second influential event was the death of my grandmother, who used to tell me stories of my ancestors and homeland. But by the time I was in junior high school, she stopped telling me these stories, I assumed, because she did not want to feel the sorrow of being so far away from her homeland. After she died, I realized I had taken her for granted and that it was more likely that she had stopped telling me stories because I had been indifferent to them. How could I have been so insensitive? Not only did I lose a wonderful grandmother but also a chance to learn about my cultural identity.

Then, my father died in early 1989—an event that had a huge impact in changing my attitudes. He had spent his whole life dedicated to giving my sister, brother, and me a better life. Not only did he work hard, but he also longed to go back home. He missed my grandmother after her death, as well as the jungles and mountains. Whenever he told me about our homeland, he felt so homesick that he became depressed. It seems that having lost the love of life, my father also lost the will to live. As I look back, I can feel the pain and suffering that my father went through. Another cause of my father's sorrows was the changes he saw in our family. His heart was saddened by the fact that his children were becoming Americanized. We were slowly losing our heritage as we were surrounded by American customs so different from ours. His feelings were similar to those of other Asian parents who see their children losing their identities. My father, however, was comforted by the fact that I was trying my best to preserve my culture. I took better care of my animals and stayed close to nature. I looked at our family albums and asked my parents questions.

For the first two weeks after my father's death, I was in a state of shock, pain, and guilt. I could not believe that my father, the man who loved us so much and dedicated his life to keeping us alive, was no longer with me. I felt tremendously guilty because I had not seen the pain and homesickness he endured. As I look back, I realized, once again, as I did after my grandmother's death, that I had been insensitive and ignorant. How I wish I could have spent more with my father in order to learn about Chru and Vietnamese cultures. I should have spent less time at work and in school. It is so sad that we do not realize how much we would miss someone until after he or she is gone. Now there is a burning hole in my soul that can never be filled. I am in a never-ending search to find ways to bridge the chasm between my lost former identity and me. Because of these losses, I have finally stopped degenerating and am trying to rebuild my identity and preserve my heritage. I now ask my mother many questions about our family history. I am also trying to learn to read and write Vietnamese.

I am proud to be a Chru-Vietnamese. Living in America, I am also an Asian American. Being Asian American does not mean we have to lose the Asian parts of our identity. I am trying to be a person with a broader view, open to the loftier parts of Chru, Vietnamese, and American cultures. I believe that people with a knowledge of different ways of life are more adaptable and can live more easily in different societies. Another advantage that such people have is that they are more sensitive about other people's feelings. Because of all the prejudice and discrimination I have experienced, I know what it feels like to be different and to have xenophobes mock me. I know what it feels like when someone calls another person "fresh off the boat,"

"Chink," "China girl," "boat person," or "dog eater." But these cruelties have also enriched me: I can understand and sympathize with people who are different from the majority group in society. I am always willing to lend a hand to aliens, strangers, people who are different. I would never judge or classify a person based on his or her race, creed, or other traits. The beauty of our world comes from the differences, as well as the uniqueness, that people of different cultures possess.

I have finally learned to think of my life as beautiful because I am the bearer of three cultures. I cook and eat American and Vietnamese food, while my love of plants and animals reflects my Chru heritage. I listen to some of the old folk songs and practice some of the old customs, such as paying respect to our ancestors by cooking special food and preparing a special dinner table for them. During this ceremony, we light candles and pray to honor our ancestors. I am proud that I can speak more than one language. While living in America, I have also learned to associate with people of all races.

It was Mrs. T., a Nisei [second-generation Japanese American] woman, who first helped me appreciate the advantages I enjoy as a multicultural person. Telling me about her own life, she helped me realize that I am not the only person who has experienced alienation and injustice. Despite the obstacles she faced, Mrs. T. finished college with a BA in English. She has a respectable career as a freelance writer. She told me that anybody—Asian, Black, or White—can overcome injustice. She also taught me to be proud of myself and never to be ashamed of my culture or anything else about me. She regrets that she does not know Japanese. During her childhood, her parents did not teach her the language because they were afraid she would be looked down on if she spoke Japanese. Not only do Asian Americans face obstacles but so do other minority ethnic groups, such as Hispanic Americans and African Americans. By learning about our own cultural origins, as well as those of others, we can better understand both ourselves and them.

While writing this paper, many emotions and feelings that I had forgotten or even assumed had never existed were aroused. This assignment enabled me to better understand myself, my heritage, the homeland I left, and the society I live in today.

CHAPTER FIFTEEN

Integrity through Change

The author left Saigon with her family in a U.S. helicopter that delivered them to a U.S. Navy ship on April 30, 1975, when she was thirteen years old. Her mother had worked for the U.S. Air Force for twelve years; that connection was what qualified the family for evacuation. Part of this narrative is based on diary entries and reveals a little-known fact: after the runways at Tan Son Nhut Airport were damaged, the International Control Commission, formed in 1954 to monitor events in Vietnam, managed to negotiate with the Communist forces that were poised to enter the capital to allow the Americans a few hours to lift out, by helicopter, all the people still waiting at the airport who could no longer be evacuated by fixed-wing aircraft. Her family, whose members were Buddhists, left North Vietnam, where her grandfather had been a mandarin (a government official), in 1954 following the signing of the Geneva Accords. The author explains that because of her grandfather's occupation and social status, she understood the key elements of Vietnamese culture clearly and could pinpoint the differences between Vietnamese culture and Communism. She wrote this family history in 1980 when she was a seventeen-year-old freshman. It is apparent that she was very mature for her age.

The story of my family is a classic example of a family affected by the destructive forces of war and a series of historical events that undermined a stable family structure. Although my family's origins reflect the importance of preserving Vietnamese culture, the lives of its members show the influence of Western culture on a people forced to leave their homeland.

My family originated in North Vietnam. We were landowners who possessed farmland and produced agricultural goods. Tenant farmers worked our land. My grandparents also owned other kinds of property. My grandfather was a city magistrate—a mandarin in the king's court. He and some of our other relatives were active in making local government decisions. Their status influenced the values of our family, which were passed down from generation to generation. We were greatly influenced by Confucian values that imbued us with a sense of elitism because of our high social position. Confucianism, a philosophy that originated in China, defined the roles and mutual expectations of various members of society with the goal of maintaining harmony and providing guidelines for social interactions. It filtered into other countries in Asia; Vietnam was one of the countries greatly influenced by Confucianism, which supported a strict social stratification of society, in which people in the upper classes were revered and respected. These ideas persist among many Vietnamese.

Communism, in contrast, is an ideology that calls for the eradication of social stratification. It attempts to dissolve class differences and to achieve equality of classes and sexes. Because the values and expectations of Vietnamese families had been largely determined by the historical and cultural influences of Confucianism and Buddhism, Communism posed a definite threat to the ideas that formed the foundation of our value system. However, more than the fact that we disagreed with Communist ideology, survival was a concern that superseded all other considerations during a time in a war when revolution was imminent. Survival was the impetus that made us decide to leave our homeland.

My family was a typical extended family in Vietnam. It was composed of my grandmother, my mother, my uncle, two aunts, my brother, two cousins, and me. All of us lived in a big house under the same roof. My grandmother did not work; she devoted most of her time to Buddhist temples, where she did humanitarian work. My older aunt, V., and my uncle, T., worked part time. Aunt V. majored in Chinese linguistics and philosophy in college, Uncle T. majored in sociology, while my younger aunt, T., majored in law. My family's income came primarily from my mother's salary. She worked for the U.S. Air Force for twelve years as an office personnel manager. That was a high position for a Vietnamese woman. Her salary was about two hundred U.S. dollars a month. When changed into Vietnamese piasters, that was a lot of money. My brother and I went to junior high school while my two cousins went to elementary school.

As my grandfather was a mandarin, all of us were exposed to Vietnamese literature and customs. My mother worked all the time so I was mostly influenced by my uncle and aunts—especially my aunts. Aunt T., who was studying law, always talked about international and domestic legal issues. Aunt V., meanwhile, taught me the philosophy of life and told me how people should behave. From them, I learned a lot about how to treat people and to be aware of those around me. Sometimes we talked about my mother's life—how she had met my father and how bad my father was. She left him when I was only one year old; as a result, the other members of my family depended heavily on her. I respected my mother a lot even though she was not close to me. I have always imitated her and have a strong personality as a woman. With my aunts and my mother as my role models, I am an active, involved, and outspoken individual.

In Vietnam, I had many friends from school and from my Buddhist Girl Scouts troop. My teachers loved me very much because I was their best student in class. The values and philosophy I learned in school have shaped my life, my attitudes, and my future. The culture and traditions of my native land are deeply ingrained in me. Being Vietnamese means I must follow the ideologies, values, and beliefs that have persisted for thousands of years, upon which the entire history and social and familial structures of Vietnam are based.

Two main factors forced my family to leave Vietnam. First, as the North Vietnamese invaded more and more South Vietnamese territory, we knew that my mother, who had worked for the Americans for twelve years, would be the first person in our family to be killed because the Communists fiercely hated the United States and anyone associated with that country. If my mother died, then my family would live a nightmare and my brother and I would become orphans—both fatherless and motherless. Second, most of my family had been born in North Vietnam. We had moved to the South in 1954 to get away from the Communist regime in the North. My family, a prosperous family, knew what life would be like under Communism. We feared that the Communists might kill our whole family in revenge because we had moved to the South back in 1954. My mother decided that our family should go to the United States, while my two cousins would remain in Vietnam with their mother and stepfather. The following paragraphs are from the diary I kept, which tells about my adventures as we escaped to America.

April 27, 1975

Boom! Boom! My house was reverberating. It was about 9:00 P.M. Darkness and fear overwhelmed the whole city of Saigon. The news kept coming that the North Vietnamese and their allies, the Viet Cong, were coming closer and closer to the capital. They started shelling the city. Everybody ran around, not knowing what to do.

Everyone wanted to find a way to escape from Saigon. American officials were providing airplanes and ships to evacuate those Vietnamese who had been affiliated with them or with American businesses. But not many people had American connections, so they ran to the harbor and just jumped on any ship they saw. My family was also searching for a way to leave. My mother managed to obtain passports and exit permits for us. We packed our suitcases although we did not know what to bring. We could not say goodbye to our friends and relatives because we feared that if we failed to escape, they might report us to the Communists when the latter captured Saigon in order to curry favor with the new rulers. This entire day has been filled with terror and chaos.

April 28, 1975

When we arrived at Tan Son Nhut, about eight thousand people were jammed into that small airport. We were waiting for our passport numbers to be called when suddenly, Boom! Boom! again. Everyone ran into the airport's hangars. The building into which my family ran was shaking, the windows were cracking, and glass was falling on the floor. We sat under a big table and prayed to Buddha. Some helicopters caught fire when bombs dropped on them. People cried with frustration as they thought the Americans would leave all of us behind. Some impatient people left the airport to return to their homes. Around 7:30 P.M., the bombing stopped. People spread out blankets in what little space was available and ate the food they had brought with them. Everyone stayed up through the night with the hope that the Americans would take all of us. My grandmother, who had come to the airport with us simply to wish us bon voyage, ended up leaving with us because she could not return home with bombs falling.

April 29, 1975

It rained. Perhaps Buddha was crying with us. Everybody was desperate because there were no signs of when the Americans would evacuate us. More people returned to their homes. Fortunately for us, an organization called the International Control Commission reached an agreement with the Communists to allow the Americans a few hours to pick up all the people at the airport. When we heard that news, everyone was happy and hastily got in line to board the helicopters.

Each person was allowed to bring only two pieces of clothing and nothing else so that the helicopters could take more people.

April 30, 1975

The helicopters delivered people to several big U.S. Navy ships. About 11:00 A.M., my aunt turned on the radio. The news said that our government had given up and now the Viet Cong and North Vietnamese had taken over. We were shocked. Many people cried. There was no longer any hope that we might return to our homeland. Living on the navy ship was to live like animals. People fought for space on the ship, the food was terrible, and the toilet was just three pieces of wood hanging over the edge of the ship. Some people fell through the hole in the toilet into the sea.

May 5, 1975

We have landed in Subic Bay, an American naval station in the Philippines. We felt much relief as the living conditions on land were much better than at sea. The food tasted good but we had to wait in long lines for it. After spending two days at Subic Bay, we flew to Guam where the climate was very hot. My mother was busily taking care of the paperwork so our family could go to a camp on the U.S. mainland.

After three days in Guam, we flew to Fort Chaffee in Arkansas. We lived in a barrack. Every day we had three meals and went to a learning center to learn English. Life in that camp was like a vacation. We were relaxed with nothing to do. We lived at Fort Chaffee for three months. Then a Lutheran church in Washington, D.C., sponsored us. But we could not bear the freezing snow in the winter, so we moved to San Francisco after living in Washington, D.C., for only a year.

We have lived in San Francisco ever since. My grandmother, who is now sixty-six years old, is living on social security payments. She spends her time in Buddhist temples and in Chinatown shopping and visiting friends. My mother is now forty-four years old and working as a head teller in a bank. My uncle is twenty-eight years old and working as an electronics technician in San Jose. He will marry Miss B. next month. They had been together for four years before they got separated in 1975. He waited for five years for her to come to the United States. She escaped with her brothers and sisters as "boat people." Aunt V. is thirty-eight years old, married, and has two kids. Her family is living with us. She stays home to take care of her children. My brother is nineteen and is a freshman at San Francisco State University. I am seventeen and a freshman at the University of California.

My family has made the transition from North Vietnam to South Vietnam and then to the United States. We hope the United States is the last place in which we make our home. Members of my family feel quite settled and we are satisfied with our lives. In time, my other aunt will also marry, and my brother and I will finish college and have our own families, too. Although we are comfortable in our new home, still our hearts yearn to return to our homeland—a place that presently exists only in our imagination. Historical events and the present government in Vietnam have changed my country enormously. It is no longer the country we remember. So, for now, we must accept America as our home.

My experiences with American people have been largely influenced by the situations in which I have encountered them. I have come to see that people tend to be more influenced by the circumstances in which they find themselves than by some inner drive. It seems that individuals are greatly influenced by their environment and act according to its constraints.

In Vietnam, my first contact with Americans occurred in 1965 when I met Jean and Betty who had come to Vietnam as Baptist missionaries. They became close friends with my mother and aunts. Jean and Betty taught my mother and aunts English; in return, my mother and aunts taught them Vietnamese. I remember that they took my family out to eat several times. They were lovable people. In 1966, another aunt of mine, M., married Bill, an American soldier. They now live in Maryland. Because I had considerable contact with Americans even before I left Vietnam, the American lifestyle—movies, music, and clothing—has influenced me quite a lot.

While I was still living in Vietnam, I developed a positive image of Americans at school, through watching television, and reading newspapers. People in South Vietnam regarded America as the most powerful country in the world. In addition to supporting democracy in South Vietnam, Americans supplied food for the poor, so we thought of the United States as a benevolent ally. However, the American involvement also created an unequal relationship in which Vietnamese felt indebted to the United States. That worked at times to the detriment of South Vietnam. Although American weapons were very modern and powerful, in the end the Americans failed to win the war because they did not know how to fight highly motivated guerrillas. Many antiwar organizations in the United States, eager to end the war in any way possible, in effect became partners with the Viet Cong, which led to the collapse of the South Vietnamese government. War is a most ugly phenomenon that brings out the worst in people. No one wins a war; all are victimized by its devastation. War affects people's personalities in an insidious way: as fear turns inward, it destroys the sense that people have of themselves. War distorts interactions between people in an unhealthy way.

Even though South Vietnam received a great deal of help from the United States, I would have to say that America failed in its attempt to help our country. Americans weakened and almost destroyed the entire younger generation. They introduced drugs such as marijuana and heroin and many young Vietnamese became addicts. Wherever Americans went, prostitution always appeared, resulting in a large number of mixed-blood orphans, abandoned by both their fathers and mothers. Americans also ruined the Vietnamese economy because it became too heavily dependent on American dollars. After the GIs left Vietnam, prostitutes remained, trapped in a cycle of heroin addiction and poverty. Homeless orphans roamed the streets. There was also a large number of unemployed citizens.

In 1975, I felt thankful to Americans for helping my family get out of Vietnam and start a new life. But I cannot appreciate America fully because this atonement is not enough compared with all the suffering that Americans had caused the Vietnamese who now live under Communism. My image of America as a superior, benevolent, and grandiose nation has disappeared. Despite its military power, the United States could not defeat the much smaller army of North Vietnam. Though some Americans are indeed benevolent, many think of themselves first and do not care about other people. Americans may be grandiose in terms of their physical appearance, but often their minds are selfish and immature. However, I *have* met many nice Americans who impressed me with their kindness and openness. As I juggled these different images, I began to realize that American society contains a great variety of people with many different perspectives on life. Not only that, but there are many races and nationalities in the United States.

Perhaps my attitude toward America is too negative. In my opinion, American morality has declined because America does not have a stable culture. Rather, it is made up of many different cultures. The strength of America lies predominantly in its technological and economic achievements, but capitalism's emphasis on profit-making has resulted in avarice. People judge each other according to how much money they have. Although wealth can reflect one's status in society, it does not indicate one's true personality. Americans tend to focus on money-making more than on moral development.

I came to the United States when I was thirteen years old. I have lived here for almost five years now and will soon become an American citizen. However, because of my moral and cultural heritage, I will still consider myself a Vietnamese and not a Vietnamese American. Vietnamese culture is so deeply ingrained in me that I do not think I can be Americanized. There are many Vietnamese cultural values I will try to preserve. At the beginning of Vietnamese history, two beings, Lac Long Quan from the "dragon lineage" and Au Co from the "fairy lineage" became the founders of Vietnam. The dragon and fairy have been national symbols in Vietnam for thousands of years. The dragon represents a grand, imperious force, undefeatable perseverance, and ingenious talent. The fairy represents grace, beauty, freshness, delicacy, gentleness, and vivaciousness. Those two beings symbolize a distinctive Vietnamese philosophy—to live powerfully and gracefully. Our culture points to the union of two contrasting elements: father and mother, yin and yang, high and low.

I believe that the family is the best school for educating the young and is the best nursing home for elders. The family is also a court in which a small group of people can mediate their differences. The family is a fundamental institution in Vietnamese society. For foreigners to destroy Vietnamese society, they must first destroy the family. All Vietnamese have been taught to respect their parents, elders, and teachers, and to protect their younger brothers and sisters and never fight with them. Vietnamese children learn to listen to, instead of talking back to, their elders. They should be polite to everybody and never violate the laws that might disgrace a family's reputation. These beliefs form the core of my identity. For an ideology to persist, it must be lived and not merely remembered. I must therefore follow the fundamental values of my country in every respect of my life if I am to retain my identity as a Vietnamese and to maintain my integrity as an individual.

After coming to the United States, I have gone through many transitions, confronting culture shock and language differences. It took me quite a while to adjust to the new society. I am pursuing my academic career with diligence and determination. I am majoring in electronic engineering, a major that enrolls only a small number of women. My mother and other members of my family place no demands on me with regard to what major I should choose. All they want is that I have a successful professional career.

I am the one who must fulfill my family's dreams for a variety of reasons. My brother has been handicapped since he was one year old. He had polio in his leg. At the time he was afflicted, medical treatment for polio was still in its developmental stage. He thinks he is different from ordinary people because of his physical appearance; his handicap has affected his perception of the world. He has many dreams but he makes little effort to work toward his goals. Neither my aunts nor my uncle had a chance to finish their college education. They were in their third and fourth years of college when the events of 1975 dashed their hopes. They feel too depressed to start over again in this country. Besides, they have to work to support themselves instead of depending on my mother's earnings as they had done in the past. So, I am the one who must fulfill my family's hopes by finishing college. Although many women are discouraged from majoring in engineering because of its difficult courses, engineering is a worthwhile major: after four years of study, we can earn a high income. Sometimes I worry that I may not be able to pursue my engineering major because I am only seventeen years old and my preparation in some technical areas is very weak. If my ability is not suited to engineering, then I shall study law.

The opportunities afforded me in this country are vastly different from those in my homeland. Whatever choices and commitments I make in order to benefit from these opportunities must take into consideration some facts related to my ethnicity. I am a Third World woman in a predominantly White, male-dominated society. I must contend with language differences. I will face racism, both personal and institutionalized. I must fight such discrimination throughout my professional career. In addition to these obstacles, I must satisfy the desires and expectations of my family, particularly my mother. It is important to me to maintain my "Vietnameseness," but at the same time, I must succeed in American society. This is true for most immigrants and it necessitates that we, as individuals and as ethnic minorities with distinct cultural backgrounds, must make certain compromises if we wish to succeed in America.

CHAPTER SIXTEEN

A Place to Call Home

The author and her family left Saigon on April 30, 1975, on a boat belonging to the South Vietnamese Navy commanded by one of her father's friends when she was eight years old. Like the author's family, about half of the people who fled Saigon were not evacuated by U.S. aircraft, as commonly assumed. Rather, they made their own way on whatever boats were available to ships of the U.S. Seventh Fleet anchored in the South China Sea. This account tells a three-generational story about a family of mixed Chinese and Vietnamese ancestry. The narrator's poverty-stricken grandfather was orphaned at age six in China. His grandmother raised him until he was fourteen and then sent him to live with his aunt in Vietnam. He worked as a coolie to put himself through school. His wife died young, leaving him with six motherless children to raise. Despite these hardships, all these children, including the author's mother, became medical professionals. Both the author's parents were doctors. They, as well as the author's aunts, managed with great effort to reestablish themselves in their professions in the United States. Perhaps for that reason, the author, unlike many of the other narrators, did not express a desire to return to Vietnam when she wrote this family history in 1988.

When Americans look at Asians, they probably do not notice much except that our skin is yellow and our eyes are slanted. They may see us as friends or competitors. Taking a closer look, they may realize that behind every Asian American there is a story. If Americans perceive us as competitors, perhaps they realize that what makes Asians strong are the very hardships we have experienced and the close family ties that keep us together, give us support, and help us survive.

Born in 1967 in Saigon, South Vietnam, I am one of three children born to two doctors. I have been living in the United States for almost thirteen years and I consider America my home. That does not mean that I am not proud of my origins because I am. I am more than proud to tell anybody who asks that I am three-eighths Chinese and five-eighths Vietnamese. Where did I come from? How did I get here? Although thousands of refugees have arrived in the United States since 1975, we each have our own story to tell.

When South Vietnam fell to the Communists, I was only eight years old. I remember being sent home from school several times in the spring of 1975 because of the bombings. I remember the awful loud noises the bombs made and the screams of people running for cover. At home, we all ran into the cellar and sat under a long wooden table. We waited and prayed. The war had less of an impact on me than on other members of my family because I was still too young to understand much. I even thought it was exciting to rush out of school with my classmates, to visit fortune-tellers to find out what our future would be, and for our family to get together to talk about whether we should leave South Vietnam. Little did I understand that the war was killing thousands of people. Only on the day that Saigon was captured by the Communists did my family hastily pack up to leave. To a little girl, that still did not mean much. I was only dimly aware that I might never see my friends again and I had few possessions to leave behind. To the adults in my family, however, Vietnam was their homeland, where most of them were born, grew up, married, and established families. Vietnam was their life—the place where they had struggled hard and accomplished much.

To my maternal grandfather, Vietnam was the place where he received an education. Born in the city of Amoy (Xiamen) in Fukien (Fujian) Province, China in 1896, he was one of three children. His parents died when he was only six and he went to live with his grandmother until he was fourteen. She then sent him to live with his mother's sister who was in Vietnam. Working as a coolie, he sent most of his meager earnings to his grandmother to thank her for all the years she had taken care of him. While working, he also went to a school that was a mile from where he lived. School was hard because he had difficulty learning Vietnamese. His classmates teased him because he wore his hair in a queue as the ruling Qing dynasty required all Chinese men to do. Whatever little money he could save, he spent on books. In time, he learned both Vietnamese and French through self-study.

He married my grandmother when he was thirty. She was the youngest of three children. Her parents passed away when she was nineteen, so she went to live with her sister who was married to a man of wealth. Unlike some rich men, he did not look down on others; instead, he gladly helped those less fortunate than himself. He took his wife's younger sister in with open arms. However, his mother and older sister did not like having an extra mouth to feed. So, he opened a small shop where his sister-in-law could earn a living sewing and altering clothes. It was in this shop that my grandfather met my grandmother. When she was twenty-three, they got married. Their love for each other helped them overcome hardships. According to my grandfather, those were the best years of their lives. Tragically, she died at age thirty-five giving birth to their seventh child, who also died.

Once again, my grandfather was on his own. This time, however, his struggles were even more difficult because he now had six children to take care of all by himself. At that time, my grandfather was not yet successful in his business dealings. How was he going to manage? Fortunately, his sister-in-law and her generous husband took him and all his children into their home. The couple had no children, so they treated the children as their own. My grandfather told the children to make the best of the opportunities offered them. In time, the eldest daughter, my aunt, completed her education and became a pharmacist, opening her own pharmacy in Saigon. My grandfather was more than proud. He helped his daughter manage the pharmacy and it flourished. His other children also eventually became professionals: in addition to my aunt, the pharmacist, three of her siblings, including my mother, became doctors, one a chemist, and one a radiologist. Although my grandfather still loved China, Vietnam had become his home. It was here that his wife was buried; it was here that his children grew up and thrived.

My mother thought of Vietnam as her home because she was born and went to school there. She fought against many odds to become a doctor. She remembers her struggles—how hard she had to study, how poor she was, and how her schoolmates teased her because she was not a full-blooded Vietnamese. Despite all the hardship, she was always the top student in her class. She graduated from the School of Medicine in Vietnam, where she met my father and married him. When she received her medical degree, she opened her own clinic in Saigon.

My father was the eldest of five children in a lower-middle-class family. When he was young, his parents sent him to live with some friends of the family because their own house was far away from any school. Even though he lived at the house of his parents' friends, he still had to walk miles a day to get to school. He remembers that his lunch consisted of rice and fish sauce. At night, when his hosts turned off the kerosene lamps and went to bed, he went outside to study under the faint light of street lamps. Through years of hard work, he also managed to graduate from the School of Medicine. He practiced medicine in Saigon as well.

My family found it very difficult to decide whether to leave Vietnam in 1975. If we left we would be free from Communist oppression, but where would we go? Would we survive a journey that might be filled with horrors and dangers? Would we be able to remain together as a family? The older members of my family were still pondering these questions when April 30, 1975, dawned. On that day that changed our lives, South Vietnam surrendered to North Vietnam. We realized that should we stay, life would never be the same again. Even if we did not know what the future might hold, we knew it would still be better than if we stayed. As educated professionals, my parents and aunts and uncles might all be killed.

With a few suitcases containing some clothing and old photographs, we left our house in two cars and headed to the port. As we neared the dock, we saw that the ship we had hoped to catch was already heading out to sea. Luckily, there was a little Vietnamese Navy boat commanded by one of my father's friends, which took us out to the big ship. With about two hundred and fifty people on board, the conditions on the ship were terrible. People threw up all around me—*that* I definitely remember clearly. Some people even died. We sustained ourselves by eating dry noodles.

After three or four days at sea, an American ship rescued us. I remember seeing a sailor throw out a twinelike ladder for people from another boat to climb up on. My mother and aunt whispered to each other in fright as some people fell off into the sea, which took their lives. Would the same thing happen to my grandfather and grandaunt who were old and weak? Fortunately, as the American ship came closer to our boat, it let down a gangplank, which was a lot easier to climb onto. Sighing with relief, we boarded the big ship, where we stayed for three or four days. I remember we had to line up to get food and drinks. I did not mind doing that but I was horrified by the fact that men and women had to take showers in the same area with only a flimsy curtain separating them. The toilets were just boards placed on the side of the ship, where the waste simply dropped into the sea. We slept on the bare decks holding on tightly to our belongings.

We arrived at Subic Bay in the Philippines where we stayed for two months. It was there that I learned my first few words of English and a little bit about American culture. My grandfather and grandaunt were not happy at all. What helped ease their anxieties were their fellow refugees. The old folks got together to talk about their lives in Vietnam—a source of entertainment as well as spiritual comfort.

From Subic Bay we went to Guam, where we learned more English. An event that took place there made me realize that even among our own people there was jealousy and dishonesty. I remember lying on my cot as a robber crawled from under one cot to the next. Seeing a small knife in his hand, I dared not scream. When he got under my mother's cot, he grabbed her purse. She woke up screaming while holding on to her purse. My uncle leaped out of his cot and chased him off with a stick. Even as an eight-year-old, I asked why we could not help each other instead of robbing what few belongings each of us had. I guess the answer is a concept I learned many years later: survival of the fittest.

After two and a half months on Guam, we flew to Indiantown Gap in Pennsylvania. We had finally arrived in America! We felt excitement as well as fear. Would America fulfill our hopes, dreams, and expectations? The elders missed their homeland very much and longed to return to Vietnam one day. The adults wondered how they could start a new life. I was terrified of going to school and not being able to understand my teachers or make friends with my classmates. Some friends of my uncle sponsored us and we went to live with them in Philadelphia. I remember how crowded our apartment was—ten people crammed into two small rooms. My brothers and I went to a special school where we learned English. The adults had a hard time adjusting. My parents and my aunt had to relearn everything and take licensing examinations before they could practice as doctors in the United States. In Vietnam, they had all been well established; now, they were poor and had to start over. In their forties, they felt weary but giving up was the last thing in their minds.

My brothers and I found school difficult at first. When I did not understand anything, I cried, but my classmates were very helpful. During recess, they started picking up different objects and teaching me the names for them. I repeated over and over what they tried to teach me to say. Once, when I was in class, I had to go to the restroom but I did not know the English word for it. In desperation, I raised my hand and said, "pee pee." The whole class laughed but at least they understood and I got to use the restroom. Incidents such as this made me determined to master the English language. By my second year, I had learned English well enough to win every spelling bee we had in class. The only word that tripped me up was *coffee*.

After passing their licensing examinations, my parents found jobs in Rome, Georgia. Moving away from my grandfather, grandaunt, uncle, and aunt was the hardest thing we ever had to do. We had been together all these years no matter what. Now, we had to separate as we each tried to find new beginnings for ourselves. Tears rolled down my eyes as we said goodbye. Was this the American dream—a life apart from our loved ones? Georgia, where my parents practiced medicine for the first time in the United States, did provide my family with a better life. My parents worked long hours to earn enough to send my brothers and me to private schools. Socially, however, I think we were treated more kindly in Pennsylvania; in Georgia, people stared at us in supermarkets and on the street. Was there something wrong with us? I soon realized there was nothing wrong with us. People stared because they lacked an understanding of who we were and where we came from.

After four years in Georgia, my father decided to see what opportunities California might offer. He took my two brothers with him while I stayed in Georgia with my mother—just in case things did not work out in California as planned. But things did work out and a year later my mother and I also moved to California. Today, my father has his own clinic and so does my mother. Most of their patients are Vietnamese, Cambodians, Laotians, and Chinese. My parents are very happy and I am so proud of them. My aunt has moved to California also. She now works as a pharmacist in a hospital in Riverside. One weekends, we go to visit her and my grandaunt and all the adults talk about the good old days. They tell us children how lucky we are— how very easy our lives are. In a way, I wish my life were not so easy so that I must strive harder to reach my goals.

Last year, before my grandfather passed away, he had a chance to visit China, his original homeland. He came back with tales of how wonderful everything is in China. I think the image of China had been imprinted in his mind when he was still a boy. No matter where he was, he always thought China was the most beautiful place in the world. My grandaunt also passed away last year within two months of my grandfather's death. She was a very outspoken woman and left us with a lot of stories to pass down to our children. I miss them both greatly. Although they are no longer with me, they will always have a place in my heart.

America has given my family a chance to rebuild our lives. It has made us appreciate what we have and taught us not to take anything for granted. Today, members of my family are scattered all over the United States. I even have an uncle in France. Distance is the only thing that separates us, for the hardships and struggles we have been through have made us stronger and closer to one another. These ties can never be broken. The American dream has come true for us but we will always remember and cherish Vietnam.

CHAPTER SEVENTEEN

The Coming of Age of a
Chinese-Vietnamese American

The author came from a large, well-to-do ethnic Chinese family in South Vietnam. The seventh child in a family of eleven children, she recalls how government officials "visited" them, took an "inventory" of the family members, and confiscated their car, bicycles, and television set after three of her older sisters and oldest brother escaped in 1977. The second batch of family members to escape, in 1978, included the narrator, another brother, two sisters, an aunt, and a cousin. The narrator was only seven years old at the time but she has vivid recollections of the journey, their shipwreck, and the harsh living conditions in the refugee camp at Pulau Bidong, Malaysia. A little later, when her parents and three younger siblings tried to escape, their boat capsized and her mother's body was never recovered. Pinning her hopes on the fact that her mother might not have perished after all, the author began a poignant, futile search for her. This richly textured account also chronicles the tensions that surfaced after the author's father and surviving younger sibling finally rejoined the rest of the family in California. Written in 1990, this reflexive autobiography of a strong-willed young woman concludes with a discussion of her determined efforts to express her individuality.

Our family came to this country to escape from the inequality and differential treatment that we had experienced under the Communists in Vietnam who regarded us Chinese-Vietnamese as people with too much wealth and whose properties should be confiscated. In 1977, two years after the fall of Saigon, I was sitting on the stairs eavesdropping on a conversation between my mother and our maid, Mai. Mom told Mai that our family was deeply grateful for her service through the years but now we had no choice except to let her go because the new government had reduced the value of the currency. Mai protested and insisted that she be allowed to remain with us even if we could not pay her. However, my mother ordered Mai to take the money my mother gave her and use it to buy her way out of the country. I could not understand what my mother meant by "leave the country." Why should Mai leave? Where would she go? I knew of only one country—Vietnam. Later, when I questioned my mother, all she said was, "You're too young to understand."

A few days later, I saw a scene that was even more confusing. Even though I asked, no one told me what was happening. My parents, oldest brother, and three oldest sisters were standing before the Buddhist altar that we had in our house and praying. Their eyes were red and wet from crying. My father gave some money to my brother and told him to use it as needed. He emphasized the importance of remaining alive and instructed my brother and sisters to give "them" the money and jewelry if "they" demanded it. My mother, who was kneeling before the altar with joss sticks between her palms, sobbed so hard that she could not say a word. Finally, they all hugged and my brother and sisters left. I thought they must be going to visit our grandparents. I did not realize they were leaving the country forever.

A year passed. In 1978, I entered first grade at an elementary school but I hated school because we were required to wear a red scarf around our neck as part of our school uniform. One day, when I took the scarf off during recess, I was sent to the principal's office. He wanted to know why I had taken my scarf off and who had taught me to do so. He asked whether my parents had told me to do that. I answered, "I took it off because it is ugly." He sent me home and told me I would remain on detention for two days. To my surprise, my parents did not punish me but only advised me to keep my mouth shut from then on. I did not understand why.

In the spring of 1978, two "visitors" from the government came to our house to take an inventory of my family members. They asked me for the names of all my brothers and sisters. My response was, "I don't know." It was an honest answer because I did not, in fact, know their names as I always called them "older brother" or "older sister." When my mother smiled at me, I realized I must have given the correct answer. I overheard my dad tell the visitors that there were only seven children in the family. I was puzzled because I thought there were eleven of us. What about the other four? I asked myself. Fortunately, I did not ask that question out loud in front of the visitors or my father would have had a lot of explaining to do. The visitors searched every room in the house—the living room, dining room, four bedrooms, bathrooms, sewing room, storage room, and garage. I noticed they paid special attention to the bicycles, the car, and the television. They came back the next day and confiscated those items. They told us we no longer needed those things because there was no time for leisure in the new society. My little brother cried for days afterward because he loved watching television. I was afraid they would visit us again in the future. Who knows? Maybe they would take my dolls and picture books next.

One foggy morning, my mother woke up my older brother, sister, me, and my younger sister. Silently, she bundled us up in long pants, shirts, sweaters, and jackets. I felt like a stuffed turkey. One by one, my dad took each of us on his motorcycle to the port. Everything was happening so fast that my head was spinning. My aunt and one of my cousins met us at the port and led us to a wooden boat. We all got in. Only when the motor began to roar did my aunt tell us that we were going to visit my grandparents. I believed her. As the boat moved into deeper waters, I looked out of the window in the ship's cabin and saw my mom with her face buried in my dad's chest. His arms were wrapped tightly around her. At that instant, I realized we were probably not going to visit my grandparents, but instead, to someplace far away. Suddenly, I wept because I feared I would never see my parents and other brothers and sisters again. Could this be our last farewell?

The boat moved into the endless sea. For three days, huge waves splashed violently against our boat and soaked my body. I recall crying constantly, craving water, and vomiting. My mouth was dry as a rice cake. I tried to swallow my own saliva but there wasn't any in my mouth. My older sister scooped up saltwater for us. It was most inviting at first but the salt left in my mouth and throat made my weak stomach feel worse. I vomited even more until there was nothing left in my stomach. All I could do was groan.

On the fourth night, a loud crash woke us up. People started screaming as the boat tilted to one side. Everyone rushed up the stairs, pushing their way out of the cabin. People pulled each other's hair and fistfights broke out. As the water rose up to my neck, someone grabbed my wrist and pulled me out. I thought my arm was being yanked off. It was pitch dark but somehow I managed to climb on to the rocks that had punctured our boat. I was so relieved when I found my brother, sisters, aunt, and cousin. We realized we had just experienced a shipwreck and might have lost everybody. By the time everyone had climbed on to the rocks, the fuel tanks were leaking rapidly. Soon, the sea was a shimmering black. A dead baby was still lying on the deck. Two women wrapped their arms around the bawling mother and held her back as she cried, "Just let me be with my baby!" Tears came to my eyes as I remembered my younger brother and sisters who were back in Vietnam with my parents.

We sat on the rocks for a day until a fishing boat found us. The fishermen contacted a large ship that came to pick us up. It took us to an island housing Vietnamese prisoners who had tried to escape from the country. We stayed there for about a month until the government decided to let us go. My aunt told us we were lucky because we had left Vietnam as Chinese who had obtained legal permits to depart. So, after a month in prison, we were allowed to leave in a boat that the government provided us. This time, we had more water and more food on board. I vomited and cried less but every time I closed my eyes my mind flashed back to our kitchen at home. The image was so real and vivid that I was surprised that my mother, who was cooking, did not seem to see me or speak to me. I was invisible to her. When I opened my eyes, I realized I was still on the boat.

Five days later, we found land. It was a rocky island called Pulau Bidong in Malaysia. The fishermen we had met at sea advised us to destroy our boat once we got near the island. Otherwise, they said, the Malaysian authorities would tow us back to sea. The captain headed directly to shore and some men punctured a large hole in the bottom of the boat with an ax. We all jumped into the water and waited for further instructions. The Malaysian officials led us to a camping area. There were no built structures and we had to sleep under the stars until we could construct our own shelter. Unfortunately for us, a harsh wind howled all night as needlelike rain pelted us. I thought there was no God to answer our prayers. It was up to us to make the best of everything. My belief in God ceased to exist.

For months, all we had to eat were noodles and watery congee [rice porridge] for both lunch and dinner. We were not given any breakfast. Worse, millions of black flies settled on everything we ate and drank. Diarrhea was a common illness. As for our shelter, the brilliant sun was our cover. My once pale complexion transformed into dark brown skin and my once straight hair turned into an entwined bird's nest where hundreds of lice made their home. Only three months later were we supplied with metal sheeting that enabled us to construct a long building to house fifty families. The building had only a roof and no walls. Our "home" reminded me of a swap meet in Saigon.

While living on this small island, I learned to behave like an adult. My daily chores included cooking, washing clothes, and sprouting green beans. When I was sick, I went to the doctor myself. The sick people could not simply walk in or make appointments. Rather, we had to line up starting at 2:00 or 3:00 A.M. and wait until the doctor's office opened, usually around 9:00 A.M. The line was always as long as a dragon. Another duty I had was to guard all the new boats that arrived. Some friends who arrived after us told us that most of my relatives, including my grandmother, had also managed to leave the country. Since they never showed up at Pulau Bidong, we figured they must have gone to another island.

Dying was a common event on Pulau Bidong. Each day, numerous people died of various diseases or accidents. A few were killed when falling coconuts struck them on the head. Others slipped off rocks while trying to fish. Nothing was a surprise anymore. One day, we received a letter from my dad. As my aunt read the letter, her hands shook violently and after she finished reading, she screamed. Tears flooded her eyes, rolling down her hollow cheeks, dropping to the ground. Everyone gathered around us and demanded to know what was in the letter. When my aunt did not respond, a woman picked up the letter that my aunt had thrown on the ground and read it to us. My dad wrote that the boat that he, my mother, my younger brother, and two sisters were on sank before it even left port. More than half of the passengers died. The Communists did not allow my dad to return to the boat until three days after the accident. He found the bodies of two of my siblings and buried them, but he never found my mother's body. He did not know where it had drifted. The woman could not continue reading because she was sobbing so hard. However, no tears poured out of my eyes. I pinched myself to cry, but because I had cried so much since I left Vietnam, there were no more tears left. Although I felt as if a sharp needle was stabbing my chest, my eyes were dry.

My aunt wept for one long week; she did enough crying for all of us. She could not eat and drank only a few sips of water. She cursed the Communists and my mother's stupidity. She said my mother would not have died had she left with us. But, no, my mother had insisted that she would only leave with my dad. At times, my aunt screamed and begged Buddha to take her life so that she could reunite with her mother. Later, however, she changed her mind and asked Buddha not to take her life because she was stuck on this island with the son and daughters of her brother. I felt as though she hated us and was blaming us for her misfortunes.

After eight months on the island, we were informed that we would be admitted into the United States where my oldest brother and sisters already were. As my aunt prepared for our departure, she wanted to take the pots and pans we had accumulated to the United States but my cousin talked her out of doing so. She managed to grab only a soup pot to take with her. I explored the island one last time and found more graves than I had expected. I was grateful that none of the graves belonged to the people I knew.

While waiting for a 747 jet to transport us to our destination, I mentally rehearsed the little bit of English I had learned on the island. "How are you?" "I am fine." "Thank you." "You're welcome." "I don't know." Even though I sounded alien and funny, I hoped that I would soon be able to speak English fluently. In May 1979 we arrived in Texas. During the reunification with my older brother and sisters, I felt overwhelmed with excitement. For the first time, I learned their names and found out how old they were. They told me I was the seventh child in a family of thirteen people and that only my dad and our baby sister were still in Vietnam. While we ate dinner, we shared our experiences on our respective journeys to the United States. Since I left Vietnam, I had never felt so complete. Now, there need be no more worries about dying of starvation or disease.

Having heard how warm the weather is in California and how many Asians live in that state, we decided to move there. After three months in Texas, we packed our bags again, climbed aboard a Greyhound bus, and headed to the Golden State. When we arrived in Glendale in southern California, I expected to see lots of Asians but, instead, most of our neighbors were White. I did not feel comfortable among them because they often stared or frowned at us. At times, I heard "they're Vietnamese" whispered behind my back. A Spanish-speaker called me "China." Those remarks made me feel like a dirty kid who lived in a trash dump and smelled like shit. Although I was upset, I could not defend myself. This feeling of helplessness was most depressing.

When fall arrived, I entered second grade. I was terrified by the language barrier and the fact that I had never encountered people of other races. What if they hated me because I was an alien? On the first day of class, the teacher did a roll call. I felt my heart pumping a thousand times faster than normal. When the Caucasian teacher called my name, I could not recognize it because I had never heard my name pronounced in English before. I glanced around the classroom: all eyes were on me. My cheeks became flushed as I stood up and shrieked feebly, "he-e-e-re," which caused a few giggles. The teacher smiled at me. Unsure of myself, I did not know whether to smile back or to ignore her. Back in Vietnam, teachers do not smile at their students during roll call, which was performed in a very strict and formal way.

During lunchtime, everyone ate sandwiches and drank milk. I was reluctant to take out my rice but my hunger could not wait. So, I got my container and removed the lid. The smell of rice and spicy fish sauce wafted across the lunch area. A couple of students covered their noses while others moved away. I was embarrassed and desperately wished the earth would swallow me up. Instead, I pretended not to notice and waited until everyone had left the lunch area to dump my container and its contents into the trash can. Even though I was very hungry, I felt I had to get rid of all the evidence for the crime I had committed.

I gradually adjusted to my new life by trial and error. I learned from observing my classmates and by enduring the laughter of those who thought I was stupid. By the end of the school year I knew how to eat burritos and drink cold milk. My English had improved to such an extent that I could ask directions to the library or the restroom. My sister and I tried speaking English to each other but the language still sounded strange to us. We laughed at our own accents. After a while, we unconsciously got into the habit of slipping a few English words and phrases into our conversations in Vietnamese. I tried to forget about the past—until the night my father flew to the United States.

It was eight o'clock in the evening when the phone rang. One of my brothers picked it up. The call was from my father who said he would arrive in the United States the next morning. Our family was so excited. One of my sisters went to the supermarket to buy food for the celebration and my aunt kept thanking Buddha as she knelt in front of the altar. Later that night, my aunt warned us not to mention the dreadful past. I could not sleep at all that night as I began to feel guilty. I felt I was a terrible person because I had not been able to cry when I heard about my mother's death. I was not excited like everyone else about the reunion with my father. One half of me was afraid of him while the other half wanted to see him again. I feared that members of my family would have difficulties readjusting to one another. I also worried that I would not be able to have a conversation with my dad since I was now speaking mostly English. I was afraid I might upset him.

My father and my youngest surviving sister arrived the next morning. We had a grand dinner that evening. Everyone was cautious of what he or she said. Finally, my dad broke the ice as he retold the shipwreck story, except this time it was more detailed. The only sentence I remember was, "Your mother's body was never found." This suddenly gave me hope that she might have been saved by someone. From then on, I commenced a secret investigation to find my mother. During the search, I encountered many difficulties, but because I had a deep faith that she had somehow survived, I was extremely upset when my aunt insisted I go to a Buddhist temple with her to pray for my mother's soul so that she could enter heaven. I refused to go. My aunt thought I had become too Americanized and she told my father how disobedient I was. My dad, who is not as religious as my aunt, let her remark pass. However, he did begin to worry that his children were becoming too Americanized. So, he set down regulations. We were not allowed to speak English at home and could speak only Vietnamese or Cantonese. We were not allowed to participate in extracurricular activities after school. The only thing we could do was to go to the library to study. He also enrolled the younger children in a Chinese-language school that held classes on the weekends.

These rules hampered my search for my mother as I could no longer go to Chinatown by myself to peer at the women there to see if one of them might be my mother. I also could not buy newspapers to look through all the ads for announcements of women who survived their escapes. Almost every night, I dreamed that my mother had come back to us. Sometimes she appeared very distant while at other times I could almost touch her. Some nights she talked to me, telling me to give up my search and crying before her image faded. These dreams continued on and off for at least a year.

Then, things suddenly changed. One night, my father announced his decision to remarry. Everyone in the family was shocked but we did not dare object. We felt we had no right to interfere with his personal life. Moreover, it had already been three years since our mother's disappearance. We hoped his new wife would make his life merrier. Although I did not dare voice an objection, I was afraid that my dad would not love us anymore. It was bad enough that I was the number-seven child—a middle child who had received little attention. Now, I would have to compete with another person for my father's love. I was scared. That night, I saw my mother again in my dreams. I remember vividly how I watched her sitting in a tree, crying. Then another dream overlapped with the first dream. I saw another of my aunts who had also died in the shipwreck. She advised me to forget about my mother because she had already reached heaven and was happy there. This was the last time I saw my mother in a dream. From then on, I gave up all hope of her survival.

I finally graduated from the sixth grade. Elementary school was over. As I entered junior high school, I became more aware of my appearance, especially the clothes I wore and the cosmetics other girls my age used. My Caucasian friends wore the latest fashions and started using makeup. I wanted to be like them but my older brothers and sisters forbade me to use lipstick, eye shadow, or eyeliner. My clothes were hand-me-downs from my older sisters. Unable to keep up with my white friends, I switched to Asian, mainly Chinese-Vietnamese, friends. I found I could relate to them better because we had the same experiences as "boat people" and their parents were similarly strict and stubborn. We also shared the same difficulties in terms of the language barrier, our taste in food and music, and values.

By 1987, Glendale had become more densely populated and our rent rose rapidly. The landlady suggested that we move because she wanted to remodel the house. My father was angry with her because he thought she was discriminating against us. The house, from his point of view, was not that old. We were the only Asian family in that neighborhood; our neighbors on both sides were old Caucasian ladies who often complained about the noise we made. They accused us of playing our music too loudly even though the biggest "stereo" we could afford at that time was a Walkman that could not possibly have produced the loud music they complained about. As we felt more and more unwelcome, my father decided we should move to Los Angeles in order to be close to its Chinatown that has a large Chinese community. He said that living among White people was too frustrating because they did not respect us. I objected to the move because I was finally feeling that I had adapted to American life. I could communicate better in English than in Cantonese or Vietnamese. Moreover, moving meant I would have to make new friends. The thought of another move brought painful memories of my departure from Vietnam.

My dad insisted we move and we did so in the summer of 1987 after I completed ninth grade. When school started in September, I encountered culture shock. I had not seen so many Asians since I left Vietnam. Although I had visited Chinatown, I had never lived among Chinese or Vietnamese in the United States. As my dad was satisfied with our new environment, I did not dare to complain. I feared my dad would get angry at all his children. Whenever one of us did something wrong, all of us got into trouble. He never saw us as individuals. So, I kept quiet for the sake of my brothers and sisters.

Upon entering high school, I decided I could no longer attend the Chinese-language school because even after four years of study, I still had not learned the language. I could not concentrate on what the teachers were saying and kept wishing I could skip class. I went to class only because I was afraid my dad would find out if I played hooky. Sometimes, I brought my homework from public school to do while I was sitting in the Chinese class. Finally, going to Chinese school became so intolerable that I got up the courage to tell my dad I no longer wanted to attend. My aunt, who was listening in on the conversation, started lecturing me harshly. She blamed my dad for being too lenient with me and my siblings. She reminded us that there are important traditional values we should treasure and that we could retain those values only if we knew the language. She accused me of wanting to be an American and of abandoning my roots. Then she blamed my dad for not watching over us and for allowing us to do too many things freely. The bottom line, in her eyes, was that my dad did not know how to be a proper father. She said she regretted taking some of his children, including me, out of Vietnam. She declared she would never have done so if she had known we would become so disobedient and disrespectful.

That night, our house was filled with tension. We all went to bed early. I crawled into my only private space—my bed—and cried in anger and confusion. I felt completely alone. Half of me wanted to give up the fight and follow all of my dad's and aunt's expectations, while the other half wanted to find the inner me, to do the things I wanted to do and not what others expected of me. Up to that point, all my actions had been directed by other members of my family. Whatever I wanted to do had to be approved by the entire family. That was really difficult because there was always at least one person who opposed my desires. It was so frustrating to try to please *everyone*. I asked myself, if I were to disobey them, would I then be considered a selfish person?

As I lay in bed, I thought of something one of my dad's friends had confided to him: this friend was afraid that his children would send him to an old folks home as they went on with their lives. He thought they would probably visit him only on weekends. He warned my dad how easily Chinese or Vietnamese children became Americanized and once they did, they would no longer care for their parents. They would become totally selfish, he said.

Despite my father's and my aunt's objections, I discontinued Chinese school. I felt I was mature enough to make such a decision. At age fourteen, I felt like an adult because of all I had been through. Not only was I working at a part-time job, but I had also long ago learned to go see the dentist or the doctor by myself. I cooked for my family, studied hard, and did not socialize. I did not feel like a normal teenager who still needed her parents' guidance. Thus, I thought I should be allowed to make decisions because I understood their consequences. The sentence, "You're too young to know or understand" no longer existed in my world.

During high school, I rebelled against all the expectations that my family and friends placed on me. After being on the tennis team for a year, I developed a new interest and enrolled in the Junior Reserved Officers' Training Corps (JROTC), which caused countless objections from the people who tried to shape my life. I joined JROTC to avoid going to physical education classes, which I despised because there were so many unmotivated students who hated to exercise. I soon became committed to JROTC, which inspired and motivated me to participate in all its extracurricular activities. I was on the exhibition drill team and the staff team. It is difficult to explain the satisfaction I derived from this program. At home, I had no space I could call my own: every corner of the house belonged to everyone. There was no space in which I could recognize myself as an individual. JROTC gave me an opportunity to gain insight into myself, my likes and dislikes, my hidden skills and talents, and my real personality.

From my family's perspective, JROTC reminded them of the Communists who had forced us to leave our country. My green uniform especially troubled them. My father strongly discouraged my participation because he felt ashamed and disturbed as I proudly wore my neatly pressed uniform in public. He could not understand why I wanted to show my patriotism when the United States is not our "original" country. He also objected because I was a young woman. Even though my father is not an overly dominating male who believes women belong only in the kitchen, he felt the army is not the right place for women. I also sensed that my military uniform brought back painful memories of the war and of my mother's death. Because of my inability to express myself well in Chinese, I did not succeed in explaining to him what JROTC meant to me.

Some of my friends also disapproved of my participation in JROTC. They even accused me of becoming a violent person because I was learning to spin rifles while not shooting them. They thought I was too gung-ho for war. Others felt I was trying to imitate Americans by participating in an American program. The proof they offered was that I was not active in ethnic cultural organizations.

All these objections forced me to reconsider my priorities. Although I managed to remain in JROTC for three years—until I graduated from high school—I often wondered if I was being too selfish. I felt ashamed about my father's displeasure; at the same time, my ability to stick it out gave me a sense of accomplishment and victory. I had proven to my father that JROTC did not automatically lead to my joining the "real" army and that I was simply educating myself through an uncommon venue. Following my example, both my younger sisters are also in JROTC. The pressure that other members of my family impose on them is not as great as what they inflicted on me. I presume it is because my family is slowly accepting the fact that their most strenuous objections will not always make us change our minds.

The next step I took toward independence was in my choice of which college to attend. I wanted to go to a college that would not be too close to Los Angeles, which would require me to live at home, but at the same time was not too far away so that I could visit my family on holidays. My father wanted me to live at home and attend a local college, possibly the same one that all my older siblings were attending, California State Polytechnic University in Pomona. But I was determined to be "unlike" any other member of my family. I also wanted to be a role model for my younger sisters. I wanted to prove to my father that I could get admitted into a University of California campus, which is harder to get into than a California State University campus. As for my intended major, recalling my experience as a junior counselor and a teacher's aide, I thought that I would like to major in psychology.

When I was accepted at this university, the only members of my family who supported my decision to enroll here were one of my older sisters and my two younger sisters. They agreed with me that it was best to go away to college so that I would not have to worry about family problems all the time. My sisters and I feel that we can become more independent if we move away from our huge family. By doing so, we will have a chance to learn to rely on ourselves. However, my father and older brothers and sisters thought I had gone insane. They claimed that the campus I chose was not the right college for me because so many of its students are European Americans and it is famous as a "party school." They thought if I wanted to attend a University of California campus, I should go to UCLA. They also opposed my desire to study psychology, telling me that I should study medicine or dentistry—more "practical" professions that ensure a high income—instead.

Since coming to this university, I have made many new discoveries about myself. At the beginning of the first quarter, I felt homesick and lonely because everywhere I saw unfamiliar faces and heard unfamiliar voices. Though I yearned to see the faces of my family members, I did not go home often because I could not allow them to assume that I had made a wrong decision. I did not want them to force me to return home. I also had trouble eating bland American food in the dormitory dining rooms. I even missed washing the dishes because I was so used to doing them. What frustrates me most now is the loss of my identity. I often feel as if I do not know who I am. When people ask me what kind of music I like, I have no answer because at home I always listened to whatever my brothers and sisters wanted to hear. Now I have to make decisions about even trivial matters.

Although I fought for this freedom for many years, I am not sure I enjoy it now that I have it. In addition, there is no longer pressure to do anything I do not want to do, like go to a Buddhist temple to pray. It is devastating not knowing what I believe in. Now, when people ask me what religion I belong to, I tell them I am an agnostic.

When I visited my family in Los Angeles after being in this school for a few months, they told me I had changed radically. They complained that I had become too Americanized because I could not speak Chinese well and now ate pizza for dinner instead of rice, or angel cake instead of moon cakes as snacks. My father and older brothers and sisters still oppose my desire to major in psychology. They say it is a "useless" major that is full of "bullshit." They claim it is an "American" major, something inappropriate for a Chinese to study. My father and aunt want all of us to become doctors and engineers as those professions would bring honor to the family. So far, I have not yet succeeded in convincing them that I really enjoy what I am studying and that I cannot major in something they like but I don't. My plan is to continue studying psychology. My family needs to realize that psychology is *my* major.

My closest friends, who are Chinese and Vietnamese, tell me I have matured too quickly and that I am becoming too "liberal." Yet, they still support my decision to go away to college. I guess this is what makes us close friends. Having gone through some of the same experiences, they understand where I am coming from.

On this campus, I feel more Chinese than American. Although I do things most Americans do, such as go to football and basketball games, I still interact mainly with Asian Americans. Sometimes I yearn for Chinese food and miss the Chinese holidays. Many of my values are still traditional. For example, I do not believe in premarital sex, but at the same time, I think it is fine for young people of both sexes to live together without having to marry or even to date each other. Whenever my "old" and "new" values conflict, I choose what makes the most sense to me. Therefore, I classify myself as a Chinese-Vietnamese American: I live in between not two, but three worlds.

CHAPTER EIGHTEEN

My Father and I

The author's family originated in North Vietnam. He, his mother, and sister escaped from Vietnam in October 1978 when he was seven years old while his father, an official in the South Vietnamese government, was incarcerated in a re-education camp. The most amazing aspect of their flight was that it was the father who managed to make the arrangements for the escape even though he was under close surveillance. The narrator tells a moving story of his father's confinement, offering graphic glimpses of the varying conditions in the several re-education camps in which his father was imprisoned, and reveals the corruption and mercilessness of the camp wardens who kept for themselves the food that family members sent the prisoners who were barely surviving on starvation diets. This narrative is also notable for the father's efforts to teach his son something about the political history of Vietnam, in contrast to many other parents who simply stressed the importance of preserving Vietnamese culture. The father, a humane man who attributed his sufferings not to the Communists, but to "fate," declined for several years after he rejoined his family in 1986 to tell his son what he had endured. He said he wanted to wait until he thought his son was old enough to cope with the gruesome details. This account was written in 1992.

My relationship with my father sometimes confuses me because it is more like a friendship than a father-and-son relationship. It isn't that I don't respect my father, because I really do, but I feel so intimate with him that he seems like the best buddy I have ever had. He is not like the usual Asian father who is often portrayed as an authoritarian figure.

I was four years old when the North Vietnamese army conquered South Vietnam. After the fall of Saigon, my father, along with other high-level government officials, military commanders, and the employees and dependents of Americans, was put into re-education camps. I remember vividly the night Communist officials came to our house in Saigon and took my father away. Even though the officials said that my father would be away for only a ten-day seminar, my father sensed that things would not be that simple. He whispered something to my mom and then he hugged my sister and me as the Communist officials dragged him away from us. I cried the cry of an innocent boy when someone he loves is out of sight. I did not know that the Communists had stolen my father and that I would have to grow up without him. I was too young to understand how many families in our country were broken apart by the Communist government, how thousands of children would grow up fatherless, and how thousands of women would have to, for the first time, find ways to support themselves and their children, as well as their loved ones in the re-education camps.

Ten days passed but my father did not come back by nightfall. My paternal grandfather died late that night. I do not know what caused his death because he was very healthy. Later on, I heard rumors that my grandfather had committed suicide because he did not want to live under Communist rule. Others said that my grandfather missed my father so much that he must have had a heart attack. My mother had to hide the sad news from my father because she did not want him to suffer even more. The government did not allow anyone to visit my father. We could only send him a letter and a package of food once a month. Letters were the only means of communication between my father and us, but we could not say much because the government usually read the letters before they reached his or our hands, in their effort to find out whether we had any plans to escape or any thoughts against them.

After my father was taken away, my mother, for the first time in her life, had to go out to find a job in order to feed and clothe us. After many months of searching, she found a job as a seamstress. The money she made was barely enough to pay all the bills. So we had to sell things in the house, starting with our television, refrigerator, and stereo. The last items to be sold were our bed frames and mattresses. The house was now empty and we slept on the floor. I still remember waking up in the middle of the night to find my mother crying. She told me she had bad dreams and I believed her then. Only when I became older did I understand that she was crying over our future, our means of survival, and my father's life in prison.

As the Communist government started to pressure us to move to the New Economic Zones in mid-1978, we received a letter from my father asking us to contact a friend of his in Saigon. I did not find out until later that he had arranged for us to leave Vietnam. My mother, sister, and I escaped in October 1978. Every year, thousands of Vietnamese were escaping to find freedom in other lands. Many, like my mother, my sister, and me, left in small fishing boats. Thousands of people in small boats attempted to reach the refugee camps in Thailand, Malaysia, or Indonesia. However, the "boat people's" journey to freedom was extremely dangerous. Violent storms destroyed some boats and buried people at the bottom of the ocean. Some boats got lost and the people on board died of hunger or thirst before they could be rescued by merchant ships. Yet other boats were captured by pirates. After robbing the refugees' belongings, the pirates raped the women, tortured the men, and threw people off the boat if they showed any kind of resistance. Only a small number of these fishing boats were fortunate enough to find their way safely to a refugee camp. Despite hearing about the horrible incidents, people still did not give up hope of finding freedom somewhere else. They would rather take their chances and risk their lives than be oppressed and enslaved by a Communist government. When my father heard from my aunt that my mother, I, and my sister had made it safely to a refugee camp in Indonesia, he felt both sad and happy. Sad, because his wife and children were now even farther away, but happy, because we were safe and would have a bright future.

After a year in a refugee camp in Indonesia, we came to San Jose, California. After we settled down in the United States, the contact between us and my father became even less frequent. Every night before I went to sleep, I prayed to God to help him get out of the re-education camp and reunite with us as soon as possible. The image of my father in my mind, however, grew dimmer and dimmer as I adjusted to a new life in America and began to face problems of my own when I became a teenager.

My father was released from the re-education camp in 1985. In 1986, he escaped from Vietnam in a boat and landed in Malaysia. I did not get to really know my father until October of that year when he came to live with us in America. While we were waiting at the airport for him, I tried to remember how he looked, how he walked and talked. My younger sister was as anxious as I was. Only my mom looked calm. She kept staring at the gate. Once in a while, she looked at her watch and then turned her eyes to the gate again. As people started coming out of the gate, we all stood up. I searched the crowd and spotted a small figure moving slowly toward us. My mother was very surprised to see this person. She stood there with her mouth open and both of her arms wide open. I was surprised also because my father looked so different from what I had expected. I could not believe that the man standing in front of me, a rather old man with lots of grey hair, was my father. He had changed so drastically that no one in my family expected how he would look. He hugged and kissed my mom for a long time. I could not keep the tears of joy from running down my cheeks the minute my father turned around and asked, "Is this big young man my son?" "Yes, papa," I quietly replied. He then hugged me and I could feel his skinny arms shivering on my back. I wanted him to hug me tighter. For a moment, it seemed as though my father and I were one. I had prepared many things to say to him, but at that moment, the words were just stuck in my throat. He also hugged my sister. Then we all walked to the car. On the way home, everyone was quiet. Not having seen each other for so long, we did not know where to begin a conversation.

There were many things I did not know about my father, such as his experiences growing up during the wars in Vietnam and the suffering he went through in the re-education camps. I had read and heard about the kinds of things that happened in those camps but I wanted to hear directly from my father. Many times I asked him about his experiences. At first, he hesitated to tell me anything. He said I should wait until I was a little older, then he would tell me everything about his life.

Aside from my curiosity about my father's life, which he did not wish to tell me until I was older, we got along very well. He helped me with my homework every day. He is very good in calculus and French. We usually watched sports events together. I remember the first time I explained to him the rules of football, basketball, and baseball. He did not like football or baseball as much as basketball. He said football is too violent while baseball is too slow and boring. On weekends, I helped him in our front and backyards, where he gardened and did carpentry. He is very good at fixing things around the house.

The summer before I left for college, my father and I finally had the conversation I had been waiting for. We stayed up very late drinking tea and eating Vietnamese cookies. He said he was very proud that I had been admitted into a good university. He reminded my sister and me how important education is. He said, "Education is the master key that opens all the doors of opportunity." He asked me what I planned to major in. He suggested that I consider becoming a premedical student. "Just give it a try, son," he said. "If you don't like it, then study whatever you want to. But remember, whatever career you choose, you should put yourself into it. Always try your best. The question is not how difficult something is but how hard you try to get it done." He told me how valuable education had been when he was growing up. He then started to tell me his life story.

My father began by telling me some facts in the history of Vietnam. He told me that Vietnam is located in Southeast Asia—south of China and east of Thailand. According to French scholars, the Vietnamese are direct descendants of a people called the Viet who inhabited a large region of China south of the Yangzi River. As the Chinese empire expanded in the third century B.C., the Chinese destroyed the Viet kingdom and the remaining people gradually made their way southward. It is believed that one group of Viet entered the Red River Valley where the first Vietnamese state was founded. In the early centuries of its existence, Vietnam was controlled by the Chinese. Then the French colonized it. Vietnam has always fought to regain its independence, my father told me proudly.

My father was born in 1940 in a small village in North Vietnam and grew up during the period when Japan occupied Indochina and left the French colonial government intact. My father remembers the famine that gripped the country. Many people died from starvation in his village. Around 1945, when it became apparent that the Japanese were losing the war, they did not allow people to cultivate or harvest rice. They also threw the rice in the storehouses into the river. Many people were so hungry that they streamed out of the cities looking for food. My paternal grandfather was a wealthy man in the village, so the family had just enough to eat to get by. There was no schooling for the children in that period because people worried more about getting food than an education.

After the Japanese surrendered, my father continued, the Viet Minh and the French fought to gain control over Vietnam. The French held on to the cities as the Viet Minh withdrew into the jungles. The Viet Minh only came out at night to persuade villagers to follow and support them. My father's family did not want to follow the Viet Minh, so they moved to Hanoi. In 1954, the Viet Minh defeated the French forces at Dien Bien Phu. The Geneva Agreements divided Vietnam in half at the seventeenth parallel, with North Vietnam being controlled by the Communists and South Vietnam by the Saigon government, which received aid from the United States. Under the agreement, both parties allowed people to move to whichever half of Vietnam they chose within a certain time. After the period ended, they could no longer cross the border for any reason. My father's family, along with about a million others from the North who did not want to live under a Communist government, moved to the South to start life over. Most of the people who left North Vietnam were rich, or well educated, or Catholics. The rich people knew that if they remained in the North, the government would confiscate their properties. To the Communists, it was a crime to be rich. The well-educated people left because they knew that Communism would make people suffer and that the Communist leaders were liars. The Catholics left because the Communists would not allow them to practice their religion. My father's family left for all the above reasons.

My father continued his schooling in Saigon. He attended a business school, where he met my mother and they fell in love. At first, my grandfather objected to the relationship because my mother was a Southern girl. Northerners used to think that all the women in the South were flirtatious, nontraditional, and would not become good housewives. Despite my grandfather's objections, my father married my mother after he received his accounting degree. They bought a house in Saigon and my father worked as an accountant for the South Vietnamese army. He was the sole supporter of our family. Even though my mother also had a good education, she stayed home to take care of the children. In Vietnam in those days, a man's salary was sufficient to support a whole family. Few women had jobs because their primary responsibility was to be good wives and mothers. Life was good until the civil war broke out between the North and the South.

The war ended on April 30, 1975, when the Communists from North Vietnam took over South Vietnam. A year later, Vietnam was reunified under a new name: the Socialist Republic of Vietnam. Because my father had worked for the South Vietnamese government, he, along with many others, was sent to re-education camps. During the ten years in those camps, my father was transferred to many different places. He was imprisoned first in the South, then was moved to the North, and finally back to the South again. Every time he was moved, he was blindfolded and handcuffed together with the other prisoners because the Communists were afraid they would try to escape.

Life in the re-education camps was like "hell on earth," my father told me. When he was still in the South, he was put into a room full of people. Each person had only enough space to lie down—six feet long and one foot wide. The prisoners were kept in total darkness. My father told me he could not even see his own hand. They could not tell the difference between night and day. Time seemed to have stopped. The room was also very stuffy as there were so many people in it. Whenever anyone moved, he would bump into somebody else. The inmates received only one meal a day—usually two thin slices of sweet potato. The Communists wanted to weaken these people so that they could not fight against the government. My father and the other prisoners could not do anything or move around in the camp. Even when they had to go to the restroom, each person had to go to his own assigned spot. The inhumane Communists treated my father and the other prisoners as though they were animals. They beat up anyone who showed the slightest resistance to their rule.

Some prisoners died because they could not take it anymore. The guards often whipped the prisoners with bamboo canes until the prisoners "confessed" to whatever the guards wanted to hear. They also starved the prisoners by not giving them any food or water for days. At other times, the Communists put the prisoners in a metal box called a connex and took off all their clothes. At noon, when the sun was directly overhead, it was so hot inside the connex that it felt as though their bodies were on fire. At night, as the temperature dropped rapidly, the prisoners suffered from the cold. Many got sick and died. Anyone punished by the Communists was more likely to die than to survive.

A year after his first incarceration, my father and some of his friends were transferred to another re-education camp that was near a mountain, deeper within southern Vietnam. When my father was taken out of the room to be transferred, he could not open his eyes because the light hurt them so much. He had lived in darkness for so long that he felt his eyes were going to pop out if he looked directly at the sun. At the new camp, the prisoners had to get up at five o'clock every morning and work in the fields until sunset. They were chained together because the government was afraid some might try to escape. In fact, some prisoners did run away to live in the jungle, but nobody ever heard what happened to them. The work consisted of breaking up rocks from the mountain to create more arable land. Then the prisoners had to plant vegetables on that piece of land. Sometimes they cut down trees to construct houses for the government officials and their families. The work was hard but the prisoners were fed only a little food. They started looking for "anything that moved" to fill their stomachs. Some ate cockroaches, ants, and rats, while others ate leaves and mushrooms in the forest. These people did not survive long because the raw food made them sick. Those who ate poisonous mushrooms died immediately. The government officials usually kept for themselves the packages of food that the prisoners' families sent them every month.

My father was in this second re-education camp for two years. In 1978, he was transferred to another camp. This time, he was put on a train that took him to the North. The weather there was much colder than in the South, especially near the mountains along the border with China. The government did not give the prisoners any warm clothing except a pair of pajama-like prison uniforms for each person. At this time, after my mother, sister, and I had escaped from the country, my aunt (my father's sister) started sending food packages to him but he never received them. The officials kept the packages for themselves but they did give the prisoners a little bit of the food on Communist holidays or the Vietnamese New Year.

In early 1979, soon after my father moved North, China invaded Vietnam. During this border war, my father was moved to another camp located on another mountain in the North. A minority tribe named Meo [Hmong] lived in that area. Next to the re-education camp was a cemetery where hundreds of prisoners were buried. Since the location was so high up in the mountain, there was not enough water to allow the prisoners to wash themselves. The camp was covered in clouds all the time. The weather was super cold, with the temperature often below the freezing point. My father said that sometimes when he woke up in the morning, he found that the person lying next to him had frozen to death. In this camp, my father lost all contact with my aunt. It was also the period when almost all his friends died. Despite the severe punishment, my father never gave up hope that someday he would reunite with his wife and children.

After the war between China and Vietnam ended, my father was taken back to the lowlands, where he became very sick and weak. Also, his eyesight got worse. But working outside in the fields in this new re-education camp, his health improved a little. My aunt sent him some food for the New Year, which helped him to recover somewhat. My aunt wrote my father to tell him that my paternal grandmother was dying of cancer. He also learned about the death of my grandfather. He wanted to see his mother one last time, so he and another man escaped from the camp. But they were caught. A soldier whipped them with a bamboo cane and put them into the connex. My father said that the punishment did not hurt him as much as not being able to be next to his parents when they passed away. At that moment, my father just wanted to die but the image of his wife and children gave him the strength to continue living. His hope of seeing us again made my father determined to stay alive. After one month in the connex, the Communists let him out. The friend who had escaped with him could not survive the punishment and died in the connex.

In 1983, my father was transferred back to the South where he was imprisoned in several camps. He was finally released in 1985. He went to live with my aunt's family. A few months later, he escaped from Vietnam. He spent about a year in a refugee camp in Malaysia, where he studied English, before he was allowed to come to the United States to live with us. The first few months here were very difficult for him. My mother was no longer a housewife as she had been in Vietnam. She was working from eight to five at a beauty parlor. My sister and I went to school in the morning and usually had lunch in school. My father was all alone until my sister and I came back from school. He looked for things around the house that needed repair and he planted and took care of flowers and plants in the yard. I could sense that my father was getting restless. My mother and I comforted him but he wanted to look for work because he was not used to sitting around and doing nothing. Growing up in a male-dominated society where men were the supporters of their families, he told me he felt inferior to my mom who was now supporting him. He did not want to depend on anyone.

My father had a very hard time finding employment. Most companies usually required their employees to be fluent in English and to have at least a few years of related work experience. As a middle-aged refugee, my father did not meet those requirements. Finally, my uncle, who has been in the United States since 1975, helped my father get a job as a technician in an electronics company.

As I learn about my father's life, I realize what a lot of pain he has gone through. Deep in his eyes, I can see his past suffering. It hurts me every time I think about all the things that have happened to him. One time, I asked him if he blamed the Communist government for his sufferings; he looked me straight in the eye and said, "It's nobody's fault, son. It is fate." I felt as though something was stuck in my throat. I love him even more for his ability to forgive. My father told me that what would make him most happy is to see his children succeed in becoming whatever they want to be. As his only son, my father has high expectations of me. He told me I must never forget my heritage, where I came from, and that I should always be proud of who I am. He hopes I can become a doctor and return to Vietnam someday to help the people there.

I am trying my best to fulfill my father's expectations. My undergraduate education has broadened my mind and I now have a wider perspective on life. Living away from home, I have had the opportunity to explore the world on my own and I have gained some valuable experiences, regardless of whether they came from pleasant or unpleasant situations. During my first two years of college, I lived in a dormitory and was exposed to people from many different cultural and ethnic backgrounds. By interacting with them, I learned to appreciate my own individuality and I am proud of my ethnic identity. However, the path that has led me to appreciate my own uniqueness has not been smooth. Because of my race, I am sometimes discriminated against in the classroom, the campus cafeteria, and on the street. But what I have learned from my father has helped me look beyond other people's ignorance. After taking a variety of courses, I feel I have become more creative and have greater clarity about my goals.

As a senior this year, I am looking forward to my graduation. Meanwhile, I am preparing to apply to medical schools. I am determined to get into at least one even though I am fully aware that a medical education is costly and time-consuming. And once I am admitted, I shall be patient in my studies. As a doctor, I shall be able to help the general public. My dream is to go back to Vietnam to serve my people.

CHAPTER NINETEEN

The Pain in My Heart

This is a rare account of an ethnic Chinese family that lived in a village in rural North Vietnam and escaped to the People's Republic of China in early 1979 when the author was eight years old. The existing literature to date has failed to include the approximately quarter million people who sought sanctuary in China, rather than in the countries of first asylum in Southeast Asia, as part of the refugee exodus from Vietnam. Another revealing detail is that the author's family spoke only Cantonese, unlike the Sino-Vietnamese in South Vietnam who usually knew both the Chinese and Vietnamese languages. This is perhaps a reflection of the differences between North Vietnam's and South Vietnam's policies regarding citizenship and assimilation vis-à-vis the ethnic Chinese. Though life was relatively easy in China, the narrator's mother (his father had died by then) thought her children would have a better future in another country. So, the family fled a second time, from China to Hong Kong, in October 1979. Though the refugee camp in Hong Kong is seen through the eyes of an eight-year-old boy, the account suggests that in the early years of the exodus at least, refuge-seekers had more "freedom" in Hong Kong's "open camps" than those housed in the camps in Southeast Asian countries. This memoir was written in 1991.

None of my friends knows much about my family history. Sure, they know where I am originally from, how many siblings I have, what language I speak at home, and how long I have been in the United States. But beyond that, few know any of the events I am about to tell you.

I am one of the so-called boat people from Vietnam. Nearly every refugee has a story to tell and I am no different. I came from a pretty rich family, compared with other families in the village in North Vietnam where I was born. In those days, few families could afford to eat chicken and duck because they were quite expensive. However, my family ate chicken or duck at least once a week. At other times, we ate seafood and vegetables. We could afford seafood because my grandparents were fishermen. My father was a businessman who also worked on a ship. He had business friends who asked him to sell their goods for them. Thus, he earned a profit by taking goods from the village to the city and selling them there at higher prices. With the profit he made, he bought goods in the city and sold them in the village, also for a profit. While my father was away doing business, my mother took care of us children and did some trading in the village herself. We children had no responsibilities except to have fun. The village was like a big family because we knew everyone who lived there. There were rocks, sand, and water at the back of my house and people, young and old, swam there. Overall, my life in the village was good.

Who would have imagined that those happy days would soon be gone forever? One day in December 1978, we received news that my father had died. My mother, who was pregnant at the time, was shocked half to death. She gathered her five children together and told us that our father was going to someplace far away and would never return. I could not figure out what my mother was saying but I sensed something unpleasant had happened from the tone of her voice and the look in her eyes. Two days later, some family friends brought my father's dead body back to the village. My entire family burst into tears. We five helpless brothers and sister sobbed as our mother went crazy. She was crying and yelling, "My dead husband, why do you have to leave us so soon? Our sons and daughter, who is going to take care of them? Why? Why do you have to be the one who died?"

Only years later did I learn that my father had been electrocuted as he ran out of his cabin to lower the ship's anchor as it reached the harbor. A metal pole crossed a wire above and electricity flowed through the pole to the chains of the anchor. There were five other men with my father in the cabin but since he came out first, he was the one who touched the anchor's chain and got electrocuted, while the other men were able to jump off the ship into the water. I was only seven years old then; it has been hard living for the past thirteen years without my father. No one will ever understand how I feel. I lack the comfort and happiness of families with fathers. I really miss my father's love and support.

Hostility between China and Vietnam was really intense in late 1978. At that time, the Vietnamese government was pushing Sino-Vietnamese [ethnic Chinese living in Vietnam] out of the country. At the beginning of 1979, not long after my father's death, China and Vietnam fought a border war. People from my village started leaving. Four months later, after mourning my father, my mother realized that we also had better leave because nearly half of our fellow villagers had already departed. If we stayed, our lives would not be the same as before now that my father was dead and conditions in Vietnam had got worse. In addition, we knew the Vietnamese really wanted us to leave because we were Sino-Vietnamese. My family, which consisted of my seven-months-pregnant mother, my older sister and brother, myself, my two younger brothers, and my grandparents and their youngest son (my uncle) and their daughter (my aunt), left on a small fishing boat. Most of my other relatives—my aunts and uncles from both sides of my family—had already left and those still in the village planned to go away soon.

To leave, we had to pay the Vietnamese guards in gold. The voyage did not take long because North Vietnam is not far from the southeastern border of China. On our way to China, I lost a younger brother. One hot and humid night during the trip, he climbed on top of the cabin in the boat to sleep with my uncle. Originally, he was sleeping on the deck but my aunt and uncle had an argument, so my aunt traded places with my brother. The next morning, when my mother called for him, there was no answer. She came out of the cabin to look for him and suddenly she started screaming, "Where is J.M.?" Everyone searched but he was nowhere to be found. Thus, he must have fallen into the deep sea and drowned. We rowed the boat around for hours trying to find him, but it was hopeless. The current was strong and he probably had already been carried someplace miles away. When dusk came, we finally gave up. My mother stared into the sea. Even though she was quiet, her grief cannot be described in words. I, for my part, was scared. My heart beat rapidly and I wanted to cry but could not. So I cried, instead, in my heart over my brother's death.

When we reached China, we were temporarily put inside a big warehouse. There were hundreds of other people from Vietnam in there. A few days later, along with other families, we were transported on a boat to a small village in southeastern China. Different groups of families were taken to different villages. In the village where we landed, people worked in sugarcane fields. My family was given a small house to live in. My grandparents, aunt, and uncle were given another small house. After we had been there for two months, my mother gave birth to her last child, a boy. We named him "Ah Loke," which in Cantonese means number six. Life in the village was simple. My mother did not have to work in the sugarcane plantation because she had two small children to look after. Instead, she was given a job in a childcare center. My older sister, older brother, and I went to school. On our way home from school, we gathered sugarcane leaves that my mother used as fuel for the fire over which we cooked our food. Sometimes we stole some pieces of sugarcane so we could chew and suck out the sweet juice. Once in a while, my family went to a crowded city nearby to shop and look around. We got along with our neighbors very well. Sometimes they gave us some of the edible plants they grew; in return, whenever my mother cooked something good, she gave them a share.

Even though life was pretty good in China, my mother wanted to go to Hong Kong because she did not see a future for us in China. She knew her children would most likely grow up to work in the sugarcane fields or we would have to work very hard at some menial job in the city. China is so overpopulated that poor people there have a hard time earning a living. Had my mother thought only of herself, she would have remained in China because life there was quite satisfactory for her. However, she wanted her children to have a better life. She heard that refugees from Vietnam who went to Hong Kong had a chance to go to the United States. So, my mother urged my grandparents to help find some other people who wanted to leave also.

A chance came when my grandfather met a friend in the city who said he was planning to escape to Hong Kong. The man had a boat and knew how to navigate it but he needed one more person to help him. Luckily, since my grandfather was a fisherman, the man had bumped into the right person. My grandfather told his friend that he wanted to bring along his wife, his daughter-in-law, and his five grandsons and one granddaughter. His friend agreed to take us but said that while my grandfather could travel for free, the rest of us had to pay. When my grandfather came home and told my mother the news, she said she was willing to pay, no matter how much it would be.

My grandfather and his friend planned to escape in October on a day when none of us had to report for work or go to school. Thus, if we did not show up, no one would suspect anything. On the appointed day, my grandparents first took me and my next-to-youngest brother to the city. Some hours later, my mother, older sister, older brother, and youngest brother followed. We left the village at different times because we did not want anyone to get suspicious. We brought along dry biscuits and water for the journey. We traveled all afternoon to get to the outskirts of the city to meet the other families who would be escaping with us. We boarded the boat at twilight. As it sailed away, many sentimental thoughts ran through my mind. I knew I would miss the exciting days I had spent stealing and eating sugarcane. I would miss the tranquility of the countryside. At the same time, I had new hope even though I had no idea what would lie ahead.

On the first night at sea, even though there were about a hundred and twenty people in the boat, everything felt peaceful. Everyone seemed to enjoy the first night munching on cookies and dried biscuits and drinking water. The next morning, however, our boat bumped into a rock and shook violently. Everyone was scared. Luckily, no one was thrown overboard, but the rock made a hole in the boat and water rushed in. The men took turns bailing it out. When night came, we saw city lights on the horizon. We were so excited, but suddenly, the boat stopped moving forward. Instead, it kept going round and round in the same spot. The boat was caught in a whirlpool and we could not get out of it. My older brother was nearly thrown off the boat as it swirled. Luckily, he grabbed on to a stranger. Everyone was panicking. Fortunately, a big ship came our way and pulled us out of danger. We were saved! Everyone felt grateful and we gave some gold to the captain of the ship that had rescued us. The big ship towed us toward Macao, the crew gave us instructions on how to get there, and then it left. We beached our boat on the sand at Macao and spent the night on the beach. The next morning, a guard told us we had to leave and pointed out the direction to Hong Kong. When we neared Hong Kong, we ran into two other boats, one in front of us and one behind. One could say we were all "in the same boat" because we were all refugees.

We had to wait a long time before we could get off the boat in Hong Kong because guards questioned every single family. We told them we had come directly from Vietnam and showed them some Vietnamese documents as proof. If they had known we had departed from China, they would have sent us back. We all went into a big warehouse to be processed. The warehouse was packed with people. Many seemed to be starving and everybody smelled bad because we had no water to wash ourselves. After processing, we were taken to a refugee camp where we slept on bunk beds. Hundreds of people shared a common bathroom. We had to stand in long lines for every meal. However, we received three meals a day, mostly rice and canned fish, so we neither starved nor felt completely full. Sometimes, we were fed rice and vegetables.

At first, we were not allowed to go outside the refugee camp, which made us feel as though we were in jail. We disliked our living conditions but we could not do anything about them. We could only hope. We did not know exactly what to hope for—only that something better would come. Later, we were permitted to go outside the refugee camp and to look for work. My mother got a job in a toy factory. The work was hard at first, but she adapted to life in Hong Kong as a working woman. What helped was that she could speak Cantonese. Our family's sense of well-being increased.

Living in Hong Kong was exciting. I saw tall buildings and fast cars for the first time. People in Hong Kong like to go out at night to eat all kinds of food sold by vendors in the streets. They also shop at the marketplace, which is open until very late. Hong Kong's high-rise buildings look so beautiful at night. Because I was only nine years old, I did not have much to do. My friends and I walked around picking up empty soda cans in the streets. We sold them and used the money to buy things to eat. I played in the streets all day because there was nothing else to do.

While we were living in the refugee camp in Hong Kong, one of my mother's younger brothers was admitted into the United States as a refugee. He wrote my mother to tell us that he would be willing to sponsor us and that he had already started doing the necessary paperwork. Day after day, we waited to hear whether our admission into the United States had been approved. Before that lucky day came, something dreadful happened. My youngest brother, the one born in China, caught a childhood disease. By the time my mother took him to the hospital, the doctors told her it was too late. Losing another brother was painful. The pain felt like fire burning in my heart. I also saw the pain my mother suffered as she coped with another death in the family.

In March 1981 my family flew to the United States to live with my uncle in Los Angeles. When we arrived, we had to go through medical examinations. My uncle then helped my family apply for Aid to Families with Dependent Children (AFDC). We were eligible because my mother was a widow with four dependent children. My uncle rented a house for us near where he lived. He also helped enroll me and my two brothers in a public elementary school and my sister in junior high school. My mother went to an adult school to learn English.

I entered the third grade. On my first day at school, my teacher, a blond woman in her early thirties, asked me what my name was. I could not understand a word she was saying. I turned my head and saw the other kids looking at me. I turned my head back to look at my teacher. She smiled at me and I suddenly felt shy. I put my head down and furtively looked at her by rolling my eyeballs upward. After a while, she asked a little Asian girl to translate. Her Cantonese sounded weird but I did understand what she said. Seeing a piece of chalk at the blackboard, I got out of my seat, went to the blackboard, grabbed the chalk, and wrote my name in Chinese characters on the blackboard. When I finished, I turned around and saw all the kids laughing hard at me. I felt so confused and scared. My palms were sweating. I glanced at the teacher and she seemed amused. She led me to a seat next to the little girl so she could help me. I did not mind because she was cute. I shall always remember that first day at school. I quickly realized that in order to fit in with the other kids and to communicate with them, I had to learn English.

There were a lot of Spanish-speakers in my neighborhood. There were also some Asians but very few Whites. The dominant Asian groups were Cambodians and Vietnamese. There were far fewer Chinese. Even though my family was from Vietnam, we spoke only Cantonese. As a result, I had almost no one to talk to. In school, I was quiet and felt left out. I could not participate in discussions because I did not know anything about the topics. The only thing I could do outside of class was to participate in sports. I picked up English slowly in the third, fourth, and fifth grades. I was allowed to skip sixth grade, not because I was smart, but because the school thought I was too old to remain in elementary school. In seventh and eighth grades, I was put into English as a Second Language (ESL) classes because I still did not know much English. Only when I got to ninth grade could I attend regular English classes. In eleventh grade, I had an honors course in Asian American literature. My teacher was very hard on us because he wanted us to be prepared for college. He gave us a novel called *Lonesome Dove* to read and told us we had to write a seventeen-page paper summarizing the novel. I was lazy at the time so I never read that thick book or wrote the paper. When I enrolled in the same teacher's class in world literature the second semester, he refused to admit me. So, I attended a regular class, which was so easy that I got an A.

During those four years in high school, I began to see changes in myself. I gradually assimilated into American culture. I listened to American music, mostly pop. I liked to listen to Debbie Gibson, Roxette, Paula Abdul, Janet Jackson, Tommy Page, Stevie B., and Timmy T. I also watched American movies. I liked movies starring Arnold Schwarzenegger, Jodie Foster, Andie McDowell, Patrick Swayze, Demi Moore, Jean-Claude Van Damme, Julia Roberts, and Michael J. Fox. I also went to see American plays and I ate American food at Pizza Hut, McDonald's, and Carl's Jr. I watched sitcoms on television. I liked *Three's Company*, *Charles in Charge*, *Cheers*, and *Married with Children*. I also liked watching game shows, especially *Wheel of Fortune* and *Jeopardy!*. I watched the Los Angeles Lakers and felt so sad when I heard that Magic Johnson has HIV. I went to picnics at the beach on nice days. I listened to news and talk shows. Thus, I basically did everything that Americans do. In short, Asian Americans *are* Americans. But I can also do things they cannot: I go to Chinese movies and celebrate Chinese New Year. Even though Asians and Americans are similar in many ways, Asians tend to express their ideas and feelings in a different way. Many American youth engage in premarital sex; far fewer Asian Americans do.

During my last two years in high school, my friends and I constantly chased after girls, both in class and after class. I was interested only in Korean and Filipina girls. I had a Korean friend who chased after only Filipina and Mexican girls. Another friend, an American-born Chinese, was interested in any kind of girl. It was funny that we did not chase after girls belonging to the same ethnic groups as ourselves. I guess we felt it was more fun to chase after girls who were different. However, most of the male friends I have are Chinese or Sino-Vietnamese.

Although I often fantasize about getting together with a girl from a different ethnic background, I know that in the end I will very likely end up with someone from the same background as mine. In my first year at the university, I met some beautiful blonds. One whom I particularly liked had a gorgeous body and a cute face, but I knew I had no chance to date her because she was taller than me. I have met many non-Asian girls and I have talked to them, but that's all. I do not see many Asian guys going out with Caucasian girls but there are a lot of Caucasian guys going out with Asian girls. Why is that?

This year, my second year in college, I have become more interested in Asian girls. I am actually narrowing my choices down to Chinese or Sino-Vietnamese girls. However, there is a problem even here: most of the Chinese girls speak Mandarin [*putonghua*], but I speak only Cantonese. So, we often talk to each other in English. However, when we are in a group, they like to speak Vietnamese or Mandarin and I feel left out. I am looking for a young woman who can speak Cantonese because if we ever get serious, I shall have to take her to meet my mother. If the two of them cannot communicate, then there will be problems.

When I found out that I could change my name when I became a naturalized American citizen, I did just that. Now I have both a Chinese and an American name. Having a first name that other people can pronounce makes life easier for me. I remember how other kids used to laugh at my name when I was young. My friends found it awkward to introduce me to their other friends because they had to say my name two or three times before their friends got it. Even my teachers mispronounced my Chinese name.

I have another problem as an Asian American. Most Asian parents expect a lot from their children because they have made so many sacrifices to bring their children to the United States. My mother does not make many demands on me but she does have high hopes for me.

I cannot let her down because she has suffered so much and worked so hard. She works twelve hours a day, five days a week, in a sewing factory. I cannot even imagine myself sitting in a chair for twelve hours a day. To excel in my major, business economics, I must improve my communication skills. In my major, being an Asian American is a disadvantage because Caucasian Americans have a competitive edge over us in terms of language skills. I know that no matter how hard I try, I cannot catch up to them, but I must try to narrow the gap.

I have learned a lot from writing this paper. My past is clearer to me than before. I now appreciate better my mom's situation—what she has gone through for my siblings and me. While I was growing up, as the communication gap between my mother and me widened, she knew less and less about my life in school. She never asked me many questions and I told her only a little. But as I wrote this paper, I realized I should talk to my mother more often and tell her how much I appreciate all the hardships she has endured for the sake of her children.

CHAPTER TWENTY

The Never-Ending Struggle

The author's ethnic Chinese family lived comfortably before the fall of Saigon. Even though her father was poverty-stricken during his youth, in time he owned the largest automobile dealership in town. After the Communists captured Saigon, the family's socioeconomic status declined drastically when her father was forced to become a common laborer. Communist cadres also confiscated whatever they wanted in her home. The family escaped from Vietnam in March 1979 when she was seven years old. She recounts how her mother had ingeniously sewn gold jewelry into the elastic waistbands and collars of their clothing and in the handles of their luggage and how callously Indonesian officials treated them after their boat reached an island in that country. The narrator and her fellow refuge-seekers were kicked out of seven different islands in a nine-month period. The family was eventually resettled in Portland, Maine, where the author adapted to life in America. She experienced a second uprooting when her parents decided to move to Oakland, California. Fearing a complete loss of the children's cultural heritage, the parents enrolled her and her siblings in a Chinese-language school where, as she put it, "the Chinese part of me slowly returned." She wrote this account in 1992.

Tens of thousands of people from Vietnam have escaped clandestinely from their homeland on boats under extremely unsafe and violent conditions. They left for various reasons, ranging from political persecution to social discrimination. My family and I were among the fortunate ones who managed to leave Vietnam in search of freedom and a better life as conditions within Vietnam deteriorated. We were a wealthy family as my father owned an automobile dealership in partnership with his brother. Every day, he came home with piles of money. Sometimes he talked about the old days when he was so poor that the only thing he had to eat was a palmful of rice with rock salt and chili pepper. He had only one pair of shorts and a T-shirt that he wore for five years. His mother had to keep patching both garments with bits of rags she gathered in the market.

I have six siblings and we lived luxuriously and happily. Every morning, my mother drove us to school in an elegant family car. My teacher was very strict and mean. One time, he whipped me because I could not recite the sayings of Confucius. It was my first painful punishment. However, I had lots of fun after school. I usually played in the playground with my siblings and other little children as we waited for our mothers to pick us up. My mother drove us to my father's company where we did our homework. Then she took us shopping or to the park to play. This luxurious life ended when the Communists invaded South Vietnam.

The invasion caused tremendous chaos and lowered the standard of living of many people. The country was short of foreign exchange and the cities were polluted, poorly lit, and unsanitary. The new government used two methods to raise money. It issued a new currency and the old currency became worthless. A law prohibited people from using the old currency. People with money began to buy gold as gold can always be exchanged for money anywhere. All owners of privately owned businesses and those who worked in them were forced to work for the government at a pay of thirty dollars a month. The government also replaced all Chinese teachers with Vietnamese teachers and changed the school curriculum.

With an income of only thirty dollars a month, my father was exasperated and felt restricted. Because he went from being the owner of the largest automobile dealership in Saigon to a common laborer with a fixed income, he lost his ambition and the desire to work. During this period, the government drafted any male it could find so long as he could lift a rifle and pull the trigger. Every so often, Communist soldiers showed up at our house without prior notice and took whatever possessions they pleased. My parents really hated the Communist attempts to redistribute the wealth of the bourgeoisie. They thought the Communists were thieves who stole from the people. They decided this would not be the country where they wanted to raise their children. Fleeing the country was the only way out.

Since my father was a well-known businessman, the captain of a boat planning to take people out of the country asked my father to join his crew because my father knew how to repair engines. The escape plan had to be absolutely secret because anyone trying to flee would surely be put into a labor camp and that person's entire family or group would also be imprisoned. The cost of the trip was four thousand dollars' worth of gold for each person regardless of age. The captain collected the money before the departure date to ensure that no one was a spy. Only the captain and a few of his crew members knew where people were supposed to embark. Everyone had to be ready to depart at any time. My father kept the entire escape process secret from his family until the morning we left in March 1979. He told my mother to pack a few essential belongings and to take all the gold we had hidden in the house. My mother quickly sewed gold necklaces and jade jewelry inside the elastic waistbands on our pants, inside the collars of our shirts, and inside the handles of our luggage. At two o'clock in the morning, my parents woke us up and told us we were going on a trip to a faraway land. They told us we must move quickly and be absolutely quiet. When we arrived at the dock, there were at least thirty other families waiting in line. Standing in line as my father loaded our luggage, I thought the boat was enormous. However, once inside, I began to cry as I saw the huge crowd squeezed tightly together in this suffocating, dark, and gloomy vessel. I wanted to return home to our cozy beds. Because we were among the last people to board, we sat at the back of the boat near the exit door and the bathroom.

The journey was seemingly endless as we sailed across the ocean. It took us three weeks to reach Indonesia. The trip was a horrible and frightening experience. We were robbed by pirates who, fortunately for us, only wanted our valuable items and did not kill anyone. The condition within the boat was hell. Because of the large number of people, no one could make his or her way to the bathroom. So, when mother nature called, we used some kind of jar or container. Many times, children could not wait for the containers and urinated on the deck. In addition to the smell of urine, there were body odors and the foul smell of vomit from those who were seasick. To make matters worse, we lacked water and food the entire time we were at sea. Although the crew circulated five-liter bottles of water from one passenger to the next, there were only a few drops left by the time the bottles reached our hands. Fortunately, my father, who was working with the captain, sneaked some water and food to us once in a while. The sight of people suffering from hunger and thirst made me long for home. However, nothing frightened me more than the death of the person sitting next to me. As we were so tightly squeezed together, I thought he was asleep. I did not know he was dead until I tapped on his shoulder to ask if he wanted any water. Instead of responding to me, his cold and pale face fell against mine. I was in such a state of shock that I screamed and wetted my pants. Then a few volunteers dragged his body to the edge of the boat and tossed the corpse into the open sea. For many nights after that incident, I was afraid to sleep. Every time I closed my eyes and began to fall asleep, the image of the man's cold, pale face and dark purple lips awakened me. This event continued to terrify me for years. Because of this, I am afraid to attend funerals.

It was a dark and cold night when we reached Indonesia. Indonesian soldiers sailed toward our boat and pushed everyone into the water when we were about twenty yards from shore. They stood in the water and watched as we struggled ashore. My father, who had me and one of my younger brothers in his arms and my grandmother on his back, somehow managed to swim toward the beach. My mother, who was carrying my one-year-old baby brother on her back and my little sister on her front who clung to her neck, and holding on to my older brother and sister with her two arms, waited for my father to return to help her. She stood in the ocean for half an hour, soaking wet, before my father came back. Meanwhile, some Indonesian soldiers standing nearby saw my mother, pitied her, and once in a while swam to her to help push my brothers and sisters above the water for air.

After everyone went ashore, the soldiers ransacked our belongings and took whatever treasures they could find. They accidentally wrecked the boat's engine when they were looking for hidden valuables there. They allowed two men to board our boat to take the remaining baggage ashore. People gathered around them to claim their belongings. Because of my mother's wit in hiding the gold in our clothing, we managed to retain our fortune. But since my father and the captain did not have the necessary tools to repair the boat's engine, we were stranded on the island for several months.

Life on the island was regimented and full of sorrows. The refugee camp we lived in was surrounded by barbed wire and armed sentries. The rules in the camp were very strict. Anyone caught escaping was brutally punished and placed into a cage that was submerged in the cold ocean for a night. Each person received a small sack of rice, potatoes, beans, and a few cans of tuna fish—our food supply for a month. Desperate people stole from one another. At night, hungry people wandered around kicking dirt on people's faces while snatching their food. My parents took turns sleeping every night in order to guard our food and to keep us children from danger. During our stay on the island, my parents made many sacrifices similar to those made by Carlos Bulosan's parents [described in *America Is in the Heart*]. They starved for days in order to fill their children's empty stomachs. I was too blind to notice their sacrifices until my mother collapsed one day. She fainted because of the lack of food. Fearing she might die of hunger, I reduced my appetite and controlled my growling stomach. My parents' sacrifices had a great impact on me. It was in Indonesia that I first learned to be sensitive and empathetic. Now, in California, every time I encounter a homeless mother and her children, I always give her some money or I buy some food for them to eat.

After three months of dreadful hardship on that island, we were forced to leave. An Indonesian Navy ship dragged our half-fixed boat and another refugee boat at a very high speed into the ocean and released the towropes. Because the naval vessel was still speeding when it released the ropes, the other refugee boat flipped over and sank. Many people who could not swim drowned. Others desperately struggled toward our boat for help. But our captain just sailed away. I could not understand why we did not try to help those people. I was confused and angry at the captain's horrible, evil action. My mother tried to explain that our boat was already too crowded and its engine was weak. If we had allowed those people to board our boat, it might have sunk and everyone would have drowned. Nonetheless, I resented my father for not doing anything and did not speak to him for a long time after that incident. Years after we arrived in the United States, I finally felt thankful that such a terrible decision had been made; otherwise, I would not be alive today to enjoy the beautiful country called America. I realized that the opposite thing could have happened to us—that is, our boat might have sunk and the other boat might not have rescued us. So, I apologized to my father for not speaking to him for such a long time. Sadly, I learned that it is human nature to be selfish when one's life is at risk.

After two days at sea, our boat's engine stopped running. We landed at a nearby island, where we were treated the same way as in the first island. After living in the refugee camp there for a few weeks, we were forced to leave again. In nine months, we were driven out of seven different islands. Our hope for freedom and democracy was fading fast; my parents were losing faith. Luckily, at our last stop in Malaysia, immigration officials examined and interviewed us. Our interviewers did not go into microscopic details in the same way that U.S. immigration officials who interrogated Chinese immigrants on Angel Island had done. Instead, we were asked where we would like to go and why. In contrast, the health examination was similar to what Asian immigrants went through on Angel Island. Anyone who was sick or had some kind of communicable disease was prohibited from entering the United States. Those who passed the examinations had to wait patiently to be told when they could leave. Fortunately, everyone in our family was healthy and we did not have to wait long. Two weeks after our interview, we boarded a plane in the middle of December 1979 that took us to the United States.

The flight aboard the Pan American jet was wonderful. When I looked out the window, I saw white puffs of clouds and felt like I was in heaven. The service was terrific and the food was appetizing. At the sight and smell of chicken, I became a wild and hungry beast. I tore the chicken apart quickly and shoved it down my throat, fearing that it might be the last time I would have such a decent meal. My father, who was disgusted with my rude manners, snatched the food from me. He said that Chinese people must always be well mannered. What he said stayed in my mind and that is why I now have excellent manners while I eat.

Like many immigrants and particularly refugees, adjusting to life in a new country has been very difficult. We were fortunate to have the Trinity Lutheran Church as our sponsor. Upon our arrival in Portland, Maine, a group of Caucasians from the church greeted us. They even brought a Vietnamese interpreter. But since the interpreter had lived in the United States most of her life, she did not look Vietnamese and spoke Vietnamese with an American accent. Nevertheless, my parents managed to communicate with her. When I first saw the Caucasians, they frightened me and I began to cry. Because their hair and complexion were so pale and their hands so cold, I instantly remembered the cold, pale face of the dead man on the boat. I refused to look at them or follow them as we walked out of the terminal. The interpreter bribed me with a piece of candy and told me the Caucasians were alive, not dead. It took her a long time to get the message across to me because every time she spoke, I made fun of her Vietnamese. Looking back, I regret laughing at her because "what goes around comes around." Now people make fun of my Vietnamese accent when I speak English.

The sponsors took us to a huge house, which was furnished and nicely decorated. The refrigerator was filled with various kinds of meat and other food. It made me think of our home in Vietnam and I missed it terribly. The strangest thing happened as I toured the house. Inside one of the rooms, I found an oval-shaped chair with a cover and an opening in the center half-filled with water. Next to this oval chair was a sink parallel to my forehead. Beside the basin was a long, wide tub. I knew the tub was for bathing but I could not distinguish the toilet from the sink. Thus, I used the sink as a toilet and washed my hands in the water in the toilet. The color of the water varied—sometimes it was clear and other times it was yellow. I thought that was strange so I asked our sponsor what the oval chair was. She demonstrated by pulling down her pants and sitting down over the hole in the oval chair. She said, "Shhhhrrrr," as she imitated the sound of releasing urine. Then she pressed a button on the side of the oval chair and the yellow water disappeared as clear water replaced it. After that, she twisted the knobs on the basin and rinsed her hands in the running water. I laughed at my stupidity.

On my first day at school, I was in culture shock. My brothers, sister, and I stuck out like sore thumbs in a sea of Caucasian faces. I felt inferior and useless because I was so different. My hair was the wrong color, my nose was flat, and I did not speak English. I felt angry and ashamed at the same time. Although the Caucasians around me were very patient in trying to help me learn the language, I often felt offended by their facial expressions that signified to others how stupid they thought I was. Every day brought uneasiness and an endless supply of humiliation and degradation. I wondered if I could ever be as good as white people. I thought of myself as a short, yellow alien. I hated myself and wished that I had blond hair and blue eyes. I struggled and tried to learn the language so that I could be like everyone else—White.

As my English improved, I was gradually accepted and was treated like all the white kids in the school and the neighborhood. As time passed, my native tongues, Chinese and Vietnamese, became almost foreign languages to me. Two languages that had been so familiar since I was a baby were now a distant memory. Our traditional culture also vanished into thin air. As a result of my Americanization, great conflicts arose between my parents and me. It got to a point where we could not communicate or understand each other at all. My father, fearing that his children might lose whatever was left of our language and culture, decided to move to California where Asians are plentiful. I myself was lured by California's warm climate and beautiful beaches.

When we first arrived in Oakland, California, I was very disappointed because we lived nowhere near the beach. Furthermore, I was appalled by the large number of Asians and all kinds of other people in the city. My parents, on the contrary, were delighted. They felt so overwhelmed that they cried. They began to feel at home again. Seeing my parents' happiness made me happy. However, I was also angry at them because I felt they had moved for their own best interests and not those of their children.

On my first day of school in Oakland, I did not know whether I should cry or rejoice when I saw that Asians formed an overwhelming majority in the class. In Maine, I had always been the only Asian in my classes, so I did not know how to associate with Asians. Mentally, I felt I was superior to them because they could not speak English properly. This proved to be a grave mistake on my part because they also thought I was inferior—I now could speak only one language, English, while they knew Chinese, English, and Vietnamese. Some branded me a "banana"—White inside and yellow outside. I was ridiculed for trying to be white when I was not. I did not know what to do. I had learned to act like the white kids in Maine in order to be accepted by them, but here, I was unacceptable. I made no friends and felt very isolated and depressed. I wanted to tell my parents my feelings but I knew that with my broken Chinese, there was no way to express how I felt. Fortunately, my dad saw how confused I was and enrolled me in a Chinese-language school.

In the Chinese school, I made some friends, regained my native language, and learned the value of Chinese customs and traditions. At the beginning, it was very difficult. I was reminded of my first day of school in Maine where I had to overcome a communication barrier. However, after a month of strict discipline and teaching, the Chinese part of me slowly returned. I began to understand that hundreds and thousands of Asians had immigrated into the United States in the same way as I had done, yet they managed to retain their ethnic identities and cultural traditions while adapting to a Western way of life. After six years in the Chinese-language school, I realized that my parents had moved to California not simply for their own best interests but also for the best interests of their children. They wanted us to be proud of who we are.

Indeed, my journey to America, the land of freedom and liberty, was an unforgettable experience. But it was in the United States that I was forced to open my eyes and to understand my past. I learned that nothing is impossible if one sets one's mind and heart to it. Since America is a land of opportunity, I should always aim high and never be biased and judgmental toward anyone or anything. America is my new home and I shall try my best to achieve the American dream, but I shall always remember my roots and never forget where I came from.

CHAPTER TWENTY-ONE

An Unfinished Journey

The author escaped from Vietnam with his uncle's family in mid-1979 when he was twelve years old. Since his father was a judge, the Communist authorities sent him to a re-education camp. To feed her children, his mother scraped together earnings from various jobs and from selling sandwiches on the street. She sent her children out of the country one by one—a common practice to ensure that at least some family members would survive and find safe haven. All the narrator's family members failed in their first attempts to flee, but that did not stop them from trying again. The most gripping part of this chapter is the author's recollection of how pirates robbed the refuge-seekers and raped women and girls on the island of Kokra, where they stayed for three weeks, surviving ironically on the food that the pirates had given them. Officials from the United Nations High Commissioner for Refugees rescued the group and took them to the refugee camp at Songkla, Thailand. After the author's father was released from the re-education camp, his parents failed repeatedly in their escape attempts, which made the author realize that he was "their only ticket out of Vietnam." He therefore filed a petition to sponsor their entry into the United States via the Orderly Departure Program. He was still waiting to hear the result when he wrote this essay in 1988.

I was born in Saigon, the capital of South Vietnam. When I was five, my father accepted a post as a judge in a province on the outskirts of Saigon. Part of my early childhood was spent in the countryside, away from the bright lights of Saigon but close enough to that city so that my family could feel the sense of security that seemed to radiate for miles around the capital. Life in the countryside, as I remember, was pleasantly easy. A maid helped my mother with the household chores and a chauffeur drove us children to school. Sometimes on the weekends, the whole family went out for ice cream. On rare occasions, we went to Vung Tau, a seaside resort where we had a vacation home. I enjoyed swimming in the ocean, playing in the wet sand, and watching fishermen as they pulled in their nets filled with fish. Each trip to Vung Tau was like going to heaven.

New Year—Tet, as it is called in Vietnam—was a festive time of celebration. Everyone put on his or her best clothes. All kinds of food especially prepared for this occasion covered the dining tables in most families. Little children wished their elders a happy New Year; in return, they received little red envelopes containing money to wish them good luck. In 1975, Tet came in early February. As people in the town where we lived welcomed the year of the cat in the spirit of peace amid the sound of firecrackers, one hardly noticed the sound of artillery firing in the distance. As the celebration came to an end, the sound of gunfire became more audible. News of terrible battles began to dominate the newspaper headlines. In March, the battle of Ban Me Thuot suddenly became the topic of adult conversations. The South Vietnamese soldiers fought hard but morale was at an all-time low because the United States had cut its military aid to the South Vietnamese government. After a week of fighting, Ban Me Thuot fell. New battles started in twelve different provinces all over central and southern Vietnam. I was only eight years old at the time but I could feel that something was wrong. My father became intensely quiet, while my mother did her best to disguise her deep worries. Late one night as I lay in bed unable to sleep, I looked through the narrow opening of my bedroom door and saw my mother writing our names on some cotton bags with shoulder straps and my father burning documents and family photographs in an old metal container. The next morning, my parents told me to pack my clothes in one of the cotton bags so that we could go to Saigon. I felt immediately that this was not going to be a normal visit to my grandmother's house and that I might not return home for a long time. A week after we arrived in Saigon, the South lost to Communist forces.

On the morning of April 30, 1975, Communist soldiers marched through the gates of the presidential palace, waved North Vietnam's flag from the balcony, and declared victory. The streets in Saigon were filled with people. South Vietnamese soldiers stripped off their uniforms as armed North Vietnamese troops marched along the streets. My father and I were in our car trying to move through the mass of people to get back to my grandmother's house. I saw hundreds of military uniforms, along with guns and ammunition, scattered all over the streets. Distinctive amid a jumble of incoherent sounds was the roar of victory chants and of little children crying for their mothers. Our car moved very slowly and was forced to halt at times by the crowds. As we passed by a squad of marching Communist soldiers, one of them waved at us. I noticed that my father flashed a quick grin back at him. This, I could not understand. For all I knew, these soldiers were our enemies. At another street corner, another soldier from the North waved at us. Again, a grin appeared quickly on my father's face. Then his face turned grim as the soldier looked the other way.

Two weeks after the fall of Saigon, the uproar had calmed down somewhat. Our family moved into the house of my aunt, who had left for France a year earlier. The new government called in men who had worked under the previous regime to report to camp. They were told they had to readjust their way of thinking. We learned that judges and other high-ranking officials of the judiciary branch of government would be sent to re-education camps for twenty-five days. My father reported to the local authorities and was taken away. He was imprisoned in a re-education camp for more than five years.

After my father was taken away, my mother gathered us together and warned us about what was ahead. I was nine years old then and did not understand the full impact of the changes, but some aspects of our new lifestyle were noticeably different from the days before Saigon fell. The prices of pork, beef, and chicken skyrocketed and we no longer had meat on our dinner table. Most of the time, we ate rice and vegetables and occasionally fish. My mother always ate the meat left on the bones, telling us that that was the best part of the fish. We believed her. Only years later did I realize she was letting her children eat the best part of the fish while she sucked out the tiny bits of flesh left on the bones. At first, we had plenty of rice to eat but soon, rice, too, became expensive. So we mixed the rice with less expensive yams and potatoes. My wardrobe consisted of two pairs of pants and three shirts. Before April 1975, each of us children received a new outfit sewn by our mother every New Year. But now, there was no income and our savings drained as the days passed by. My mother tried to make ends meet by selling off some of our possessions. First went the car, then the motorcycle, after that the piano, and finally just about everything except the absolute necessities. We had come to grips with this harsh new reality.

In 1978, my mother decided we had to find a way to generate an income in the absence of my father. We opened a sandwich stand. Every morning, we children woke up at six to help our mother make sandwiches. In those early hours, the streets were often empty as the sun came out. Pushing the cart containing the sandwich stand down the street alone when all was still quiet was something I really enjoyed.

Our sandwiches did not bring us much money, so my mother took on a second, then a third job. She made wedding cakes, sewed, and handmade artificial flowers in order to provide for our family.

We were allowed to visit my father once every four or five months. The last few times I saw my father, he appeared pale and frail as a result of the harsh conditions in the re-education camp. His hair had turned grey and his eyes were sunken deep in their sockets. He always smiled as he saw us. My mother usually cried as she told my father not to worry about us and to take care of his health. My father knew how hard it was on her to provide for the family. They comforted each other and hoped that everything was going to be better soon. But they knew nothing short of a miracle could turn our lives around. Our visits usually lasted only fifteen minutes before my father had to go back to his cell, carrying the food we had brought him. My mother held tightly on to my hand as she waved goodbye and watched him disappear behind the gate of the camp.

As early as 1976, South Vietnamese began escaping from the country by sea in small boats. By the beginning of 1979, the number fleeing the country had grown much, much larger. Those who decided to escape faced great risks. About half of them were caught by Communist policemen before they even set foot in their boats. After spending time in prison, they returned home empty-handed, their possessions having been confiscated by the government as punishment for their crimes. As for those who made it out to sea, the possibility of never reaching land was as great as their chances of surviving. Most of the boats were not made for ocean travel. Many sank. Some boats with broken engines drifted for weeks as people on board died of thirst and hunger. Most of the women faced the possibility of being raped by pirates. This was the price they had to pay for freedom.

As we gathered around the dinner table one night, my mother told us that she planned to send us overseas—especially my brother and me before we approached the age when we would be drafted. We listened as she assured us that once we got out safely, she and my father would join us as soon as he was released. So, one by one, she sent us away. We all failed in our first few escape attempts. My brother was the first among us to escape successfully. He was rescued by a Norwegian ship and was taken safely to Norway. My mother burst into tears when she received his telegram. The suspense was over: my brother had made it. A few months later, I tried again. This time, I felt something that told me that I would succeed. We said our usual casual goodbyes. We smiled as we exchanged words of farewell. My sister jokingly said, "See you home soon." But not this time. This time

I would be gone for good. As my thoughts wandered, my tears started to pour. Soon, everyone was crying.

Along to take care of me on this trip was my uncle and his family. He had a wife and two little children, one aged four and the other four months. After two hours on a bus, we found ourselves in a rural area. The road was narrow with no poles for electric wires along the side. Houses were built of bamboo and leaves, surrounded by fields of crops. We stayed in the back of a small house, our hideout until midnight. In that house were several people also waiting to escape. At midnight, a guide led us to our clandestine rendezvous spot by the river's edge. It was pitch dark. The only source of light was the moon. The guide had a flashlight but would use it only in case of an emergency. He did not want the police to see us. The walk in the dark was long. There were thorny bushes along the way and potholes in the ground. We tried our best to avoid them. When we arrived at the water's edge, we saw many others sitting quietly on the ground. As soon as everyone had arrived, we hopped on little canoes that took us to the "mother boat," which used to be a fishing boat. We were told to stay in the lower level of the boat. When there was no more room on the lower level, some of the passengers had to lie down under a large sheet of plastic on the deck. The boat measured about thirty-six feet by ten feet. It was smaller than the size of a tennis court but held eighty-one people.

We hit a storm the first night at sea. We all became sick and vomited all over the deck. At dawn, the captain told us we had made it—we had slipped past the patrol along the shore and also survived the storm. Everyone was happy. But we discovered that during the storm, two of the four water tanks had fallen into the ocean. We had only the two tanks that were on the lower level left. Exhausted from vomiting, I was glad to breathe the fresh air of the ocean. I looked around and saw water everywhere. For the first time, I realized how big the ocean was and how dangerous it could be. This was not the same ocean as the one I had known in Vung Tau.

On the third day of our journey, our engine broke down. At first, everyone panicked. Then we slowly settled down and gazed at one another for now it would be up to faith to get us out of this ordeal. Someone started to say a prayer and soon a small group formed. They sat and prayed together. Each person's allotment of water was now cut in half. We would get only half a cup a day. We tried not to eat much because most of the food we had brought with us was dry and eating it would increase our thirst. We drifted for six days. During this time, we saw a number of commercial ships but none stopped to rescue us.

On the sixth day, a Thai fishing boat approached us. The fishermen climbed into our boat and gestured that they would help us. They were our saviors. They gave us food and water and fixed our engine. In return, they searched through our bags and took most of our valuables. No one objected because the fishermen had given us hope. They told us we were approximately three hours from Thailand. We felt excited as we headed in the direction they had pointed out to us.

Two hours later, we saw a thin strip of land and shouted with joy. We thought we had finally reached our destination safely—our hardship had ended. But we were wrong. The hardship was just beginning. Two fishing boats approached us from the rear. We did not stop and kept moving forward toward the land. They caught up with us and threw ropes over our boat to force it to stop. We knew these were not the same kind fishermen whom we had met earlier. These men were pirates. Because most of our valuables had been taken earlier, they found little they wanted. They looked disappointed as they returned to their boats. One of the boats charged straight at our boat at full speed. As the two boats collided, the front of their boat smashed our top cover into little pieces. Women screamed and little children cried. We knew this would be the end of our journey. Suddenly that boat sailed away. The second fishing boat pulled us away and dumped us on a deserted beach on an island named Kokra. We spent the next twenty-one days there until a boat sent by the United Nations High Commissioner for Refugees rescued us.

Those twenty-one days on the island were living hell for all of us, especially the women. The first night we were there, pirates came with knives and guns. They separated the women from the men as they searched everybody thoroughly. They punched a man in the face who had hidden a ring in his pocket; as he fell to the ground, the pirates kicked his chest and face. As it was dark, some of the women managed to sneak away and they hid as the pirates took the rest of the women away to rape them.

The next morning, we found graffiti on a wall warning us about the pirates. The graffiti included maps that showed us where the hideouts for women were. We followed the instructions and hid all the women. My aunt had to abandon her four-month-old daughter and hand her to my uncle as she herself went into hiding. Husbands took food to their wives when the pirates were not present. Ironically, it was the pirates who had given us this food. I suppose they wanted to keep us alive so that they could torture the men and rape the women.

I came to know a girl from our boat. She looked about twelve years old. She had short hair and round eyes and was about five feet tall. Her father put soot on her face with the hope that she would resemble a boy so that the pirates would leave her alone. With soot covering most of her face, she did look like a boy but when I looked closely, I saw the face of a pretty, fearful, innocent girl. One night, she and I sat on the sand and talked about what we planned to do if we made it to America. She did not say much; in Vietnam, girls do not converse with boys. Even when two young people are going steady, they do not hold hands in public. Even after they are married, it is not acceptable for them to kiss in public. As we were talking, I saw Thai pirates jumping off their boat and heading toward us. The girl also noticed them and I saw the fear in her eyes. The pirates shone their flashlights directly into our faces. One of the pirates noticed the soot on the girl's face. He wiped it off, turned to the others, and smirked in victory: he had found a girl. Three pirates dragged her to a nearby bush and took turns raping her as the whole camp watched in horror. A long time passed before they emerged from the bush. Her father ran into the bush and carried her out. She had fainted. Crying, he pulled his hair and repeatedly wailed, "Why, God, why?" For the first time in my life, I felt disgusted by human cruelty. I was afraid to approach her again because I did not know how she felt. After that night, she went into hiding with the rest of the women.

One of the young women in our group found a hiding spot in a tall grass field. She lay flat on her stomach and covered her back with dried grass as she hid herself from the pirates. One day, as she was running to her hideout, a pirate saw her. They searched the grassfield, determined to find her. After a long search, they still had not succeeded in finding their prey. So they burned the grassfield down as they waited for her to run out, but there was no sign of the young woman. Eventually they gave up their search. After they left, her father, along with some other people, rushed to the spot where she was hiding. There, they found her still lying on her stomach with her back burned severely.

On the twenty-first day, representatives of the United Nations High Commissioner for Refugees rescued us. They took us to a refugee camp at Songkla in southern Thailand. We stayed there as we waited for our paperwork to be processed. The camp was situated along the seashore. It was small and filled with refugees. We were given a spot in one of the bungalows. Our family of six and two other people occupied a small space that was about fifteen feet long and seven feet wide. This was to be our shelter for the next nine months. Because of the tiny space we had, I slept outside on the sand. Before I went to sleep, I always filled up our water tank, which had to be filled daily. There were only about ten water pumps in the camp and the lines were very long in the daytime as people waited to get water. Life in the camp was slow. I was bored as there was not much to do except to wait and hope that the next serial number to be called for departure would be ours.

My aunt received some money from her parents who had reached the United States earlier. We used the money to buy food and clothing. We were lucky: not everyone had relatives abroad. One big problem in the camp was the restrooms, which were located behind the camp about three blocks from our bungalow. My little cousin, who was only four years old at the time, had difficulty coping with the distant restrooms. I often walked her to the restrooms as she was too weak to carry the bucket of water to be used to dispose of the waste. At times, she just could not wait until we got there and she relieved herself in her pants.

For Catholics in the camp, mass was said every Sunday. Most of the churchgoers had the same prayer that they repeated week after week: let their serial number be called next. My own prayers were finally answered when our number was called. We were on our way to America! My uncle and his family and I woke up early to get ready. A bus took us to the airport. All our bags were searched thoroughly before we could get on the airplane. It was a long flight. As the plane was about to land, I said to myself, "Now we have found freedom."

When we got off the plane, my aunt's family was there to greet us. She drove us to her father's home. I sat quietly in the back of the car and watched the scenery go by. Everything looked so beautiful but somewhat strange to my eyes. The streets were wide, the buildings were tall, and people had all kinds of hair color. When we arrived at Grandpa's house, he showed us around. The things I saw in that house in the next few days amazed me. The floor of the whole house was covered in red carpet. In the living room were an electric organ, a color television, and a tall grandfather clock. The kitchen was big, equipped with an electric stove, a refrigerator with an ice-maker, and a microwave oven with funny little buttons. I whispered to my aunt, "Grandpa is so rich." As we gathered around the kitchen table, my little cousin ran in and shouted, "Mommy, Mommy, we have a bathroom right here in the house. I won't have to walk so far anymore." My aunt smiled and bent down to hug her as all of us burst out laughing.

I had a few weeks to enjoy my new life in America before school started. Because I did not speak English, I was placed in the sixth grade—a grade I had already passed in my homeland. I had problems with all the subjects except math. I could understand math with ease except, of course, for word problems. As my English improved, I quickly skipped to seventh grade, then eighth grade, all in the same year. In eighth grade, I studied new subjects, such as biology and history. By the time I got to high school, I could understand everything and did well in all my classes. I started to associate with my American classmates and got involved in many school activities. I was a member of various clubs and held office in some of them. When I graduated from high school, I ranked third in my class and was recognized as the most active student on campus.

In 1981, I received great news: my father had been released from the re-education camp. I was so happy and hoped that my parents would be able to escape as I had done. But after several failed attempts, they lost everything they had and were forced to give up trying. I realized that I am now their only ticket out of Vietnam. So I filled out sponsorship forms and I am still waiting for the Vietnamese government to allow my parents to leave the country via the Orderly Departure Program.

Since I came to the United States, my parents have written me to remind me constantly to do well in school. I have tried to do so, and hope that when I graduate from college, I shall find a job and build a successful life here, a life that many people in Vietnam would envy. However, no matter how successful I turn out to be, I shall never be completely joyous until I am reunited with my family once again.

CHAPTER TWENTY-TWO

From Vietnam to Germany to the United States

The author's parents owned a photography studio in Saigon and had a booming business during the war as they had a contract with the U.S. Army. His family failed in their first attempt to escape from Vietnam in 1978, but his mother and two of his brothers succeeded in a second try in 1979 and made their way to Germany. The author, his sister, and his father finally managed to escape in 1982 when he was thirteen years old. The two brothers who had gone to Germany first then moved to the United States and later sponsored the rest of the family for entry. This account, written in 1991, contains a vivid description of the family's first escape when they were caught and imprisoned. The narrator, his mother, and his siblings were released after several weeks but his father was kept for another year and a half. However, because the father was in a prison camp, and not a re-education camp, his family could visit him every three weeks and he was allowed to keep the food they brought. The wardens finally released the man when they realized the family had no more money to offer bribes—another indication of the corruption in the post-1975 government. This account is notable for its description of how kindly the West German government, as well as the German people, treated Vietnamese refugees during a period when Germany had relatively few nonwhite immigrants.

I was born in Saigon and have three brothers and one sister. I am the third child. My parents owned a photography studio. During the Vietnam War, business boomed because my parents had a contract with the U.S. military. So, we were a rather affluent family. Unlike many Vietnamese, my parents did not like to store gold and jewelry at home. Instead, they spent most of the money they earned on us, the children. They wanted us to have a good life and fulfilled all our wishes. My father did put aside a large portion of his earnings, however, so that he could design and build a very large house in Saigon. Every month, we closed the photo shop for a few days and went to Vung Tao to visit my grandparents. Life in those days was peaceful and remarkably beautiful.

My parents sent my brothers, sister, and me to the best private schools, hoping that we would accomplish things that they themselves never could. They asked for nothing in return for all the love and care they showered on us except that we study hard and respect them. Before I entered the first grade, my mother spent several hours a day teaching us arithmetic, reading, writing, and French. It was a terrible experience because my mother has a very hot temper and at that time I was too young (about four) to understand how important an education would be. Every day, she evaluated how much each of us had learned. If we were negligent in our studies, she punished us in painful ways. Thus, by the time I entered elementary school, I already knew how to multiply and divide as the multiplication table had been forced into my brain. Unlike my classmates, I could also read and write fairly well, so there was not much for me to learn at school.

Before 1975, every year we had a grand family reunion during the Tet festival. All my relatives gathered at my grandparents' house and we spent several days celebrating New Year. It was on those occasions that I had a chance to meet many relatives from far away. No matter where they lived—in Vietnam or in another country—they all came to the reunion. The women cooked delicious dishes, while the men washed the dishes and helped in various other ways. The children were not asked to do anything, so we just ran around the village and played with one another until we were called to lunch or dinner. There was not enough room in my grandparents' house to sleep some two hundred people. The children slept in the available beds and the adults slept on the floor. Although sleeping on the floor was not very comfortable, a feeling of warmth, love, and unity filled the air. Adults talked about their lives and offered to help those who needed it. Everybody took care of everyone else.

After the fall of Saigon, even though some of my uncles and aunts had supported the Viet Cong, the Communists from North Vietnam accused them of having been U.S. Central Intelligence Agency (CIA) agents. The new government put them in jail for several years. The Communist officials harassed us often because my father was related to the "accused." They frequently came to our house, confiscating our property so that they could, they said, share our wealth with the poor. Some of my relatives had fled the country with their American friends just before the war ended, so that was another black mark against us. The Communists used a currency-exchange program to limit the amount of wealth that people could retain. Each family was allowed to exchange only a certain amount of the old currency for the new. This hurt my family more than some others because we did not stock gold but only cash at home. We could not sell any of our possessions because we did not want the government to get suspicious.

My grandfather passed away in 1976. A moderately large number of family members gathered to mourn him. My grandparents had many friends in Vung Tau who also participated in the funeral. As children of the oldest son (my father), we had to march from my grandparents' house to the cemetery dressed in white, the color of mourning in Vietnam. Each of us carried a picture of my grandfather in our arms. More than four hundred people attended the funeral.

In 1978, my parents decided to escape from Vietnam with the hope that we could enjoy the freedom and opportunities we would not have under Communism. We went to Vung Tau frequently to plan our escape. One day, we packed everything we might need and went to "visit" my grandmother. I still remember vividly our first attempt to flee Vietnam. It was a moonless night. I crouched inside a wooden shack that was somebody's home. By the dim light of three lanterns, I observed my surroundings. We were in a large room with four dirt-brown walls that was crowded with people huddled next to the few possessions they brought along to start new lives in some foreign land. Everyone was quiet because we were afraid to speak. It was so quiet that I could hear the sound of waves murmuring. The coconut palms surrounding the house shrieked as they swayed in the ocean breeze. Parents watched their children and kept them quiet. Most slept peacefully on their parents' laps. Nobody said a word. We were all waiting to get on the boat and slink away in the darkness to safety. A baby's cry broke the silence. Other babies awoke and started crying also. The parents tried desperately to calm their babies. The anxiety on their faces spoke for itself.

Then, BANG! all four walls shook as they were being kicked in. Men rushed in and commanded, "Stay where you are! Put your hands behind your head!" The intruders demolished the walls. I saw policemen everywhere. I did not understand what was happening but I was very scared. I turned to my dad for reassurance. He whispered, "There is nothing to worry about," as he took me into his bosom. All the children were shaken up by the gunshots the policemen fired and began to cry. At gunpoint, the policemen forced us to leave the room. They put us in a huge, rusty, military camion and hauled us away. It was about 1:00 A.M. The area we were in was covered in total darkness. "Daddy, where are they taking us?" I asked. "I don't know yet, but we will all be fine," my dad whispered in my ear. On the way to the prison, my dad took all his valuable cameras and threw them into the bushes along the road. He did not want the Communists to confiscate them.

Finally, we arrived at a prison camp. The whole area was lit up by a huge beam shining from the guard tower. We were unloaded and taken to a large hall where each of us was strip-searched for anything valuable that we might have hidden. The policemen took my dad's belt buckle because they believed it was made of gold. Despite my fear, I fell asleep while they were trying to decide where to put us. When I awoke, I saw that we were in another hall. No one told us how long we were going to stay there. We guessed that our arrest was part of a great scam. The owner of the boat had apparently stabbed us in the back by promising the police they would get whatever gold we had.

I ran around the hall looking for my dad. "Mom, where is Daddy?"

"They have taken him away," she answered. I cried. That whole day, I did nothing but cry. I did not even feel like eating. My mouth was dry, my throat hurt, and my stomach was empty. When my mother told me she thought they would release us soon, I felt better. Another day went by; we just sat and waited. A few days later, I began to play with some of the other kids. Another two weeks went by. I lost hope that we would ever be released. I missed my dad so much.

Then, one afternoon, while I was playing with the other kids, I noticed my dad working on the other side of the prison yard. We ran toward him but the fence that divided the yard into two stopped us. He turned around, looked at me, smiled, and asked how we were doing. He told us to take care of ourselves and Mom. None of us children said a word. My eyes were dewy with tears. "Daddy, when are they going to let us go?" I finally managed to blurt out. "Pretty soon. Don't worry," he reassured me. He always smiled when he talked to us but I could see the sadness deep in his eyes. When the guard shouted at him to get back to work, he told us to go back to our hall. That night I cried again. Everyone in my family did. We missed my dad so much. My mother looked so sad as she worried about him. She wondered how the guards were treating him. Several times a day she prayed that we would all be released soon.

It was boring in the prison camp. Every day we woke up about the same time. We just sat around and talked to each other. We got the same food for lunch every day—noodles, uncooked on top and burned on the bottom. Some days, they gave us a little bit of fish for dinner. There was no running water in the camp and we had to get water from a well, which did not have much water in it. So, we could not wash ourselves. In the afternoons, the other kids and I played until exhaustion overcame the ache in our hearts. Many people in the camp got sick. The smell of fresh and old vomit permeated the air, mixed with the stench of sick, unwashed bodies and the reek of manure from a nearby potato patch. In the daytime, flies dominated the hall. Everywhere I turned, there were thousands of them. They sat on people's food and on little babies. At night, it was the mosquitoes' turn. We covered ourselves with whatever we could find to protect us but nothing hindered the cockroaches that crawled over our bodies. I hated the cockroaches. I stepped on them whenever I could. But when I slept, they crawled wherever they wished.

Two more weeks went by and I still did not see my father. I thought they would never release us and we would have to spend the rest of our lives in this ugly prison camp. That thought really scared me. Then, one day, while I was playing with the other kids, we heard our names announced on the loudspeaker hanging in a corner of the hall. We were informed that we would be released in the next two days. We were all so happy until my mother noticed that they had not called out my father's name. That night, I had a very strange feeling. I was glad we could finally leave but the thought that my father would not be coming with us made me sick. We learned that they had decided to transfer my father to another camp where prisoners were locked together in small cells and were rarely released until they had been there for at least a year.

When we got home, we discovered that the government had confiscated all our property. We lost our house and everything else we had. Because we had attempted to escape from Vietnam, we had to face the government officials who gave us a lot of trouble. They forced us to move around quite often. My mother decided to take us to my aunt's house, which was located near the camp my father had been transferred to, so that it would be convenient to visit him. Every three weeks, the officials allowed us to bring him some food and other necessities. Sometimes we even got to talk to him, but only after my aunt gave the guard a bribe.

A few months later, my mother and two brothers made a second attempt to escape from Vietnam. This time they succeeded. They left my sister and me behind to wait for my father's release. After my mother's departure, our home always seemed so quiet. Every day, we waited for a letter from my mother. My sister, aunt, and I could not afford to leave Vietnam because we had no more gold left. The only thing we could do was wait. I found it hard to study because as I sat in class, my mind kept wandering off. I visited my father quite often. The guards knew me so they did not give me much trouble. My father told me to study hard, take good care of my sister, and be nice to my aunt.

A year later, when it became clear to the authorities that we had no money left to bribe them, they released my father from prison. With his support and care, I began to study again. It was during this period that I met the best friends I have ever had. There were four of us: a very beautiful and smart girl; a lively, cute, intelligent, and short girl; the best boy student in our school; and me. We studied and played together. Every day at lunch, we ate the same food. Whatever each of us had, we shared it with the others.

My mother and my two brothers were allowed to go to Germany after spending six months in the Pulau Bidong refugee camp in Malaysia. A year later, my brothers left for Florida under the sponsorship of another aunt of mine. Three years after that, my dad, sister, and I managed to leave Vietnam and reunited with my mother in Germany.

Coming from Vietnam, an underdeveloped country, everything I saw in Germany surprised me. The weather was very cold—it was twenty-five degrees Celsius below zero when we arrived at the Frankfurter Flughafen [Frankfurt Airport]. I was so excited as I touched snowflakes for the first time. Everything in sight was covered with snow and looked so beautiful. But it took only a few minutes for the cold to penetrate through my clothing. German officials took us to a reception center for refugees and they tried to help us get in touch with my mother to inform her that we had arrived. While we were in the center, the Germans gave my father some money and he took us to a nearby supermarket to buy food. I was amazed at the plentiful products and the nice decorations in the supermarket. I ran around looking at and touching everything. I was especially surprised to see a price tag on every item. There were many items on the shelf that I had never seen or heard of before. That first visit to the supermarket was an intriguing experience.

After staying at the refugee reception center for a few weeks, we moved out to live with my mother. We moved to a neighborhood in Frankfurt where only a few Vietnamese families lived. In compliance with the German regulations on education, we had to go to school immediately. We did not get a chance to take any language preparation classes. The school had no German classes for foreign students. At that time there were not many foreign students in Germany. It was very hard on my sister and me because we could not communicate with anybody. Each day, I went to school, sat in class, listened to what the teachers said without understanding any of it, and waited for the recess bell to ring so I could leave.

At home, there was virtually nothing for me to do. We had a television but I could not understand a word regardless of what channel I switched on. My mother bought us a German-Vietnamese dictionary. Every day after school, my sister and I spent time memorizing words from the dictionary. Doing so was not particularly fun, but it was the only way we could learn to communicate with other students in school. Some kids in my class were very nice and kind. They offered to help me learn their language and do my homework. They went over with me whatever I did not understand in class. Each time I pronounced a German word wrong, they gently corrected me in an effort to eliminate my accent. Thus, even though I did not fully understand what they said, I felt as though I was among my best friends.

A German lady in our neighborhood also devoted some time to help us daily after school. Each day, right after school, we dropped by her house. She cut out pictures from magazines and newspapers and put them together in a booklet, which she used to teach us German, because she believed that conventional readers designed for little children would not serve us well. She had two kids—a girl my sister's age and a little boy. Her family treated us so well that they even took us along on vacations, during which we had ample opportunities to practice speaking German.

After living for a year in Frankfurt, our teachers recommended that my sister and I be transferred to Liebig Gymnasium—a school that prepares students to go to college after they finish the thirteenth grade. The new school was a lot harder than the first one we had attended. Aside from my sister and me, there was only one other Vietnamese in a school that enrolled more than two thousand students. However, I had no problem making new friends there. The classes were very difficult—we studied fourteen subjects each semester. The Germans put heavy emphasis on teaching science and foreign languages to their children at an early age. By the time students graduate from a gymnasium, they will have studied eight years of biology and six years of chemistry and physics, and their mastery of mathematics will be superb. Besides, they will know several foreign languages.

As time went by, I grew accustomed to the German way of life. Mr. J., a Danish-German, became a friend of my parents. He was interested in Vietnam, its people, and its culture. He often came to visit us. When he found out that we used to play the mandolin when we were young, he gave my sister and me each a violin. He also found us a violin teacher and paid for the two lessons we had every week.

Soon, I felt like Germany had become my second homeland. There, I got almost everything I needed—good friends, people I could always count on, and a good education hard to find anywhere else in the world. One of my favorite hobbies was skiing. Every Christmas, my two best friends and I went to Austria for a few weeks. We had pen pals in Neukirchen and Vienna, so we often spent Christmas vacation with them. Germans work hard but they spend a lot of money on vacations because they consider vacations an essential part of their lifestyle. No matter how poor they are, they still go on vacation at least once a year. The government gives even Germans who are unemployed and are living on welfare money to go on vacation, as well as supplies them with winter and summer clothing.

Just when my life began to look so rosy, my parents told us that my aunt in the United States was sponsoring us for admission and that we would be leaving Germany in a few months. I was disappointed as I had come to think of Germany as my second homeland. But the thought of seeing my two brothers again helped convince me that the move was the right thing to do.

I arrived in the United States in 1986. It was the first time in almost eight years that I had seen my brothers. They looked so strange. I did not know what to say to them. All I could do was to prevent tears from rolling down my cheeks. None of us said a word. Only my father was strong enough to hug them and ask them questions. During the years we had been separated, I often wondered what they were like, but now, standing in front of them, I felt too awkward to talk to them. Everything I had planned to say to them got stuck in my throat. It took days before we began to feel reasonably comfortable with one another. Unfortunately, things did not work out well in my aunt's place, so my parents decided to move to Orange County in California.

Having spent virtually all our money to pay for our airfare from Germany, we had little money left. My brothers gave us eight thousand dollars that they had saved over the years, which enabled us to move across the country. My fifty-four-year-old father found it difficult to learn English at his age. The unemployment rate was also fairly high at that time and my father had never had any formal training in photography even though he was a talented photographer who had won several photography contests held in Japan, Paris, Hong Kong, and elsewhere. Unfortunately, he lost all his negatives during our first failed escape attempt. Despite his talents, he found it very difficult to get a job. Some of his friends found him a job delivering furniture from a store owned by Chinese to the homes of customers. However, he did not have enough strength for this kind of heavy work so he stayed on that job for only a few months. Then he tried delivering newspapers early every morning. Later, he worked as a kitchen helper. Finally, he found a job working in the darkroom of a photo shop.

My mother had a somewhat easier time for she had worked for Americans for several years in Vietnam. She had also worked as a bookkeeper at the U.S. Rhein-Main Air Base in Frankfurt. However, she could not find a job as a bookkeeper in the United States because she did not have a formal certificate. She learned from one of her friends that she could work as a seamstress at home. Every day, she sat for fourteen hours sewing pants, shorts, and shirts and was paid about seventy-five cents for each item. Because of our financial difficulties, there was a lot of tension in our house. Eventually, my mother found a position working for the federal government as a bookkeeper. To help my family, I took a job ironing clothes for a few dollars a day. As my English improved, I got a job at McDonald's and worked fifteen to twenty hours a week. The pay was low but I had a chance to practice my English with my co-workers.

When I first went to high school, I was shocked to see some students carrying their babies to school. Back in Vietnam, people usually do not get married at such a young age and premarital sex is almost unheard of. Vietnamese consider relationships too important to be developed overnight. Getting divorced is considered a disgrace. I also did not understand what a "drug" is. The words *cocaine, marijuana,* and so on were all strange to me. Another surprise I had was how important sports are to Americans. Some kids don't do well in school but they don't care; all they worry about is whether they can play certain sports well. They know that professional athletes can earn much more money than college graduates. Everything in America seems to revolve around good, easy money.

Once again, I had to sit in classes where I could not understand anything. I felt so left out. Some of my teachers told me that maybe I did not belong in their classes; this really upset me. I spent nights and days studying, looking up words in the dictionary for almost every word in the books I had to read. Unlike the German kids who tried to help me so much, many of the American students, especially Hispanic students, made fun of me and my accent. I studied really hard because I knew we had risked our lives to escape from Vietnam and members of my family had been separated for many years so that we could come to a place where we could begin our lives anew. After a while, I got to know some of the students in my classes, among them two nice, helpful, and intelligent Korean American students. They had come to the United States when they were three years old and knew English as well as any American-born student. They offered to teach me English and to help me with my homework.

I remember clearly a day when I went up to the blackboard to solve a chemistry problem. I saw a copper plaque hanging on the wall and asked my teacher what the plaque was for. "That's the plaque we use to keep a record of the best students in chemistry each year. If you work hard enough, your name may well be on it this year." All the students broke out laughing. They obviously did not think it would be possible for me to do well in chemistry because of my poor English. Or maybe they thought that since I came from Vietnam, a country that has never produced a talented scientist, I could never be one. I resolved to work hard to show them my abilities. In contrast to the students' reaction, my chemistry teacher was very helpful. He believed I had the potential to achieve anything if I put my mind to it. He was just like a father to me. Discovering my interest in science, he gave me several books to read and offered to help me as often as I needed. With the help of my Korean American friends, I improved significantly as time went by. At the end of my second semester in high school, I ranked first in my chemistry class with a score of 99.8 because I had a perfect score on almost all my tests.

At the end of the school year, each high school sends three of its best students to compete against approximately four hundred other students from other high schools in the examination given by the Southern California Section of the American Chemical Society. I was among the chosen. This was my chance! I was one of the five highest scorers on the exam and of course my name was engraved on the copper plaque. This may not seem like much to other people, but this achievement was very significant to me because I did not let my teacher or my friends down. Other students now seemed to have more respect for me. But then some began calling me "nerd."

During my second year in high school, I learned that many of my fellow students did not even know where Vietnam is located on the map. That really bothered me. Our culture is four thousand years old. How can a culture that teaches children to respect their elders and how to behave before they can even talk be so unknown in the United States? Vietnam has spent a thousand years fighting for independence from foreign powers that controlled it, yet all that the kids in my school knew was that Americans had fought in something called the Vietnam War, during which more than fifty thousand Americans were killed. The more I thought about this, the more I realized why people in other countries know so little about Vietnam.

It is because there has been no world-famous Vietnamese. We have not produced a Mozart, an Albert Einstein, or anyone equally well known. To most people, Vietnam is just an underdeveloped and primitive country. This realization helped me set an important goal in my life.

My goal is to invent or discover something in science that will contribute greatly to meeting the world's needs. I dream of winning the Nobel Prize and establishing an Institute of Technology to educate young Vietnamese. I want to help put Vietnam on the world map in order to show others that we Vietnamese can do anything if given the opportunities. After my parents both found the jobs they wanted, I decided to quit my job and spend more time on my studies. While still in high school, I enrolled in evening classes at a nearby university to study science and mathematics. My workload was very heavy. I spent almost fourteen hours a day in class or at the library. By my senior year in high school, my English had improved quite a bit and I no longer needed to spend so much time studying. I joined the track team and became photo editor of the yearbook staff. For the first time, I had many opportunities to get involved in American life. I got to know a lot of people and became fairly popular on campus as I had to attend most school events to take pictures for the yearbook.

There were a few Vietnamese students at my high school. After I made their acquaintance, I felt disappointed in the Vietnamese girls I met. They seemed to have changed so much after they came to the United States. The image I have of Vietnamese girls was shaped by two of my best childhood friends who were always nice, helpful, innocent, easy to talk to, and fun. They never asked for much. To my surprise, the Vietnamese girls I met in high school in the United States were talkative, demanding, and calculating. They seemed to lack Vietnamese characteristics. However, in my senior year I met T. Even though her family had left Vietnam in 1975, her knowledge of Vietnamese culture and her ability to speak Vietnamese amazed me. She was not only fluent in the language, she could even write poetry in our mother tongue. We got along very well because we had many things in common. We are still the best of friends. She was the only Vietnamese girl I liked and dated when I was in high school. (I also dated non-Vietnamese girls.)

I finally graduated from high school and was accepted into this university. I am triple-majoring in mathematics, physics, and chemistry. Life is very nice on this campus. The students are very open-minded and helpful. My chemistry professor offered me a position as his research assistant the summer before I even entered college. In the last two years, he has taught me a lot of science, but most important of all, he has given me a most valuable gift: self-confidence. After working for two years as a research assistant in chemistry, I decided to find a similar job in physics. With the help of my physics professor, I published an original paper in astrophysics and became an undergraduate teaching assistant for the Astronomy 1 course.

To further increase my knowledge about Vietnamese culture, I joined the Vietnamese Students Association and became its vice president. I also participated in activities of the student government. I took part in Project Ngoc, a program designed to raise funds to support the refugee camps in Hong Kong and Malaysia. We send books to the refugee camps so that children can be educated, as well as medicine to those in need. We formed a Southern California Vietnamese Students Union so that we can raise our voices to ask the pertinent governments to help our people who had risked their lives on the ocean only to be confined in the camps for years before being repatriated to Vietnam. I can never do enough but I continue to try to do the best I can.

I have also kept in touch with my best friends in Vietnam. One is studying chemical engineering in Russia; another was forced to go to a New Economic Zone with his whole family because his father was a former senator and his brother had escaped from Vietnam; the third, as the daughter of a military officer in the former regime, was not allowed to go to college. All she can do is help her family sell things in the black market in Vung Tau. Life is so unfair to them; they are so intelligent and would have such bright futures if only they had a chance. I send some money to them from time to time because we are still close friends. As for me, I feel quite settled. There is nothing more I desire; I now have everything I need—good friends, a good job, a car, and most important of all, knowledge about many things, freedom, and the chance to determine my own future.

I am taking this class to learn more about Asian immigration and to find out what American college students know about Asia. As I expected, many of them are so ignorant—they had never heard of the Khmer Rouge in Cambodia and the Hmong in Laos until they took this class. Their surprised faces and the astonishment they expressed when they saw the films that Professor Chan showed in class suggests that there is a real need to help them learn more about Asian societies so that they can better understand them, as well as the refugees and immigrants from those countries who now live in the United States.

CHAPTER TWENTY-THREE

Vietnam Memories in America

The author's father worked for the U.S. Central Intelligence Agency and the South Vietnamese government, so he was a prime candidate for imprisonment in a re-education camp. Though the family tried to flee just before Saigon fell, their attempt failed. After seven years of incarceration, the authorities released the narrator's father but forced the family to move to a New Economic Zone. Finding life "unbearable" in the NEZ, the family resolved to escape even if they might die at sea. Or if they survived but were thrown into jail, her father said, the entire family would commit suicide together. After the narrator's sister and seven brothers were caught and imprisoned during their escape, her parents decided to send her away alone in 1983 when she was fourteen years old. This account contains a touching recollection of how she fended for herself during the two years she spent in a refugee camp in Malaysia. While there, she received a letter from her father telling her that he, her sister, and one of her brothers had successfully reached Hong Kong. Two months after that, her mother and the rest of her brothers showed up in the camp where she was. The entire family was reunited when they were sent to the Refugee Processing Center in the Philippines. Insightful and wise beyond her years, she wrote these reminiscences in 1992.

On April 30, 1975, North Vietnam took over South Vietnam. It was a shattering moment. Thousands of people tried to escape in search of freedom. People who managed to leave in 1975 faced a lot of difficulties. Those who escaped later in overcrowded boats faced even more problems. I am one of the refugees who left on a boat. Before my departure, I faced many hardships under a Communist government and later in a refugee camp. I had great expectations of America, but since my arrival in 1985 I have faced many unexpected disappointments and realize that my dreams were little more than illusions.

We are a family of eleven: in addition to my parents and myself, I have an older sister, four older brothers, and three younger brothers.

We were a middle-class family. My father worked for the U.S. Central Intelligence Agency (CIA) and the South Vietnamese government. My dad also owned a gas station and a rice warehouse that my uncle managed. My mother was a housewife. Maids took care of us children. We lived in a big beautiful house near the river, which we crossed every day to go to a private school. I had a happy and peaceful childhood until one day when my dad came home and said we had to leave because the Communists would be taking over the country soon. Given his occupation, he knew we had to leave as soon as possible before the Communist army reached Saigon.

I was seven years old at the time and was excited about traveling, seeing new things, and visiting different places. However, I was immediately disappointed when my family of eleven piled into an overcrowded automobile with our luggage. It took an entire day to reach our destination, a town located along the coast of South Vietnam. My father originally wanted to go to Saigon because he thought it would be safer there; also, he had friends there who could help us find a way to leave. To our dismay, one of the bridges to Saigon had been bombed; the bombs destroyed not only the bridge but our plans as well. We stayed in that coastal town for a week, during which I saw thousands of dead people on the streets. Bombs and grenades exploded everywhere. As we left the house where we were staying, I saw a wounded lady holding two children in her arms. All three were lying on the street. She mumbled for help but we walked away and ignored her because we were trying to leave as quickly as possible as our own lives were in danger. I thought we were so selfish and felt guilty for not doing anything to save the woman and her children. Therefore, whenever I think of Vietnam, I think about her. Her bloody image always appears in my mind and I get so scared. Since that day, every night I have prayed for her forgiveness.

As we kept walking and walking, more people continued to drop dead in front of our eyes. Finally, my father decided we had to turn back. One night, I saw a bright light shining on the house where we were staying. I asked my sister, "Are we going to die?" When my father heard my question, he called us over and made us sit next to each other. He said, "No matter what, we will live together, and if we die, we will die together." My mom started to cry. We children followed suit. It was a touching and memorable night that I shall never forget. Luckily, a week later, when the Communists captured all of South Vietnam, we were still alive. My father decided to move back to our hometown in central Vietnam.

A few days after we got there, my father was arrested. That tragedy will always remain deep in my memory. We children were sleeping when it happened. When my mother woke us up, I was so surprised to see dozens of Communist soldiers and military officers with guns in their hands as they surrounded my father. I did not know what was going on. My mother was crying as she knelt down and begged them, "Please don't take my husband away. He is innocent. He never hurts anyone." We all tried to hold on to my father but they pulled him out of our house and took him away. I thought my father was gone forever but I kept hoping and wishing that one day we would be reunited with him.

After that, our life became harder. Before 1975, my whole family lived on my father's salary and his business income. After he was arrested, my mom had to work day and night as a laborer to support her nine children by herself. She faced many difficulties under the Communist government. For example, she had to go to "seminars" every other night. She was told how we had to behave while we were on probation. We were on probation because my father had been a military officer in the former government. We children were isolated in school and prohibited from participating in various activities. Soldiers and officials came over to our house frequently without telling us ahead of time. They dug around our house to look for gold and jewelry but they found only part of our wealth. My mother knew how greedy the Communists were, so she had hidden our valuables in many different secret places. The Communists then kicked us out of our house and gave us a small hut located in a rural area. They took not only our house, but also our car and furniture. We lost almost all the gold we had (worth three hundred thousand U.S. dollars at the time) because it was in our house and yard. We only had a little gold left that my uncle was keeping for us. Since we received no rations, we had to buy food, which was very expensive, in the black market. The government did not care if we starved to death. They did not allow my mother to visit my father often.

At that time, I was too young and naive to realize the truth about Communism. In theory, Communism stands for people's rights, but in truth, that is only a lie. Before 1975, the Viet Cong went from town to town to convince people that they would do their best to protect them and bring equality to everyone. They flattered people and helped them do their farmwork and housework. Therefore, most peasants and poor people believed them and supported them. But after 1975, we learned that Communists are cold-blooded murderers. As a child, I learned this truth the hard way firsthand. I saw that under Communism people in fact did not have any rights. Even friends and families were afraid to gather in groups to socialize because they feared the Communists would suspect them of plotting against the new government. The Communists had absolute power over our lives. They could take us away from our family any time they wished. They could even shoot us without any reason and no one would dare to say a word to challenge their actions.

The Communist government prohibited people from doing all sorts of things, particularly if the adults had worked for the former government. They had a special policy for the children of such parents, such as us. We were told we could never receive a college education. In 1978, they announced a five-year plan and said that there would be no more private ownership of anything, and that people had to pay higher taxes. Worst of all, they forced women to use diaphragms as part of their birth control program that aimed to reduce the number of babies women could produce. During that period, many women became very ill. My mother was one of them. The Communist doctors were not really professional doctors. They took only a few classes and trained for only a few months, after which they were recognized as doctors, dentists, and nurses. During the years when my family lived under Communist rule, the Communists indirectly killed a lot of people because of their lack of health care experience. For example, a friend of mine had a stomachache from eating the wrong food. Her family took her to the hospital but she died a few days later. I could not believe it: people died from easily curable ailments. Our lives were worth very little in the eyes of our new rulers.

In 1980, when my father was still in a re-education camp in the northern part of Vietnam, he got very sick because the weather in the North was dismal and he had suffered a heart attack in earlier years. He almost died. The guards neither took him to the hospital nor allowed my mother to visit him. All we could do was to wait nervously for news of his recovery. We thought we would never see our father again. We cried, prayed, and begged those cold-blooded people for help, but their unspoken philosophy was: "Too bad you die. Who cares?" Luckily, when they allowed my mother to visit him three months later, he was still alive.

In 1982, after seven years of imprisonment, my father was released from the re-education camp. But my family was forced to leave our hometown and relocate to a New Economic Zone (NEZ) in the middle of nowhere. The living conditions in the NEZs were unbearable. Our entire family worked in sugarcane fields from 6:30 A.M. to 6:00 P.M. every day. The NEZ had no school, no hospital, and no electricity. Our future looked so bleak that we finally risked our lives and escaped to Saigon to live illegally with my aunt's family. We were determined to escape from Vietnam at whatever cost even if it meant we might lose our lives, just as two of my cousins who tried to escape lost theirs. My father planned ahead: if we failed and could not get out of Vietnam, he said, our entire family would commit suicide together. No matter how many times we might be arrested and put in jail to rot, we never gave up the idea of escaping. The fact that we no longer had any money did not deter our determination to flee from Communist Vietnam.

In 1983, my older sister and seven brothers tried to escape but were caught and put in jail. Even though my parents lost all the gold they had paid the boat owner, they were determined that at least one member of our family should leave. So, they decided that I should escape alone. At that time, I did not know anything about what was involved in an escape attempt. The only information I had was what my parents told me. I left Vietnam when I was fourteen in a small boat with a huge number of people in it. During our journey across the ocean, we had no thoughts of anything else except food and water. The boat owner gave each of us a very small cup of water and an uncooked yam each day. But we could not eat the raw yam because we were so tired that our teeth had become too weak to chew anything. We sat in the boat exhausted as we waited to get to our destination. After seven days at sea, we ran out of water. About half the people in the boat became disoriented. They fought with one another as they desperately tried to see who had food and water. The last few days on the boat, I was so sick that I became almost unconscious. As I lay on the deck, people stepped over me.

Eventually, to my disbelief and immeasurable joy, our boat finally reached Malaysia. Many people on my boat, including me, were taken to a hospital in Kuala Lumpur, the capital of Malaysia. We were so sick that we stayed there for a month. Only after we recovered and had been checked carefully did they take us to a refugee camp. It was so sad to leave behind in the hospital five people who had come on the same boat with me.

On the same day that I arrived at the refugee camp, representatives from World Relief interviewed me. They asked me about my family and wrote down everything I told them on a refugee application form. Luckily, I had memorized the full names of my parents, sister, and brothers, as well as all their birthdays. I also told them my father's background and military identification number. They looked at me in surprise because I remembered every little detail. They said I could enter the United States easily because my father's background fitted the priority categories they had established with regard to what kind of people would qualify for admission into the United States.

They gave me my own identification number and took me to live in the Minors' Center in the camp.

During my first week in Malaysia, I experienced a storm of mixed emotions and had no sense of direction. I was both happy and sad—happy because I had almost reached the America my parents had dreamed of, but sad because I was separated from my family and had no idea when or even if I would ever see them again. I felt sorry for myself because I was all alone in a foreign country at age fourteen. Back in Vietnam, I had a big family to take care of me. Now, I had no one. Being alone, I had plenty of time to sulk.

Conditions in the camp during the first few weeks were chaotic. I lived with other children who were under age eighteen whose parents were not with them. I never saw so many kinds of people as I did at the Minors' Center. Boys and girls lived together in one big, long house. Most of them used slang words and a lot of girls were pregnant. Seeing them scared me. As soon as I came in, a girl came up to me and said, "You have to be careful at night." Therefore, every night I tried to stay awake and I only dared to sleep in a corner in the daytime. I tried not to bother or talk to anyone. I was afraid of being beaten up. I was nervous every single minute because I had no idea what would happen to me. I knew nothing about sex until I entered that camp and learned that many of the pregnant girls had been raped. To make matters worse, during my second week there, I began to menstruate. I thought something was wrong with me. I did not know what to do except sit in a corner and cry. That evening, while everyone was busy watching television, I went to the clinic. Along the way, people looked at me strangely and laughed. When the doctor explained to me why I was dripping with blood, I became so embarrassed that I did not want to go back to the Minors' Center. But I had to because I had nowhere else to go. In the days that followed, I felt so uncomfortable that I was afraid to meet people. I had only one pair of pants and one shirt, so I always had to wash my clothes while taking a shower and put them back on when they were still wet. I smelled bad. I cried and cried because I missed my family so much and felt so sorry for myself.

Three months later, I met a lady who had been on our boat. I told her about my situation and she felt so much sympathy for me that she invited me to live with her and her two children. I felt a lot safer with her but everything was still so foreign and strange. However, when I recalled my life in the NEZ, my memories gave me the strength to overcome whatever obstacles I might encounter. After that, I stopped feeling discouraged and started to learn English and French at the school in the refugee camp. I also learned to cook and to sew. In time, I became self-sufficient. It was a little scary, though, to think how much I had grown up in such a short time. I could now take care of myself, I was more confident about my ability to survive, and my circle of friends grew larger as time passed. I got used to my environment and was even getting used to the idea that I might never see my family again. In late 1983, I was informed that I would be allowed to go to the United States under my father's priority category. However, I had to wait for someone to sponsor me, so I had to keep waiting.

In 1985, to my amazement, I received a letter from my father telling me that he, my sister, and one of my brothers had just escaped to Hong Kong by boat. Even more miraculously, two months later I met my mother and the rest of my brothers who had also made it to Malaysia. After two years of separation, it felt like heaven to see their faces. Our happiness was beyond belief. I had changed so much—I had become an adult. Four months later, our family was reunited in the Philippines [at the Philippine Refugee Processing Center], where we had to learn English before being allowed to enter the United States. While there, I envisioned an America based on the stories that other people told me. I thought it must be a beautiful "land of the free," a country full of natural wonders and immeasurable wealth. People can walk on gold, I was told, because it is so plentiful that there is enough gold for everybody. I heard that in America everything is possible. All I had to do was to reach out and grab it. Based on such fanciful visions, I began making plans for my future. I dreamed of going to school, making a lot of new friends, and becoming an artist and a professor of music.

This vision of America failed to materialize when we left the Philippines and arrived in the United States in 1985. As the plane touched down, we began to get the jitters. We were scared because we did not know anyone. Our sponsor and a representative from IOM [International Organization for Migration] met us at the airport. America looked so beautiful and prosperous. Americans also looked so different—they had shiny, silky, golden hair instead of black hair. What impressed me the most was their gigantic size, which made us feel small, insignificant, and invisible. I gazed at them with much curiosity. As our sponsor drove us to the apartment she had rented for us, I began to daydream about my wonderful future—a future full of material things: cars, clothes, money, schooling, and a career. When we arrived at a dirty, run-down three-bedroom apartment, we saw the food that our sponsor had prepared for us. It was so kind of her to have done so. The only problem was that we could not understand what she said to us, so we had to communicate by body language.

It took us a while to adjust to the new time zone and the cold weather. We slept while other people went to work and were awake at night when other people slept. Two weeks later, our sponsor took us to the Welfare Department to apply for welfare and Medicare. She also enrolled me and my siblings in school and found me a part-time job in a Vietnamese restaurant. I worked four hours a day after school was out. I was a waitress and helped clean up the premises and chop things for the cooks. As my cooking skills improved, I became an assistant cook. I made $4.50 an hour and sent most of my earnings to our relatives in Vietnam. A year later, I met a lady at a bus station and she told me that I could get a job in a garment factory. I left the restaurant and started sewing clothes. Even though I earned the same amount of money, I liked sewing better. My parents also thought that sewing was a more desirable job than waitressing. They told me they felt so sad when I was working as a waitress. They asked me to set my eyes on a more prestigious occupation as all of us had risked our lives to escape from Vietnam. Everyone in my big family had problems with the English language and with adapting to American culture just as all newcomers do.

America seemed particularly strange to my parents. They refused to face the fact that we were here to stay. They were trapped in their own world, a world of the never-forgotten past. They now devote their lives to raising their children. They are obsessed with one goal and one goal only: to raise us to become decent, self-supporting individuals. Once, I commented on their lack of a social life. I asked them, "How come you never go out? Why don't you ever do things with friends?" I was not mature enough at that time to realize how painful those questions were to my parents. As I grew older, I became more sensitive to the circumstances that inhibit my parents from being happy and enjoying life. I pictured myself being in my parents' place and came to the conclusion that I would rather die than be so dependent on other people. Even though we have been in the United States for seven years, my parents' knowledge of English consists of broken segments of sentences. They depend on their children to translate and interpret for them. Finding work is out of the question because they have no marketable job skills. They also depend on us for transportation because they cannot drive. Therefore, they are restricted to the boundaries of our home and all they can do is housework.

Welfare payments and a free public education helped us children start our lives over. My first day at school was nerve-wracking. I did not understand anything the teacher said. All I had learned in the Philippines were words like "hi," "bye," "how are you?" and "hell."

When I was in the tenth grade, I had to take English as a Second Language (ESL) classes. I studied very hard. Every night, I stayed up until 3:00 or 4:00 A.M. doing my homework because I had to look up almost every word in the dictionary. Only when I entered eleventh grade did my English get better. It was very difficult for me to learn English because I came to the United States when I was sixteen years old, so I could not learn the language quickly as little kids can. I eventually got used to the American school system, however, and made friends with students of many different national origins. After three years, I graduated from high school and was accepted by several universities. I chose to attend this university and am majoring in business economics with an emphasis in accounting. College is challenging but not as difficult as high school used to be when I first arrived. I shall be graduating in June 1992. My three older brothers have already graduated from college and now work as engineers. My three younger brothers are now at UCLA. They all want to be doctors and are majoring in biochemistry. My eldest sister got married and works in a nail salon. Her husband works in the construction industry. Even though she is married, she continues to help take care of our parents.

Our family's economic condition is now much better and my siblings and I have adapted quite well to American culture. However, no matter what we do, Vietnam is still in our hearts. We respect older people, including our teachers. We speak Vietnamese at home, read Vietnamese newspapers and magazines, watch Vietnamese movies, and eat Vietnamese food. Vietnam will always be in our brains and blood.

At the same time, I am now an American. I became a naturalized citizen in 1990. Sometimes I still feel an impulse to return to Vietnam where I imagine myself sinking blissfully into all the happiness we had experienced when I was young. But these impulses do not last long because I know the past that I treasure can never be retrieved. Acknowledging this truth, as well as my determination to succeed in whatever I do right here in America, I know I *am* an American.

The way my parents live their lives still saddens me. I don't know why but every time I think about that I cry and cry. Maybe I am crying for two people who eat and breathe but are, in fact, dead. They died the instant they left their native land. Perhaps I am also crying for two people whom I call my parents but who are alienated from their children simply because they refuse to accept the fact that America is their new home and not merely a temporary refuge. I cry because I do not really know what my parents feel and think. The most important reason I cry is that I have to watch my parents die a little each day and there seems to be nothing I can do about it.

CHAPTER TWENTY-FOUR

My Transition to Being an Asian American

After two failed escape attempts, the author and his grandmother came to the United States via the Orderly Departure Program in 1984 when he was fifteen years old. He is the only author in this book who arrived via that venue. The narrator painfully reveals that not all Vietnamese families are as close knit and harmonious as Vietnamese would like the world to think. After his parents divorced when he was only six months old, he seldom saw his parents and developed no fondness for them. Fortunately, his extended family—his grandmother, uncles, and aunts—took good care of him. This chapter, written in 1989, contains a compelling account of the author's two failed escapes, what conditions were like in the two prisons in which he was confined after being caught, and his observations about Amerasians whom he met in a transitional camp in Thailand where he and his grandmother stayed before they came to the United States. A telling detail concerns why his uncles tried to flee: they wanted to evade conscription. This is a reason that is seldom mentioned in writings by and about the "boat people." This life story also indicates how an Asian American Studies class helped the narrator come to terms with the tragedies he had experienced at a young age. Unlike many of the other narrators in this book, he has no desire to return to Vietnam.

Nineteen sixty-nine. Richard Nixon was sworn in as the thirty-seventh president of the United States. Senator Edward Kennedy drove his car off a bridge on Chappaquiddick Island. Astronaut Neil Armstrong was the first human to walk on the moon. The first reports of the My Lai Incident were published. Nineteen sixty-nine was also the year in which I was born. Along with other important events in the world, Vietnam, a small country on the east coast of the former French Indochina, had added a new citizen. As the baby grew up, his life was full of joy, wonder, stress, and sorrow.

The stage was set in a small city located about forty kilometers from Saigon. In mid-October, the weather changed as the tropical heat and humidity began to lessen, bringing the fresh coolness of early winter. The natives knew it was time to take out their warm clothes. But not everyone realized that winter was coming. A young South Vietnamese naval officer and his wife did not notice the change in weather because something special was going on in their lives: the young couple welcomed their first child. Unfortunately, their joy and excitement did not last very long. After a few months, all their plans for the child's future were forgotten as they realized they were still young and preferred an active social life rather than staying home and taking care of their baby. From being a symbol of joy, the baby became a burden. Constant arguments ensued as they blamed each other for whatever problems they had. When the baby was six months old, they got a divorce and sent their son to live with his paternal grandmother and her children. That baby is me.

My childhood at my grandmother's house was enjoyable and care-free. Unlike other children who do not live with their parents, I was fortunate to grow up in a disciplined and respectable environment. Since my uncles and aunt were not married at the time, they all treated me like their own child. Not living with my parents made me more special. My extended family did everything to make me happy. But they also tried hard to keep me away from the negative factors in our neighborhood. They never allowed me to go outside to play with other kids even though I really wanted to. I still remember how I used to stand at the window every day and watch other kids my age playing outside. Besides being overprotective, my family also wanted to take care of me themselves—my grandmother, aunt, and uncles did not let the maid take care of me. They wanted me to become a respectable person in society, a person with class. They taught me how to behave at the dinner table, to respect older people, to get along with everyone, and to act properly in public. They also paid a great deal of attention to my future education. They planned to send me to a private school and then to France for college. All I had to do was to eat a lot and grow bigger.

Before my parents sent me away, I never had a careful look at my mother's face. While I was growing up, I met her only five times. Not seeing her did not bother me at all until I was a teenager. To me, my grandmother and my aunt were my mothers and my uncles were my fathers. One day, when I was coming home from school, I saw my aunt talking to a strange lady. I came up to them and greeted them in the usual manner. My aunt told me to say hello to my mother in a more sincere way. Although I had not seen my mother since I was a baby, I was not too excited about meeting her. The word *mother* did not give me any special feeling at all. I was too young to realize how much that word means to everybody. The strange lady, my mother, kept staring at me and saying repeatedly, "He looks like me!" I felt embarrassed. How could we look alike when I did not even know her?

I did not see my mother again until a couple of years later. She came to visit my grandmother and me. This time, we went out for dinner and had our picture taken. I felt very uncomfortable sitting next to her. I tried to behave properly but felt that she was not my mother; rather, she was just a stranger. The third time I saw my mother was two years later when she came again to visit my grandmother and me. I saw her two more times, after which I never saw her again. But by now, at least I knew I had a mother. However, her image in my mind was never clear enough to enable me to remember what she looked like. I wish I had taken a good look at my mother the last time we met. Instead, what I see when I think of her is a picture of her and me that I accidentally found when I was fifteen years old.

My father visited me more often. He came home every three months to visit his mother, brothers, sister, and me. For some reason, I was always afraid of his military uniform (he was a high-ranking officer at the time) and of the way he acted and talked. Because of that fear, I used to stay away from him during his visits. That did not bother him because he did not seem to care about his only son. In 1974, my father remarried. That event did not affect me at all. Besides, my stepmother seemed very nice. (Years later, I realized the impression I had of her was dead wrong.) A year after her marriage, my stepmother gave birth to a baby boy. She, my father, and their son left the war in Vietnam behind them in 1975 and went to the United States.

April 30, 1975, was a very sad day. For the North Vietnamese and their allies in South Vietnam, the Viet Cong, it was a day to celebrate their victory over the South Vietnamese government and the United States. But for the South Vietnamese, it was the beginning of the "Dark Ages." The Communist takeover affected everyone's life. Family members were separated from one another and people's standard of living became worse. We, too, were greatly affected by the political changes as some members of my family had worked for the former regime. Communist officials constantly came to our house to search it and to question us. Although my father could have taken us to the United States with him, for some reason he did not. A few years later, my grandmother told me why we had been left behind: my father's new wife was not sufficiently fond of her own family to take them along, so she asked my father to treat his family the same way. He listened to her. After I found this out, my attitude toward my stepmother changed completely. I lost all respect for her because she was so selfish. It was not until 1977 that I was able to get in touch with my father.

In 1978, my oldest uncle escaped by boat to Singapore. While at sea, an American oil tanker rescued him and the other passengers in his boat. In early 1980, as the number of people fleeing Vietnam increased dramatically, my grandmother, uncles, and aunt also decided to take our chances at escaping. After the fall of Saigon, they had suffered a great deal as the local police harassed them. The policemen kept trying to get information about my father out of his mother and siblings. They came two or three times a week and walked around the house looking for things they considered helpful to the new government's intelligence service. I think they were also trying to see if we still had any gold or money in our house.

Another factor in our decision to flee was the living conditions at the time. The Communists printed new paper money to replace the currency of the fallen regime. Each family was allowed to exchange a certain amount of money based on the number of persons in that family. The change in currency affected us a great deal. We could no longer use the cash we had on hand or in our bank account. To make matters worse, my uncles' and aunt's salaries were not enough to feed the entire family. Each of them made fifty *dong* a month, which was only enough to buy each of them one big breakfast. My grandmother started selling our furniture and jewelry. We worried that we would soon run out of furniture and jewelry to sell.

The most important factor of all was that my uncles were told they had to join the army. As the Vietnamese invasion of Cambodia came to a climax [in late December 1978 and early January 1979], a large number of young men were forced to become soldiers. The government wanted my uncles to join the army but my uncles had no desire whatsoever to help the Communists. Realizing the dangers they faced, they persuaded my grandmother that we should all leave the country.

Five months after purchasing a boat and preparing for our journey, my family, some of our more distant relatives, and close friends decided that it was the appropriate time to leave. We divided ourselves into three groups and agreed to meet at a certain location at midnight. We secretly left our house and made our way to a quiet pier about five kilometers from Saigon. I was in a group of elderly people and children. Before the appointed time, our navigator purposely ran the boat along the river to distract people's attention. After we all boarded and the boat started moving, suddenly there was a loud noise as our boat shook violently from hitting some underwater object. The engine stopped running and our boat got stuck in the middle of the river. The propeller had broken. All the passengers thought that was a bad omen. It took our mechanic nine hours to fix the propeller. We thought we had brought along a spare propeller but no one could find it. Because of the delay, our plan to slip by the patrol boats under the cover of darkness no longer worked. However, we had no desire to go back so we continued our journey.

A patrol boat stopped us two hours later. I was awakened by a scream and heard the unfamiliar sound of another engine. I tried to look outside but it was too dark to see. Suddenly, a bright beam of light swept across the waves in the water. The light stopped moving abruptly as it found our boat. I heard a stranger ask, "Where are you going? We need to see your travel permits." Nobody on board answered. Instead, after a moment our navigator shouted, "Press on the gas! Press on the gas at full speed!" The gunshots that followed startled me. As I peeked out, I saw bullets flying toward our boat, which started to jerk and slowed down as its engine stopped. Our boat's engine had been hit. A few second later, a patrol boat pulled up alongside us. Nobody in our boat said a word. We were in a state of shock and wondered what the police would do to us. The police tied our boat to theirs and some of them jumped over to our boat. They shouted and asked who the leader was but no one answered. Finally, my aunt begged the patrolmen to let us go but she was stopped by a round of gunfire. The policemen warned us not to talk or else they would shoot us and throw us overboard.

The policemen towed our boat to a patrol station nearby. They tied up all the men and questioned each one thoroughly. After spending a day at that patrol station, they transferred us to a jail. As we approached the prison, many children ran around the truck we were on. Local people surrounded us as we walked from the truck to the prison. They laughed at us probably because they enjoyed the thought of another victory over those who tried to escape. Unlike other jails, this one had no bars. It only had a large windowless room in which they locked us. A majority of the people in that prison had been arrested for the same reason as we had been. Only a few prisoners were there because of other crimes, such as stealing or murder, they had committed. Since all escapees were considered deserters, the wardens confiscated all our belongings. They searched each of us carefully to make sure we had not hidden anything. According to my aunt, a policewoman stuck her finger into my aunt's rectum to see if my aunt had hidden anything within her body. Because I was only a kid, they did not search me. Since one of my uncle was the organizer of the escape attempt, they locked him up in a separate room and tortured him. Luckily, he did not suffer any permanent or serious injury.

Living conditions in the jail were not too bad except we were fed the same food day after day and mosquitoes constantly bit us. No one had to do any hard labor. In the daytime, we were allowed to walk around and do whatever we wanted, but after 6:00 P.M., everyone was locked inside the large room. As there were only a few women and children in our group, they were put in the same incredibly crowded room as all the men and boys.

After being in jail for two weeks, my grandmother and I were released. We returned to our house but when we got there we could not get inside. It was no longer our house: the government had taken it over right after we left. My grandmother and I went to the house of our relatives and stayed there until the rest of our family was freed. Living in Saigon without a house and without identification papers was not easy. My grandmother and I hid inside our relatives' house all the time. We were afraid that the neighbors might report our presence to the local police. After a year, everyone in my family was released and we were allowed to buy another house. We purchased one near our old neighborhood.

Two years later, in 1982, one of my uncles and I tried to escape again. We were the only two members of our family who got to go because the people who organized the escape had only two spaces left on their boat. Besides, my family did not have enough gold left to pay for the other family members' passage. In addition, we thought some people in our family should stay behind in case my uncle and I got arrested again. My uncle and I took a bus to a place called Rach Gia, which is located at the southern tip of Vietnam very close to the Vietnamese-Cambodian border. After our arrival, we stayed with a family for five days before we were taken in the middle of the night to a secret place where we were to hide until we could embark on the boat. It took us hours to walk to that secret place. It was very dark and the country road was narrow. I fell into the rice paddies on both sides of the road many times. By the time we reached the secret place, I was covered with mud. People waiting at that place were not allowed to talk in their normal tone of voice. Everything was done in silence. There were no electric lights at that place and the water was dirty. The organizers also did not give us enough to eat. All we had each day was a small amount of rice seasoned with salt or fish sauce. When our departure night came, we walked for about two hours to hide in various locations to wait for the boat that was supposed to pick us up. But no boat showed up, so we had to go back to the secret place. Walking was no easy task. The paths in the pineapple fields that we walked on were very narrow and slippery because the mud was wet. Worse, the leaves of the pineapple plants, which have very sharp edges, constantly cut our flesh. The pineapple leaves are so sharp they can even penetrate our clothes, including the thick fabric that jeans are made of. Day after day, we were divided into groups and told to hide in the pineapple fields so that the local people would not see us. We suffered the heat of the sun all day long; when night came, it was the mosquitoes' turn to torment us by sucking our blood.

After having to repeat this procedure day after day and night after night, people began to complain about our miserable condition and the fact that no "mysterious boat" ever appeared as promised. After one and a half months, we finally saw the boat. As we had done on other nights, we walked across a big muddy field. Once again, I was covered with mud. But a boat was indeed waiting for us. I realized immediately that it was too small to carry our entire group of about forty people. But it was too late. We could not do anything. All of us had to sit on the lower deck, which was so crowded that my legs were pressed against my chest. After a few minutes, my legs began to feel numb. It was also hard to breathe. Feeling that I could not sit like this for more than an hour, I wished a patrol boat would stop us. I told myself that if we were caught, I would never try to escape again. I received my wish when a patrol boat appeared fifteen minutes later and arrested all of us.

In contrast to the jail we were confined in after my first failed escape attempt, the prison this time was huge, probably because the policemen were arresting many more people who were trying to flee. The prison was divided into two camps, one for men and the other for women. High walls surrounded the prison, so we were allowed to walk around freely inside. At night, we were not locked up because the huge structure that housed us had only a roof but no walls. This prison also served the same kind of food every day. We had only a small bowl of rice for each meal. People who still had money with them could buy additional food. My uncle and I had no money and no one from our family came to visit us because they had not yet heard that we had been caught, so we were hungry all the time. Unlike the situation in the other prison, the men in this one had to work in the fields all day long. Since my uncle knew how to fix electrical appliances, he did not have to work in the fields. Instead, he was asked to fix appliances for the families of the policemen.

After a month, I was freed but my uncle was not. On the day I was told I could go home, my aunt coincidentally came to visit us. She gave my uncle some money and then took me home. However, going home did not make me happy because I knew my uncle was still a prisoner. At home, any time I saw food being set on our dining table, tears came to my eyes. I wished that my uncle was home to enjoy the food with us. Nine months later, my uncle was finally allowed to come home. Later that year, 1983, the uncle who was with me on our second escape attempt and his older brother tried to get out of the country again. But once more, they failed. Because my family had lost so much money in these three failed attempts, we decided to wait for my father to sponsor us through the Orderly Departure Program.

The local officials did not allow me to continue my schooling because of my attempted escapes. So, my family had to hire a tutor to teach me math at home. One day, he did not show up. At first I was really happy because I would have the day off. He did not come the following day, either. When he finally appeared after a week's absence, he looked very unhappy. I asked him why he had not come last week and he slowly told me that he had to take care of a funeral for his baby boy who died a few hours after he was born. He told me that the baby did not die from sickness; rather, he died because the oxygen supply system in the clinic was not working properly. Tears ran down his cheeks. Seeing his pain, I asked him to stay home and rest for a week and said we would still pay his salary. The tragedy saddened me greatly. Just the week before, my teacher was a happy father, but in an instant, he was reduced to a mourner. I could not understand why such a tragedy should happen to him because he had never hurt anybody. Life is so unfair.

I received more bad news a few months after the death of my teacher's baby. Someone from my mother's side of the family came to tell us that my mother had died. The messenger did not know any specific details about the cause of her death. All he knew was that my mother had been sick for a short time. I was so sad that I could not be with her during the last minutes of her life. All the dreams I had of getting to know my mother were shattered. I would never have a chance to find out how it feels to have a mother. I was full of hatred and sorrow. I hated life because it had been so unfair to me and the people I knew. I hated myself because for some unknown reason I had to suffer one crisis after another. I repeatedly asked, "Why me?" I had never done any harm to anybody, yet tragedy engulfed me. I thought that by being a virtuous person, one could prevent tragedies from happening.

In 1984, the U.S. government allowed my grandmother and me to come to America via the Orderly Departure Program. I was so excited that I felt as though I had been reborn. But along with the excitement was also sorrow. On the day I left, as my grandmother and I were walking toward the airplane, I stopped and looked back at my uncles and aunt—the only family I had known. Our other relatives and friends also came to the airport to say goodbye. Everyone smiled and waved at us. Even though they were sincerely happy that we could leave, I could also see sadness behind those smiles. While they were happy for us, they must have felt sorry for themselves because they had to continue living miserable lives. I burst into tears. How I wished that everyone could leave the country as we were doing. I did not know if I would ever see those people again as I left the life I had lived for the past fifteen years behind.

Sitting in the airplane, I wondered how the American soldiers had felt when they left Vietnam—a place where they had fought, lived, and seen their comrades die, a place that gave them painful and unforgettable memories. I also wondered why so many Asians had to leave their countries and be separated from their loved ones. I told myself that in my next life, I wanted to be born somewhere else. When the plane arrived in Thailand, I was shocked by the "hospitality" the officials extended us. They treated us like prisoners, they fed us as though we were animals, and they made us feel inferior. Was it all because we came from a poor country? Or was it because we were foreigners? I had no answers but I hoped that I would not be treated like that in America. The month we spent in Thailand while we were being processed by U.S. immigration officials was terrible. However, along with the poor treatment, I got something very special out of my stay there: I became acquainted with Amerasians.

In Vietnam, people discriminated against the mixed-blood children whose fathers were American soldiers. "Pure blooded" Vietnamese kids called them names and said nasty things about them. Because of such ill treatment, the mixed-blood children, Amerasians, formed their own groups and tried to avoid interacting too much with other people. Not only did Vietnamese kids taunt them, but adults also criticized them for being unfriendly, rude, and immoral. Until now, I still do not know where Vietnamese got such ideas. In Thailand, when I stayed in the same room as the mixed-blood youngsters, I discovered that they are not as bad as people in my country had claimed they are. We got along very well together and we had fun hanging out together. I found them to be friendly, polite, and respectful to others. I wondered why my people had such negative and wrong ideas about these children. Was it because they are different? Was it because they do not have black hair and slanted eyes as we do? Was it because these kids have foreign blood in them? I had no answers. I kept hoping that

Americans would not treat me the same way my people treated these Amerasians.

After we arrived in the United States, we went to my father's house. Along the way, the streets looked so big, the buildings so tall, and the cars so beautiful. Riding in a car—something I had never experienced before—felt magnificent. The rich materialism of American life amazed me. The shopping malls, supermarkets, color television—everything was new and fascinating to me. I believed that this new place was a land that gives everybody a chance to make his or her dreams come true. I told myself I should learn the language and work hard to take advantage of the many opportunities waiting for me.

However, after only a few weeks, I realized that there were problems waiting for me, too. After the death of my mother, I continued to believe that my father loved me. I thought of him as someone I could turn to whenever I needed help. I thought he would take good care of me after I came to America in order to make up for all the years we were apart. But after living with him and my stepmother for a month, I realized my presence was not welcome. My stepmother criticized me constantly. She told my stepbrother and stepsister that I had been adopted. The worst was yet to come. One day, my father told me I should not call him "Dad" in the presence of his friends. What he said hurt me very much. All the positive thoughts I had about him disappeared. I could not believe my father could actually say such a thing to me. I wondered what I had done wrong to make him so angry. Or was he just embarrassed by the fact that he had a child with some woman other than the one he was living with? Since I was so upset, I told my uncle what my dad had said to me. My uncle was so furious that he would not talk to my dad for the next two years.

Meanwhile, the relationship between my stepmother and me got worse and worse. She was not comfortable having me around and she told me about other places where I could live. Fortunately, my uncle invited me to live with him. However, as he had his own family to support, my uncle asked me to pay for the food I ate but said that he would not charge anything for my room. I asked my father for some money but he never responded to my request. Luckily, I managed to find a part-time job to help pay my bills. From then on, I realized that the only person I can rely on is myself. Because I had always depended on my family, living independently was not easy. I had a very hard time keeping up with school because I had to work so many hours. I usually fell asleep when I returned home from work and the bad grades I got did not make my uncle happy. He pushed me to study harder despite the fact that I was working. He did not let me watch television at all except for the evening news. He told me that the only way I can have a better life is to bury myself in my studies.

Before I came to the United States, I never imagined that my life in this country would be so tough. Having no choice, I decided I had better follow my uncle's advice. I kept pushing myself to study harder because I knew it was the only way I had to make my life better. I also worked hard because I wanted to show my father that I could survive without his support. In the high school I attended, a few of the White students were very nice to me but most of them were not friendly at all. They made fun of the foreign-born students by calling them names. I was, of course, one of their victims. Once, one of them asked me what my ethnicity was. Since I knew they said nasty things about Vietnamese, I told them I was Japanese. They still made fun of me anyway.

When the first semester of ninth grade ended, I was relieved I had survived my first few months in America even though my grades were not good. By the time the second semester ended, I no longer had any problems because I had learned to manage my time. In fact, I often set the test curves in my classes. Because of my academic performance, the White kids became more friendly to me. They even helped me with English. In return, I helped them with their math and science homework. After a while, I became quite popular in school and nobody made fun of me anymore. During weekends, I was very anxious to go back to school on Monday. I even received some awards for my outstanding academic achievement.

During the summer after my ninth grade, my uncle moved to a small city in Ventura County, California, and I moved with him. Its population is mostly white and middle class. In the high school I attended, there were hardly any Asians. The first time I set foot in that school, I did not feel comfortable. I had never seen so many white students in one place before. I thought I would be a prime target for all their jokes. Fortunately, everything turned out well. The students were friendly and helpful. As I had done before, they helped me with my English and I helped them with their math and science.

In that high school, I met M., a guy whose family had come from the Philippines when he was three years old. We became best friends. Even though he could not speak any Filipino language at all, his family has managed to help him retain Asian culture and attitudes. We got along so well because we thought about life the same way. Besides, he tried to help me in every respect because he knew my life had not been pleasant. At the end of sophomore year, he and I found a new friend named J. to hang out with. J. is a 100 percent hardcore American. He is funny and brilliant and always helps me with my English. At the end of our junior year, the three of us became friends with a Vietnamese guy, T.Q. The four of us hung out and studied together. We all decided to go to the same university after we finished high school.

The recognition I received in high school gave me strong feelings about my ethnic origins. The fact that I did well in school even though I came from a poor country and had to start from scratch made me proud of the work ethic that Asians have. Although I finished high school successfully, I did have to deal with differences between American culture and Vietnamese culture. For a long time, I felt very uncomfortable about the two different ways of life. The first thing I had to adjust to was the food. I could not stomach American food at all when I first arrived. Cheese smelled so strong that I could not swallow it. The hot dogs, pizza, and ham all seemed tasteless. Because I love food, this problem upset me a lot. I was disappointed that I had to live in a place whose food I did not like. The second problem was that I could not understand why American parents allow their children to date when they are still too young for such relationships. I was bothered by the way that American teenagers act. They have no discipline or respect for their teachers or parents. My classmates were rude and showed tremendous disrespect toward our teachers. I also could not understand why teenagers want to move out of their parents' house right after their eighteenth birthdays.

As I was busy trying to survive, I did not begin to miss my homeland and its people until a year after I first set foot on American soil. It happened on Near Year's Eve. My uncle and his family were already sound asleep and there I was, wearing my pajamas and watching television to see how Americans celebrate their New Year. What a sad feeling I had! I wished I could go out and celebrate with those people. Then I realized it was not my holiday as Vietnamese New Year was still a month away. When Tet came, the only thing my uncle's family did was to eat a big dinner that my aunt cooked. That day was a school day so I had to go to school and my uncle and aunt had to go to work. I felt so sad because I realized I would never have another New Year celebration like the ones in Vietnam.

However, after being here for two years, I no longer had such feelings. I had adapted to the American way of living and was fast becoming a part of the system. In other words, I had become Americanized before I even knew it. I began to love American food, enjoyed the Western way of celebrating New Year, and no longer paid any attention to how teenagers behave. I guess as long as their parents accept them, they can do whatever they please.

A majority of the Vietnamese who came to the United States pay a great deal of attention to developments within Vietnamese ethnic

communities. In that respect, I am entirely different. I do not enjoy going to the events organized by Vietnamese. I discovered that
some Vietnamese actually kill or cheat other Vietnamese out of their
money. I read and heard about many cases of Vietnamese families
being robbed or killed by Vietnamese gangs. I stayed away from
Vietnamese because I felt unsafe not knowing who was a gang member and who was not. I did not give even my best Vietnamese friend
my address and phone number until after I had known him for a year.
Furthermore, since I will have to work with Americans all my life, I
want to explore American society rather than stay within my own
ethnic community. The fact that I do not want to be overly involved
with Vietnamese people does not mean that I am ashamed of being a
Vietnamese. Whenever I am asked what I am, I say proudly that I am
Vietnamese.

Many times I have asked myself if I would go back to Vietnam to
live if I were allowed to. Most of the time, my answer is "no." I will
go for visits but I would not want to live there for the rest of my life
because there is no one and nothing left there for me to live for. The
country is tightly controlled by a Communist government. However,
if I become a doctor, I shall go back to help my people from time
to time. Before the 1989 academic year started, I used to feel sorry
for myself because I had experienced so much hardship. After taking
this Asian American Studies class, however, I realized that what I
and other Vietnamese refugees and immigrants are going through is
nothing compared with what other Asian immigrants faced in the
nineteenth and early twentieth centuries. From what I have learned
in this class, I feel lucky to have a chance to live here during a period
when more and more people are given a chance (more or less) to
achieve their dreams. This class has greatly increased my respect for
the strength of all Asian people. I wish similar classes could be offered
at the high school level. I am happy that I can survive in this society
entirely on my own efforts.

As I end this paper, I have a strange feeling that perhaps everything
that has happened to me was planned by some higher spirit. Since
I believe in predestination, as well as the Buddhist concept that one
can change one's life by the way one lives, I will try to live in such a
way that my life will not be full of sorrows in the future.

[Some years after the author wrote this paper, he discovered that his
mother had not died after all. In fact, she had managed to immigrate to
the United States. He went to visit her but still felt awkward around
her. Since that reunion, mother and son have kept in touch only
sporadically.]

CHAPTER TWENTY-FIVE

At That Time in My Life

This autobiography contains one of the most detailed accounts we have of what children learned in school in Vietnam after 1975. Two days before Saigon fell, the author's father, a captain in the South Vietnamese Army, asked his wife to take their children out of the country. The family managed to get on one of the last American ships to leave, but just as the gangplank was being pulled up his mother ran back with her children to the pier because she simply could not bear to leave her husband behind. The narrator's father spent nine years in re-education camps. Only after he was released did his son begin to learn the "truth" about Communism. Informed by the authorities that he would not be allowed to go to college because of his bad "family record" and certain that he would soon be drafted, the author escaped alone in 1986 when he was seventeen years old. In this essay, he fearlessly denounces the cowardice of South Vietnam's leaders, the cruelty of the Communist regime, and the selfish behavior of his fellow refuge-seekers on the boat that took him to Malaysia. Written in 1992, the narrative also explains why the author joined the U.S. Army—an ironic act, he notes, in light of the fact that one reason he escaped was to avoid being conscripted into the Vietnamese Army.

What do people in the world know about Vietnam? Fighting against the French colonial regime? Fighting a civil war with United States involvement? Invading Cambodia? The Vietnamese people have fought against many nations, not just France, the United States, and Cambodia. They fought against the Chinese for almost a thousand years, the French for almost a hundred years, and then waged a thirty-year civil war that began at the end of World War II. Today, some people might want to forget about the Vietnam War. Many Americans purposely do not want to remember that war because they think it was a shameful experience for the American people. Not many people know how much the Vietnamese suffered during the civil war. And how many people are aware of the hardships that Vietnamese who risked their lives to escape from their country suffered? Even some Vietnamese who were not in the country during that period do not know how terrible life was. But many refugees, including me, can never forget what an unbelievable price we paid on our way to find freedom. We will never forget our losses as we live as refugees in many countries all over the world.

In 1975, I was a six-year-old boy living peacefully and happily with my parents and sister until April 30, a day that no Vietnamese anywhere on the face of this planet can ever forget. When Saigon succumbed to the might of the North Vietnamese army, I was too young to understand fully what had occurred. All I sensed was that it was bad, very bad, for a lot of people, including my family.

Two days before the Communists took Saigon, my father was still at the front lines with his troops. He was a captain in the South Vietnamese Army. He sent a message to my mother and told her to take us out of Vietnam by any means possible. He knew that Saigon was about to fall into Communist hands once President Nguyen Van Thieu and Premier Nguyen Cao Ky fled the country, taking a lot of the government's money with them. Even though my father was still on duty, he did not want his family to be stuck in Saigon when the Communists captured it. My mother at first listened to my father's advice and started packing a few belongings. She could not take much because she had to hold on to me as she ran while carrying my one-year-old sister in her arms. People were running around all over the streets of Saigon trying to find a way to get out. The sound of explosions put more pressure on people. Children cried for their parents and wives and husbands called out to their spouses as they got lost in the crowd. We were definitely in a war zone. My mother, sister, and I managed to get on one of the last American ships to leave the harbor. But suddenly my mother changed her mind and ran off the ship just before the gangplank was pulled up because she could not bear to leave my father behind.

While the country was in danger, President Thieu and Premier Ky resigned and fled. Both left the country with the government's money even though hundreds of thousands of troops and officers like my father were willing to give up their lives to defend their nation. I am really ashamed of what President Thieu and Premier Ky did. They fled when they were most needed. During their years in office, they always wanted to look good, to be respected by the people, but their flight made all Vietnamese look bad. Many soldiers and officers, in contrast to the leaders' irresponsibility, stayed and fought bravely until President Duong Van Minh, who served only a few days before Saigon fell, called on the troops to surrender. I am proud of those soldiers. They did everything they could to save the country. Most of them would suffer greatly as the Communists put them into prisons called re-education camps but I think what they did was the honorable thing to do. Thus, I respect my father not only because he is my father, but also because he was a true soldier and managed to survive ten years of harsh imprisonment.

Life in Saigon was not easy after its fall. A few days after the Communist victory, the new officials told my father he had to go for a ten-day seminar to be "re-educated" so that all "capitalist ideas" could be washed out of his mind. Ten days passed by; a month, then a year passed by. We heard nothing from my father. We had no idea whether he was dead or alive. Yet we hoped and prayed as we waited for his return. My mother could not find a job because she was the wife of a prisoner. I was still too young to help her. Because a Communist tank had virtually demolished our house, my mother had to sell whatever we had so that we could use the money to fix the house.

In school, I learned new songs celebrating the victory of the North over the South. Other songs were about how Vietnamese kids loved Ho Chi Minh. I was taught that the North Vietnamese had fought unselfishly for many years to "kick out" the Americans and to unify the country. My first-grade teacher also taught us how Communists define "freedom." My six-year-old mind was like a blank sheet of paper so anybody could write anything they wanted on it. We learned a sentence that Ho Chi Minh had written: "Nothing is more valuable than independence and freedom." That sentence was posted everywhere. We kids knew it by heart. "Did we really have any independence?" was a question I would repeatedly ask in later years.

My mother was unemployed and had two children to support. The government told her to take us somewhere else to live, either with some relatives in the countryside or in areas designated as New Economic Zones. We had no choice. We could not survive in Saigon. So, in 1976 we went to live with my grandparents in a small town in the countryside. I was only seven years old so I did not really understand why we had to move. As I grew older, I asked why the Communists said they were doing everything for the sake of the people, yet they kicked us out of our house and took over the houses of many other people. Was this doing something for the people? They also executed people and put tens of thousands in prison. Was this also doing something for the people?

Life in the countryside was not easy. By the time my mother, sister, and I went to live with my grandparents, the Communists had already taken their rice field. A few months later, the government returned a small plot to my grandparents saying that they would not need more land because they did not have enough manpower to work a larger field. My grandparents became sick more often and both of them died within a year. Now my family had no one to turn to for advice or financial support. Fortunately, by now I was eight years old—old enough to work in the fields with our neighbors. I went to school in the mornings and worked in the fields in the afternoons. I learned to be responsible because I wanted so much to help my mother as I watched her running around every day trying to borrow a little money to buy food to feed us.

During the years that Vietnam and Cambodia fought a border war, followed by another border war between Vietnam and China, many families that were already poor became poorer because Vietnam drafted tens of thousands of its young men to fight those wars, leaving old people and children to fend for themselves. Even though the economy was becoming more depressed by the day, the government raised taxes and the prices of basic necessities. That was why I became a fisherboy. Some other kids and I bought a little net to catch fish in the canal. We pulled the net in the opposite direction as the flowing water and caught a lot of fish. But soon, other people saw what we were doing and they began to catch fish the same way. Our catch became smaller and smaller, but the fish we caught helped our families survive. My dream at that time was to have two meals a day. Later, I realized why the people could not rise up against the government: we were too busy trying to stay alive. Moreover, many people became dependent on the food rations that the government doled out, so they had no choice except to obey its cadres.

When I started high school, I went to school six, and sometimes seven, days a week. I studied very hard because I hoped to go to college. I respected my teachers as they taught us the history of Vietnam and its war against Americans. I learned how great the Russians were during World War II. My teachers told us we should be grateful to the Russians for helping us kick the Americans out of our country. They also taught us that Americans are selfish and did nothing to help win World War II except drop atomic bombs on Hiroshima and Nagasaki that killed hundreds of thousands of Japanese people. Since I had not yet been born during World War II, and no one else told me anything different, I believed what my teachers taught us. I came to like and admire the Russians for their bravery and did not like the Americans at all. I had nothing else with which to compare what the teachers said because we were not allowed to read newspapers and magazines from Western countries. My mother was so worried about keeping her children alive that she never asked me what I was learning in school.

Consequently, I believed in Communism. It sounded terrific to me. My teachers also taught us that in a Communist society, everyone is equal. People treat each other as brothers and sisters and share everything with other people. In terms of the economy, they said that "the people are the bosses of everything in the country and the government just helps to administer the system." I believed what they said. I was so stupid and naive that I did not look at the reality of life under Communism. Only later did I see the truth of what President Thieu once said: "Don't ever listen to what the Communists say, but take a careful look at what they do."

The teachers in my high school were members of the Communist Party and they deceived their students with "sweet talk" as they painted a picture of an ideal society in which people would have what they need. There would be no thieves or fights in this ideal society. We, the young people, should look forward to a day when money will drop from the sky but no one will bother to pick it up because people already have everything they want. I believed this also. I hated the Americans for bombing my country and killing innocent people. My teachers said that Americans were greedy and that was why they tried to colonize Vietnam, which has rich resources. No adult ever told me what had really happened during the war. The only person who could have told me without feeling afraid was my father, but he was in a prison somewhere in northern Vietnam near the Chinese-Vietnamese border.

I did not see the real face of Communism until my father was released and returned home in 1984 when I was a sophomore in high school. He looked so old that my mom could hardly recognize him. He did not have a single black hair left. He was so thin that he was skin and bones. His eyes looked tired. He did not look at all like the man in my parents' wedding picture. Seeing what had happened to my father, who had done nothing wrong except to carry out his duty as a military officer at the front line, suddenly made me question everything I had learned in school about Communism. Why was my father punished so severely? While he was in the military, he had been so nice to me, my sister, my mother, our relatives, and our neighbors every time he came home on a pass. At first, I resisted the thought that the Communists had beaten prisoners of war like my father. Yet, they had done so and I could not deny that cruel fact. I felt so bad about what nine years in re-education camps had done to my father: he was afraid of everything when he came home because the Communists kept on watching everything he did. He had to report to the police station every three days to tell the cadres what he had done and said during the three preceding days. They wanted to know whether he had visited anyone and if so, what he and the persons he visited had talked about. Why did they not give him some free time now? Every day when I came home from school and looked at his worried face, I asked myself where was the freedom that the Communists talked about? Where was the freedom that the Communists said they would give us after they took over South Vietnam?

Reality taught me another lesson. When I applied for college at the end of my junior year in high school, I was told I could not be admitted because I had a very bad "family record" as my father had gone to the United States for officer training seventeen or eighteen years earlier. Also, they said he had been in prison for too long. Was that my father's fault? I didn't think so. The school officials also called my mother a "capitalist" because she was buying and selling things. Capitalists, they told me, cannot be allowed to exist in Vietnam's new society. They did not care that I was one of the best students in my school. I had won a regional math contest and played in the school band. They did not look at me as an applicant with a good academic record; rather, they looked at the "records" of my parents and even my grandparents. I felt really hurt. My dream of becoming a marine engineer was gone. All the work I had put into my studies vanished.

At first, it was hard for me to give up hope. But my father kept telling me the truth about Communism. He told me how he had been treated in prison. Communists do not hesitate to kill people in the name of freedom, he said. I did not want that kind of freedom. I knew I would soon be drafted and sent to fight in Cambodia, China, or somewhere else. As I listened to my father, I finally understood that if I remained in Vietnam I would become nothing but an instrument that the Communists would use to increase their power. I realized that the Communist regime was much worse than the South Vietnamese government had ever been when Thieu and Ky were in power. Ironically, I came to understand Ho Chi Minh's famous sentence: "Nothing is more valuable than independence and freedom." Therefore, I decided to escape from Vietnam.

I left in June 1986 on a twelve-meter-long boat with 101 other people. Neither my parents nor I had been on a boat before. Even though my father made all the arrangements, he never told me anything because he was afraid that I might accidentally tell my friends. And if my friends told somebody who worked for the government, we would all be in big trouble. My father knew that we would all land in jail if the Communist cadres found out. Therefore, even though I knew I was going to escape, I did not know when or how. My parents told me only fifteen minutes before I was to leave. I did not even have a chance to say goodbye to my sister, relatives, or friends. I just stared at my parents and at every object in the house. I had a strange feeling that I might never see them again. My mother was so busy crying that she forgot to pack my clothes and other necessities. Thus, I left home with only the clothes I was wearing that day: a pair of shorts, a shirt, and slippers. I did not take any food or water with me.

The night my boat left the shore, there was a storm. Everyone was so afraid that they did not know what to do except to pray to God or Buddha. The words "holy Mary," "Jesus Christ," and "Buddha" could be heard amid the scary sound of big waves striking our boat. I also prayed. I asked God to forgive me for my sins and said I did not want to die this way. I was so tired that I eventually fell asleep. Next morning, when I woke up, I was so glad I was still alive. Like my parents, I had assumed that the organizers of the escape would provide us with food and water because we had paid them so much money. But we were wrong. We ran out of water the first day. Most of the passengers also had no food because like my parents, they also assumed it would be provided. The boat owner did have food with him, but he said it was meant only for his family and his close friends. I realized what a selfish little guy he was. He had charged everyone on board three bars of gold and he never even gave us any food or water. But what could any of us say?

By the third day at sea, I felt really weak because I had not eaten any food or drunk any water since I left home. However, I still did not want to beg anyone for anything. Though I had lost my physical strength, I still had a lot of mental strength. I felt really sorry for the children on the boat who stared with hungry eyes at people who were eating. They looked so pitiful that I could not look at them any longer as tears came to my eyes. That scene was one of the most painful things I have seen in my life. However, the people who had food and water did not seem to see what I saw. They obviously did not want to share their food and water with anyone because they wanted to live so badly. I learned a lot about my own people on this trip. I realized people are selfish because they are human beings: like animals, they know only the fittest will survive. Those who are weak will not.

Late on the third day, we ran into Thai pirates. They strip-searched everybody to look for gold and watches. After taking all our valuables, they chose seven young women on our boat and took them away as their fathers, mothers, husbands, brothers, and sisters moaned.

Even though I did not have any valuables to lose, still I felt I lost a lot that day. It was the first time that I saw my people being taken away by pirates, yet I could not do anything to stop them. Who said life is fair?

After five days on the ocean, our boat finally arrived in Malaysia with everyone still alive even though we had lost the seven women the pirates kidnapped. A few days later, everyone on my boat was taken to Pulau Bidong, a little island where the Vietnamese had to stay to be screened and processed. Like the other boat people in that refugee camp, I needed money to buy food, stamps to send letters, and so forth. Yet, after sending a few letters to my relatives who had gone to the United States, I heard nothing from them. Apparently, they did not care that I was in a refugee camp. Finally, I went to talk to a French priest who was working as a volunteer in Pulau Bidong. He did everything he could to help me. He gave me money to buy stamps and helped me get an appointment with the U.S. delegation on the island. Five months later, I was transferred to Sungai Besi, a transition camp near Kuala Lumpur. I was very lucky that I did not have to stay on Pulau Bidong long. Many people on that island had been there for more than four years. They could not leave the island because they had no relatives in "third countries" to send them money or sponsor their admission into those countries. All they had to eat was what the camp's administrators gave them, which was not much. Their lives were no different from the lives of people in Vietnam under Communism. Thus, they deserved an opportunity to resettle somewhere and I believed it was the responsibility of Vietnamese people who had reached "third countries" to support them financially and psychologically.

During the four months I spent in the transition camp at Sungai Besi, I tried to do whatever I could to help my fellow refugees. I volunteered to teach Vietnamese music to the kids in the elementary school within the camp. I had a good time with the kids and felt good that I was doing something meaningful. I thought that the help I myself had received was more than what I deserved. The woman who taught me English was a volunteer from the United States, while my supervisor at the elementary school was a Malaysian woman who really liked me and took care of me. They were like my mothers or older sisters. They not only taught me English, but also how to adapt to the new environment I hoped to encounter once I got out of the transition camp. I owe those two women a lot. I could not help asking, "How come foreigners volunteered to help us Vietnamese refugees when many Vietnamese who had been resettled hardly did anything to help?" Had they forgotten who they are and where they came from? Or did they think that once they were admitted to "third countries" and became residents there they no longer had anything to do with refugees?

Coming to America was my dream. I had heard a lot about this country from the people I met in the refugee and transition camps. I was so happy when I found out I could go to the United States. However, when I arrived, I was more afraid than happy. In my mind, I had imagined that in America, I could just walk around and make friends. But I was wrong. In the first few years, I was so afraid of going out anywhere in public that I just stayed home with my cousins who had come long before I did. I felt embarrassed about my Vietnamese accent as I tried to talk to "real" Americans. My dream of becoming a marine engineer began to seem unrealistic to me. I lost all the self-confidence I once had. However, I had no choice except to go to school because I was only seventeen and had never finished my senior year in the high school in Vietnam. I had to repeat my junior year in San Jose in order to get enough units to graduate. I was lucky that I got into a high school with great and helpful teachers. Because I spoke and wrote very poor English, I did not understand the jokes my classmates told. When Americans talked to me, even when I did not understand them I pretended I understood. I tried to do everything possible to hide my weakness, but I felt very alienated when people spoke to me in a language I could hardly understand. I did not like that feeling. Other students from Vietnam could speak and write English well, so why couldn't I? I regained my self-confidence when one of my teachers, who taught both Spanish and English, began to help me. With her help, I graduated from high school in two years with straight A's. I had overcome the biggest stumbling block in my life.

Another big change came the day I joined the U.S. Army. It seemed so ironic because I had escaped from Vietnam to avoid the draft. I joined ROTC, the Reserved Officers Training Corps, not because I needed money for college but because I wanted to. I was proud I could do something for this country because I owe it so much. I feel I can never repay it even if I give my life for it. I escaped from Vietnam with just a shirt and a pair of shorts; now I am in college as an electrical engineering major. Some of my Vietnamese friends on campus asked me why I joined ROTC when I will not earn much money in the army after I graduate from college. Why not work for a private company instead, they asked. They also asked me to think of what might have happened had I been sent to the Middle East during the Persian Gulf War. I simply said, "I want to honor a flag, the American flag. You'll understand why I want to be in the army if you understand what it stands for."

Having lived in the United States for five years now, I think I have changed a lot. I am still learning the language, adapting to American customs, and encountering new things every day. I can never forget that I am a Vietnamese refugee living in a country not my own, but I have also learned to think of myself as an Asian American. If Vietnam ever becomes a democratic country, I hope to return to it. I will not forget my responsibility as a Vietnamese who cares about other Vietnamese, especially those who are still in refugee camps in Hong Kong, Malaysia, Indonesia, and the Philippines. As the president of the Vietnamese Students Association this year, I have tried my best to help the refugees financially and psychologically. We raised a lot of money from the community around the campus and sent it to the refugee camps. We also put together a yearbook with poems and essays written by some of the Vietnamese students on campus. I will never forget where I came from, but I am also very proud to be an Asian American in the United States.

Epilogue

Even though the life stories in this book are not representative, in the sociological sense, of all the refuge-seekers who fled Vietnam for the reasons discussed in the Preface, several common themes can be discerned: the immense suffering, deprivation, loss, and violent uprooting that every family who fled Vietnam experienced; the resolute manner in which the authors struggled to overcome the English-language barrier; and the pledge that they made to themselves to do well in school and become well-paid and respected professionals in order to please their parents by compensating for the latter's downward social mobility. But the authors had a broader vision as well: they wanted to acquire skills that would enable them to help their ancestral land should they ever return there.

There are also several implicit themes that run through the narratives. One is the strength and courage of Vietnamese women. Unlike the common images that depict Asian women either as docile beings or as power-hungry "dragon ladies," the grandmothers and mothers portrayed in this book are competent, independent, decisive, brave, and tenacious women who made important decisions that affected their families in profound ways. One grandmother left her husband, who could not bear to leave the land of his birth, in North Vietnam and migrated with her children to the South after the 1954 Geneva Agreements because she did not want to live under Communism. Two of the mothers divorced their husbands even though divorce was condemned in traditional Vietnamese society and became the breadwinners in their extended families. All of the mothers whose husbands were imprisoned after the Communists came to power found ways to feed their children in the face of extreme deprivation. The stories told by the young women narrators show the determination with which they confronted and overcame the hurdles in their path during their flight, their confinement in refugee camps, and after their arrival in the United States. The war and the socialist revolution that followed tore many families apart. Were it not for the dauntless mothers, some of their children might not have survived.

A second implicit theme that emerges in some, though not all, of the life stories is how Asian American Studies classes helped the narrators find a place for themselves in America. Several compared their own experiences to those of earlier Asian immigrants whose persistence in the face of discrimination inspired them. Thus, Asian American Studies courses helped ease the adaptation of refugee students by showing them that there *is* room in American society for young people like themselves. They learned that their desire to "fit in" and be "accepted" need not mean they have to abandon their heritage or unquestioningly adopt every aspect of American society. Inhabiting an in-between space permits them to evaluate both Asian and American societies as they decide which aspects to retain, reject, accept, or change. Asian American Studies classes encouraged them to think that *they themselves* can create culture and fashion identities that feel "true" to who they are at each particular stage in their lives—a comforting thought in a world constantly in flux.

There are also differences that can be teased out of the life stories. Those who came in 1975 were more nostalgic and lamented the "loss" of their homeland with greater sorrow. They expressed a strong desire to return to Vietnam, which they continued to refer to as "my country" even after some of them had become U.S. citizens. In contrast, while the narrators who arrived in the late 1970s and 1980s as "boat people" also said they wanted to return to Vietnam to "serve my people," they expressed that goal in less sentimental ways. Instead, a sense of obligation, rather than an inconsolable sense of loss, compelled them to consider going back to their ancestral land. Compared to the Vietnamese, the ethnic Chinese expressed less desire to return. The culture that their elders insisted they preserve was Chinese, and not Vietnamese, even though the narrators themselves thought of Vietnam, and not China, as their "homeland." It is the ethnic Chinese, the ethnic Chru, and the Vietnamese who came at a very young age who most easily identified themselves as "Vietnamese Americans" or "Asian Americans." They accepted the United States as their new "home." One author even declared emphatically, "I *am* an American." All the narrators recognized that if they wished to become successful professionals, they had to do so in the American context. Several narrators expressed gratitude to the United States for taking them in, for the education they were receiving, and for the job opportunities that awaited them upon completion of their college education.

Such sentiments reflect the mindsets of people who had come from Vietnam during the refugee exodus between 1975 and the late 1990s. However, as one of the reviewers of the manuscript that became this book pointed out, both the *doi moi* policy that Vietnam's leaders adopted in the late 1980s and the resumption of trade and diplomatic relations between the United States and the Socialist Republic of Vietnam in 1994 and 1995, respectively, have had a profound impact on Vietnamese resettled in countries around the world. If to be a refugee means that one cannot return to one's homeland, this scholar observed, the fact that *Viet Kieu* (overseas Vietnamese) can now do so with ease renders them "less and less like refugees." Instead, they have become transnational migrants (or transmigrants for short) living in diasporic communities they have built around the globe. As more and more former refugees go to Vietnam for visits or to do business, they are no longer exiled from one country and forced to adapt to life in another. Transmigration is now a physical reality and not just an ever-present longing in their hearts and imaginations.

However, there *are* constraints on an unfettered transnationalism. Among the most daunting is the deep hatred for Communism that many Viet Kieu continue to harbor. Some Vietnamese still fly the South Vietnamese flag on festive occasions. In Westminster and Garden Grove in Orange County, California, residents of Vietnamese ancestry have gained sufficient political clout to persuade the city councils to pass resolutions to ban the visits of officials from the Socialist Republic of Vietnam. They also severely criticize anyone— including former Prime Minister and Vice President Nguyen Cao Ky who took a sentimental journey to Vietnam in 2005—who dares to visit Vietnam because they think people who go there show implicitly that they approve of the current Communist regime. Therefore, these fervently anti-Communist individuals object strongly to both the Viet Kieu who wish to visit Vietnam and Communist officials who come to the United States. To them, any manifestation of a thaw—be it diplomatic, economic, social, or cultural—must be prevented by all means necessary.

Mandy Thomas, an Australian anthropologist, has understood these sentiments better than have most American scholars. Until Vietnam's reentry into the world, she observed, it had been "an irretrievable country—a place of memory only, with everything they knew now extinguished by an intruding and foreign political system." As one of her interviewees told her, "I think of Vietnam as having been locked away. ... The real Vietnam is here in freedom. It is our duty here in Australia to maintain the true Vietnam with its values

intact." Vietnamese Australians who feel this way are making "a cus-
todial claim for an essential and original identity," one unblemished or
erased by Communism. Moreover, "an anti-Communist stance should
be seen partly as a strategy for claiming legitimate refugee status . . . to
challenge the image of migrants as opportunists."[1] The Vietnamese
in the United States are behaving and thinking in a similar way.

However, there is also a countervailing force at work: many young
Vietnamese Americans do not see present-day Vietnam the same way
as their elders do. Long before legal transpacific travel became possible, some of my Vietnamese American students who came to the
United States at a young age or who were born in America were already telling me that they wanted to visit Vietnam someday simply
to satisfy their curiosity—to see for themselves what life there is like.
They wished to find out whether the present government is as "bad" as
their parents claimed it is. The parents of one of my students forbade
her to participate in a summer study tour to Vietnam and threatened
to disown her should she defy their orders. In despair, she asked me
how she could convince them that she would not be showing any
sympathy for Communism by going there. I told her that there was
nothing she could say to change their minds and that she would never
understand the intensity of her parents' feelings because, having been
born in the United States herself, she has no personal memories of the
sufferings that refuge-seekers like her parents endured. I urged her to
be tolerant of her parents' "stubbornness" and to be patient: perhaps a
day will come when she will be able to go to Vietnam without rousing
her parents' ire.

I understand the interpersonal dynamics in refugee families because
even though I am not Vietnamese, I, too, was once a refugee.

Notes

Preface

1. Pham Cao Duong, "Vietnamese-in-America Studies: A Proposal Submitted to the Asian American Studies Program, Department of Ethnic Studies, University of California, Berkeley" (El Cerrito, Calif.: Author, October 16, 1978).

2. The full text of this statement may be found in Sucheng Chan, *In Defense of Asian American Studies: The Politics of Teaching and Program Building* (Urbana: University of Illinois Press, 2005), 9–20.

3. See the bibliography for anthologies of short autobiographies and oral histories: James A. Freeman (1989), Lucy Nguyen-Hong-Nhiem and Joel M. Halpern, eds. (1989), Joanna C. Scott (1989), Katsuyo K. Howard, comp. (1990), John Tenhula (1991), Steven DeBonis (1995), De Tran, Andrew Lam, and Hai Dai Nguyen, eds. (1995), Robert S. McKelvey (1999 and 2002), Mary T. Cargill and Jade Quang Huynh (2002), James M. Freeman and Nguyen Dinh Huu (2003), Daniel F. Dentzer (2004), and Trin Yarborough (2005). For book-length memoirs, see Truong Nhu Tang (1986), Wendy E. Larson and Tran Thi Nga (1986), Bui Diem (1987), Le Ly Hayslip (1989 and 1993), Nguyen Qui Duc (1991), Jade Ngoc Huynh (1994), Bui Tin (1995), Nguyen Minh Thanh (1996), Lucy Nguyen-Hong-Nhiem (1996; electronic book 2004), Kim Ha (1997), Van Thanh Lu (1997), Lam Quang Thi (2001), Nguyen Cao Ky (2002), Kien Nguyen (2002), Trinh Do (2004), and Quang X. Pham (2005).

Chapter One

1. For a detailed discussion of the origins of Vietnam, see Keith Weller Taylor, *The Birth of Vietnam* (Berkeley and Los Angeles: University of California Press, 1983), particularly Appendix D, "The Archeological Record of Dong-son," 312–13.

2. Joseph Buttinger, *Vietnam: A Political History* (New York: Praeger, 1968), 22–23; and John F. Cady, *Southeast Asia: Its Historical Development* (New York: McGraw-Hill, 1964), 5.

3. Truong Buu Lam, "Comments and Generalities on Sino-Vietnamese Relations," in *Historical Interaction of China and Vietnam: Institutional and Cultural Themes*, comp. Edgar Wickberg (Lawrence: University of Kansas, Center for East Asian Studies, 1969), 36.

4. Buttinger, *Vietnam*, 30–32; D.G.E. Hall, *A History of Southeast Asia*, 3rd. ed. (New York: St. Martin's Press, 1968), 196–97; John K. Whitmore, "Vietnamese Adaptations of Chinese Government Structure in the Fifteenth Century," in *Historical Interaction of China and Vietnam: Institutional and Cultural Themes*, comp. Edgar Wickberg (Lawrence: University of Kansas, Center for East Asian Studies, 1969), 1–10; and William J. Duiker, *Vietnam: Revolution in Transition*, 2d ed. (Boulder, Colo.: Westview Press, 1995), 17.

5. Taylor, *Birth of Vietnam*, 39.

6. Buttinger, *Vietnam*, 33–34.

7. For details about these revolts, see Hall, *History of Southeast Asia*, 197–98.

8. For an exposition of the Vietnamese worldview, see Neil L. Jamieson, *Understanding Vietnam* (Berkeley and Los Angeles: University of California Press, 1993), 9–41.

9. David G. Marr, *Vietnamese Anticolonialism, 1885–1825* (Berkeley and Los Angeles: University of California Press, 1971), 11.

10. Mark W. McLeod, *The Vietnamese Response to French Intervention, 1862–1874* (New York: Praeger, 1991), 2.

11. David Joel Steinberg, ed., *In Search of Southeast Asia: A Modern History*, rev. ed. (Honolulu: University of Hawaii Press, 1987), 69–73; and Hall, *History of Southeast Asia*, 200, 203–4.

12. Hall, *History of Southeast Asia*, 199–202.

13. McLeod, *Vietnamese Response*, 8–9; Duiker, *Vietnam*, 22; and Hall, *History of Southeast Asia*, 421–22.

14. Bunroeun Thach, "The Khmer Krom," in *Not Just Victims: Conversations with Cambodian Community Leaders in the United States*, ed. Sucheng Chan (Urbana: University of Illinois Press, 2003), 259–65.

15. Hall, *History of Southeast Asia*, 201.

16. Truong Buu Lam, *Resistance, Rebellion, Revolution: Popular Movements in Vietnamese History*, Occasional Paper No. 75 (Singapore: Institute of Southeast Asian Studies, 1984), 10–15; Buttinger, *Vietnam*, 47–54; Steinberg, *In Search of Southeast Asia*, 74–75; and Cady, *Southeast Asia*, 281.

17. Hall, *History of Southeast Asia*, 426.

18. McLeod, *Vietnamese Response*, 4–5; and Buttinger, *Vietnam*, 62–63.

19. John F. Cady, *The Roots of French Imperialism in Eastern Asia* (Ithaca, N.Y.: Cornell University Press, 1967), 2–3; and Hall, *History of Southeast Asia*, 417–18.

20. Buttinger, *Vietnam*, 63–69.

21. Buttinger, *Vietnam*, 70–73; Hall, *History of Southeast Asia*, 426–32; Cady, *Roots of French Imperialism*, 12–14; and McLeod, *Vietnamese Response*, 9–12.

22. McLeod, *Vietnamese Response*, 13–24.

23. McLeod, *Vietnamese Response*, 35–36.

24. Hall, *History of Southeast Asia*, 644–47; Buttinger, *Vietnam*, 77–82; and Milton E. Osborne, *The French Presence in Cochinchina and Cambodia: Rule and Response (1859–1905)* (Ithaca, N.Y.: Cornell University Press, 1969), 25.

25. McLeod, *Vietnamese Response*, 26–33.

Chapter Two

1. For a discussion of the factors that led to the French decision to take joint action with the British, see Cady, *Roots of French Imperialism*, 160–206.

2. Cady, *Roots of French Imperialism*, 268.

3. McLeod, *Vietnamese Response*, 43.

4. Truong Buu Lam, *Patterns of Vietnamese Response to Foreign Intervention: 1858–1900* (New Haven, Conn.: Yale University, Southeast Asia Studies, 1967), 5–6; McLeod, *Vietnamese Response*, 47, 49–51; and Buttinger, *Vietnam*, 89–91.

5. Lam, *Patterns of Vietnamese Response*, 8–14.

6. Marr, *Vietnamese Anticolonialism*, 29.

7. Marr, *Vietnamese Anticolonialism*, 30–34.

8. Lam, *Patterns of Vietnamese Response*, 16–17.

9. Buttinger, *Vietnam*, 82–92; and Cady, *Roots of French Imperialism*, 269–79.

10. For details about the French takeover of Cambodia, see David P. Chandler, *A History of Cambodia*, 2d ed. (Boulder, Colo.: Westview Press, 1992), 137–72; and Osborne, *French Presence*, 175–260. Milton E. Osborne, *River Road to China: The Mekong Expedition, 1866–1873* (New York: Liveright, 1975) chronicles how the French hoped to find a back door to China by sailing upstream on the Mekong.

11. Truong, *Resistance, Rebellion, Revolution*, 18–20; and Marr, *Vietnamese Anticolonialism*, 44–76.

12. Hue-Tam Ho Tai, *Radicalism and the Origins of the Vietnamese Revolution* (Cambridge, Mass.: Harvard University Press, 1992), 15–18.

13. Osborne, *French Presence*, 63.

14. For a history of the French colonization of Laos, see Alfred W. McCoy, "French Colonialism in Laos, 1893–1945," in *Laos: War and Revolution*, eds. Nina S. Adams and Alfred W. McCoy (New York: Harper Colophon Books, 1970), 67–98; Arthur J. Dommen, *Laos: Keystone of Indochina* (Boulder, Colo.: Westview Press, 1985), 25–47; Geoffrey C. Gunn, *Rebellion in Laos: Peasant and Politics in a Colonial Backwater* (Boulder, Colo.: Westview Press, 1990), 1–98; and Arthur J. Dommen, *The Indochinese Experience of the French and the Americans: Nationalism and Communism in Cambodia, Laos, and Vietnam* (Bloomington: Indiana University Press, 2001), 14–20.

15. For detailed discussions of the administrative structure the French set up, see Osborne, *French Presence*, 59–130; Buttinger, *Vietnam*, 108–147; and Dommen, *Indochinese Experience*, 21–27.

16. Buttinger, *Vietnam*, 103–7.

17. For an in-depth analysis of how the French exploited their Indochinese colonies economically, see Martin J. Murray, *The Development of Capitalism in Colonial Indochina (1870–1940)* (Berkeley and Los Angeles: University of California Press, 1980). Rubber plantations are discussed in Chapter 6 and mining operations in Chapter 7. Readers without a basic knowledge of Marxist theory may find this work difficult to understand. Dommen, *Indochinese Experience*, 27–31, and David G. Marr, *Vietnamese Tradition on Trial, 1920–1945* (Berkeley and Los Angeles: University of California Press, 1981), 4–8, are two short and readable accounts of the same topic.

18. For an autobiographical account of the harsh life on a rubber plantation, see Tran Tu Binh, trans. John Spragens, Jr., ed. David G. Marr, *The Red Earth: A Vietnamese Memoir of Life on a Colonial Rubber Plantation*, Monographs in International Studies No. 66 (Athens: Ohio University, Southeast Asia Series, 1985).

19. Ngo Vinh Long, *Before the Revolution: The Vietnamese Peasants under the French* (Cambridge, Mass.: MIT Press, 1973) is the most detailed analysis of how the lives of peasants became truly destitute under French colonial rule.

20. Marr, *Vietnamese Anticolonialism*, 95–97.

21. Tai, *Radicalism*, 25.

22. The most detailed discussions of Phan Boi Chau's life, political-intellectual activities, and historical significance are Marr, *Vietnamese Anitcolonialism*, 83–86, 98–155, 225–28, 238–41, 258–68; and Tai, *Radicalism*, 27–28, 58–67, 140–42.

23. Details of Phan Chu Trinh's life and philosophy are told in Maar, *Vietnamese Anticolonialism*, 127–28, 156–57, 159–63, 195–201, 244–48, 268–76; and Tai, *Radicalism*, 154–57.

24. For statistics on school enrollment, see Marr, *Vietnamese Tradition*, 35–44; Tai, *Radicalism*, 34; and Duiker, *Vietnam*, 33.

25. For the fascinating history of these decades of intellectual discovery and political and social foment, see Tai, *Radicalism*; Marr, *Vietnamese Anticolonialism*, 156–277; Marr, *Vietnamese Tradition on Trial*; and Scott McConnell, *Leftward Journey: The Education of Vietnamese Students in France, 1919–1939* (New Brunswick, N.J.: Transaction, 1989).

26. For brief histories of these political organizations, see Huynh Kim Khanh, *Vietnamese Communism, 1925–1945* (Ithaca, N.Y.: Cornell University Press, 1982), 39–53; William J. Duiker, *The Communist Road to Power in Vietnam*, 2d rev. ed. (Boulder, Colo.: Westview Press, 1996), 10–12; and James P. Harrison, *The Endless War: Vietnam's Struggle for Independence* (New York: Columbia University Press, 1989), 42–44.

Chapter Three

1. Huynh, *Vietnamese Communism*, 58, note 37, offers the most detailed discussion of Ho's many aliases and his uncertain year of birth. Of the several biographies of Ho Chi Minh available, the most detailed is Jean Lacouture, trans. Peter Wiles, translation ed. Jane C. Seitz, *Ho Chi Minh: A Political Biography* (New York: Vintage Books, 1968).
2. Lacouture, *Ho Chi Minh*, 24.
3. Lacouture, *Ho Chi Minh*, 46.
4. As is true of many other aspects of Ho's life, the exact dates of these journeys are not known. Lacouture, *Ho Chi Minh*, 42 and 46.
5. The most detailed discussion of Thanh Nien's activities is in Huynh, *Vietnamese Communism*, 63–89. Also see Duiker, *Communist Road to Power*, 17–29.
6. Duiker, *Communist Road to Power*, 30; Huynh, *Vietnamese Communism*, 88; and Lacouture, *Ho Chi Minh*, 69–70.
7. Huynh, *Vietnamese Communism*, 120–26.
8. Huynh, *Vietnamese Communism*, 126–41; and Harrison, *Endless War*, 53–60.
9. This paragraph and the next are based on Duiker, *Communist Road to Power*, 33–45; Harrison, *Endless War*, 53–60; and Huynh, *Vietnamese Communism*, 151–71.
10. Lacouture, *Ho Chi Minh*, 64–65.
11. Duiker, *Communist Road to Power*, 52–58; and Huynh, *Vietnamese Communism*, 179–86.
12. Huynh, *Vietnamese Communism*, 238–40; Dommen, *Indochinese Experience*, 52–53; Duiker, *Communist Road to Power*, 63; and Buttinger, *Vietnam*, 184–86.
13. Huynh, *Vietnamese Communism*, 249–56; and Duiker, *Communist Road to Power*, 60–62.
14. Duiker, *Communist Road to Power*, 63–67; and Buttinger, *Vietnam*, 189–90.
15. Harrison, *Endless War*, 88.
16. Huynh, *Vietnamese Communism*, 264.
17. Huynh, *Vietnamese Communism*, 269–80.
18. Buttinger, *Vietnam*, 193–98; and Dommen, *Indochinese Experience*, 53–54.
19. Buttinger, *Vietnam*, 200–201; Lacouture, *Ho Chi Minh*, 78–85; Duiker, *Communist Road to Power*, 81; and Harrison, *Endless War*, 88–89. These authors do not agree on the dates of Ho's capture and his release.

Chapter Four

1. Huyhn, *Vietnamese Communism*, 280–84.
2. Buttinger, *Vietnam*, 205–6; Dommen, *Indochinese Experience*, 66–86; Huynh, *Vietnamese Communism*, 294–96; and David G. Marr, *Vietnam 1945: The*

Quest for Power (Berkeley and Los Angeles: University of California Press, 1995), 50–69, 113–26.

3. While most authors mention the famine in passing, Huynh Kim Khanh and David G. Marr are the only scholars who analyze the skill with which the Viet Minh turned the famine into a political issue. Huynh, *Vietnamese Communism*, 299–302, 312–15; and Marr, *Vietnam 1945*, 96–107. A short discussion is also in Ellen J. Hammer, *The Struggle for Indochina, 1940–1955: Viet Nam and the French Experience* (Stanford, Calif.: Stanford University Press, 1966), 145–46.

4. Marr, *Vietnam 1945*, 150; and Huynh, *Vietnamese Communism*, 314.

5. The most detailed and nuanced discussion of these weeks in August is Marr, *Vietnam 1945*, 345–401. Shorter accounts are in Huynh, *Vietnamese Communism*, 322–26; and Duiker, *Communist Road to Power*, 95–104.

6. Harrison, *Endless War*, 95; and Duiker, *Communist Road to Power*, 91–93.

7. For the identities of important people that the Viet Minh "liquidated," see Dommen, *Indochinese Experiences*, 120–21; for an estimate of the number of people imprisoned or detained, see Marr, *Vietnam 1945*, 518–19.

8. Dommen argues that the so-called August Revolution was in fact a coup d'état. See *Indochinese Experience*, 103–10. The most intricate and nuanced chronicle of these heady days that analyzes both the similarities and the differences in various regions and cities is in Marr, *Vietnam 1945*, 373–472, 520–37. Shorter accounts include Duiker, *Communist Road to Power*, 98–104; Lacouture, *Ho Chi Minh*, 93–108; Hammer, *Struggle for Indochina*, 98–105; and Harrison, *Endless War*, 96–97. For the American involvement in Indochinese affairs during this transitional period, see Archimedes L. Patti, *Why Vietnam? Prelude to American's Albatross* (Berkeley and Los Angeles: University of California Press, 1980). Patti was the head of the OSS-Indochina Mission.

9. For a list, see Dommen, *Indochinese Experience*, 117.

10. Marr, *Vietnam 1945*, 503, 516–17.

11. Dommen, *Indochinese Experience*, 125–26; and Duiker, *Communist Road to Power*, 118–19. For more detailed accounts, see Hammer, *Struggle for Indochina*, 113–21; and Buttinger, *Vietnam*, 221–26.

12. Dommen, *Indochinese Experience*, 131–32; and Hammer, *Struggle for Indochina*, 120, 124.

13. Hammer, *Struggle for Indochina*, 132–38, 146–47; and Buttinger, *Vietnam*, 234–40.

14. Dommen, *Indochinese Experience*, 134–35; and Hammer, *Struggle for Indochina*, 138–45.

15. Duiker, *Communist Road to Power*, 122–25; Hammer, *Struggle for Indochina*, 150–56; and Dommen, *Indochinese Experience*, 145–52.

16. Dommen, *Indochinese Experience*, 154–60; Hammer, *Struggle for Indochina*, 170–74; and Buttinger, *Vietnam*, 246–53.

Chapter Five

1. Hammer, *Struggle for Indochina*, 182–94. Moutet's quote is from p. 194.
2. Hammer, *Struggle for Indochina*, 203–22.
3. Hammer, *Struggle for Indochina*, 222–25 and 230; Buttinger, *Vietnam*, 277–93; and Dommen, *Indochinese Experience*, 187.
4. Hammer, *Struggle for Indochina*, 234–35; Buttinger, *Vietnam*, 308–9; and Dommen, *Indochinese Experience*, 188–90.
5. Dommen, *Indochinese Experience*, 200.
6. Phillip B. Davidson, *Vietnam at War: The History, 1946–1975* (Novato, Calif.: Presidio Press, 1988), 58–59; and Dommen, *Indochinese Experience*, 195–96.
7. Davidson, *Vietnam at War*, 76, 91; and Duiker, *Communist Road to Power*, 151–53.
8. Harrison, *Endless War*, 118; and Davidson, *Vietnam at War*, 107–8, 121. For military buffs, a blow-by-blow account of these battles may be found in Davidson, *Vietnam at War*, 109–21.
9. Dommen, *Indochinese Experience*, 207–8; and Duiker, *Communist Road to Power*, 160–62.
10. The most in-depth analysis of French domestic reaction to the First Indochina War is found in Edward Rice-Maximin, *Accommodation and Resistance: The French Left, Indochina, and the Cold War, 1944–1954* (Westport, Conn.: Greenwood Press, 1986).
11. Dommen, *Indochinese Experience*, 212–19.
12. Dommen, *Indochinese Experience*, 230.
13. Davidson, *Vietnam at War*, 165–67.
14. There are three long and gripping accounts of the battle at Dien Bien Phu: Jules Roy, *The Battle of Dienbienphu* (New York: Carroll and Graf, 1963); Bernard B. Fall, *Hell in a Very Small Place: The Seige of Dien Bien Phu* (New York: Vintage Books, 1966); and Davidson, *Vietnam at War*, 161–281, on which my cursory summary is based. Two brief accounts are in Harrison, *Endless War*, 123–24; and Duiker, *Communist Road to Power*, 162–70.
15. Harrison, *Endless War*, 124.
16. Dommen, *Indochinese Experience*, 234–36.
17. Peter A. Poole, *The Vietnamese in Thailand: A Historical Perspective* (Ithaca, N.Y.: Cornell University Press, 1970).
18. Louis A. Wiesner, *Victims and Survivors: Displaced Persons and Other War Victims in Viet-Nam, 1954–1975* (Westport, Conn.: Greenwood Press, 1988), 6.

Chapter Six

1. For details on the early years of American involvement, see Melvin Gurtov, *The First Vietnam Crisis: Chinese Communist Strategy and American Involvement, 1953–1954* (New York: Columbia University Press, 1967); Patti, *Why Vietnam?;*

Ronald H. Spector, *Advice and Support: The Early Years of the U.S. Army in Vietnam, 1941–1960* (New York: Free Press, 1985); and Andrew J. Rotter, *The Path to Vietnam: Origins of the American Commitment to Southeast Asia* (Ithaca, N.Y.: Cornell University Press, 1987).

2. Harrison, *Endless War*, 117.

3. There are two book-length biographies of Ngo Dinh Diem: Dennis Warner, *The Last Confucian: Vietnam, Southeast Asia, and the West* (New York: Penguin Books, 1964), and Anthony T. Bouscaren, *The Last of the Mandarins: Diem of Vietnam* (Pittsburgh, Pa.: Duquesne University Press, 1965). By far, the most scholarly assessment is Seth Jacobs, *America's Miracle Man in Vietnam: Ngo Dinh Diem, Religions, Race, and U.S. Intervention in Southeast Asia* (Durham, N.C.: Duke University Press, 2004), a thoroughly revisionist work. Short sketches of Diem are in Bernard B. Fall, *The Two Vietnams: A Political and Military Analysis*, 2d. rev. ed. (New York: Praeger, 1967), 234–53; Stanley Karnow, *Vietnam: A History* (New York: Penguin Books, 1984), 213–18; and Harrison, *Endless War*, 207–9.

4. Jacobs, *America's Miracle Man*, 31.

5. Jacobs, *America's Miracle Man*, 31, 58; Marilyn B. Young, *The Vietnam Wars, 1945–1990* (New York: HarperPerennial, 1991), 44.

6. Duiker, *Communist Road to Power*, 181; and Young, *Vietnam Wars*, 48.

7. Young, *Vietnam Wars*, 45; and George C. Herring, *America's Longest War: The United States and Vietnam, 1950–1975*, 2d ed. (New York: Alfred K. Knopf, 1986), 44, 51.

8. William S. Turley, *The Second Indochina War: A Short Political and Military History, 1954–1975* (Boulder, Colo.: Westview Press), 14; Herring, *America's Longest War*, 52–53; and Harrison, *Endless War*, 212–13.

9. Young, *Vietnam Wars*, 52–61.

10. For an in-depth analysis of the organization and strategies of the National Liberation Front of South Vietnam, commonly called "Viet Cong," see Douglas Pike, *Viet Cong: The Organization and Techniques of the National Liberation Front of South Vietnam* (Cambridge, Mass.: MIT Press, 1966). On the indispensable strategic importance to the Communists of the Ho Chi Minh Trail, see John Prados, *The Blood Road: The Ho Chi Minh Trail and the Vietnam War* (New York: John Wiley and Sons, 1999).

11. Wiesner, *Victims and Survivors*, 31–55, contains the most detailed discussion of the Strategic Hamlet Program.

12. One of the participants in the coup, General Tran Van Don, has told his version of the story in *Our Endless War: Inside Vietnam* (Novato, Calif.: Presidio Press, 1978), 87–118. The fullest account of the coup and the political and social contexts in which it took place is in Ellen J. Hammer, *A Death in November: America in Vietnam, 1963* (New York: E.P. Dutton, 1987). For brief accounts, see Robert Shaplen, *The Lost Revolution: The United States in Vietnam, 1946–1960* (New York: Harper and Row, 1966), 188–212; Karnow, *Vietnam*, 279–80, 279–311; Turley, *Second Indochina War*, 48–54; and Dommen, *Indochinese Experiences*, 508–30.

13. For memoirs by high-level South Vietnamese leaders about this period, see Nguyen Cao Ky, *Twenty Years and Twenty Days* (New York: Stein and Day, 1976), which was republished as *How We Lost the Vietnam War* (New York: Cooper Square Press, 2002); Tran, *Our Endless War*; Nguyen Cao Ky, with Marvin J. Wolf, *Buddha's Child: My Fight to Save Vietnam* (New York: St. Martin's Press, 2002); and Bui Diem, with David Chanoff, *In the Jaws of History* (Bloomington: Indiana University Press, 1999), 106–269. Other writings about South Vietnam include Robert Scigliano, *South Vietnam: Nation under Stress* (Boston: Houghton Mifflin, 1964); Fall, *The Two Viet-Nams*, 254–315; Shaplen, *Lost Revolution*, 213–49; Keesing's Research Report 5, *South Vietnam: A Political History, 1954–1970* (New York: Charles Scribner's Sons, 1970), 45–108; and Anthony J. Joes, *The War for South Vietnam, 1954–1975* (New York: Praeger, 1989), 53–145.

14. Fredrik Logevall, *Choosing War: The Lost Chance for Peace and the Escalation of the War in Vietnam* (Berkeley and Los Angeles: University of California Press, 1999), 23–33, makes a compelling argument that President Kennedy disagreed with his hawkish military and political advisors on what course to follow in Vietnam. On the Special Forces, see Charles M. Simpson, III, *Inside the Green Berets: The First Thirty Years—A History of the U.S. Army Special Forces* (Novato, Calif.: Presidio Press, 1983), 95–112; and Shelby L. Stanton, *Green Berets at War: U.S. Army Special Forces in Southeast Asia, 1956–1975* (Novato, Calif.: Presidio Press, 1985), 35–50. For accounts of U.S. covert operations in North Vietnam, see Sedgwick Tourison, *Project Alpha: Washington's Secret Military Operations in North Vietnam* (New York: St. Martin's Paperbacks, 1997); and Richard H. Schultz, Jr., *The Secret War against Hanoi: The Untold Story of Spies, Saboteurs, and Covert Warriors in North Vietnam* (New York: Perennial/HarperCollins, 1999). Covert operations, including assassinations, and psychological warfare carried out in South Vietnam against the "Viet Cong" are described in Douglas Valentine, *The Phoenix Program* (New York: William Morrow, 1990; repr. iUniverse, an Authors Guild Backprinting edition, 2000).

15. Herring, *America's Longest War*, 116–17.

16. Herring, *America's Longest War*, 119–22; Harrison, *Endless War*, 249; Young, *Vietnam Wars*, 117–18; and Karnow, *Vietnam*, 366–76.

17. For a nuanced analysis of whether U.S. leaders "engineered" the Gulf of Tonkin confrontation, see Logevall, *Choosing War*, 196–207. In *Tonkin Gulf and the Escalation of the Vietnam War* (Chapel Hill: University of North Carolina Press, 1996), Edwin E. Moise, in a detailed reconstruction of the events, concludes that there was no attack on the second night. However, Moise also concludes that the naval officers did not lie; rather, they genuinely thought they were under attack.

18. Jon M. Van Dyke, *North Vietnam's Strategy for Survival* (Palo Alto, Calif.: Pacific Books, 1972), 235–42. For detailed discussions of the air war, see Raphael Littauer and Norman Uphoff, eds., *The Air War in Indochina*, rev. ed. (Boston: Beacon Press, 1972); and Mark Clodfelter, *The Limits of Air Power: The American Bombing of North Vietnam* (New York: Free Press, 1989). For an analysis

by a military historian of why the air war was launched, see Davidson, *Vietnam at War*, 333–37.

19. Turley, *Second Indochina War*, 87.

20. Young, *Vietnam Wars*, 159.

21. On chemical and biological warfare in Vietnam, Laos, and Cambodia, see Steven Rose, ed., CBW: *Chemical and Biological Warfare* (Boston: Beacon Press, 1968), 19–98; Barry Weisberg, *Ecocide in Indochina: The Ecology of War* (San Francisco: Canfield Press, 1970); and J.B. Neilands et al., *Harvest of Death: Chemical Warfare in Vietnam and Cambodia* (New York: Free Press, 1972).

22. The antiwar movement has been chronicled in Charles DeBenedetti, with Charles Chatfield, *An American Ordeal: The Antiwar Movement of the Vietnam Era* (Syracuse, N.Y.: Syracuse University Press, 1990); Mitchell K. Hall, *Because of Their Faith:* CALCAV *and Religious Opposition to the Vietnam War* (New York: Columbia University Press, 1990); James W. Tollefson, *The Strength Not to Fight: An Oral History of Conscientious Objectors of the Vietnam War* (Boston: Little, Brown, 1993); and Tom Wells, *The War Within: America's Battle over Vietnam* (Berkeley and Los Angeles: University of California Press, 1994).

23. Van Dyke, *North Vietnam's Strategy*, offers a close analysis of all the methods the North Vietnamese used to cope with the destruction caused by these bombing campaigns.

24. Turley, *Second Indochina War*, 64, 72; Karnow, *Vietnam*, 682–84; and Harrison, *Endless War*, 243. For an in-depth discussion of the ground war from 1965 to 1968, see Davidson, *Vietnam at War*, 333–470.

25. Don Oberdorfer, *Tet! The Turning Point in the Vietnam War* (New York: De Capo Press, 1971) offers a gripping book-length account. For an account by a member of the Military Assistance Command—Vietnam who was intimately involved on the American side, see Davidson, *Vietnam at War*, 473–528. Ronald H. Spector, *After Tet: The Bloodiest Year in Vietnam* (New York: Free Press, 1993) analyzes the military sequel to and consequences of the Tet Offensive.

26. Turley, *Second Indochina War*, 108–10.

27. Karnow, *Vietnam*, 684–86.

28. William Shawcross, *Sideshow: Kissinger, Nixon, and the Destruction of Cambodia*, rev. ed. (New York: Simon and Schuster, 1987) has the most detailed account of the bombing campaign over Cambodia and the joint U.S.-ARVN invasion.

29. Duiker, *Communist Road to Power*, 317–18.

30. Duiker, *Communist Road to Power*, 320–22; and Turley, *Second Indochina War*, 138–43,

31. See Weisner, *Victims and Survivors*, for details.

Chapter Seven

1. For a short account of how the Ho Chi Minh campaign was planned and executed, see Nayan Chanda, "Suddenly Last Spring," *Far Eastern*

Economic Review [hereafter *FEER*], September 12, 1975, 35–39. Alan Dawson, who served in Vietnam for seven years first as a soldier and then as a journalist, provides a gripping book-length day-by-day chronicle in *55 Days: The Fall of South Vietnam* (Englewood Cliffs, N.J.: Prentice Hall, 1977). Dawson was the last full-time Western journalist permitted to remain in Saigon and did not leave until six months after its fall.

2. Vo Nguyen Giap, *How We Won the War* (Philadelphia: Recon Pub., 1976); and Van Tien Dung, trans. by John Spragens, Jr., *Our Great Spring Victory: An Account of the Liberation of South Vietnam* (New York: Monthly Review Press, 1977). Two eminent scholars of the Vietnam War agree that it was "people's war," a war that combined political and military struggles and used flexible tactics, that held the key to victory. See Douglas Pike, *PAVN: People's Army of Vietnam* (Novato, Calif.: Presidio Press, 1986), 213–53; and William J. Duiker, *Sacred War: Nationalism and Revolution in a Divided Vietnam* (New York: McGraw-Hill, 1995), 251–58.

3. Bui Diem, with David Chanoff, *In the Jaws of History*. The five quotes are from pp. 275, 289, 277, 341, and 334.

4. Nguyen, *How We Lost*, 101–16; and Nguyen with Wolf, *Buddha's Child*, 158–82.

5. Nguyen, *Buddha's Child*, 307.

6. Nguyen, *How We Lost*, 137.

7. Tran *Our Endless War*, 168–71.

8. Tran, *Our Endless War*, 241.

9. Tran, *Our Endless War*, 230.

10. Tran, *Our Endless War*, 231.

11. Tran, *Our Endless War*, 222.

12. Cao Van Vien, *The Final Collapse* (Honolulu: University Press of the Pacific, 2005), 116.

13. Cao, *Final Collapse*, 154–66.

14. The U.S. attorney general's parole authority is delineated in section 212(d)(5) of the Immigration and Nationality Act, as amended on October 3, 1965, 8 *U.S. Code* 1182(d)(5), which provides that "the Attorney General may in his discretion parole into the United States temporarily under such conditions as he may prescribe for emergent reasons or for reasons deemed strictly in the public interest any alien applying for admission to the United States, but such parole of such alien shall not be regarded as an admission of the alien and when the purposes of such parole shall, in the opinion of the Attorney General, have been served the alien shall forthwith return or be returned to the custody from which he was paroled and thereafter his case shall continue to be dealt with in the same manner as that of any other applicant for admission to the United States." Normally, only individuals are admitted under parole. However, the Indochinese were admitted as a group; they were also permitted to adjust their status from "parolee" to "permanent resident" after two years on U.S. soil. For further explication, see Marvin Samuel Gross, "Refugee-Parolee: The

Dilemma of the Indochina Refugee," *San Diego Law Review* 13, no. 1 (1975): 175–91.

15. U.S. Congress, House of Representatives, Committee on International Relations, Hearings: "The Vietnam-Cambodia Emergency, 1975, Part I—Vietnam Evacuation and Humanitarian Assistance," 94th Cong., 1st sess., April 9, 15, 16, 18, May 7, and 8, 1975 (Washington, D.C.: Government Printing Office, 1976); and U.S. Congress, Senate, Committee on the Judiciary, Subcommittee to Investigate Problems Connected with Refugees and Escapees, Hearings: "Indochina Evacuation and Refugee Problems, Part II—The Evacuation," 94th Cong., 1st sess., April 15, 25, and 20, 1975 (Washington, D.C.: Government Printing Office, 1976).

16. U.S. Congress, House of Representatives, Committee on International Relations, Special Subcommittee on Investigations, Hearings: "The Vietnam-Cambodia Emergency, 1975, Part III—Vietnam Evacuation: Testimony of Ambassador Graham A. Martin," January 27, 1976 (Washington, D.C.: Government Printing Office, 1976).

17. For eyewitness accounts of the fall of Saigon and some of the events immediately preceding it, see Dawson, *55 Days*; Thomas G. Tobin, Arthur E. Laehr, and John F. Hilgenberg, *Last Flight from Saigon*, United States Air Force Southeast Asia Monograph Series, vol. IV, monograph 6 (Washington, D.C.: Government Printing Office, 1978); Larry Engelmann, *Tears before the Rain: An Oral History of the Fall of South Vietnam* (New York: Oxford University Press, 1990); James Fenton, "The Fall of Saigon," *Granta* 15 (1985): 27–119; David Butler, *The Fall of Saigon: Scenes from the Sudden End of a Long War* (New York: Dell Books, 1986); Oliver Todd, trans. from the French by Stephen Becker, *Cruel April: The Fall of Saigon* (New York: W.W. Norton, 1990). *The Fall of Saigon*, a documentary film made by the Discovery Channel to commemorate the twentieth anniversary of that event, documents the fact that it was the munitions dropped by the pilots in the South Vietnamese Air Force as they flew their families and friends to safety that ultimately destroyed Tan Son Nhut's runways.

18. The chaos was captured in the footage of *The Fall of Saigon.*

19. Frank Snepp III, *Decent Interval: The American Debacle in Vietnam and the Fall of Saigon*, 1st ed. (New York: Random House, 1977), discusses the "delusions" and "fantasies" that shaped U.S. policy in Vietnam and criticizes the CIA for failing to protect its own agents there, especially those of Vietnamese ancestry, and for not shredding all its classified documents before leaving. The CIA sued Snepp, who was its principal policy analyst in Saigon during the war, for this criticism and won a punitive judgment against him.

20. Barry Wain, *The Refused: The Agony of the Indochinese Refugees* (New York: Simon and Schuster, 1981), 38.

21. U.S. Department of Health, Education, and Welfare, Task Force for Indochina Refugees, *Report to the Congress, June 15, 1976*, typescript (Washington, D.C.: Task Force for Indochina Refugees, 1976), 14–17.

22. The story of these ill-fated repatriates is told in Tracy Dahlby, "South Vietnamese in Limbo-Land," *FEER*, October 10, 1975, 26; Louis Halasz,

"Vietnamese on a Sea of Uncertainty," FEER, October 17, 1975, 30–31;
and Louis Halasz and Stephen Barber, "Sailing on a Sea of Trouble," FEER,
October 31, 1975, 24–25.

23. For details on the re-education camps, see Nguyen Van Canh with
Eric Cooper, *Vietnam under Communism, 1975–1982* (Stanford: Hoover Institu-
tion Press, 1983), 188–25, 197–98, 202; James A. Freeman, *Hearts of Sorrow:
Vietnamese-American Lives* (Stanford: Stanford University Press, 1989), 201–54;
and Robert S. McKelvey, *A Gift of Barbed Wire: America's Allies Abandoned in South
Vietnam* (Seattle: University of Washington Press, 2002).

24. Nayan Chanda, "Towards Socialism—On the Double," FEER, July 9,
1976, 10–11.

25. *New York Times*, June 8, 1976, 30, col. 3; July 22, 1976, 2, col. 5.

26. Peter Weintraub, "Slow Boat to Nowhere: Plight of the Indochinese
Refugees," FEER, December 16, 1977, 30–33; and *Newsweek*, April 17, 1978,
70.

27. Michael Richardson, "For Freedom's Sake," FEER, March 10, 1978,
20–21.

28. *Washington Post*, April 9, 1978, 4, col. 1.

29. U.S. General Accounting Office, "Report to the Congress of the
United States by the Comptroller General—The Indochinese Exodus: A
Humanitarian Dilemma" (Washington, D.C.: Comptroller General of the
United States, 1979), 49–50.

30. U.S. General Accounting Office, "Report—Indochinese Exodus," 50–
51.

31. U.S. Department of State, Immigration and Naturalization Service,
Indochinese Refugee Program Processing Guide (Washington, D.C.: Government
Printing Office, 1978).

32. U.S. General Accounting Office, "Report—Indochinese Exodus," 61.

Chapter Eight

1. Nayan Chanda, "Comrades Curb the Capitalists," FEER, April 14,
1978, 11–12.

2. Nayan Chanda, "Hanoi Takes a Grip on the South," FEER, May 26,
1978, 78–81.

3. Charles Benoit, "Vietnam's 'Boat People,'" in *The Third Indochina Conflict*,
ed. David P. Elliott (Boulder, Colo.: Westview Press, 1981), 139–62.

4. Elizabeth Becker, *When the War Was Over: The Voices of Cambodia's Revolution and Its People* (New York: Simon and Schuster, 1986), 367.

5. Benoit, "Vietnam's Boat People"; and Nayan Chanda, "Cholon's Merchants Feel the Border Backlash," FEER, May 5, 1978, 10–11.

6. Nayan Chanda, "Peking Says It Out Loud to Hanoi," FEER, May 12,
1978, 9–10.

7. Chang Pao-min, *Kampuchea between China and Vietnam* (Singapore:
Singapore University Press, 1985), 72–91, provides the most succinct

account available of these two wars. For a short account, see Nayan Chanda, "Cambodia: Fifteen Days That Shook Asia," FEER, January 29, 1979, 10–13. Also see Thu-truong Nguyen-vo, *Khmer-Viet Relations and the Third Indochina Conflict* (Jefferson, N.C.: McFarland, 1992), 125–44; Nayan Chanda, *Brother Enemy: The War after the War* (San Diego, Calif.: Harcourt Brace Jovanovich, 1986), 339–47; David Bonavia, "Changing the Course of History," FEER, March 2, 1979, 8–10; Russell Spurr, "A Quick Bout . . . or a Sluggish March," FEER, March 2, 1979, 10–11; David Bonavia, "Sowing the Seeds of a Bigger War," FEER, March 9, 1979, 12–13; Russell Spurr, "Holding Back the Angry Giant," FEER, August 9, 1979; Nayan Chanda, "End of the Battle but Not of the War," FEER, March 16, 1979, 10–12; idem, "Rallying Round the Flag," FEER, March 16, 1979, 10–12; and idem, "A Breather between Rounds," FEER, April 20, 1979, 18–19.

8. David Bonavia, "Mother China's Homecoming Problem," FEER, June 30, 1978, 8–9.

9. David Bonavia, "Please Take Your Partner," FEER, August 4, 1978, 11–12.

10. See the citations in note 7.

11. Peter Weintraub, "Propping Up the Half-Way House," FEER, August 11, 1978, 36.

12. *New York Times*, August 11, 1980, 7, col. 1; and "Towing Out to Sea Has Been Going On since 1975," FEER, August 31, 1979, 40–41.

13. Michael Richardson, "Singapore Slams the Door," FEER, November 10, 1978, 24–28; Peter Weintraub, "The Exodus and the Agony," FEER, December 22, 1978, 8–11; and K. Das and Guy Sacerdoti, "Digging in for a Long Stay," FEER, December 22, 1978, 11–12. For two oral histories collected by Lesleyanne Hawthorne from "boat persons" on Pulau Besar and Pulau Bidong, which describe the conditions on these islands in some detail, see Lesleyanne Hawthorne, ed., *Refugee: The Vietnamese Experience* (Melbourne: Oxford University Press, 1980), 263–84.

14. K. Das, "A Rising Tide of Troubles," FEER, December 15, 1978, 15–16.

15. K. Das, "Malaysia Will Take No More," FEER, January 26, 1979, 10.

16. Peter Weintraub, "The Exodus and the Agony," FEER, December 22, 1978, 8–11; and Susumu Awanohara et al., "The Lure of an Island," FEER, April 27, 1979, 18–22.

17. Wain, *The Refused*, 74.

18. Mary Lee, "Putting Up the Barriers," FEER, January 19, 1979, 32.

19. Mary Lee, "Angry, Determined but Impotent," FEER, February 3, 1979, 21–22.

Chapter Nine

1. Wain, *The Refused*, 17–20.

2. Guy Sacerdoti, "Plight of the 'Ship of Gold,'" FEER, November 24, 1978, 36; idem, "An Ultimatum by Malaysia," FEER, December 1, 1978,

11–12; K. Das, "Answer to a Desperate Plea," FEER, December 8, 1978, 13–14, 19; K. Das and Guy Sacerdoti, "Economics of a Human Cargo," FEER, December 22, 1978, 10–11; and Wain, *The Refused*, 20–35.

3. Wain, *The Refused*, 69, 108–22; Mary Lee and Paul Wilson, "A New Shipload of Problems," FEER, February 16, 1979, 32–34; Susumu Awanohara et al., "The Lure of an Island," FEER, April 27, 1979, 19–22.

4. Anonymous, "The Shoot-on-Sight Story That Found Refugees Homes," FEER, August 31, 1979, 42–44.

5. Wain, *The Refused*, 84–106.

6. U.S. General Accounting Office, "The Orderly Departure Program from Vietnam," Report to the Chairman, Subcommittee on Immigration, Refugees, and International Law, Committee on the Judiciary, House of Representatives (Washington, D.C.: Government Printing Office, 1990).

7. Wain, *The Refused*, 2–3.

8. Mary Lee, "The Slow Road to Recovery," FEER, August 24, 1979, 18; and idem, "Long Wait for the Promised Land," FEER, November 9, 1979, 30. Analyses of the Orderly Departure Program a decade after it began can be found in Robert L. Funseth, "Orderly Departure of Refugees from Vietnam," *Current Policy* no. 1199 (Washington, D.C.: U.S. Department of State, Bureau of Public Affairs, 1989); U.S. General Accounting Office, "The Orderly Departure Program," 4–10; and International Catholic Migration Commission, "The Orderly Departure Program," *Migration World* 20, no. 4 (1992): 34.

9. *New York Times*, October 15, 1979, 8, col. 3.

10. Richard Nations, "Hanoi's Test of Civilization," FEER, August 3, 1979, 18–19.

11. Both quotes in this paragraph are from Helen Ester, "A Hardening of the Heart," FEER, August 10, 1979, 22–23.

12. *New York Times*, June 12, 1980, 3, col. 1.

13. *New York Times*, August 11, 1980, 7, col. 1.

14. Wain, *The Refused*, 214–16; Gil Loescher and John A. Scanlan, *Calculated Kindness: Refugees and America's Half-Open Door, 1945–Present* (New York: Free Press, 1986), 154–55; and Valerie O. Sutter, *The Indochinese Refugee Dilemma* (Baton Rouge: Louisiana State University Press, 1990), 166–69.

15. U.S. Senate, "The Refugee Act of 1980," Report No. 96–590, 96th Cong., 2d sess. (Washington, D.C.: 1980).

16. For discussions of the 1980 Refugee Act and the new features that set it apart from earlier U.S. refugee policy, see Edward M. Kennedy, "Refugee Act of 1980," *International Migration Review* 15, no. 1 (1981): 141–56; Deborah E. Anker and Michael L. Posner, "The Forty Year Crisis: A Legislative History of the Refugee Act of 1980," *San Diego Law Review* 19, no. 1 (1981): 9–89; Dennis Gallagher, Susan Forbes, and Patricia Weiss Fagen, *Of Special Humanitarian Concern: U.S. Refugee Admissions since Passage of the Refugee Act* (Washington, D.C.: Refugee Policy Group, 1985); Loescher and Scanlan, *Calculated Kindness*, 1–101; Norman L. Zucker and Naomi Flink Zucker, *The Guarded Gate: The Reality of American Refugee Policy* (San Diego, Calif.: Harcourt

Brace Jovanovich, 1987); Ricardo Inzunza, "The Refugee Act of 1980, Ten Years After—Still the Way to Go," *International Journal of Refugee Law* 2, no. 3 (1990): 413–27; Lawyers Committee for Human Rights, *The Implementation of the Refugee Act of 1980: A Decade of Experience* (New York: Lawyers Committee for Human Rights, 1990); Juan P. Osuna and Christine M. Hanson, "U.S. Refugee Policy: Where We've Been, Where We're Going," *World Refugee Survey, 1993*, 40–48; and Kathleen Newland, *U.S. Refugee Policy: Dilemmas and Directions* (Washington, D.C.: Carnegie Endowment for International Peace, International Migration Program, 1995).

17. Gallagher, Forbes, and Fagen, *Of Special Humanitarian Concern*, 23 and 49.

18. For a history of the UNHCR and the constraints and changing conditions under which it operates, see Shelly Pitterman, "International Responses to Refugee Situations: The United Nations High Commissioner for Refugees," in *Refugees and World Politics*, ed. Elizabeth G. Ferris (New York: Praeger, 1985), 43–81; United Nations High Commissioner for Refugees, *The State of the World's Refugees, 2000: Fifty Years of Humanitarian Action* (New York: Oxford University Press, 2000), 1–35; Howard Adelman, "From Refugees to Forced Migrations: The UNHCR and Human Security," *International Migration Review* 35, no. 1 (2001): 7–32; Michael Barnett, "Humanitarianism with a Sovereign Face: UNHCR in the Global Undertow," *International Migration Review* 35, no. 1 (2001): 244–77; Gil Loescher, "The UNHCR and World Politics: State Interests vs. Institutional Autonomy," *International Migration Review* 35, no. 1 (2001): 33–56; idem, *The UNHCR and World Politics: A Perilous Path* (New York: Oxford University Press, 2001); and Astri Suhrke and Kathleen Newland, "UNHCR: Uphill into the Future," *International Migration Review* 35, no. 1 (2001): 284–302.

19. Charles B. Keely, "The International Refugee Regime(s): The End of the Cold War Matters," *International Migration Review* 35, no. 1 (2001): 303–14.

20. For discussions of the savage pirate attacks, see Joseph Cerquone, *Vietnamese Boat People: Pirates' Vulnerable Prey* (New York: American Council for Nationalities Service, U.S. Committee for Refugees, 1984); idem, *Uncertain Harbors: The Plight of Vietnamese Boat People* (New York: American Council for Nationalities Service, U.S. Committee for Refugees, 1987), 20–26; *New York Times*, June 7, 1987, 22, col. 1; Stuart B. Kleinman, "Terror at Sea: Vietnamese Victims of Piracy," *American Journal of Psychoanalysis* 50, no. 4 (1990): 351–62; and W. Courtland Robinson, *Terms of Refuge: The Indochinese Exodus and the International Response* (London: Zed Books, 1998), 166–71.

21. U.S. Committee for Refugees, *World Refugee Survey, 1987* (Washington, D.C.: American Council for Nationalities Service, 1988), 51.

22. Robinson, *Terms of Refuge*, 171–75.

23. U.S. Committee for Refugees, *World Refugee Survey, 1987*, 53; *World Refugee Survey, 1988*, 54; and *New York Times*, January 30, 1988, 4, col. 2.

24. U.S. Committee for Refugees, *World Refugee Survey, 1988*, 52; and Robinson, *Terms of Refuge*, 190.

25. *New York Times*, May 1, 1988, 17, col. 1.

Chapter Ten

1. Robinson, *Terms of Refuge*, 183.

2. Lawrence S. Eagleburger, "Indochinese Refugee Situation: Toward a Comprehensive Plan of Action," *Current Policy*, no. 1184 (Washington, D.C.: U.S. Department of State, Bureau of Public Affairs, 1989); "Fresh Hope in South-East Asia," *UN Chronicle* 28, no. 3 (1991): 53–55; Phyllis E. Oakley, "Comprehensive Plan of Action for Indochinese Refugees," U.S. Department of State *Dispatch* 6, no. 31 (1995): 600–602; U.S. Congress, House of Representatives, Committee on International Relations, Subcommittee on International Operations and Human Rights, Hearing, *Comprehensive Plan of Action for Indochinese Asylum Seekers*, 104th Cong., 1st sess., July 25 and 27, 1995 (Washington, D.C.: Government Printing Office, 1996); and Robinson, *Terms of Refuge*, 187–230.

3. *Christian Science Monitor*, October 14, 1997, 1, col. 2.

4. Borje Ljunggren, ed., *The Challenge of Reform in Indochina* (Cambridge: Harvard Institute for International Development, 1993); William S. Turley and Mark Selden, eds., *Reinventing Vietnamese Socialism: Doi Moi in Comparative Perspective* (Boulder, Colo.: Westview Press, 1993); Benedict J.T. Kerkvliet and Doug J. Palmer, eds., *Vietnam's Rural Transformation* (Boulder, Colo.: Westview Press, 1995); Adam Fforde and Stefan de Vylder, *From Plan to Market: The Economic Transition in Vietnam* (Boulder, Colo.: Westview Press, 1996); and James W. Morley and Masashi Nishihara, eds., *Vietnam Joins the World* (Armonk, N.Y.: M.E. Sharpe, 1997).

5. Robinson, *Terms of Refuge*, 193; and *World Refugee Survey 1993*, 86.

6. Robinson, *Terms of Refuge*, 193–94.

7. Eagleburger, "Indochinese Refugee Situation," 2.

8. William S. Ellis, "Hong Kong's Refugee Dilemma," *National Geographic Magazine*, November 1979, 709–23, 762; Kristen G. Hughes, "Closed Camps: Vietnamese Refugee Policy in Hong Kong" (Ph.D. diss., University of California, Berkeley, 1985); Lawyers Committee for Human Rights, *Inhumane Deterrence: The Treatment of Vietnamese Boat People in Hong Kong* (New York: Lawyers Committee for Human Rights, 1989); Chan Kwok Bun, "Hong Kong's Response to the Vietnamese Refugees: A Study in Humanitarianism, Ambivalence and Hostility," *Southeast Asian Journal of Social Science* 18, no. 1 (1990): 94–110; Linda Hitchcox, "Repatriation: Solution or Expedient? The Vietnamese Asylum Seekers in Hong Kong," *Southeast Asian Journal of Social Science* 18, no. 1 (1990): 111–31; idem, *Vietnamese Refugees in Southeast Asian Camps* (New York: St. Martin's Press, 1990), 96–105, 115ff.; Leonard Davis, *Hong Kong and the Asylum-Seekers from Vietnam* (New York: St. Martin's Press, 1991); and Ronald Skeldon, "Hong Kong's Response to the Indochinese Influx, 1975–93," *Annals of the American Academy of Political and Social Sciences* 534 (July 1994): 91–105.

9. Davis, *Hong Kong*, 16.

10. Davis, *Hong Kong*, 9.

11. Davis, *Hong Kong*, 48–77; and Hitchcox, *Vietnamese Refugees*, 165–67.

12. Davis, *Hong Kong*, 200–221.

13. Robinson, *Terms of Refuge*, 216.

14. Robinson, *Terms of Refuge*, 216–18.

15. U.S. Congress, House of Representatives, Committee on International Relations, Subcommittee on Asia and the Pacific and Subcommittee on International Relations and Human Rights, Joint Hearing, "Indochinese Refugees: Comprehensive Plan of Action," 104th Cong., 1st sess., July 25, 1995 (Washington, D.C.: Government Printing Office, 1996), 2.

16. U.S. State Department, Bureau of Population, Refugees, and Migration, Department of Justice, and Department of Health and Human Services, *U.S. Refugee Admissions Program for Fiscal Year 1998* (Washington, D.C., 1998), 8–9.

17. U.S. Department of State, Department of Justice, and Department of Health and Human Services, *Proposed Refugee Admissions for Fiscal Year 2000* (Washington, D.C., 1999), 12; and idem, *Proposed Refugee Admissions for Fiscal Year 2001* (Washington, D.C., 2000), 9–11.

18. *World Refugee Survey 1997*, 114–15; *World Refugee Survey 1998*, 108; *World Refugee Survey 1999*, 106; and *World Refugee Survey 2000*, 137–38.

19. On the difficult lives of Amerasians in both Vietnam and the United States, see Chung Hoang Chuong and Le Van, *The Amerasians from Vietnam: A California Study* (Folsom, Calif.: Folsom Cordova Unified School District, Southeast Asia Community Resource Center, 1994); Steven DeBonis, *Children of the Enemy: Oral Histories of Vietnamese Amerasians and Their Mothers* (Jefferson, N.C.: McFarland, 1995); Thomas A. Bass, *Vietnamerica: The War Comes Home* (New York: Soho Press, 1996); and Robert S. McKelvey, *The Dust of Life: America's Children Abandoned in Vietnam* (Seattle: University of Washington Press, 1999).

20. Amerasian Homecoming Act, P.L. 100–202.

21. U.S. Coordinator for Refugee Affairs, "Proposed Refugee Admissions for Fiscal Year 1989," Report to Congress (Washington, D.C.: U.S. Coordinator for Refugee Affairs, 1988), 11.

22. McKelvey, *Dust of Life*, 7–8, 34, 75–77, 109–10, 120; and U.S. General Accounting Office, letter to Congressmen Robert J. Mzarek and Thomas J. Ridge assessing the Amerasian Resettlement Program, November 16, 1992 (Washington, D.C.: U.S. General Accounting Office, Program Evaluation and Methodology Section, 1992), 12 pages.

23. U.S. Department of State, Department of Justice, and Department of Health and Human Services, *U.S. Refugee Admissions for Fiscal Year 2000* (Washington, D.C., 1999), 13.

24. *World Refugee Survey 1989*, 57; and U.S. Coordinator for Refugee Affairs, "Proposed Refugee Admissions for Fiscal Year 1991" (Washington, D.C.: U.S. Coordinator for Refugee Affairs, 1990), 12; and *World Refugee Report* (Washington, D.C.: U.S. Department of State, 1990), 310.

25. U.S. Department of State, Department of Justice, and Department of Health and Human Services, *U.S. Refugee Admissions for Fiscal Year 2000* (Washington, D.C., 1999), 13.

26. Peter Bui-Xuan-Luong, "South Vietnamese Officer Prisoners of War: Their Resilience and Acculturation Experiences in Prison and in the U.S." (Ph.D. diss., The Fielding Institute, 2000); and McKelvey, *Gift of Barbed Wire.*

27. *World Refugee Survey 1989,* 57; *World Refugee Survey 1992,* 66, and *World Refugee Survey 1993,* 86.

28. U.S. Coordinator for Refugee Affairs, *Proposed Refugee Admissions for Fiscal Year 1991,* 12–13; idem, *Proposed Refugee Admissions for Fiscal Year 1992,* 9–10; idem, *Proposed Refugee Admissions for Fiscal Year 1993,* 11; idem, *Proposed Refugee Admissions for Fiscal Year 1994,* 9–10; idem, *Proposed Refugee Admissions for Fiscal Year 1995,* 8–9.

29. U.S. Congress, House of Representatives, "To Extend Eligibility for Refugee Status of Unmarried Sons and Daughters of Certain Vietnamese Refugees," *107 House Report 254,* 107th Cong., 1st sess. (Washington, D.C.: Congressional Information Service, 2001).

Epilogue

1. Mandy Thomas, *Dreams in the Shadows: Vietnamese-Australian Lives in Transition* (St. Leonards, Australia: Allen and Unwin, 1999), 179–80.

Selected Bibliography: The Vietnam War and the Exodus of Refuge-Seekers from Vietnam

Unlike most bibliographies that list the works authors have consulted, this bibliography is the first part of a stand-alone compilation to help readers find existing writings on various aspects of the Vietnam War, the exodus of refuge-seekers, their detention in refugee camps, and their resettlement abroad, particularly in the United States. The last bibliography on the Vietnamese in America, *Emergence of the Vietnamese American Communities: A Bibliography of Works Including Selected Annotated Citations*, was published by the Asian American Studies Center at the University of California, Los Angeles, in 1996. It did not include studies of the Vietnam War. Many new works on Vietnamese communities in the United States have appeared since then, so a more up-to-date bibliography is warranted.

Listed here are selected books and government documents about the Vietnam War; books and journal articles about Vietnamese and Sino-Vietnamese refuge-seekers in the countries of first asylum in Southeast Asia and in Hong Kong; overviews of the first phase of Vietnamese resettlement in the United States, Canada, Australia, New Zealand, Great Britain, France, Norway, and Sweden; the American public's perception of and response to the refugee influx; books written in English by South Vietnamese and North Vietnamese political and military leaders who have retrospectively assessed the outcome of the Vietnam War; and book-length memoirs and short autobiographies and oral histories collected in anthologies.

Studies of the postresettlement period will be listed in the second part of the bibliography, which will appear in my forthcoming book on the interactions between Vietnamese newcomers and the institutional structures that both facilitated and constrained their settlement in the United States. It will include books, government documents, and articles on U.S. policies regarding refugee resettlement; the bureaucracy created or modified to handle the influx; the economic, social, cultural, psychological, medical, and educational challenges the refugees confronted as they adapted to life in the United States; and studies of the elderly, women, and youth.

There are two big gaps in the existing literature. There are no systematic, large-scale studies of how the socioeconomic status of the refugees, immigrants, and transmigrants has changed over time. (There exists only a handful of studies on how they fared during the early years of their resettlement.) Even scarcer are works that analyze the political differences among Vietnamese in the United States and in other countries in the Vietnamese diaspora.

Several hundred PHD dissertations and MA theses have been written about the Vietnamese who have come to the United States, but because of space limitation I list only those on topics not well covered in published writings. These include unaccompanied minors placed into foster homes after their arrival; Amerasians; former political prisoners who had been incarcerated in so-called re-education camps; the ethnic Chinese from Vietnam; and Vietnamese interactions with other racial and ethnic minorities in the United States. Space limitation also prevents me from including tens of thousands of short articles published in newspapers and popular periodicals about the American phase of the wars in Vietnam, Laos, and Cambodia, as well as the refugee exodus. Of these short articles, only those I cite in the Endnotes are included in the two parts of the Bibliography.

Adelman, Howard. 1980. *The Indochinese Refugee Movement: The Canadian Experience*. Toronto: Operation Lifeline.

———. 1982. *Canada and the Indochinese Refugees*. Regina, Canada: L.A. Weigl Educational Associates.

Adelman, Howard, Charles Le Blanc, and Jean-Philippe Therien. 1980. "Canadian Policy on Indochinese Refugees." In *Southeast Asian Exodus: From Tradition to Resettlement*. Ed. Elliot L. Tepper, 135–50. Ottawa: Canadian Asian Studies Association.

Agency for International Development. 1975. "Operation Baylift: Report on the Emergency Movement of Vietnamese and Cambodian Orphans for Intercountry Adoption." Washington, D.C.: Author.

Allen, Rebecca and Harry H. Hiller. 1985. "The Social Organization of Migration: An Analysis of the Uprooting and Flight of Vietnamese Refugees." *International Migration* 23, no. 4: 439–52.

Anker, Deborah E. 1981. "The Forty Year Crisis: A Legislative History of the Refugee Act of 1980." *San Diego Law Review* 19, no. 1: 9–89.

Ashworth, Georgina. 1979. *The Boat People and the Road People: Refugees from Vietnam, Laos, and Cambodia*. Sunbury, England: Quartermaine House.

"Asia." 1978. *World Refugee Survey, 1978*. New York: U.S. Committee for Refugees, 20–26.

"Asia and the Pacific." 1982. *World Refugee Survey, 1982*. New York: U.S. Committee for Refugees, 25–28.

Asia Watch. 1991. "Indefinite Detention and Mandatory Repatriation: The Incarceration of Vietnamese in Hong Kong." New York: Human Rights Watch.

————. 1992. "Refugees at Risk: Forced Repatriation of Vietnamese from Hong Kong." New York: Human Rights Watch.

Asselin, Pierre. 2002. *A Bitter Peace: Washington, Hanoi, and the Making of the Paris Peace Agreement*. Chapel Hill: University of North Carolina Press.

Australia. Parliament. Senate Standing Committee on Foreign Affairs and Defense. 1982. "Indochinese Refugees Resettlement—Australia's Involvements." Canberra: Australian Government Publications Service.

Bach, Robert L. 1990a. "Third Country Resettlement." In *Refugees and International Relations*. Ed. Gil Loescher and Laila Monahan, 313–31. Oxford: Clarendon.

————. 1990b. "Transforming Socialist Emigration: Lessons from Cuba and Vietnam." *In Defense of the Alien* 12: 89–103.

Baer, Florence E. 1982. "'Give Me . . . Your Huddled Masses': Anti-Vietnamese Refugee Lore and the 'Image of Limited Good.'" *Western Folklore* 41, no. 4: 275–91.

Baker, Nicholas G. "Substitute Care for Unaccompanied Refugee Minors." *Child Welfare* 61, no. 6: 353–63.

Baker, Reginald and David S. North. 1984. *The 1975 Refugees: Their First Five Years in America*. Washington, D.C.: New TransCentury Foundation.

Bass, Thomas A. 1996. *Vietnamerica: The War Comes Home*. New York: Soho.

Beach, Hugh and Lars Ragvald. 1982. *A New Wave on a Northern Shore: The Indochinese Refugees in Sweden*. Norrkoping, Sweden: Statens Invandrarverk, Arbetsmarknadsstyrelsen.

Beck, Melinda et al. 1985. "Where Is My Father?" *Newsweek*, April 15, 54–55 and 57.

Beiser, Morton. 1999. *Strangers at the Gate: The "Boat People's" First Ten Years in Canada*. Toronto: University of Toronto Press.

Beiser, Morton and Ilene Hyman. 1997. "Southeast Asian Refugees in Canada." In *Ethnicity, Immigration, and Psychopathology*. Ed. Ihsan Al-Issa and Michel Tousignant, 35–56. New York: Plenum.

Benoit, Charles. 1981. "Vietnam's 'Boat People.'" In *The Third Indochina Conflict*, 139–62. Ed. David P. Elliott. Boulder, Colo.: Westview Press.

Bergerud, Eric M. 1991. *The Dynamics of Defeat: The Vietnam War in Hau Nghia Province*. Boulder, Colo.: Westview Press.

Berman, Larry. 1982. *Planning a Tragedy: The Americanization of the War in Vietnam*. New York: W.W. Norton.

————. 2001. *No Peace, No Honor: Nixon, Kissinger, and Betrayal in Vietnam*. New York: Free Press.

Blackburn, Robert M. 1994. *Mercenaries and Lyndon Johnson's "More Flags": The Hiring of Korean, Filipino, and Thai Soldiers in the Vietnam War*. Jefferson, N.C.: McFarland.

Borresen, C. Robert. 1982. "An Exploratory Survey of the Development of a Vietnamese Stereotype." *Psychological Reports* 50, no. 1: 159–66.

Bouscaren, Anthony T. 1977. *Diem of Vietnam: The Last of the Mandarins*. Pittsburgh, Pa.: Duquesne University Press.

_____, ed. *All Quiet on the Eastern Front: The Death of South Vietnam.* Old Greenwich, Conn.: Devin-Adair.

Bousquet, Gisele. 1987. *Behind the Bamboo Hedge: The Impact of Homeland Politics in the Parisian Vietnamese Community.* Ann Arbor: University of Michigan Press.

_____. 1991. "Living in a State of Limbo: A Case Study of Vietnamese Refugees in Hongkong [sic] Camps." In *People in Upheaval.* Ed. Scott M. Morgan and Elizabeth Colson, 34–53. Staten Island, N.Y.: Center for Migration Studies.

Bradshaw, Adrian. 1989. "Amerasians Left Behind." *Geographical: Monthly Magazine of the Royal Geographical Society* 61, no. 7: 25–28.

Brigham, Robert K. 1999. *Guerrilla Diplomacy: The NLF's Foreign Relations and the Vietnam War.* Ithaca, N.Y.: Cornell University Press.

Brown, William A. 1988. "Indochinese Refugees and Relations with Thailand." *Current Policy,* no. 1052. Washington, D.C.: U.S. Department of State, Bureau of Public Affairs.

Bui, Diana D. 1980. "The Indochinese Mutual Assistance Associations." Washington, D.C.: Indochina Resource Action Center.

_____. 1990. "Detention in Hong Kong: Women's Voices." *Migration World* 18, no. 3–4: 18–26.

Bui, Diem with David Chanoff. 1999. *In the Jaws of History.* Bloomington: Indiana University Press.

Bui-Xuan-Luong, Peter. 2000. "South Vietnamese Officer Prisoners of War: Their Silence and Acculturation Experiences in Prison and in the United States." PH.D. diss., The Fielding Institute.

Burchett, Wilfred G., 1965. *Vietnam: Inside Story of the Guerrilla War.* New York: International Publishers.

Butler, David. 1985. *The Fall of Saigon: Scenes from the Sudden End of a Long War.* New York: Dell.

Buttinger, Joseph. 1968. *Vietnam: A Political History.* New York: Praeger.

Buzzanco, Robert. 1996. *Masters of War: Military Dissent and Politics in the Vietnam Era.* New York: Cambridge University Press.

Cady, John F. 1954. *The Roots of French Imperialism in Eastern Asia.* Ithaca, N.Y.: Cornell University Press.

_____. 1964. *Southeast Asia: Its Historical Development.* New York: McGraw-Hill.

Cao, Van Vien. 2005. *The Final Collapse.* Honolulu: University Press of the Pacific.

Cao, Van Vien and Dong Van Khuyen. 1978. *Reflections on the Vietnam War.* McLean, Va.: U.S. Army Center of Military History.

Cargill, Mary T. and Jade Quang Huynh, eds. 2000. *Voices of Vietnamese Boat People: Nineteen Narratives of Escape and Survival.* Jefferson, N.C.: McFarland.

Carlin, James L. 1981. "The Development of U.S. Refugee and Migration Policies: An International Context." *Journal of Refugee Resettlement* 1, no. 4: 9–14.

Casella, Alexander. 1989. "The Refugees from Vietnam: Rethinking the Issue." *World Today* 45, no. 8–9: 160–64.

Cerquone, Joseph. 1984. *Vietnamese Boat People: Pirates' Vulnerable Prey*. New York: American Council for Nationalities Service, U.S. Committee for Refugees.

————. 1986. "Southeast Asian Refugees: Back to the Future." *World Refugee Survey, 1986*. Washington, D.C.: U.S. Committee for Refugees, 34–35.

————. 1987. *Uncertain Harbor: The Plight of Vietnamese Boat People*. New York: American Council for Nationalities Service, U.S. Committee for Refugees.

Chan, Kwok Bun. 1990a. "Getting through Suffering: Indochinese Refugees in Limbo 15 Years Later." *Southeast Asian Journal of Social Issues* 18, no. 1: 1–18.

————. 1990b. "Hong Kong's Response to the Vietnamese Refugees: A Study in Humanitarianism, Ambivalence and Hostility." *Southeast Asian Journal of Social Science* 18, no. 1: 94–110.

Chan, Kwok Bun and Kenneth Christie. 1995. "Past, Present and Future: The Indochinese Refugee Experience Twenty Years Later." *Journal of Refugee Studies* 8, no. 1: 75–94.

Chan, Kwok Bun and Doreen M. Indra, eds. 1987. *Uprooting, Loss and Adaptation: The Resettlement of Indochinese Refugees in Canada*. Ottawa: Canadian Public Health Association.

Chan, Kwok Bun and David Loveridge. 1987. "Refugees 'in Transit': Vietnamese in a Refugee Camp in Hong Kong." *International Migration Review* 21, no. 3: 745–59.

Chanda, Nayan. 1986. *Brother Enemy: The War after the War*. San Diego, Calif.: Harcourt Brace Jovanovich.

Chang, Pao-min. 1985. *Kampuchea between China and Vietnam*. Singapore: Singapore University Press.

Chanoff, David and Doan Van Toai. 2001. *Vietnam: A Portrait of Its People at War*. London: I.B. Tauris.

Charlton, Michael and Anthony Moncrieff. 1989. *Many Reasons Why: The American Involvement in Vietnam*. New York: Hill and Wang.

Chen, Edwin E. 1975. "The Last 'New Life Hamlet.'" *Progressive* 39 (November): 20–24.

Chen, King C. 1969. *Vietnam and China, 1938–1954*. Princeton, N.J.: Princeton University Press.

Chermayeff, Ivan. 1998. "The Vietnamese Migration." *World Policy Journal* 15, no. 1: 68–76.

Chung, Hoang Chuong and Le Van. 1994. *The Amerasians from Vietnam: A California Study*. Folsom, Calif.: Southeast Asian Community Resource Center.

Clodfelter, Mark. 1989. *The Limits of Air Power: The American Bombing of North Vietnam*. New York: Free Press.

Cohen, Roberta. 1990. *Introducing Refugee Issues into the United Nations Human Rights Agenda*. Washington, D.C.: Refugee Policy Group.

Coles, Gervase. 1990. "Approaching the Refugee Problem Today." In *Refugees and International Relations*. Ed. Gil Loescher and Laila Monahan, 373–410. Oxford: Clarendon.

Colombey, Jean-Pierre, ed. 1995. *Collection of International Instruments and Other Legal Texts Concerning Refugees and Displaced Persons.* Geneva: Office of the United Nations High Commissioner for Refugees, Division of International Protection.

"Comprehensive Plan of Action for Indochinese Refugees." 1995. *U.S. State Department Dispatch* 6, no. 31: 600–602.

Congressional Research Service. 1980. "Review of U.S. Refugee Resettlement Programs and Policies," a report prepared at the request of Edward M. Kennedy, Chairman, Committee on the Judiciary, U.S. Senate, by the Congressional Research Service. Washington, D.C.: Government Printing Office.

Davidson, Phillip B. 1988. *Vietnam at War: The History, 1946–1975.* Novato, Calif.: Presidio Press.

Davis, Leonard. 1991. *Hong Kong and the Asylum-Seekers from Vietnam.* New York: St. Martin's Press.

Dawson, Alan. 1977. *Fifty-five Days: The Fall of South Vietnam.* Englewood Cliffs, N.J.: Prentice Hall.

DeBenedetti, Charles, with Charles Chatfield as assistant author. 1990. *An American Ordeal: The Antiwar Movement of the Vietnam Era.* Syracuse, N.Y.: Syracuse University Press. [Chatfield finished the book after DeBenedetti's death in 1987.]

DeBonis, Steven. 1995. *Children of the Enemy: Oral Histories of Vietnamese Amerasians and Their Mothers.* Jefferson, N.C.: McFarland.

DeMonaco, MaryKim. 1989. "Disorderly Departure: An Analysis of the United States Policy toward Amerasian Immigration." *Brooklyn Journal of International Law* 15, no. 3: 641–709.

Desbarats, Jacqueline. 1985. "Indochinese Resettlement in the United States." *Annals of the Association of American Geographers* 75, no. 4: 522–38.

Detzer, Daniel F. 2004. *Elder Voices: Southeast Asian Families in the United States.* Walnut Creek, Calif.: AltaMira Press.

DeVecchi, Robert P. 1982. "Politics and Policies of 'First Asylum' in Thailand." *World Refugee Survey, 1982.* New York: U.S. Committee for Refugees, 20–24.

De Voe, Dorsch M. 1981. "Framing Refugees as Clients." *International Migration Review* 15, no. 1: 88–94.

Dillard, Walter S. 1982. *Sixty Days to Peace: Implementing the Paris Peace Accords, Vietnam 1973.* Washington, D.C.: National Defense University.

Diller, Janelle M. 1988. *In Search of Asylum: Vietnamese Boat People in Hong Kong, a Report.* Washington, D.C.: Indochina Resource Action Center.

Do, Hien Duc. 1999. *The Vietnamese Americans.* Westport. Conn.: Greenwood Press.

Do, Trinh Quang. 2004. *Saigon to San Diego: Memoir of a Boy Who Escaped from Communist Vietnam.* Jefferson, N.C.: McFarland.

Dommen, Arthur J. 2001. *The Indochinese Experience of the French and the Americans: Nationalism and Communism in Cambodia, Laos, and Vietnam.* Bloomington: Indiana University Press.

Duc, Thich Minh. 1999. "The Shadows of War and the Vietnamese in the United States." *ReVision* 22, no. 1: 21–27.

Duiker, William J. 1976. *The Rise of Nationalism in Vietnam, 1900–1941.* Ithaca, N.Y.: Cornell University Press.

———. 1995a. *Sacred War: Nationalism and Revolution in a Divided Vietnam.* New York: McGraw-Hill.

———. 1995b. *Vietnam: Revolution in Transition.* 2d ed. Boulder, Colo.: Westview Press.

———. 1996. *The Communist Road to Power in Vietnam.* 2d ed. Boulder, Colo.: Westview Press.

Duke, Karen and Tony Marshal. 1995. "Vietnamese Refugees since 1982," Home Research Study no. 142. London: Home Office.

Duling, Gretchen A. 1977. *Adopting Joe: A Black Vietnamese Child.* Rutland, Vt.: Charles E. Tuttle.

Duong, Lloyd. 2000. *The Boat People: Imprints on History.* Boston: Optimal World Publishers.

Eagleburger, Lawrence S. 1989. "Indochina Refugee Situation: Toward a Comprehensive Plan of Action." *Current Policy* no. 1184. Washington, D.C.: U.S. Department of State, Bureau of Public Affairs.

"East Asia and the Pacific." 1984. *World Refugee Survey, 1984.* New York: U.S. Committee for Refugees, 48–51.

———. 1985. *World Refugee Survey, 1985 in Review.* New York: U.S. Committee for Refugees, 52–55.

———. 1986. *World Refugee Survey, 1986 in Review.* Washington, D.C.: U.S. Committee for Refugees, 51–56.

———. 1987. *World Refugee Survey, 1987 in Review.* Washington, D.C.: U.S. Committee for Refugees, 46–53.

———. 1988. *World Refugee Survey, 1988 in Review.* Washington, D.C.: U.S. Committee for Refugees, 49–55.

———. 1989. *World Refugee Survey, 1989 in Review.* Washington, D.C.: U.S. Committee for Refugees, 51–59.

———. 1990. *World Refugee Survey, 1990.* Washington, D.C.: U.S. Committee for Refugees, 1990.

———. 1991. *World Refugee Survey, 1991.* Washington, D.C.: U.S. Committee for Refugees, 60–67.

———. 1992. *World Refugee Survey, 1992.* Washington, D.C.: U.S. Committee for Refugees, 56–57 and 60–63.

———. 1993. *World Refugee Survey, 1993.* Washington, D.C.: U.S. Committee for Refugees, 78–86.

———. 1994. *World Refugee Survey, 1994.* Washington, D.C.: U.S. Committee for Refugees, 76–89.

———. 1995. *World Refugee Survey, 1995.* Washington, D.C.: U.S. Committee for Refugees, 84–98.

———. 1996. *World Refugee Survey, 1996.* Washington, D.C.: U.S. Committee for Refugees, 78–91.

_____. 1997. *World Refugee Survey, 1997.* Washington, D.C.: U.S. Committee for Refugees, 110–23.

_____. 1998. *World Refugee Survey, 1998.* Washington, D.C.: U.S. Committee for Refugees, 104–17.

_____. 1999. *World Refugee Survey, 1999.* Washington, D.C.: U.S. Committee for Refugees, 100–121.

_____. 2000. *World Refugee Survey, 2000.* Washington, D.C.: U.S. Committee for Refugees, 130–57.

_____. 2001. *World Refugee Survey, 2001.* Washington, D.C.: U.S. Committee for Refugees, 124–51.

_____. 2002. *World Refugee Survey, 2002.* Washington, D.C.: U.S. Committee for Refugees, 110–41.

Eastman, Lloyd E. 1967. *Throne and Mandarins: China's Search for a Policy during the Sino-French Controversy, 1880–1885.* Cambridge, Mass.: Harvard University Press.

Edholm, Felicity, Helen Roberts, and Judith Sayer. 1983. *Vietnamese Refugees in Britain.* London: Commission for Racial Equality.

Egan, Maura Goggin. 1984. "Social Adaptation in Foster Families Caring for Unaccompanied Refugee Minors from Vietnam." PH.D. diss., University of Washington.

Eisenbruch, Maurice. 1986. "Action Research with Vietnamese Refugees: Refugee, Befriender, and Researcher Relationships." *Journal of Intercultural Studies* 7, no. 2: 30–51.

Elliott, David W.P., ed. 1981. *The Third Indochina Conflict.* Boulder, Colo.: Westview Press.

Elliott, Duong Van Mai. 1999. *The Sacred Willow: Four Generations in the Life of a Vietnamese Family.* New York: Oxford University Press.

Ellis, William S. 1979. "Hong Kong's Refugee Dilemma." *National Geographic* 156, no. 5: 709–23 and 732.

Employment and Immigration Canada Commission. 1982. "Indochinese Refugees: The Canadian Response, 1979 and 1980." Ottawa: Employment and Immigration Canada.

Engelmann, Larry. 1990. *Tears before the Rain: An Oral History of the Fall of South Vietnam.* New York: Oxford University Press.

Evans, Grant and Kelvin Rowley. 1990. *Red Brotherhood at War: Vietnam, Cambodia, and Laos since 1975.* London: Verso.

"Fact Sheet: U.S. Expands Orderly Departure for Vietnamese Refugees." 1991. *U.S. Department of State Dispatch* 2, no. 13: 225.

Fall, Bernard B. 1966. *Vietnam Witness, 1953–66.* New York: Praeger.

_____. 1967. *The Two Vietnams: A Political and Military Analysis.* New York: Praeger.

_____. 1968. *Hell in a Very Small Place: The Siege of Dien Bien Phu.* New York: Vintage Books.

_____. 1972. *Street without Joy.* New York: Schocken Books.

Fall, Bernard B., ed. and with an introduction. 1967. *Ho Chi Minh on Revolution: Selected Writings, 1920–66.* New York: Praeger.

Fanning, Louis A. 1976. *Betrayal in Vietnam*. New Rochelle, N.Y.: Arlington House.

Feen, Richard H. 1985. "Domestic and Foreign Policy Dilemmas in Contemporary U.S. Refugee Policy." In *Refugees and World Politics*. Ed. Elizabeth G. Ferris, 105–19. New York: Praeger.

Fein, Helen. 1987. *Congregational Sponsors of Indochinese Refugees in the United States, 1979–1981*. Cranbury, N.J.: Associated University Presses.

Fenton, James. 1985. "The Fall of Saigon." *Granta* 15: 27–119.

Ferris, Elizabeth G. 1985. "Overview: Refugees and World Politics." In *Refugees and World Politics*. Ed. Elizabeth G. Ferris, 1–25. New York: Praeger.

———. 1990. "The Churches, Refugees, and Politics." In *Refugees and International Relations*. Ed. Gil Loescher and Laila Monahan, 159–77. Oxford: Clarendon.

Fforde, Adam and Stefan de Vylder. 1996. *From Plan to Market: The Economic Transition in Vietnam*. Boulder, Colo.: Westview Press.

Fielding, Nick. 1987. "The Boat People: Still Adrift." *New Society* 82 (November 18): 16–18.

Fields, Rona M. 1992. "Life and Death on a Small Island: Vietnamese and Cambodian Refugees in Indonesia." *Migration World Magazine* 20, no. 5: 16–20.

Fitzgerald, Frances. 1972. *Fire in the Lake*. New York: Vintage.

Forbes, Susan S. 1984. "U.S. Refugee Resettlement: A Program at the Cross-roads." *World Refugee Survey, 1984*. Washington, D.C.: U.S. Committee for Refugees, 32–36.

Freeman, James M. 1989. *Hearts of Sorrow: Vietnamese American Lives*. Stanford, Calif.: Stanford University Press.

———. 1993. *Changing Identities: Vietnamese Americans, 1975–1995*. Boston: Allyn and Bacon.

Freeman, James M. and Nguyen Dinh Huu. 2005. *Voices from the Camps: Vietnamese Children Seeking Asylum*. Seattle: University of Washington Press.

"Fresh Hope in Southeast Asia." 1991. *UN Chronicle* 28, no. 3: 53–55.

Friesen, Evelyn as told by Phu Sam. 1985. *Freedom Isn't Free: A Boat People Story*. Hillsboro, Kans.: Kindred.

Funseth, Robert L. 1987. "Aspects of U.S. Resettlement Programs for Vietnamese Refugees." *Current Policy* no. 1037. Washington, D.C.: U.S. Department of State, Bureau of Public Affairs.

———. 1989. "Orderly Departure of Refugees from Vietnam." *Current Policy* no. 1199, Washington, D.C.: U.S. Department of State, Bureau of Public Affairs, 1–4.

Gaiduk, Ilya. 1996. *The Soviet Union and the Vietnam War*. Chicago: Ivan R. Dee.

Gallagher, Dennis, Susan Forbes Martin, and Patricia Weiss-Fagen. 1985. *Of Special Humanitarian Concern: U.S. Refugee Admissions since Passage of the Refugee Act*. Washington, D.C.: Refugee Policy Group.

_____. 1990. "Temporary Safe Haven: The Need for North American-European Responses." In *Refugees and International Relations*. Ed. Gil Loescher and Laila Monahan, 333–53. Oxford: Clarendon Press.

Gallienne, Robin. 1991. "The Whole Thing Was Orchestrated: New Zealand's Response to the Indo-Chinese Refugee Exodus, 1975–1985." Centre for Asian Studies resource paper no. 2. Aukland, New Zealand: University of Aukland.

Garvey, Jack I. 1985. "Toward a Reformulation of International Refugee Law." *Harvard International Law Journal* 26, no. 2: 483–500.

Gettleman, Marvin E., Jane Franklin, Marilyn B. Young, and H. Bruce Franklin, eds. 1995. *Vietnam and America: A Documented History*. Rev. enl. 2d ed. New York: Grove Press.

Gibney, Mark. 1988. "A Well-Founded Fear of Persecution." *Human Rights Quarterly* 109, no. 1: 109–21.

Gilbert, Mark J. and William Head, eds. 1996. *The Tet Offensive*. Westport, Conn.: Praeger.

Golsan, Lucy B. 1977. "Liem's Story: A Vietnamese Woman Recalls Life before the Fall of Saigon." *Christian Century*, October 26, 976–82, 994.

Goodwin-Gill, Guy S. 1988. *The Refugee in International Law*, 2d ed. New York: Oxford University Press.

Gordenker, Leon. 1981. "Organizational Expansion and Limits in International Services for Refugees." *International Migration Review* 15, no. 1: 74–87.

_____. 1987. *Refugees in International Politics*. London: Croom Helm.

Gordon, Linda W. 1983. "New Data on the Fertility of Southeast Asian Refugees in the United States." *P/AAMHRC Research Review* 2, no. 1: 3–6.

Gow, Anne W. 1991. "Protection of Vietnamese Asylum Seekers in Hong Kong: Detention, Screening and Repatriation." Working paper submitted to the United Nations Economic and Social Council, Commission on Human Rights, Subcommission on Prevention of Discrimination and Protection of Minorities. 43rd sess. Berkeley, Calif.: Human Rights Associates.

Gowlland-Debbas, Vera, ed. 1996. *The Problem of Refugees in the Light of Contemporary International Law Issues*. The Hague: Martinus Nijhoff.

Grant, Bruce. 1979. *The Boat People: An 'Age' Investigation*. London: Penguin Books.

Ha, Kim. 1997. *Stormy Escape: A Vietnamese Woman's Account of Her 1980 Flight through Cambodia to Thailand*. Jefferson, N.C.: McFarland.

Haines, David W. 1983a. "The Commitment to Refugee Resettlement." *Annals of the American Academy of Political and Social Science* no. 467: 187–201.

_____. 1983b. "Southeast Asian Refugees in the United States: An Overview." *Migration Today* 29, no. 2: 8–13.

Haines, David W., ed. 1985. *Refugees in the United States: A Reference Handbook*. Westport, Conn.: Greenwood Press.

_____. 1989. *Refugees as Immigrants: Cambodians, Laotians, and Vietnamese in America*. Totowa, N.J.: Rowman and Littlefield.

————. 1997. *Case Studies in Diversity: Refugees in America in the 1990s.* Westport, Conn.: Praeger.

Haley, P. Edward. 1982. *Congress and the Fall of South Vietnam and Cambodia.* East Brunswick, N.J.: Associated University Presses.

Hall, D.G.E. 1968. *A History of Southeast Asia,* 3rd. ed. New York: St. Martin's Press.

Hall, Mitchell K. 1990. *Because of Their Faith: CALCAV and Religious Opposition to the Vietnam War.* New York: Columbia University Press.

Hammer, Ellen J. 1966. *The Struggle for Indochina, 1940–1955.* Stanford, Calif.: Stanford University Press.

————. 1987. *A Death in November: America in Vietnam, 1963.* New York: Oxford University Press.

Hanson, I.R. 1990. "Hong Kong's Screen Door Policy: An Analysis of Hong Kong's Screening Procedures in the Context of International Law." *Brooklyn Journal of International Law* 16, no. 3: 583–619.

Harding, Richard K. and John G. Looney. 1977. "Problems of Southeast Asian Children in a Refugee Camp." *American Journal of Psychiatry* 134, no. 4: 407–11.

Harrell-Bond, Barbara E. and Eftihia Voutira. 1992. "Anthropology and the Study of Refugees." *Anthropology Today* 8, no. 4: 6–10.

Harris, David W. 1994. "The Indochinese Refugee Problem in Thailand: A Political Analysis." PH.D. diss., George Washington University.

Harrison, James P. 1989. *The Endless War: Vietnam's Struggle for Independence.* New York: Columbia University Press.

Haskins, James. 1980. *The New Americans: Vietnamese Boat People.* Hillside, N.J.: Enslow.

Hatfield, Mark O. 1984. "U.S. Refugee Policy and Southeast Asia: Time for a Renewed Commitment." *World Refugee Survey, 1984.* Washington, D.C.: U.S. Committee for Refugees, 28–31.

Hathaway, James C. 1990. "A Reconsideration of the Underlying Premise of Refugee Law." *Harvard International Law Journal* 31, no. 1: 129–83.

————. 1991a. *The Law of Refugee Status.* Toronto: Butterworths, 1991.

————. 1991b. "Reconceiving Refugee Law as Human Rights Protection." *Journal of Refugee Studies* 4, no. 2 (1991): 113–31.

————. 1993. "Labeling the 'Boat People': The Failure of the Human Rights Mandate of the Comprehensive Plan of Action for Indochinese Refugees." *Human Rights Quarterly* 15, no. 4: 686–702.

Havens, Thomas R.H. 1990. "Japan's Response to the Indochinese Refugee Crisis." *Southeast Asian Journal of Social Sciences* 18, no. 1: 166–81.

Hawthorne, Lesleyanne, ed. 1982. *Refugee: The Vietnamese Experience.* Melbourne: Oxford University Press.

Hayes, Jim et al. 1980. "Help for the Indochinese: How Much Is Too Much?" *Public Welfare* 38, no. 3: 4–9 and 59–64.

Hayslip, Le Ly with Jay Wurts. 1989. *When Heaven and Earth Changed Places: A Vietnamese Woman's Journey from War to Peace.* New York: Doubleday.

Hayslip, Le Ly with James Hayslip. 1993. *Child of War, Woman of Peace*. New York: Doubleday.

Hein, Jeremy. 1988. "State Incorporation of Migrants and the Reproduction of a Middleman Minority among Indochinese Refugees." *Sociological Quarterly* 29, no. 3: 463–78.

———. 1993. *States and International Migrants: The Incorporation of Indochinese Refugees in the United States and France*. Boulder, Colo.: Westview Press.

———. 1995. *From Vietnam, Laos, and Cambodia: A Refugee Experience in the United States*. New York: Twayne.

Herring, George C. 1986. *America's Longest War: The United States and Vietnam, 1950–1975*. 2d ed. New York: Alfred A. Knopf.

Hickey, Gerald C. 1964. *Village in Vietnam*. New Haven, Conn.: Yale University Press.

———. 1982. *Sons of the Mountains: Ethnohistory of the Vietnamese Central Highlands to 1954*. New Haven, Conn.: Yale University Press.

Hitchcox, Linda. 1990. "Repatriation: Solution or Expedience? The Vietnamese Asylum Seekers in Hong Kong." *Southeast Asian Journal of Social Science* 18, no. 1: 111–31.

———. 1991. *Vietnamese Refugees in Southeast Asian Camps*. New York: St. Martin's.

Hoang, Ngoc Lung. 1978. *The General Offensives of 1968–69*. McLean, Va.: U.S. Army Center of Military History.

Hoang, Van Chi. 1964. *From Colonialism to Communism: A Case History of North Vietnam*. New York: Praeger.

Hocke, Jean-Pierre. 1990. "Beyond Humanitarianism: The Need for Political Will to Resolve Today's Refugee Problem." In *Refugees and International Relations*. Ed. Gil Loescher and Laila Monahan, 37–48. Oxford: Clarendon.

Hohl, Donald G. 1978. "The Indochinese Refugee: The Evolution of United States Policy." *International Migration Review* 12, no. 1: 128–32.

Hosmer, Stephen T., Konrad Kellen, and Brian M. Jenkins. 1980. *The Fall of South Vietnam: Statements by Vietnamese Military and Civilian Leaders*. New York: Crane, Russak.

Howard, Katsuyo K., comp. 1990. *Passages: An Anthology of the Southeast Asian Refugee Experience*. Fresno: Southeast Asian Student Services, California State University—Fresno.

Howell, David R. 1982. "Refugee Resettlement and Public Policy: A Role for Anthropology." *Anthropological Quarterly* 55, no. 3: 119–25.

Hughes, Kristen G. 1985. "Closed Camps: Vietnamese Refugee Policy in Hong Kong." PH.D. diss., University of California, Berkeley.

Hugo, Graeme. 1987. "Postwar Refugee Migration in Southeast Asia: Patterns, Problems, and Policies." In *Refugees: A Third World Dilemma*. Ed. John R. Rogge, 237–52. Totowa, N.J.: Rowman and Littlefield.

———. 1990. "Adaptation of Vietnamese in Australia: An Assessment Based on 1986 Census Results." *Southeast Asian Journal of Social Science* 18, no. 1: 182–210.

Hugo, Graeme and Kwok Bun Chan. 1990. "Conceptualizing and Defining Refugee and Forced Migrations in Asia." *Southeast Asian Journal of Social Science* 18, no. 1: 19–42.

Human Rights Watch. 1997. "Abuses against Vietnamese Asylum Seekers in the Final Days of the Comprehensive Plan of Action." *Human Rights Watch/Asia* 9, no. 2(C). New York: Human Rights Watch.

Hunt, Richard A. 1995. *Pacification: The American Struggle for Vietnam's Hearts and Minds.* Boulder, Colo.: Westview Press.

Huynh, Jade Ngoc Quang. 1994. *South Wind Changing.* St. Paul, Minn.: Graywolf Press.

Huynh, Kim Khanh. 1982. *Vietnamese Communism, 1925–1945.* Ithaca, N.Y.: Cornell University Press.

Indochina Refugee Action Center. 1979. "Synopsis of Current Indochinese Refugee Situation." Washington, D.C.: Author.

Indochina Resource Action Center. 1986. "Confronting New Realities, a Report: Recommendations on the Southeast Asian Refugee Program, Community Action Strategies." A Report on the Indochinese Community Leadership Convention, June 22–24, 1986. Washington, D.C.: Author.

———. 1989. "Toward Humane and Durable Solutions to the Indochinese Refugee Problem: Statement of 160 Indochinese Organizations in North America and Europe to the International Conference on Indochinese Refugees, Geneva, June 13–14, 1989." Washington D.C.: Author.

"Indochinese Refugee Resettlement Program." 1975. U.S. Department of State Special Report no. 21. Washington, D.C.: U.S. Department of State, Bureau of Public Affairs.

"Indochinese Refugees." 1977. *Editorial Research Report* 2, no. 8: 639–59.

"Indochinese Refugees: No End in Sight." 1981. *World Refugee Survey, 1981.* New York: U.S. Committee for Refugees, 18–20.

International Catholic Migration Commission. 1992. "The Orderly Departure Program." *Migration World* 20, no. 4: 34.

Isaacs, Arnold R., 1983. *Without Honor: Defeat in Vietnam and Cambodia.* Baltimore: Johns Hopkins University Press.

Jacobs, Seth. 2004. *America's Miracle Man in Vietnam: Ngo Dinh Diem, Religion, Race, and U.S. Intervention in Southeast Asia, 1950–57.* Durham, N.C.: Duke University Press.

Jaeger, Gilbert. 1981. "Refugee Asylum: Policy and Legislative Developments." *International Migration Review* 15, no. 1: 52–68.

Jambor, Pierre. 1992. *Indochinese Refugees in Southeast Asia: Mass Exodus and the Politics of Aid.* Bangkok: Ford Foundation.

Jamieson, Neil L. 1993. *Understanding Vietnam.* Berkeley and Los Angeles: University of California Press.

Joes, Anthony J. 1990. *The War for South Vietnam, 1954–1975.* New York: Praeger.

Jones, Howard. 2003. *Death of a Generation: How the Assassinations of Diem and JFK Prolonged the Vietnam War.* New York: Oxford University Press.

Jones, Peter R. 1982. "Vietnamese Refugees: A Study of Their Reception and Resettlement in the United Kingdom." London: Research and Planning Unit paper 0262-1738:13, Home Office.

Jones, Woodrow, Jr. and Paul Strand. 1986. "Adaptation and Adjustment Problems among Indochinese Refugees." *Sociology and Social Research* 71, no. 1: 42–46.

Jorgensen, Karen K. 1989. "The Role of the U.S. Congress and Courts in the Application of the U.S. Refugee Act of 1980." In *Refugee Law and Policy: International and U.S. Responses.* Ed. Ved P. Nanda, 129–50. Westport, Conn.: Greenwood Press.

Kahin, George McT. 1986. *Intervention: How America Became Involved in Vietnam.* Garden City, N.Y.: Anchor Books.

Karnow, Stanley. 1984. *Vietnam: A History.* New York: Penguin Books.

Kayson, Carl. 1995. "Refugees: Concepts, Norms, Realities, and What the United States Can and Should Do." In *Threatened Peoples, Threatened Borders: World Migration and U.S. Policy.* Ed. Michael S. Teitelbaum and Myron Weiner, 244–56. New York: W.W. Norton.

Keely, Charles B. 1983. "Current Status of U.S. Immigration and Refugee Policy." In *U.S. Immigration and Refugee Policy.* Ed. Mary M. Kritz, 339–59. Lexington, Mass.: D.C. Heath.

———. 1995. "The Effects of International Migration on U.S. Foreign Policy." In *Threatened Peoples, Threatened Borders: World Migration and U.S Policy.* Ed. Michael S. Teitelbaum and Myron Weiner, 215–43. New York: W.W. Norton.

Keesing's Research Report. 1970. *South Vietnam: A Political History, 1954–1970.* Report No. 5. New York: Charles Scribner's Sons.

Kelly, Gail P. 1977. *From Vietnam to America: A Chronicle of Vietnamese Immigration to the United States.* Boulder, Colo.: Westview Press.

Kelly, P. 1988. "Settlement of Vietnamese Refugees." In *The Australian People: An Encyclopedia of the Nation, Its People and Their Origins.* Ed. James Jupp, 833–36. North Ryde, New South Wales, Australia: Angus and Robertson.

Kennedy, David. 1986. "International Refugee Protection." *Human Rights Quarterly* 8, no. 1: 9–69.

Kennedy, Edward M. 1981. "Refugee Act of 1980." *International Migration Review* 15, no. 1: 141–56.

Kerkvliet, Benedict J.J., and Doug J. Palmer. 1995. *Vietnam's Rural Transformation.* Boulder, Colo.: Westview Press.

Kessner, Thomas and Betty B. Caroli. 1982. *Today's Immigrants, Their Stories: A Look at the Newest Americans,* chap. 1: "I Get Homesick Every Day: Refugees from Indochina." New York: Oxford University Press, 31–70.

Kissinger, Henry. 2003. *Ending the Vietnam War: A History of America's Involvement in and Extrication from the Vietnam War.* New York: Simon and Schuster.

Kleinman, Stuart B. 1990. "Terror at Sea: Vietnamese Victims of Piracy." *American Journal of Psychoanalysis* 50, no. 4: 351–62.

Klinek, Jan H. 1989. "The Present State of the Southeast Asian Refugee under the 1980 Refugee Act: A Call for Reform." *Syracuse Journal of International Law and Commerce* 15, no. 2: 285–304.

Knudsen, John C. 1983. *Boat People in Transit: Vietnamese Refugee Camps in the Philippines, Hong Kong and Japan.* Migration Project Studies Occasional Paper no. 31. Bergen, Norway: University of Bergen.

———. 1988. *Vietnamese Survivors: Processes Involved in Refugee Coping and Adaptation.* Bergen, Norway: Migration Project, Department of Social Anthropology, University of Bergen.

———. 1990. "Prisoners of International Politics: Vietnamese Refugees Coping with Transit Life." *Southeast Asian Journal of Social Science* 18, no. 1: 153–65.

Koehn, Peter. 1991. *Refugees from Revolution: U.S. Policy and Third World Migration.* Boulder, Colo.: Westview Press.

Kolko, Gabriel. 1985. *Anatomy of a War: Vietnam, the United States, and the Modern Historical Experience.* New York: Pantheon Books.

Krepinevich, Andrew F., Jr. 1986. *The Army and Vietnam.* Baltimore: Johns Hopkins University Press.

Kritz, Mary M., ed. 1983. *U.S. Immigration and Refugee Policy.* Lexington, Mass.: D.C. Heath.

Krupinski, Jerzy and Graham Borrows, eds. 1986. *The Price of Freedom: Young Indochinese Refugees in Australia.* Sydney, Australia: Pergamon Press.

Kumin, Judith. 1987. "Orderly Departure from Vietnam: A Humanitarian Alternative?" PH.D. diss., Fletcher School of Law and Diplomacy.

Kunz, Egon F. 1973. "The Refugee in Flight: Kinetic Models and Forms of Displacement." *International Migration Review* 7, no. 2: 125–46.

———. 1981. "Exile and Resettlement: Refugee Theory." *International Migration Review* 15, no. 1: 42–51.

Lacouture, Jean. 1966. *Vietnam: Between Two Truces.* New York: Vintage Books.

———. 1968. *Ho Chi Minh: A Political Biography.* New York: Vintage Books.

Lam, Quang Thi. 2001. *The Twenty-five Year Century: A South Vietnamese General Remembers the Indochina War to the Fall of Saigon.* Denton: University of North Texas Press.

Lanphier, C. Michael. 1981. "Canada's Response to Refugees." *International Migration Review* 15, no. 1: 113–30.

———. 1987. "Indochinese Resettlement: Cost and Adaptation in Canada, the United States, and France." In *Refugees: A Third World Dilemma.* Ed. John R. Rogge, 299–308. Totowa, N.J.: Rowman and Littlefield.

Larsen, Wendy W. and Tran Thi Nga. 1986. *Shallow Graves: Two Women and Vietnam.* New York: Random House.

Lasey, Martin. 1985. *In Our Fathers' Land: Vietnamese Amerasians in the United States.* Washington, D.C.: U.S. Catholic Conference, Migration and Refugee Services.

Lavelle, A.J.C., ed. 1978. *Last Flight from Saigon.* Washington, D.C.: U.S. Air Force, for sale by U.S. Government Printing Office.

Lawrence, Mark A. 2005. *Assuming the Burden: Europe and the American Commitment to War in Vietnam*. Berkeley and Los Angeles: University of California Press.

Lawrence, Peter. 1983. "Australian Opinion on the Indo-Chinese Influx, 1975 to 1979." Centre for the Study of Australian-Asian Relations research paper 0158-586X: no.24. Brisbane, Australia: Griffith University.

Lawyers Committee for Human Rights. 1989. *Inhumane Deterrence: The Treatment of Vietnamese Boat People in Hong Kong*. New York: Author.

————. 1990. "The Implementation of the Refugee Act of 1980: A Decade of Experience." New York: Author.

————. 1991. *Uncertain Haven: Refugee Protection on the Fortieth Anniversary of the 1951 United Nations Refugee Convention*. New York: Author.

Le, Huu Tri. 2001. *Prisoner of the Word*. Seattle: Black Heron.

Le, Tang Thi Thanh Trai and Micahel J. Esser. 1981. "The Vietnamese Refugee and U.S. Law." *Notre Dame Lawyer* 56, no. 4: 656–67.

Lee, Tang Lay. 1995. "Some Gaps in the Comprehensive Plan of Action for Indochinese Refugees." *Migration World Magazine* 23, no. 1–2: 28–32.

Leibowitz, Arnold H. 1983. "The Refugee Act of 1980: Problems and Congressional Concerns." *Annals of the American Academy of Political and Social Science* 467: 163–71.

Levin, Michael. 1981. *What Welcome? Reception and Resettlement of Refugees in Britain*. London: Action Society Trust.

Lewins, Frank and Judith Ly. 1985. *The First Wave: The Settlement of Australia's First Vietnamese Refugees*. Sydney, Australia: Allen and Unwin.

Lifton, Betty Jean. 1976. "Orphans in Limbo." *Saturday Review* May 1, 20–22.

Littauer, Raphael and Norman Uphoff, eds. 1971. *The Air War in Indochina*. Rev. ed. Boston: Beacon Press.

Liu, William T., Maryanne Lamanna, and Alice Murata. 1979. *Transition to Nowhere: Vietnamese Refugees in America*. Nashville: Charter House.

Ljunggren, Borje. 1993. *The Challenge of Reform in Indochina*. Cambridge, Mass.: Institute for International Development, Harvard University.

Lo, Shih-fu. 1980. *The Reason of Exodus of Refugees from Vietnam and Its Consequences*. Taipei, Republic of China: World Anti-Communism League.

Loescher, Gil. 1990. "Introduction: Refugee Issues in International Relations." In *Refugees and International Relations*. Ed. Gil Loescher and Laila Monahan, 1–33. Oxford: Clarendon.

————. 1993. *Beyond Charity: International Cooperation and the Global Refugee Crisis*. New York: Oxford University Press.

————. 2001. *UNHCR and World Politics: A Perilous Path*. New York: Oxford University Press.

Loescher, Gil and Laila Monahan, eds. 1990. *Refugees and International Relations*. New York: Oxford University Press.

Loescher, Gil and John A. Scanlan. 1986. *Calculated Kindness: Refugees and America's Half-Open Door, 1945–Present*. New York: Free Press.

Logevall, Fredrik. 1999. *Choosing War: The Lost Chance for Peace and the Escalation of War in Vietnam*. Berkeley and Los Angeles: University of California Press.

Lu, Van Thanh. 1997. *The Inviting Call of Wandering Souls: Memoir of an ARVN Liaison Officer to United States Forces Who Was Imprisoned in Communist Re-Education Camps and Then Escaped*. Jefferson, N.C.: McFarland.

Luong, Hy V. 1992. *Revolution in the Village: Tradition and Transformation in North Vietnam, 1925–1988*. Honolulu: University of Hawaii Press.

Ly, Qui Chung. 1970. *Between Two Fires: The Unheard Voices of Vietnam*. New York: Praeger.

Lyman, Princeton. 1991. "U.S. Policy on Repatriation of Vietnamese in Hong Kong." *U.S. Department of State Dispatch* 2, no. 45: 833–34.

Marr, David G. 1971. *Vietnamese Anticolonialism, 1885–1925*. Berkeley and Los Angeles: University of California Press.

———. 1981. *Vietnamese Tradition on Trial, 1920–1945*. Berkeley and Los Angeles: University of California Press.

———. 1995. *Vietnam, 1945: The Quest for Power*. Berkeley and Los Angeles: University of California Press.

Marr, David G. and Christine P. White, eds. 1988. *Postwar Vietnam: Dilemmas in Socialist Development*. Ithaca, N.Y.: Southeast Asia Program, Cornell University.

Mabry, Philip J. 1996. "'We're Bringing Them Home': Resettling Vietnamese Amerasians in the United States." PH.D. diss., University of Pittsburgh.

Mackie, Richard A. 1997. *Operation New Life: The Untold Story*. Concord, Calif.: Solution Pub.

Majka, Lorraine. 1990. "Vietnamese Amerasians in the United States." *Migration World* 18, no. 1: 4–7.

Martin, Richard. 1989. "Vietnamese in Hong Kong Face a Voyage of the Damned." *Insight on the News* 5, no. 36: 30–31.

Masty, Stephen. 1982. "Emigration from Southeast Asia." *Mankind Quarterly* 22, no. 4: 389–96.

Matthews, Ellen. 1982. *Culture Clash*. Chicago: Intercultural Press.

McAleavy, Henry. 1968. *Black Flags in Vietnam: The Story of a Chinese Intervention, the Tonkin War of 1884–85*. New York: Macmillan.

McCarthy, John E. 1978. "The Refugees and Displaced of the Indochina Area." *Migration Today* 6, no. 1: 33–35.

McCollum, Bill. 1985. "Land Vietnamese in Thailand—An Inadequate Response." *World Refugee Survey, 1985*. Washington, D.C.: U.S. Committee for Refugees, 19–20.

McConnell, Scott. 1989. *Leftward Journey: The Education of Vietnamese Students in France, 1919–1939*. New Brunswick, N.J.: Transaction.

McCrohan, Kevin F. and John Wetterer. 1977. "Operation Babylift." *American Psychologist* 32, no. 8: 671–74.

McGurn, William. 1990. "The Scandal of the Boat People." *Commentary* 89, no. 1: 36–40.

McKelvey, Robert S. 1999. *The Dust of Life: America's Children Abandoned in Vietnam*. Seattle: University of Washington Press.

———. 2002. *A Gift of Barbed Wire: America's Allies Abandoned in South Vietnam*. Seattle: University of Washington Press.

McLean, Sheila A. 1983. "International Institutional Mechanisms for Refugees." In *U.S. Immigration and Refugee Policy.* Ed. Mary M. Kritz, 175–89. Lexington, Mass.: D.C. Heath.

McLeod, Mark W. 1991. *The Vietnamese Response to French Intervention, 1862–1874.* New York: Praeger.

McMahon, Robert J., ed. 1990. *Major Problems in the History of the Vietnam War.* Boston: D.C. Heath.

McNamara, Dennis. 1990. "The Origins and Effects of 'Humane Deterrence' Policies in South-east Asia." In *Refugees and International Relations.* Ed. Gil Loescher and Laila Monahan, 123–34. Oxford: Clarendon.

Milligan, Charles S. 1989. "Ethical Aspects of Refugee Issues and U.S. Policy." In *Refugee Law and Policy: International and U.S. Responses.* Ed. Ved P. Nanda, 165–84. Westport, Conn.: Greenwood Press.

Moise, Edwin E. 1996. *Tonkin Gulf and the Escalation of the Vietnam War.* Chapel Hill: University of North Carolina Press.

Mole, Robert L. 1970. *The Montagnards of South Vietnam: A Study of Nine Tribes.* Rutland, Vt.: Charles E. Tuttle.

Montero, Darrel. 1979a. *Vietnamese Americans: Patterns of Resettlement and Socioeconomic Adaptation in the United States.* Boulder, Colo.: Westview Press.

———. 1979b. "Vietnamese Refugees in America: Toward a Theory of Spontaneous International Migration." *International Migration Review* 13, no. 4: 624–48.

Moos, Felix and C.S. Morrison. 1981. "The Vietnamese Refugees at Our Doorstep: Political Ambiguity and Successful Improvisation." *Policy Studies Review* 1, no. 1: 28–46.

Morley, James W. and Masashi Nishihara, eds. 1997. *Vietnam Joins the World.* Armonk, N.Y.: M.E. Sharpe.

Morrison, G.S. and Felix Moos. 1982. "Halfway to Nowhere: Vietnamese Refugees on Guam." In *Involuntary Migration and Resettlement: The Problems and Responses of Dislocated People.* Ed. Art Hansen and Anthony Oliver-Smith, 49–68. Boulder, Colo.: Westview Press.

Mortland, Carol A. 1987. "Transforming Refugees in Refugee Camps." *Urban Anthropology* 16, no. 3–4: 375–404.

Muntarbhorn, Vitit. 1992. *The Status of Refugees in Asia.* Oxford: Clarendon.

Murray, Martin J. 1980. *The Development of Capitalism in Colonial Indochina (1870–1940).* Berkeley and Los Angeles: University of California Press.

Mushkat, R. 1989. "Refugees in Hong Kong." *International Journal of Refugee Law* 14: 449–80.

Nakavachara, Netnapis and John Rogge. 1987. "Thailand's Refugee Experience." In *Refugees: A Third World Dilemma.* Ed. John R. Rogge, 269–81. Totowa, N.J.: Rowman and Littlefield.

Nanda, Ved P. 1989. "Refugee Law and Policy." In *Refugee Law and Policy: International and U.S. Responses.* Ed. Ved P. Nanda, 3–19. Westport, Conn.: Greenwood Press.

Neilands, J.B. et al. 1972. *Harvest of Death: Chemical Warfare in Vietnam and Cambodia.* New York: Free Press.

Newland, Kathleen. 1995a. "The Impact of U.S. Refugee Policies on U.S. Foreign Policy: A Case of the Tail Wagging the Dog?" In *Threatened Peoples, Threatened Borders: World Migration and U.S. Policy*. Ed. Michael S. Teitelbaum and Myron Weiner, 190–214. New York: W.W. Norton.

———. 1995b. *U.S. Refugee Policy: Dilemmas and Directions*. Washington, D.C.: Carnegie Endowment for International Peace.

Ngo, Vinh Long. 1973. *Before the Revolution: The Vietnamese Peasants under the French*. Cambridge, Mass.: MIT Press.

Nguyen, Cao Ky. 1976. *Twenty Years and Twenty Days*. New York: Stein and Day.

———. 2002. *How We Lost the Vietnam War*. New York: Cooper Square Press.

Nguyen, Cao Ky with Martin J. Wolf. 2002. *Buddha's Child: My Fight to Save Vietnam*. New York: St. Martin's Press.

Nguyen, Duy Hinh. 1977. *Lam Son 719*. McLean, Va.: U.S. Army Center of Military History.

Nguyen, Khac Vien. 1974. *Tradition and Revolution in Vietnam*. Berkeley, Calif.: Indochina Research Center.

Nguyen, Kien. 2001. *The Unwanted: A Memoir*. Boston: Little, Brown.

Nguyen, Long with Harry H. Kendall. 1981. *After Saigon Fell: Daily Life under the Vietnamese Communists*. Research Papers and Policy Studies, No. 4. Berkeley, Calif.: Institute of East Asian Studies, University of California.

Nguyen, Manh Hung. 1984. "Refugee Scholars and Vietnamese Studies in the United States, 1975–1982." *Amerasia Journal* 11, no. 1: 89–99.

———. 1985. "Vietnamese." In *Refugees in the United States: A Reference Handbook*. Ed. David W. Haines, 195–208. Westport, Conn.: Praeger.

Nguyen, Manh Hung and David W. Haines. 1997. "Vietnamese." In *Case Studies in Diversity: Refugees in America in the 1990s*. Ed. David W. Haines, 34–56. Westport, Conn.: Praeger.

Nguyen, Minh Thanh. 1996. *Leaving Vietnam*. Edmonton, Canada: NeWest Publishers.

Nguyen, Qui Due. 1991. *Where the Ashes Are: The Odyssey of a Vietnamese Family*. Reading, Mass.: Addison-Wesley.

Nguyen, Thi Dinh, trans. by Mai V. Elliott. 1976. "No Other Road to Take: Memoir of Mrs. Nguyen Thi Dinh." Southeast Asia Program data paper no. 102. Ithaca, N.Y.: Department of Asian Studies, Cornell University.

Nguyen, Tien Hung and Jerrold L. Schecter. 1989. *The Palace File: Vietnam Secret Documents*. New York: Harper and Row.

Nguyen, Van Canh. 1983. *Vietnam under Communism, 1975–1982*. Stanford, Calif.: Hoover Institution Press.

Nguyen-Hong-Nhiem, Lucy. 2003. *A Dragon Child: Reflections of a Daughter of Annam in America*. Lincoln, Neb.: iUniverse (electronic book).

Nguen-Hong-Nhiem, Lucy and Joel M. Halpern, eds. 1989. *The Far East Comes Near: Accounts of Southeast Asian Students in America* Amherst: University of Massachusetts Press.

Nguyen-Vo, Thu-huong. 1992. *Khmer-Viet Relations and the Third Indochina Conflict.* Jefferson, N.C.: McFarland.

Nichols, Bruce. 1988. *The Uneasy Alliance: Religion, Refugee Work, and U.S. Foreign Policy.* New York: Oxford University Press.

Nishimoto, Robert, Kenneth L. Chau, and Robert W. Roberts. 1989. "The Psychological Status of Vietnamese Chinese Women in Refugee Camps." *Affilia* 4, no. 3: 51–64.

North, David S. 1983. "Impact of Legal, Illegal, and Refugee Migrations on U.S. Social Service Programs." In *U.S. Immigration and Refugee Policy.* Ed. Mary M. Kritz, 269–85. Lexington, Mass.: D.C. Heath.

Oakley, Phyllis E. 1995. "Comprehensive Plan of Action for Indochinese Refugees." U.S. Department of State *Dispatch* 6, no. 31: 600–602.

Oberdorfer, Don. 1971. *Tet! The Turning Point in the Vietnam War.* New York: Da Capo Press.

"Operation Babylift: Report. (Emergency Movement of Vietnamese and Cambodian Orphans for Intercountry Adoption)." Washington, D.C.: Agency for International Development (no author, no date).

Osana, Juan P. and Christine Hanson. 1993. "U.S. Refugee Policy: Where We've Been, Where We're Going." *World Refugee Survey, 1993.* Washington, D.C.: U.S. Committee for Refugees, 40–48.

Osborne, Milton F. 1965. "Strategic Hamlets in South Viet-Nam: A Survey and a Comparison." Southeast Asia Program data paper no. 55. Ithaca, N.Y.: Department of Asian Studies, Cornell University.

———. 1969. *The French Presence in Cochinchina and Cambodia: Rule and Response (1869–1905).* Ithaca, N.Y.: Cornell University Press.

———. 1975. *River Road to China: The Meking Expedition, 1866–1873.* New York: Liveright.

———. 1980. "The Indochinese Refugees—Cause and Effect." *International Affairs* 56, no. 1: 37–53.

Parker, Karen. 1989. "The Rights of Refugees under International Humanitarian Law." In *Refugee Law and Policy: International and U.S. Responses.* Ed. Ved P. Nanda, 33–41. Westport, Conn.: Greenwood Press.

Patti, Archimedes L. 1980. *Why Vietnam? Prelude to America's Albatross.* Berkeley and Los Angeles: University of California Press.

Peck-Barnes, Shirley. 2000. *"The War Cradle": the Untold Story of "Operation Babylift."* Denver: Vintage Pressworks.

The Pentagon Papers: The Defense Department History of United States Decisionmaking on Vietnam. The Senator Gravel edition. Vols. 1–4. Boston: Beacon Press, 1971. Vol. 5. *Critical Essays Edited by Noam Chomsky and Howard Zinn and an Index to Volumes One-Four.* Boston: Beacon Press, 1972.

Pham, Quang X. 2005. *A Sense of Duty: My Father, My American Journey.* New York: Ballantine Books.

Pham, Vu. 2003. "Andedating and Anchoring Vietnamese America: Toward a Vietnamese American Historiography." *Amerasia Journal* 29, no. 1: 137–52.

Phuwadol, Songprasert and Chongwatana Noppawan. 1988. *Thailand: A First Asylum Country for Indochinese Refugees.* Bangkok: Institute for Asian Studies, Chulalongkorn University.

Pierce, David C. 1987. "Resettlement as a Foreign Policy Externality: The Effects of and Local Government Responses to the Second Wave of Indochinese." PH.D. diss., University of Maryland, College Park.

Pike, Douglas. 1966. *Viet Cong: The Organization and Techniques of the National Liberation Front of South Vietnam.* Cambridge, Mass.: MIT Press.

———. 1986. *PAVN: People's Army of Vietnam.* Novato, Calif.: Presidio Press.

———. 1987. *Vietnam and the Soviet Union: Anatomy of an Alliance.* Boulder, Colo.: Westview Press.

Pitterman, Shelly. 1985. "International Responses to Refugee Situations: The United Nations High Commissioner for Refugees." In *Refugees and World Politics.* Ed. Elizabeth G. Ferris, 43–81. New York: Praeger.

Poole, Peter A. 1970. *The Vietnamese in Thailand: A Historical Perspective.* Ithaca, N.Y.: Cornell University Press.

Popkin, Samuel L. 1979. *The Rational Peasant.* Cambridge, Mass.: MIT Press.

Porter, Gareth. 1975. *A Peace Denied: The United States, Vietnam, and the Paris Peace Agreement.* Bloomington: Indiana University Press.

———. 2005. *Perils of Dominance: Imbalance of Power and the Road to War in Vietnam.* Berkeley and Los Angeles: University of California Press.

Post, Ken. 1989–90. *Revolution, Socialism and Nationalism in Vietnam.* Vol. 1, *An Interrupted Revolution;* vol. 2, *Viet Nam Divided;* vol. 3, *Socialism in Half a Century;* vol. 4, *The Failure of Counter-Insurgency in the South;* vol. 5, *Winning the War and Losing the Peace.* Aldershot, England: Dartmouth.

Prados, John. 1995. *The Hidden History of the Vietnam War.* Chicago: Ivan R. Dee.

———. 1999. *The Blood Road: The Ho Chi Minh Trail and the Vietnam War.* New York: John Wiley and Sons.

Price, Charles. 1981. "Immigration Policies and Refugees in Australia." *International Migration Review* 15, no. 1: 99–108.

Project Ngoc. n.d. "The Forgotten People: Vietnamese Refugees in Hong Kong: A Critical Report." Irvine, Calif.: Project Ngoc.

Race, Jeffrey. 1972. *War Comes to Long An: Revolutionary Conflict in a Vietnamese Province.* Berkeley and Los Angeles: University of California Press.

Rachagan, S. Sothi. 1987. "Refugees and Illegal Immigrants: The Malaysian Experience with Filipino and Vietnamese Refugees." In *Refugees: A Third World Dilemma.* Ed. John R. Rogge, 253–68. Totowa, N.J.: Rowman and Littlefield.

Rahe, Richard H. et al. 1978. "Psychiatric Consultation in a Vietnamese Refugee Camp." *American Journal of Psychiatry* 135, no. 2: 185–90.

Record, Jeffrey. 1998. *The Wrong War: Why We Lost in Vietnam.* Annapolis, Md.: Naval Institute Press.

Refugee Policy Group. 1989. "The Second International Conference on Indochinese Refugees: A New Humanitarian Consensus?" Washington, D.C.: Author.

Refugee Reports. 1979–95. Washington, D.C.: American Public Welfare Association (1979–81); American Council for Nationalities Service (1982–88); and U.S. Committee for Refugees (1988–95). (This newsletter has been published by three different organizations.)

Rice-Maximin, Edward. 1986. *Accommodation and Resistance: The French Left, Indochina, and the Cold War, 1944–1954.* Westport, Conn.: Greenwood Press.

Richmond, Anthony H. 1994. *Global Apartheid: Refugees, Racism, and the New World Order.* New York: Oxford University Press.

Robear, E.C. 1989. "The Dust of Life: The Legal and Political Ramifications of the Continuing Vietnamese Amerasian Problem." *Dickinson Journal of International Law* 8, no. 1: 125–46.

Roberts, Alden E. 1988. "Racism Sent and Received: How Americans and Vietnamese View One Another." *Race and Ethnic Relations* 5: 75–97.

Robinson, Bennie C. 1989. "U.S. Domestic Refugee Resettlement Policy." PH.D. diss., University of Denver.

Robinson, Vaughan. 1986. *Transients, Settlers, and Refugees: Asians in Britain.* Oxford: Clarendon Press.

———. 1993. *The International Refugee Crisis: British and Canadian Responses.* Basingstoke, Great Britain: Macmillan in association with the Refugee Studies Programme, Oxford University.

Robinson, W. Courtland. 1988. "Sins of Omission: The New Vietnamese Refugee Crisis." *World Refugee Survey, 1988.* Washington, D.C.: U.S. Committee for Refugees, 5–12.

———. 1992. "Ten-Year Anti-Piracy Program Closes on a Strong Note." *World Refugee Survey, 1992.* Washington, D.C.: U.S. Committee for Refugees, 64–66.

———. 1998. *Terms of Refuge: The Indochinese Exodus and the International Response.* London: Zed Books.

Rose, Peter I. 1981a. "Links in a Chain: Observations of the American Refugee Program in Southeast Asia." Part I. *Migration Today* 9, no. 3: 7–23.

———. 1981b. "South East Asia to America: Links in a Chain." Part II. *Migration Today* 9, no. 4–5: 22–33.

———. 1985a. "Long Night's Journey into Day: The Odyssey of Indochinese Refugees." *Society* 22: 75–79.

———. 1985b. "The Politics and Morality of U.S. Refugee Policy." *Center Magazine* (Sept.-Oct.): 2–14.

Rose, Peter I., ed. 1986. *Working with Refugees.* Staten Island, N.Y.: Center for Migration Studies.

Rose, Steven, ed. 1968. *CBW: Chemical and Biological Warfare.* Boston: Beacon Press.

Rotter, Andrew J. 1987. *The Path to Vietnam: Origins of the American Commitment to Southeast Asia.* Ithaca, N.Y.: Cornell University Press.

Roy, Jules. 1965. *The Battle of Dienbienphu.* New York: Carroll and Graf.

Rubin, Barry. 1976. "Vietnamese Refugees in America." *Contemporary Review* 229, no. 1327: 117–20.

————. 1978. "Indochinese Refugees: The 'New' Boat People." *Migration Today* 6, no. 5: 23, 28.

Ruiz, Hiram A. 1996. "The CPA: Tempestuous Year Left Boat People Adrift." *World Refugee Survey, 1996.* Washington, D.C.: U.S. Committee for Refugees, 82–83.

Russell, Sharon S. 1995. "Migration Patterns of U.S. Foreign Policy Interest." In *Threatened Peoples, Threatened Borders: World Migrations and U.S. Policy.* Ed. Michael S. Teitlebaum and Myron Weiner, 39–87. New York: W.W. Norton.

Rutledge, Paul. 1992. *The Vietnamese Experience in America.* Bloomington: Indiana University Press.

Ryan, Karen W. 2000. "What Became of the Airlift Orphans?" *Reader's Digest* 156, no. 937: 74–81.

Sager, Mike. 1991. "The Dust of Life." *Rolling Stone* November 14, 56–63.

Saito, Yasuhiko. 1990. "Imposter Refugees, Illegal Immigrants." *Japan Quarterly* 37, no. 1: 84–88.

Saldana, Delia H. 1992. "Coping with Stress: A Refugee's Story." *Women and Therapy* 13, no. 1–2: 21–35.

Sansom, Robert L. 1970. *The Economics of Insurgency in the Mekong Delta.* Cambridge, Mass.: MIT Press.

Santoli, Al. 1984. "The Gulf Pirates: The Boat People Face Robbery, Abduction, and Rape at the Hands of the Thai Pirates." *Atlantic Monthly* 253, no. 2: 24–28.

Scanlan, John. 1981. "Regulating Refugee Flow: Legal Alternative and Obligation under the Refugee Act of 1980." *Notre Dame Lawyer* 56, no. 4: 618–46.

Scanlan, John and Gil Loescher. 1982. "Mass Asylum and Human Rights in American Foreign Policy." *Political Science Quarterly* 97, no. 1: 39–56.

Scholer-Latour, Peter. 1979. *Death in the Rice Fields: An Eyewitness Account of Vietnam's Three Wars, 1945–1979.* New York: Penguin Books.

Schultz, Richard H., Jr. 2000. *The Secret War against Hanoi: The Untold Story of Spies, Saboteurs, and Covert Warriors in North Vietnam.* New York: Perennial.

Schulzinger, Robert D. 1997. *A Time for War: The United States and Vietnam, 1941–1975.* New York: Oxford University Press.

Schwarz, Adam. 1996. "You Can't Go Home Again." *Far Eastern Economic Review,* October 17, 29–31.

Scigliano, Robert. 1964. *South Vietnam: Nation under Stress.* Boston: Houghton Mifflin.

Scott, Joanne C. 1989. *Indochina's Refugees: Oral Histories from Laos, Cambodia, and Vietnam.* Jefferson, N.C.: McFarland.

Shaplen, Robert. 1966. *The Lost Revolution: The United States in Vietnam, 1946–1960.* New York: Harper and Row.

Simpson, Charles M. 1983. *Inside the Green Berets: The First Thirty Years—A History of the U.S. Army Special Forces.* Novato, Calif.: Presidio Press.

Skeldon, Ronald. 1994. "Hong Kong's Response to the Indochinese Influx, 1975–93." *Annals of the American Academy of Political and Social Science* 534: 91–105.

Skran, Claudena M. 1992. "The International Refugee Regime: The Historical and Contemporary Context of International Responses to Asylum Problems." In *Refugees and the Asylum Dilemma in the West.* Ed. Gil Loescher, 8–35. University Park: Pennsylvania State University Press.

Smilkstein, Gabriel. 1981. "Refugees in Thailand and Short Term Medical Aid." *Journal of the American Medical Association* no. 245: 1052–54.

Smith, R.B. 1983. *An International History of the Vietnam War: Revolution versus Containment, 1955–1961.* New York: St. Martin's Press.

———. 1985. *An International History of the Vietnam War: The Kennedy Strategy.* New York: St. Martin's Press.

Snepp, Frank III. 1977. *Decent Interval: An Insider's Account of Saigon's Indecent End Told by the CIA's Chief Strategy Analyst in Vietnam.* New York: Random House.

Solomon, Richard H. 2000. *Exiting Vietnam: U.S. Leadership of the Cambodian Settlement and Normalization of Relations with Vietnam.* Washington, D.C.: United States Institute for Peace Press.

Spector, Ronald H. 1985. *Advice and Support: The Early Years of the U.S. Army in Vietnam, 1941–1960.* New York: Free Press.

———. 1993. *After Tet: The Bloodiest Year in Vietnam.* New York: Free Press.

St. Cartmail, Keith. 1983. *Exodus Indochina.* Aukland, New Zealand: Heinemann.

Stanton, Shelby L. 1985. *Green Berets at War: U.S. Special Forces in Southeast Asia, 1956–1975.* Novato, Calif.: Presidio Press.

Starr, Paul D. and Alden E. Roberts. 1981. "Attitudes toward Indochinese Refugees: An Empirical Study." *Journal of Refugee Resettlement* 1, no. 4: 51–61.

———. 1982. "Attitudes toward New Americans: Perceptions of Indo-Chinese in Nine Cities." *Research in Race and Ethnic Relations* 3: 165–86.

Steif, William. 1992. "Trapped on the Border: Vietnamese Refugees Wait and Wait and Wait." *Progressive* 56, no. 1: 23–25.

Stein, Barry. 1979. "Legislative and Judicial Developments: The Geneva Conferences and the Indochinese Refugee Crisis." *International Migration Review* 13, no. 4: 716–23.

Steinberg, David J., ed. 1987. *In Search of Southeast Asia: A Modern History.* Rev. ed. Honolulu: University of Hawaii Press.

Stern, Lewis M. 1981. "Response to Vietnamese Refugees: Surveys of Public Opinion." *Social Work* 26, no. 4: 306–11.

Strand, Paul J. and Woodrow Jones. 1985. *Indochinese Refugees in America: Problems of Adaptation and Assimilation.* Durham, N.C.: Duke University Press.

Stubbs, Richard. 1980. "Why Can't They Stay in Southeast Asia? The Problems of Vietnam's Neighbors." In *Southeast Asian Exodus: From Tradition to Resettlement.* Ed. Elliot L. Tepper, 115–24. Ottawa: Canadian Asian Studies Association.

Suhrke, Astri. 1983a. "Global Refugee Movements and Strategies of Response." In *U.S. Immigration and Refugee Policy: Global and Domestic Issues.* Ed. Mary M. Kritz, 157–73. Lexington, Mass.: D.C. Heath.

———. 1983b. "Indochinese Refugees: The Law and Politics of First Asylum." *Annals of the American Academy of Political and Social Science* 467: 102–15.

———. 1992. *Towards a Comprehensive Refugee Policy: Conflict and Refugees in the Post-Cold War World.* Geneva: International Labor Organization/United Nations High Commissioner for Refugees.

Sully, François, ed. 1971. *We the Vietnamese: Voices from Vietnam.* New York: Praeger.

Supang, Chantavanich, E. Bruce Reynolds, and C.S.E.S. Volkswagenwerk. 1988. "Indochinese Refugees: Asylum and Resettlement." Bangkok: Institute of Asian Studies, Chulalongkorn University.

Sutter, Valerie O'Connor. 1990. *The Indochinese Refugee Dilemma.* Baton Rouge: Louisiana State University Press.

Taft, Julia Vadala. 1989. "A Call to Action for Restructuring U.S. Refugee Policy." *World Refugee Survey, 1989.* Washington, D.C.: U.S. Committee for Refugees, 7–12.

Tai, Hue-Tam Ho. 1983. *Millenarianism and Peasant Politics in Vietnam.* Cambridge, Mass.: Harvard University Press.

———. 1992. *Radicalism and the Origins of the Vietnamese Revolution.* Cambridge, Mass.: Harvard University Press.

Tai, Hue-Tam Ho, ed. 2001. *The Country of Memory: Remaking the Past in Late Socialist Vietnam.* Berkeley and Los Angeles: University of California Press.

Taylor, Keith W. 1983. *The Birth of Vietnam.* Berkeley and Los Angeles: University of California Press.

Teitelbaum, Michael S. 1980. "Right v. Right: Immigration and Refugee Policy in the United States." *Foreign Affairs* 59, no. 1: 21–59.

———. 1984. "Immigration, Refugees and Foreign Policy." *International Organization* 38, no. 3: 429–50.

Teitelbaum, Michael S. and Myron Weiner. 1995. "Threatened Peoples, Threatened Borders: Migration and U.S. Foreign Policy." In *Threatened Peoples, Threatened Borders: World Migration and U.S. Policy.* Ed. Michael S. Teitelbaum and Myron Weiner, 13–38. New York: W.W. Norton.

Tenhula, John. 1991. *Voices from Southeast Asia: The Refugee Experience in the United States.* New York: Holmes and Meier.

Thayer, Carlyle A. 1988. "The Condition of Vietnam, 1945–85." In *The Australian People: An Encyclopedia of the Nation, Its People and Their Origins.* Ed. James Jupp, 831–33. North Ryde, New South Wales, Australia: Angus and Robertson.

———. 1989. *War by Other Means: National Liberation and Revolution in Viet-Nam, 1954–1960.* Sydney, Australia: Allen and Unwin.

Thomas, Mandy. 1997. "Crossing Over: The Relationship between Overseas

Vietnamese and Their Homeland." *Journal of Intercultural Studies* 18, no. 2: 153–76.

———. 1999. *Dreams in the Shadows: Vietnamese-Australian Lives in Transition*. St. Leonards, Australia: Allen and Unwin.

Thomas, Patrick. 1981. "Indochinese Refugees in France and the U.S.: Public Policy and the Dynamics of Secondary Migration." *Journal of Refugee Resettlement* 1, no. 4: 15–21.

Thomson, Suteera. 1980. "Refugees in Thailand: Relief, Development, and Integration." In *Southeast Asian Exodus: From Tradition to Resettlement*. Ed. Elliot L. Tepper, 125–32. Ottawa: Canadian Asian Studies Association.

Thorburn, Craig. 1998. "Boat People: Vietnamese Commercial Fishermen in Los Angeles and Ventura Counties." *Intercom* 20, no. 3: 1–3 and 10–13.

Thuy, Vuong G. 1976. *Getting to Know the Vietnamese and Their Culture*. New York: Frederick Unger.

Tien, Liang and D. Hunthausen. 1990. "The Vietnamese Amerasian Resettlement Experience: From Initial Application to the First Six Months in the United States." *Vietnam Generation* 2, no. 3: 16–30.

Tillema, Richard G. 1981. "Starting Over in a New Land." *Public Welfare* 39, no. 1: 35–41.

Tobin, Thomas G., Arthur E. Laehr, and John F. Hilgenberg. 1978. *Last Flight from Saigon*. U.S. Air Force Southeast Asia Monograph Series, vol. IV, monograph 6. Washington, D.C.: U.S. Government Printing Office.

Tollefson, James W. 1989. *Alien Winds: The Reeducation of America's Indochinese Refugees*. New York: Praeger.

———. 1993. *The Strength Not to Fight: An Oral History of Conscientious Objectors of the Vietnam War*. Boston: Little, Brown.

Tonnesson, Stein. 1991. *The Vietnamese Revolution of 1945: Roosevelt, Ho Chi Minh, and de Gaulle in a World at War*. London: Sage.

Tourison, Sedgwick, Jr. 1995. *Project Alpha: Washington's Secret Military Operations in North Vietnam*. New York: St. Martin's Paperbacks.

Townsend, Peter. 1981. *The Girl in the White Ship*. New York: Holt, Rinehard, and Winston.

Tran, De, Andrew Lam, and Hai Dai Nguyen, eds. 1995. *Once upon a Dream: The Vietnamese-American Experience*. San Jose, Calif.: San Jose Mercury.

Tran, L.P. 1989. "In Search of Asylum—Vietnamese Boat People in Hong Kong." *Harvard International Law Journal* 30 no. 2: 569–72.

Tran, My-Van and Robert Holton. 1991. *Sadness Is Losing Our Country, Happiness Is Knowing Peace: Vietnamese Social Mobility in Australia, 1975–1990*. Wollongong, Australia: Centre for Multicultural Studies, University of Wollongong.

Tran, Tu Binh, trans. John Spragens, Jr., ed. David G. Marr. 1985. *The Red Earth: A Vietnamese Memoir of Life on a Colonial Rubber Plantation*. Athens: Ohio University Press.

Tran, Van Don. 1978. *Our Endless War: Inside Vietnam*. Novato, Calif.: Presidio Press.

Tranh, Yen. 1995. "The Closing of the Saga of the Vietnamese Asylum Seekers: The Implications on International Refugees and Human Rights Law." *Houston Journal of International Law* 17, no. 3: 463–517.

Truong, Buu Lam. 1967. *Patterns of Vietnamese Response to Foreign Intervention, 1858–1900.* Monograph Series No. 11. New Haven, Conn.: Southeast Asia Studies, Yale University.

———. 1969. "Comments and Generalities on Sino-Vietnamese Relations." In *Historical Interaction of China and Vietnam: Institutional and Cultural Themes.* Ed. Edgar Wickberg. Lawrence: Center for Southeast Asian Studies, University of Kansas.

———. 1984. *Resistance, Rebellion, Revolution: Popular Movements in Vietnamese History.* Singapore: Institute of Southeast Asian Studies.

Truong, Nhu Tang with David Chanoff and Doan Van Toai. 1985. *Vietcong Memoir: An Inside Account of the Vietnam War and Its Aftermath.* San Diego, Calif.: Harcourt Brace Jovanovich.

Tsamenyi, Martin. 1981. "The Vietnamese Boat People in International Law." Centre for the Study of Australian-Asian Relations, research paper 0158-586X: no. 14. Brisbane, Australia: Griffith University.

Turley, William S. 1986. *The Second Indochina War: A Short Political and Military History, 1954–1975.* Boulder, Colo.: Westview Press.

Turley, William S. and Mark Selden, eds. 1993. *Reinventing Vietnamese Socialism: Doi Moi in Comparative Perspective.* Boulder, Colo.: Westview Press.

Turner, Robert F. 1975. *Vietnamese Communism: Its Origins and Development.* Stanford, Calif.: Hoover Institution Press.

"Twenty-five Vietnamese Americans in Twenty-five Years, 1975–2000." 2000. *New Horizon: Chan Troi Moi,* no vol., no. issue.

United Nations High Commissioner for Refugees. 1995. *The State of the World's Refugees, 1995: In Search of Solutions.* New York: Oxford University Press.

———. 2000. *The State of the World's Refugees, 2000: Fifty Years of Humanitarian Action.* New York: Oxford University Press.

U.S. Air Force, 3201st Air Base Group, Office of History. 1975. *Operation New Arrivals, Eglin Air Force Base, Florida.* Washington, D.C.: U.S. Department of Defense, Department of the Air Force, Office of History, 3201st Air Base Group Headquarters, Armament Development and Test Center.

U.S. Congress. House of Representatives. Committee on Foreign Relations, Subcommittee on Asian and Pacific Affairs. 1979. "Indochinese Refugees." 96th Cong., 1st sess. Washington, D.C.: U.S. Government Printing Office.

———. 1988. "The Crisis Facing Vietnamese Refugees Seeking First Asylum in Thailand." 100th Cong., 2d sess., February 24. Washington D.C.: U.S. Government Printing Office.

———. "Indochinese Refugees at Risk: The Boat People, Cambodians under Khmer Rouge Control, and Re-education Camp Detainees." 101st Cong., 1st sess., February 8. Washington, D.C.: U.S. Government Printing Office 1989.

_____. Subcommittee on Asia and the Pacific. 1994. "Indochinese Refugees." 103rd Cong., 2d sess., April 26. Washington, D.C.: U.S. Government Printing Office.

_____. Committee on International Relations. 1975. "The Vietnam-Cambodia Emergency, 1975, Part I, Vietnam Evacuation and Humanitarian Assistance." 94th Cong., 1st sess., April and May. Washington, D.C.: U.S. Government Printing Office.

_____. Subcommittee on Asia and the Pacific and Subcommittee on International Relations and Human Rights. 1995. "Indochinese Refugees: Comprehensive Plan of Action." 104th Cong., 1st sess. July 25. Washington, D.C.: U.S. Government Printing Office.

_____. Subcommittee on International Operations and Human Rights. 1995. "Comprehensive Plan of Action for Indochinese Asylum Seekers." 104th Cong., 1st sess., July 27. Washington, D.C.: U.S. Government Printing Office.

_____. Special Subcommittee on Investigations. 1976. "The Vietnam-Cambodia Emergency, 1975, Part III, Vietnam Evacuation: The Testimony of Ambassador Graham A. Martin." 94th Cong., 2d sess. Washington, D.C.: U.S. Government Printing Office.

_____. Committee on the Judiciary 2001. "To Extend Eligibility for Refugee Status of Unmarried Sons and Daughters of Certain Vietnamese Refugees, Report accompanying H.R. 2840." 107th Cong., 1st sess. October 29. Washington, D.C.: U.S. Government Printing Office.

_____. Subcommittee on Immigration, Refugees, and International Law. 1980. "The Indochinese Refugee Problem." 96th Cong., 1st sess. Washington, D.C.: U.S. Government Printing Office.

_____. 1990. "Orderly Departure Program and U.S. Policy Regarding Vietnamese Boat People." 101st Cong., 1st sess., June 28, 1989. Washington D.C.: U.S. Government Printing Office.

U.S. Congress. Senate. Committee on the Judiciary, Subcommittee on Immigration and Refugee Policy. 1982. "Refugee Problems in Southeast Asia, A Staff Report." 97th Cong., 2d sess., Jan. 1982. Washington, D.C.: U.S. Government Printing Office.

_____. Subcommittee on Immigration and Refugee Affairs. 1989. "The International Conference on Indo-Chinese Refugees, A Staff Report." 101st Cong., 1st sess. Washington, D.C.: U.S. Government Printing Office.

_____. 1975. Subcommittee to Investigate Problems Connected with Refugees and Escapees. "Indochina Evacuation and Refugee Problems, Part II—The Evacuation." 94th Cong., 1st sess. Washington, D.C.: U.S. Government Printing Office.

U.S. Department of State and Immigration and Naturalization Service. 1978. "Indochinese Refugee Program Processing Guide." Washington, D.C.: U.S. Government Printing Office.

_____. 1989. "U.S., Vietnam Agree on Emigration of Detainees." *Bulletin* 89, no. 2152: 63.

————. 1991. "U.S. Policy on Repatriation of Vietnamese in Hong Kong." *Dispatch* 2, no. 45: 833–34.

U.S. Department of State, Bureau of Public Affairs. 1977. "Admission of 15,000 Indochinese. Statement by Assistant Secretary for East Asian and Pacific Affairs, Richard C. Holbrooke, before the Subcommittee on Immigration, Citizenship, and International Law, House Committee on the Judiciary."

————. 1980. "Indochinese Resettlement in the United States." *Serial Report* no. 68 (Feb.): 1–3.

————. 1988a. "Amerasians in Vietnam." *Gist*, August, 1–2.

————. 1988b. "UNHCR Programs to Protect Vietnam Refugees." *Gist*, November, 1–2.

————. 1989. "U.S.-Vietnam Relations and Emigration." *Current Policy* no. 1238.

U.S. Department of State, Special Refugee Advisory Panel, Marshall Green, chair. 1981. "The Indochinese Refugee Situation: Report to the Secretary of State." Washington, D.C.: Department of State.

U.S. General Accounting Office. 1979. "Report to the Congress of the United States by the Comptroller General—The Indochinese Exodus: A Humanitarian Dilemma." Washington, D.C.: Comptroller General of the United States.

————. 1985. "Problems in Processing Vietnamese Refugees from the Dong Rek Camp in Cambodia." Washington, D.C.: General Accounting Office.

————. 1990. "The Orderly Departure Program from Vietnam: Report to the Chairman, Subcommittee on Immigration, Refugees, and International Law, Committee on the Judiciary, House of Representatives, United States Congress. Washington, D.C.: General Accounting Office.

————. 1996. "Vietnam Asylum Seekers: Refugee Processing Under the CPA: Report to the Chairman, Subcommittee on International Operations and Human Rights, Committee on International Relations, House of Representatives, United States Congress." Washington, D.C. General Accounting Office.

Valentine, Douglas. 1990. *The Phoenix Program*. New York: William Morrow.

Van Dyke, Jon M. 1972. *North Vietnam's Strategy for Survival*. Palo Alto, Calif.: Pacific Books.

Van, Tien Dung. 1977. *Our Great Spring Victory: An Account of the Liberation of South Vietnam*. New York: Monthly Review Press.

Viviani, Nancy. 1984. *The Long Journey: Vietnamese Migration and Settlement in Australia*. Melbourne: Melbourne University Press, 1984.

————. 1996. *The Indochinese in Australia, 1975–1995: From Burnt Boats to Barbeques*. Melbourne: Oxford University Press.

Vo, Nguyen Giap. 1962. *People's War, People's Army: The Viet Cong Insurrection Manuel for Underdeveloped Countries*. New York: Praeger.

————. Trans. Mai Van Elliott. 1975. *Unforgettable Months and Years*. Southeast Asia Program data paper 99. Ithaca, N.Y.: Department of Asian Studies, Cornell University.

Vo, Nguyen Giap and Van Tien Dung. 1976. *How We Won the War.* Philadelphia: RECON Pub.

Wain, Barry. 1981. *The Refused: The Agony of the Indochina Refugees.* New York: Simon and Schuster.

Warner, Denis. 1964. *The Last Confucian: Vietnam, Southeast Asia, and the West.* New York: Penguin Books.

Weisberg, Barry. 1970. *Ecocide in Indochina: The Ecology of War.* San Francisco: Canfield Press.

Wells, Tom. 1994. *The War Within: America's Battle over Vietnam.* Berkeley and Los Angeles: University of California Press.

Werner, Jayne and Luu Doan Huynh, eds. 1993. *The Vietnam War: A Vietnamese and American Perspective.* Armonk, N.Y.: M.E. Sharpe.

White, Pamela M. 1990. "The Indo-Chinese in Canada." *Canadian Social Trends* 18 (Autumn): 7–10.

———. 1997. "Chinese from Southeast Asia." In *Case Studies in Diversity: Refugees in America in the 1990s.* Ed. David E. Haines, 223–43. Westport, Conn.: Praeger.

Whorton, Brad. 1997. "The Transformation of Refugee Policy: Race, Welfare, and American Political Culture, 1959–1997." PH.D. diss., University of Kansas.

Wickberg, Edgar, comp. 1969. "Historical Interaction of China and Vietnam: Institutional and Cultural Themes." Lawrence: Center for East Asian Studies, University of Kansas.

Wiesner, Louis A. 1988. *Victims and Survivors: Displaced Persons and Other War Victims in Vietnam, 1954–1975.* Westport, Conn.: Greenwood Press.

Williams, Michael C. 1992. *Vietnam at the Crossroads.* New York: Council on Foreign Relations.

Woodside, Alexander B. 1971. *Vietnam and the Chinese Model.* Cambridge, Mass.: Harvard University Press.

———. 1976. *Community and Revolution in Modern Vietnam.* Boston: Houghton Mifflin.

World Refugee Survey. (Annual). 1977–2004.

Yarborough, Trin. 2005. *Surviving Twice: Amerasian Children of the Vietnam War.* Washington, D.C.: Potomac Books.

Young, John R. 1988. "Compassion Fatigue." *Geographical: The Monthly Magazine of the Royal Geographical Society* 60, no. 12: 24–26.

Young, Marilyn B. 1991. *The Vietnam Wars, 1945–1990.* New York: Harper-Collins.

Zetter, Roger. 1985. "Refugees—Access and Labelling." *Development and Change* 16, no. 3: 429–50.

Zolberg, Aristide R. 1983. "The Formation of New States as a Refugee-Generating Process." *Annals of the American Academy of Political and Social Science* 267: 24–38.

Zolberg, Aristide R., Astri Suhrke, and Sergio Aguayo. 1989. *Escape from Violence: Conflict and the Refugee Crisis in the Developing World.* New York: Oxford University Press.

Zucker, Norman L. 1983. "Refugee Resettlement in the United States: Policy and Problems." *Annals of the American Academy of Political and Social Science* 467: 172–86.

———. 1989. "The Uneasy Troika in U.S. Refugee Policy: Foreign Policy, Pressure Groups, and Resettlement Costs." *Journal of Refugee Studies* 2, no. 4: 359–72.

Zucker, Norman L. and Naomi Flink Zucker. 1987. *The Guarded Gate: The Reality of American Refugee Policy*. San Diego, Calif.: Harcourt, Brace, Jovanovich.

———. 1992. "From Immigration to Refugee Redefinition: A History of Refugee and Asylum Policy in the United States." In *Refugees and the Asylum Dilemma in the West*. Ed. Gil Loescher, 54–70. University Park: Pennsylvania State University Press.

Selected Videography

Amerasians, Erik Gandini Multifilm, SVT Dokumentar, Stockholm, 1998, 52 minutes. Cinema Guild, info@cinemaguild.com

Anatomy of a Springroll, Paul Kwan and Arnold Iger, 1980, 60 minutes. Persona Grata and Paul Lundahl, personagrataprod.org/projects

As Seen by Both Sides: American and Vietnamese Artists Look at the War, Larry Rottmann and Mark Biggs, 1995, 58 minutes. Cinema Guild, info@cinemaguild.com

Bastards, Loc Do, 1999, 119 minutes. De/Center Communication, Inc., indierag@marginfilms.com; rottentomatoes.com

Bittersweet Survival: Southeast Asians in America, J. T. Takagi and Christine Choy, 1983, 29 minutes. Third World Newsreel/National Asian American Telecommunication Association (NAATA), distribution@naatanet.org

Bui Doi: Life Like Dust, Ahrin Mishan and Nick Rotherberg, 1994, 28 minutes. NAATA, distribution@naatanet.org

Chac, Kim-Chi Tyler, 2000, 72 minutes. Green Mango Productions, greenmangopro@aol.com; distribution@naatanet.org

Daughter from Danang, Gail Dolgin and Vicente Franco, 2002, 80 minutes. Independent Television Service, itvs.org

Dear America: Letters Home from Vietnam, The Couturie Company and the Vietnam Veterans Ensemble Theater Company, 1987, 84 minutes. HBO Video, hbo.com

Eating Welfare, Youth Leadership Project, Committee Against Anti-Asian Violence (CAAAV), 2001, 58 minutes. CAAAV, caaav.org

The Effects of War: The Indochinese Refugee Experience, 1989, 58 minutes. Insight: Multicultural Communication, Inc., insightmulticultural.com/ordering.html

Experiences of Operation Babylift Adoptees, American Museum of Natural History, 2003, 90 minutes. C-SPAN Archives, info@c-spanarchives.org

The Fall of Saigon, Discovery Channel, 1995, 60 minutes. (This excellent film is no longer available, but some libraries may own it.)

The Fall of Saigon, Michael Dutfield, 1995. Used copies available at amazon.com

The Fall of Saigon, Time Life Videos, 1998. New and used copies available at amazon.com

The Fog of War: Eleven Lessons from the Life of Robert S. McNamara, Michael Williams, Julie Ahlberg, and Errol Morris, 2004, 107 minutes. Columbia TriStar Home Entertainment, sonyclassics.com/fogofwar/

From Hollywood to Hanoi, Tiana (Thi Thang Nga), 1993, 80 minutes. Indochina Film Arts Foundation, tianatiana@aol.com

A Hand Up: The Vietnamese Nail Salon Success Story, Rob Amato and Jody Hammond, 2003, 23 minutes. Rob Amato Productions/SeaVid, rob@robamato.com

Hidden Warriors: Women on the Ho Chi Minh Trail, Phan Thanh Hao and Karen Turner, 2003, 46 minutes. Hen Hao Productions, kturner@holycross.edu

I Am Viet Hung, Vietnamese Hero, Tom Cook, Diep N. Bui, and Lenga Bui Kazan, 1997, 26 minutes. University of Southern California School of Cinema-Television; NAATA, distribution@naatanet.org

In a Strange Land: Police and the Southeast Asian Refugee, VisionWorks in association with the Community Action Agency, Portland, Oregon, 1990.

Kim's Story: The Road from Vietnam, Shelley Saywell, 1996, 48 minutes. First Run Icarus Films, mailroom@frif.com

Labor Women, Renee Tajima-Pena, 2002, 30 minutes. NAATA, distribution@naatanet.org

Letters to Thien, Trac Minh Vu, 1997, 56 minutes. NAATA, distribution@naatanet.org

The Long-Haired Warriors, Mel Halbach, 1998, 60 minutes. World Stories Film, worldstoriesfilm.com

Mai's America, Marlo Poras, 2002, 72 minutes. Women Make Movies, wmm.com

Monterey's Boat People, Spencer Nakasako and Vincent DiGirolamo, 1982, 29 minutes. NAATA, distribution@naatanet.org

My Journey Home, Renee Tajima-Pena, Jeff Bieber, and Dalton Delan, WETA-TV, Washington, D.C., 60 minutes. PBS Video, shoppbs.org

Nightsongs, Marva Nabili and Thomas A. Fucci, 1995, 107 minutes. World Artists Home Video, The Picture Palace, Inc., picpal.com

The Phans of Jersey City, Abbie Fink, Stephen Forman, John Fraker, and Dennis Lanson, 1979, 49 minutes. Documentary Educational Resources, der.org/films/phans-of-jersey-city

Precious Cargo, Janet Gardner, 2001, 56 minutes. Independent Television Service, itvs.org

The Price You Pay, Christine Keyser, 1988, 29 minutes. NAATA, distribution@naatanet.org

Reflections: Returning to Vietnam, KCSM-TV, San Mateo, 1992, 30 minutes. NAATA, distribution@naatanet.org

Regret to Inform, Barbara Sonneborn, 1998, 72 minutes. New Yorker Films, docurama.com; requesttoinform.org; and distribution@naatanet.org

Saigon, U.S.A., Lindsey Jang and Robert G. Winn, KOCE-TV, Public Broadcasting System, 2000, 91 minutes.saigonusa@earthlink.net

School Daze, Spencer Nakasako and Vietnamese Youth Development Center, 2000, 50 minutes. NAATA, distribution@naatanet.org

The Story of Vinh, Keiko Tsuno, 1990, 60 minutes. NAATA, distribution@naatanet.org

Surname Viet Given Name Nam, Trinh T. Minh-ha, 1989, 108 minutes. Women Make Movies, wmm.com

Vietnam: A Television History (a 13-part series of 60 minutes each), Richard Ellison, executive producer, 1983. Public Broadcasting System, WGBH-TV, used copies can be purchased at Amazon.com

Vietnam: At the Crossroads, Hien Duc Do and Bob Gliner, 1994, 59 minutes. NAATA, distribution@naatanet.org

Vietnam: Land of the Ascending Dragon, Video Visits, 54 minutes. Educational Video Network, Inc., info@evndirect.com

Vietnam: Picking Up the Pieces, Downtown Community Television, 1978, 58 minutes. Electronic Arts Intermix, Inc., ghunter@eai.org

Vietnam under Communism, Frontline, Public Broadcasting System, 58 minutes. PBS Video, FRON302K, shoppbs.org

The Vietnam War, Films for the Humanities and Sciences, 1992, 30 minutes. Films for the Humanities, Inc., custserv@films.com

Vietnamese-Americans, Howard Mass, 2000, 70 minutes. Films for the Humanities and Sciences, custserv@films.com

A World beneath the War, Pham Quoc Thai and Janet Gardner, 1996, 54 minutes. NAATA, distribution@naatanet.org

Xich-lo, M. Trinh Nguen, 1996, 54 minutes. NAATA, distribution@naatanet.org

* * *

The following two videos used to be distributed by the University of California Extension Center for Media and Independent Learning until it closed down permanently in June 2005. A copy of each is available at the University of California, Moffit Library, Media Resource Center, tel. (510) 642–8197.

Between Worlds, Shawn Hainsworth, 1998, 75 minutes.

Thanh's War, Elizabeth Farnsworth, 1990, 58 minutes.

Index

SUCHENG CHAN is Professor Emerita of Asian American Studies and Global Studies at the University of California, Santa Barbara. She is the recipient of many prizes and author or editor of numerous books, including, *Chinese American Transnationalism: The Flow of People, Resources, and Ideas Between China and America During the Exclusion Era* (Temple); and *Claiming America: Constructing Chinese American Identities During the Exclusion Era* (Temple, co-edited with Scott Wong), which won the award for Outstanding Book in History and Social Sciences from the Association for Asian American Studies.